Students & Families

One-Stop Inter[net]

busmanagement.glencoe.com

Content Enrichment Tools

- News Around the Globe
- Center Stage
- All-Stars
- Career City

Self-Assessment Tools

- Self-Assessment Quizzes
- Internet Treasure Hunts
- Case Studies

Glencoe

The **McGraw·Hill** Companies

GLENCOE **Business**
MANAGEMENT
Real-World Applications & Connections

busmanagement.glencoe.com

Web site includes:
- **Self-assessment quizzes**
- **Resume and interview tips**
- **Workplace connections**

In Partnership

Busines

Glencoe: Your *Real* Business Choice

Leslie W. Rue, Ph.D.
Professor Emeritus of Management
J. Mack Robinson College of Business
Georgia State University

busmana

Glen

New York, New York   Columbus, Ohio   Chicago, Illinois   Pe

About the Authors

Leslie W. Rue is professor emeritus of management at Georgia State University. He received his Bachelor of Industrial Engineering (with honors) and his Master of Industrial Engineering from Georgia Institute of Technology. He received his Ph.D. in Management from Georgia State University.

Prior to joining Georgia State University, Dr. Rue was on the faculty of the School of Business, Indiana University at Bloomington, Indiana. He has worked as a data processing project officer for the U.S. Army Management Systems Support Agency in the Pentagon, and as an industrial engineer for Delta Airlines. In addition, Dr. Rue has worked as a consultant and trainer to numerous private and public organizations in the areas of planning, organizing, and strategy.

Dr. Rue is the author of over 50 published articles, cases, and papers that have appeared in academic and practitioner journals. In addition to this book, he has coauthored seven other textbooks in the field of management. Several of these books have gone into multiple editions.

Lloyd L. Byars received his Ph.D. from Georgia State University. He also received a Bachelor of Electrical Engineering and a Master of Science in Industrial Management from Georgia Tech. He has taught at Georgia State University, Clark Atlanta University, and he is currently a professor of management at the School of Management at the Georgia Institute of Technology.

Dr. Byars has published articles in leading professional journals and is also the author of four textbooks, which are used in colleges and universities. He has served on the editorial review board of the _Journal of Systems Management_ and the _Journal of Management Case Studies_.

Dr. Byars has worked as a trainer and consultant to many organizations, including: Duke Power Company, Georgia Kraft Company, Kraft, Inc., South Carolina Electric and Gas Company, the University of Florida–Medical School, the Department of the Army, and the U.S. Social Security Administration. Dr. Byars also serves as a labor arbitrator, certified by both the Federal Mediation and Conciliation Service and the American Arbitration Association. He has arbitrated cases in the United States, Central America, and the Caribbean.

Reviewers

Christine M. Danner
Coordinator
Institute of Business and Entrepreneurship
Charles W. Flanagan High School
Pembroke Pines, Florida

Shawna S. Koger
Business Educator
Arlington High School
Arlington, Nebraska

Diane Landes
Marketing and Management Educator
Middle Bucks Institute of Technology
Jamison, Pennsylvania

Mark Matthews
Department Chair for
Business Education and Technology
University High School
Orlando, Florida

Michael Robertson
Business Educator
Marion High School
Marion, Indiana

Martin Rowley
Adjunct Professor of Business Education
Hofstra University
Hempstead, New York

Table of Contents

UNIT 1 Management Today

UNIT 3 Foundation Skills

UNIT 4 Planning Skills

UNIT 5 Organizing Skills

UNIT 6 Leadership Skills

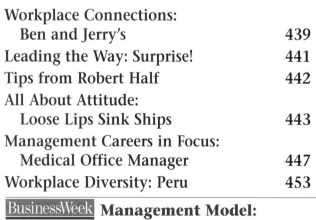

List of Features

Management Careers in Focus
Controller

Nature of the Work
Controllers are responsible for the preparation of all a company's financial reports, income statements, balance sheets, and special reports, such as depreciation schedules. They may oversee accounts payable and accounts receivable, audit, or budget departments.
In publicly traded companies, controllers make sure all reports meet federal guidelines. They monitor the flow of cash receipts and payments, and determine whether the company needs a loan to meet financial obligations. They decide when to invest extra money in interest-bearing instruments.
Controllers work in all profit-making industries and non-profit organizations. With the demand for qualified accounting professionals, experienced controllers can choose where they will work.

Working Conditions
Controllers work in comfortable, well lighted offices with a support staff. They may work long hours and sometimes work under pressure.

Training, Other Qualifications, and Advancement
To become a controller, you need a bachelor's or master's degree in finance or accounting. The CPA exam can also be helpful. Strong analytical and organizational skills are necessary,

as are computer skills in spreadsheet and word processing software.

Salary Range
Assistant controllers earn $41,000 to $81,000; controllers earn $47,000 to $138,000. Salaries vary with responsibility, experience, industry, and size and location of firm.

CRITICAL THINKING
Why are word processing skills necessary to a high-level accountant such as a controller? Why are spreadsheet skills necessary? What kind of person do you think would make a good controller?

STANDARD &POOR'S

INDUSTRY OUTLOOK
Controllers monitor the loans a company obtains from banks or other financial services companies. Like banks, financial service companies lend money at interest, charge interest, and offer many lending products that suit business needs. They are less regulated than banks and are not insured by the Federal Deposit Insurance Corporation (FDIC).

BUSINESS MANAGEMENT *Online*
For more information on management careers, go to:
busmanagement.glencoe.com

Types of Communication   Section 9.2   213

WORKPLACE DIVERSITY

International Management

WORKPLACE CONNECTIONS

LEADING THE WAY

All About ATTITUDE

BusinessWeek — Management Model

The world of business needs skilled people who can think critically, analyze information, and make important management decisions. In this book, you will have many opportunities to understand how the world of business operates and to practice making wise management decisions.

THE BENEFITS OF THE *BUSINESS-WEEK* MANAGEMENT MODEL

In every chapter, you will find a special feature called the *BusinessWeek* **Management Model.** This full-page article presents real-life case studies from *BusinessWeek* magazine.

CRITICAL THINKING

Each case study includes a **Critical Thinking** question that asks you to apply the management concepts learned in the chapter. You'll analyze interesting business topics and answer questions such as: What are the key factors of a successful business? What is the impact of community involvement in business management decisions?

DECISION MAKING

This feature concludes with a **Decision Making** activity that asks you to evaluate a situation and make an ethical business decision. You can perform these activities by using Internet-based articles, case studies from *BusinessWeek*, or articles printed in local newspapers.

The *BusinessWeek* **Management Model** will help you to:

- learn about real-life businesses.
- investigate business-related problems.
- compare and contrast different management theories.
- find creative solutions.
- learn to make wise management decisions.

BusinessWeek — Management Model

READING STRATEGIES

How can you get the most from your reading? Effective readers are active readers. As they read, they have conversations with themselves about the text; they get involved. Don't be a passive reader! Use the strategies below to help you read actively and effectively.

1. PREDICT what the section will be about.

Make educated guesses about what the section is about by combining clues in the text with what you already know. Predicting helps you anticipate questions and stay alert to new information.

Ask yourself...
- What does this section heading mean?
- What is this section about?
- How does this section tie in with what I have read so far?
- Why is this information important in understanding business management?

2. CONNECT what you read with your own life.

Draw parallels between what you are reading and the events and circumstances in your own life.

Ask yourself...
- How do my experiences compare to the information in the text?
- How could I apply this information in my own life?
- How will a manager apply this information?
- Why is this information important in understanding business management?

3. QUESTION as you read to make sure you understand the content.

Ask yourself questions to help you clarify the reading as you go along.

Ask yourself...
- Do I understand what I've read so far?
- What is this section about?
- What does this mean?
- Why is this information important in understanding business management?

4. RESPOND to what you read.

React to what you are reading. Form opinions and make judgments about the section while you are reading—not just after you've finished.

Ask yourself...
- Does this information make sense?
- What can I learn from this section?
- How will a manager apply this information?
- Why is this information important in understanding business management?

Management Today

IN THIS UNIT...

You will be introduced to the foundations of management. Included in this unit are chapters covering an introduction to management, careers in management, and management history.

Journal Writing

In your journal, assess your knowledge of
management by writing about the following:

1. What does the word *manager* mean to you?
   Make a list of five words that come to
   mind when you hear the word *manager*.
2. What does it take to be a great manager?
3. What skills and attributes do you possess
   that would make you a great manager?

CHAPTER 1

INTRODUCTION TO MANAGEMENT

LEARNING OBJECTIVES

When you have completed this chapter, you will be able to:

- Discuss changes taking place in the business world today.
- Define management.
- Explain the importance of management.
- Define entrepreneurship.
- Discuss the role of women and minorities in business today.

READING STRATEGIES

As you read

- **PREDICT** what the section will be about.
- **CONNECT** what you read with your own life.
- **QUESTION** as you read to make sure you understand the content.
- **RESPOND** to what you read.

WORKPLACE CONNECTIONS

Understanding Management

Microsoft's wealth and power seem to grow and grow. By any account, Bill Gates, one of Microsoft's founders, is one of the richest people in the world. To keep his company on the cutting edge, Gates demands that his colleagues be remarkably well-informed, logical, vocal, and thick-skinned. According to Gates, "My goal is to prove that a successful corporation can renew itself and stay in the forefront."

Analyzing Management Skills

What do you think of the demands Bill Gates places on his colleagues? What do you think of this management approach?

Applying Management Skills

At your workplace, or the workplace of a family member or friend, what types of management skills help the manager to operate the business?

BusinessWeek ONLINE

For further reading on managers and management go to: **www.businessweek.com**

THE IMPORTANCE OF BUSINESS MANAGEMENT

The Business World Today

Businesses today operate in a world of constant change. Technology and society are changing more rapidly than ever before. Concern for the environment has forced companies to think about how their actions affect the quality of the air, land, and water. Competition is fiercer than ever, because companies from all over the world now try to sell their products and services to the same customers. Workplaces have become increasingly diverse, as minorities, women, and new immigrants participate in growing numbers. All these changes have created new challenges for managers—the people who operate businesses.

▲ **INTERNATIONAL MANAGEMENT** McDonald's is one of the many U.S. companies that now have branches in many countries. *What challenges do you think McDonald's managers face in setting up an American fast-food restaurant in a foreign country?*

▲ **MANAGEMENT PROCESSES** Managers coordinate people, equipment, and money so that businesses can create products or provide services. *What are some of the things managers would have to do to set up an assembly line like this one?*

What Is Management?

Management is the process of deciding how best to use a business's resources to produce goods or provide services. A business's resources include its employees, equipment, and money.

To see why managers are important, think about the roles they play in the automobile industry. Some managers on the assembly line schedule work shifts and supervise the men and women who manufacture and assemble the vehicles. Other managers in the engineering department develop new product features and make sure that safety standards are met. Managers also plan for the future, thinking about the vehicles the company will be producing in the next decade. Without management, automobile manufacturers could not conduct business efficiently.

All organizations, from one-person businesses to giant corporations, need managers. Small businesses may be managed by one or just a few managers. Large and medium-sized companies may have many levels of management.

PREDICT

Why do you think management is an important part of the business world today?

Levels of Management

All but the very smallest organizations need more than one manager to coordinate their resources. Large companies generally have many managers at three different levels.

Senior Management

The highest level is known as **senior management**. Senior management has several important functions. First, it establishes the goals, or objectives, of the business. Second, it decides what actions are necessary to meet those goals. Finally, it decides how to use the company's resources. This level of management usually includes the chairperson of the company's board of directors, the chief executive officer (CEO), the chief operating officer (COO), and the company's senior vice presidents. Senior managers are not involved in the company's day-to-day problems. Instead, they concentrate on setting the direction the company will follow.

Middle Management

Middle management is responsible for meeting the goals that senior management sets. Middle managers include department heads and district sales managers. This level of management sets goals for specific areas of the business and decides what the employees in each area must do to meet those goals. For example, senior management might set a goal of increasing company sales by 15 percent in the next year. To meet that objective, middle management might develop a new advertising campaign for one of the company's products.

Supervisory Management

The lowest level of management is **supervisory management**. Supervisory managers make sure that the day-to-day operations of the business run smoothly. They are in charge of the people who physically produce the company's products or provide its services. Forepersons, crew leaders, and store managers are all examples of supervisory managers.

WORKPLACE DIVERSITY

EGYPT
In Egypt and other Muslim countries, it is considered an insult to display the sole of your foot when seated. Even inadvertent violations are serious. Visiting workers and managers are expected to be aware of and respect Egyptian and Muslim customs.

Large companies usually have all three kinds of managers. At JCPenney, for example, supervisory managers run stores and departments within stores. These managers are responsible for making sure that the daily operations of the store run well. Middle managers oversee districts. These managers are responsible for making sure that all store managers within their district are performing well. Middle managers also may suggest ideas for increasing sales, improving service, or reducing costs within their districts. Senior managers include JCPenney's CEO and senior vice presidents. These managers make decisions about the company's policies, products, and organization. A decision to increase salaries throughout the company would be made by senior management, for example.

The three levels of management form a *hierarchy*, or a group ranked in order of importance. As you can see in **Figure 1–1**, the management hierarchy is shaped like a pyramid, with very few

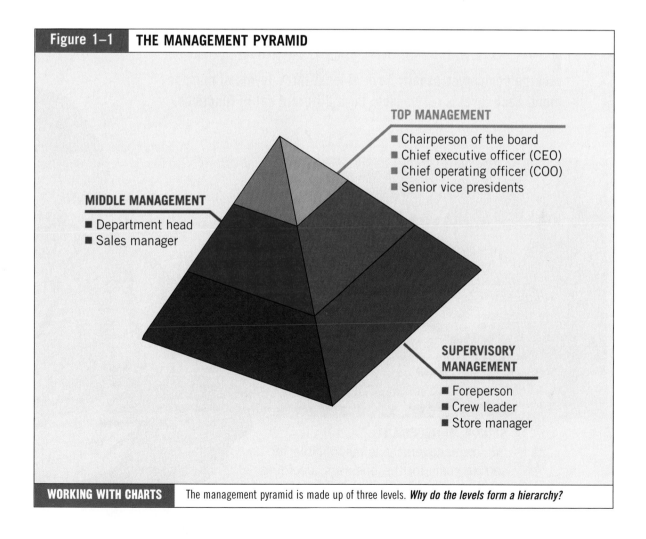

Figure 1–1 | **THE MANAGEMENT PYRAMID**

TOP MANAGEMENT
- Chairperson of the board
- Chief executive officer (CEO)
- Chief operating officer (COO)
- Senior vice presidents

MIDDLE MANAGEMENT
- Department head
- Sales manager

SUPERVISORY MANAGEMENT
- Foreperson
- Crew leader
- Store manager

WORKING WITH CHARTS The management pyramid is made up of three levels. *Why do the levels form a hierarchy?*

senior managers at the top and many supervisory managers at the bottom. Look at **Figure 1–2** to further your understanding of the different levels of management.

The Management Process

There are several ways to examine how management works. One way is to divide the tasks managers perform into categories. A second way is to look at the roles different types of managers play in a

FIGURE 1–2

Levels of Business Management

Large companies usually have at least three levels of management. Each level is responsible for a different set of functions.

1 **SENIOR MANAGEMENT**
Senior management is responsible for setting goals for the business, deciding what actions are necessary to meet them, and determining how best to use resources. This level of management usually includes the chairperson of the board of directors, the CEO, the COO, and the company's senior vice presidents.

company. A **role** is a set of behaviors associated with a particular job. A third way is to look at the skills managers need to do their jobs. Each of these ways of thinking about management will help you understand the management process.

Management Tasks

Managers in all organizations—from small businesses to large companies—engage in some basic activities. These activities can be divided into five categories:

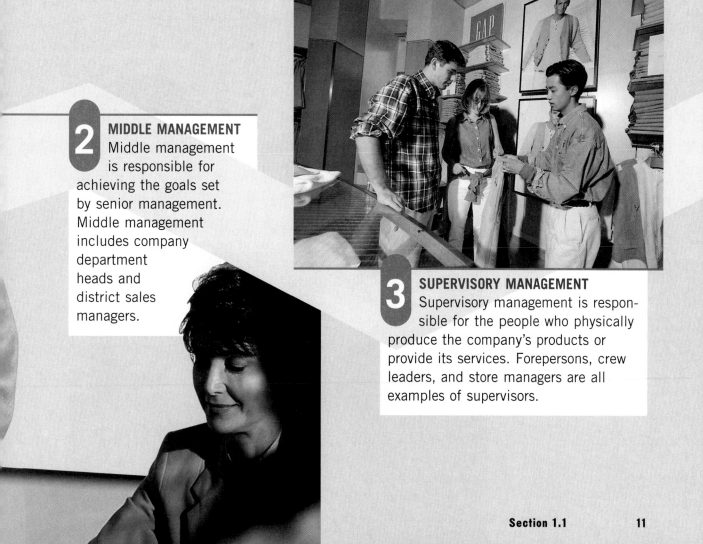

2 MIDDLE MANAGEMENT Middle management is responsible for achieving the goals set by senior management. Middle management includes company department heads and district sales managers.

3 SUPERVISORY MANAGEMENT Supervisory management is responsible for the people who physically produce the company's products or provide its services. Forepersons, crew leaders, and store managers are all examples of supervisors.

PLANNING A manager decides on company goals and the actions the company must take to meet them. A CEO who sets a goal of increasing sales by 10 percent in the next year by developing a new software program is engaged in planning.

ORGANIZING A manager groups related activities together and assigns employees to perform them. A manager who sets up a team of employees to restock an aisle in a supermarket is organizing.

STAFFING A manager decides how many and what kind of people a business needs to meet its goals and then recruits, selects, and trains the right people. A restaurant manager's staffing duties include interviewing and training waiters.

LEADING A manager provides the guidance employees need to perform their tasks. This helps ensure that company goals are met. A manager leads by keeping the lines of communication open. Holding regular staff meetings where employees can ask questions about their projects and responsibilities is a good example of leading.

▶ HIRING Staffing is one of the most important management functions. *What kinds of qualities do you think managers look for when they hire a young person for an entry-level office job?*

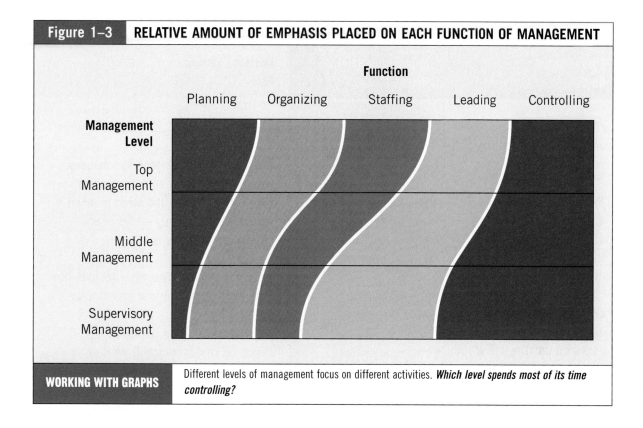

Figure 1–3 | **RELATIVE AMOUNT OF EMPHASIS PLACED ON EACH FUNCTION OF MANAGEMENT**

Function

Planning   Organizing   Staffing   Leading   Controlling

Management Level

Top Management

Middle Management

Supervisory Management

WORKING WITH GRAPHS Different levels of management focus on different activities. *Which level spends most of its time controlling?*

CONTROLLING A manager measures how the business performs to ensure that financial goals are being met. Controlling requires a manager to analyze accounting records and to make changes if financial standards are not being met.

Many management activities overlap. Organizing, for example, is difficult without a plan. Keeping good employees on the job is difficult if a workplace is poorly organized and lacks leadership.

Figure 1–3 shows how different levels of management focus on different activities. Senior managers divide their time about equally among the five activities. Middle managers spend most of their time leading and controlling. Supervisory managers spend little time planning and a lot of time controlling.

Management Roles

Managers have authority, or power, within organizations and use it in many ways. To best use their authority, managers take on different roles. Most management roles fall into one of three categories: interpersonal roles, information-related roles, and decision-making roles.

Interpersonal roles include a manager's relationships with people. A manager plays an interpersonal role by providing leadership within the company or interacting with others outside the organization.

CONNECT

Have you ever worked on a team to complete a school project? What types of organization structure did you use? Did you have leaders?

Figure 1–4	DEFINITIONS OF MANAGEMENT ROLES	
Interpersonal Roles	**Information-Related Roles**	**Decision-Making Roles**
Figurehead: Manager serves as official representative of the organization or unit. *Relationship Builder:* Manager interacts with peers and with people outside the organization to gain information. *Leader:* Manager guides and motivates staff and acts as a positive influence in the workplace.	*Monitor:* Manager receives and collects information. *Communicator:* Manager distributes information within the organization. *Spokesperson:* Manager distributes information outside the organization.	*Entrepreneur:* Manager initiates change. *Disturbance Handler:* Manager decides how conflicts between subordinates should be resolved and steps in when a subordinate suddenly leaves or an important customer is lost. *Resource Director:* Manager decides how the organization will use its resources. *Negotiator:* Manager decides to negotiate major contracts with other organizations or individuals.

WORKING WITH CHARTS	Managers take on different roles. *How does a manager play an interpersonal role?*

Source: Adapted from Henry Mintzberg, *The Nature of Managerial Work* (New York: Harper & Row, 1972), pp. 54–99.

Information-related roles require a manager to provide knowledge, news, or advice to employees. A manager fills this role by holding meetings or finding other ways of letting employees know about important business activities. *Decision-making roles* are those a manager plays when making changes in policies, resolving conflicts, or deciding how best to use resources. **Figure 1–4** gives examples and definitions of the three types of roles.

Different levels of management play different roles within organizations. Middle and supervisory managers, for example, spend more time resolving conflicts than do senior managers. Senior managers, such as the CEO, spend much of their time on interpersonal roles. These managers concentrate on representing the company in its relations with people outside the company, interacting with those people, and providing guidance and leadership to the organization.

Senior managers also determine a company's culture, or way of thinking and acting. When new management took over Sears, Roebuck and Co. in 1992, morale was low. Sales were falling, but the company refused to acknowledge that times were bad. Senior management made almost all decisions, leaving most employees feeling powerless.

To change Sears' culture, the new CEO decided to create a more open atmosphere. He began holding town meetings, where employees learned how Sears was performing. He also empowered managers at all levels by giving them more freedom to make decisions.

Management Skills

A third way of looking at the management process is by examining the kinds of skills required to perform a particular job. Three types of skills have been identified.

CONCEPTUAL SKILLS The skills that help managers understand how different parts of a business relate to one another and to the business as a whole are **conceptual skills**. Decision making, planning, and organizing are managerial activities that require conceptual skills.

HUMAN RELATIONS SKILLS The skills managers need to understand and work well with people are **human relations skills**. Interviewing job applicants, forming partnerships with other businesses, and resolving conflicts all require good human relations skills.

TECHNICAL SKILLS Managers also need **technical skills**, the specific abilities that people use to perform their jobs. Operating a word processing program, designing a brochure, and training people to use a new budgeting system are all technical skills.

◀ SMALL BUSINESS MANAGEMENT Supervisory managers often are called on to resolve problems their employees cannot handle. *What kinds of problems might a manager in a small store have to resolve?*

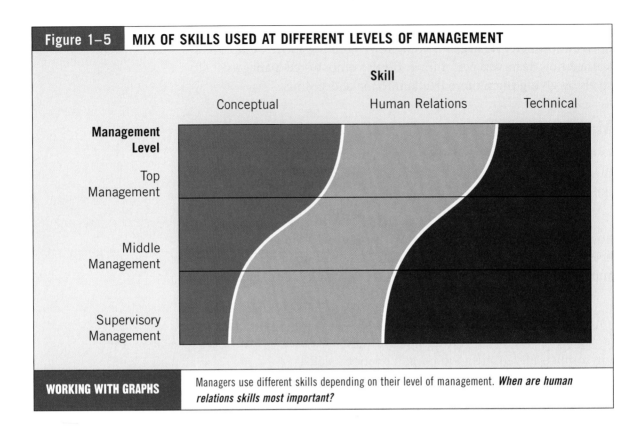

Figure 1–5 | **MIX OF SKILLS USED AT DIFFERENT LEVELS OF MANAGEMENT**

WORKING WITH GRAPHS — Managers use different skills depending on their level of management. *When are human relations skills most important?*

Not all management skills are easy to place in a single category. Most fall into more than one. In order to develop a company advertisement, for example, a manager must have conceptual, human relations, and technical skills. Managers would need conceptual skills to develop the advertisement's message. They would need human relations skills to assemble and motivate the team of people who create the advertisement. Training the team by teaching them a computer graphics program would require technical skills.

All levels of management require some combination of these skills. Different skills are more important at different levels of management, as **Figure 1–5** shows. Conceptual skills are most important at the senior management level. Technical skills are most important at lower levels of management, particularly at the supervisory level. Human relations skills are important at all levels of management.

RESPOND

Do you think a manager can succeed without conceptual, human relations, or technical skills? Why or why not?

Principles of Management

Managers often use certain rules when deciding how to run their businesses. These rules are known as principles of management.

A **principle** is a basic truth or law. The principle, or law, of gravity explains why objects fall to the ground when they are dropped. The principle of inertia explains why objects at rest remain at rest. Scientists prove that principles are true by performing controlled experiments. These experiments test a *hypothesis*, or an idea about the way something works. Once the experiment has been repeated many times with the same results, the hypothesis is accepted as a law, or principle.

Developing principles of management is more complicated than developing scientific principles. Carrying out a controlled experiment in the business world is difficult to do, because researchers cannot control all of the factors the way they can in a laboratory. To test the effect of a particular business practice, researchers would need to study companies that were exactly alike in every way except the business practice being studied. In the real world, however, companies differ in many ways. It is unlikely that researchers would find identical companies to study.

Because controlled management experiments are so difficult to carry out, most management principles are developed through observation and deduction. *Deduction* is the process of drawing a general conclusion from specific examples. For instance, a researcher may observe that employees in 15 companies work more efficiently when their supervisors treat them well. In this case, the researcher may deduce that a pleasant work environment contributes to productivity. This conclusion might then become a management principle.

▶ **DRESS CODE** Not all businesses apply the same management principles. *Why might some companies want their employees to dress formally?*

Management principles are more likely to change than physical principles. They also are likely to be interpreted differently by different people. For this reason management principles are best viewed as guides to action rather than rigid laws. A manager follows management principles most of the time. If, however, a principle clearly does not apply to a specific situation, an experienced manager will not use it. An important part of being a manager is recognizing when a principle should be followed and when it should not. Being able to change and adapt, particularly during times of uncertainty, is an important management skill.

Until recently, many managers followed the management principle that all employees need to arrive at work at the same time. They also believed that people who worked in offices needed to dress a certain way. In the past several years, managers at many companies adopted a new way of thinking about work schedules. Many companies now allow their employees to work flexible schedules, or "flex time." Some even allow their employees to work at home. Attitudes about dress codes also have changed, with many businesses allowing their employees to dress casually.

All About ATTITUDE

PITCHING IN

"I don't have to do that. It's not my job." Sound familiar? People often use this as an excuse for not taking care of business. In today's business world, businesses look for employees with a "can do" attitude. You can win points as manager or employee by being ready and able to take on any challenge when the need arises.

Women and Minorities in Management

For many years the managers of most large and medium-sized U.S. businesses were almost exclusively white males. As recently as the 1950s and 1960s, women in the workforce filled primarily service and support roles, acting as secretaries, teachers, salesclerks, and waitresses, for instance. Many minority workers, especially those lacking education, were confined to menial jobs such as custodial work and manual labor. In the last three decades of the twentieth century, however, more and more women and minorities have joined the workforce. They also have attained positions as managers in companies of all sizes.

Women and minorities now serve as the CEOs of some of the most prestigious businesses, including Avon, eBay, and Lucent. In 1999 Hewlett-Packard became the first of the 30 largest U.S. companies (the "Dow 30") to appoint a woman as its CEO. Carleton Fiorina was the first woman to win a leadership position at this very high level. Women working in the federal government also won promotions to top managerial slots. In 2000 women held 44 percent of the managerial positions in the field of public administration. In 2002 they also made up 25.1 percent of the Senior Executive Service, the federal government's highest-ranking managers.

Despite these changes, most senior managers in the country are still white men. In 2002 only 16 percent of the executives in the country's largest companies (the Fortune 500) were women, and 71 of the Fortune 500 companies had no female officers at all. African Americans, Hispanics, and other minorities fared no better: In America's top 50 corporations, ethnic minorities made up only 24 percent of the officials and managers. The problems women and minorities have had winning promotions to senior management positions gave rise to the term **glass ceiling**. This is the invisible barrier that prevents women and minorities from moving up in the world of business.

As in many other fields, such as sports and space exploration, the glass ceiling is steadily becoming a window of opportunity. Top managers, especially CEOs, are highly visible and often inseparable from

◀ **MANAGEMENT BREAKTHROUGH** Carleton Fiorina was appointed CEO of Hewlett-Packard in 1999. *Why was this significant?*

their companies. Therefore having a woman—such as Hewlett-Packard's Fiorina—in the top spot can be an advantage. It also can be the spark that is needed to trigger more promotions of women to senior managerial positions. As businesses and government agencies "downsize," or lay off workers to cut costs, many of those opting for attractive retirement benefits are senior white males. Their departure opens the door for women and minorities eager to move into the highest ranks of management.

As the glass ceiling falls, the challenges presented by a multicultural workplace increase. Workers and managers alike must be sensitive to these challenges. One example of the need for increased sensitivity involves religious holidays, which are celebrated at different times throughout the year by Muslims, Christians, Jews, and other religious groups. Managers need to be aware of the needs of their staff when it comes to these holidays, and workers need to be responsible about arranging to take these days off.

Section 1.1 Assessment

 FACT AND IDEA REVIEW

1. How have changes in modern business created challenges for managers?
2. Which management level is responsible for:
   a. Establishing a business partnership?
   b. Resolving disputes between employees?
   c. Designing a plan to meet a company goal?
3. Which role does a manager fill when resolving a dispute? Holding a staff meeting?
4. List the three types of management skills and explain why each is important.
5. Can a management principle be proven just like a scientific principle? Explain.

CRITICAL THINKING

1. **Drawing Conclusions:** Explain if a person who does a job well but has poor "people" skills would make a good manager.
2. **Determining Cause and Effect:** Should a manager fire a well-liked employee who is not performing well or keep the employee in order not to upset the other workers? Explain.

 ASSESSING MATH SKILLS

You spend 20% of an 8-hour day planning, 7.5% organizing, 7.5% staffing, 50% leading, and 15% controlling. How much time do you spend on each management function?

 CASE ANALYSIS

TechCo, a software company, tried letting some employees "telecommute," or work at home. The company's experience was not a good one, so senior management disallowed telecommuting. Janet Jefferson, team leader for a new software, broke her leg. She can work, but needs to remain home for two weeks. Management does not want to change its policy, but Janet is the product expert.

Apply: What should TechCo do? If Janet telecommutes, will management be breaking a principle? Explain your answer.

School Principal

■ Nature of the Work

Principals work with teachers to develop and maintain curriculum standards. Developing mission statements and setting performance goals help establish the academic atmosphere at the school. Principals ensure that students meet national academic standards. Many principals work with the community to develop school-to-work transition programs.

Principals hire teachers, visit classrooms to observe the teaching methods, and evaluate a teacher's work. A teacher's pay is often based on that evaluation. Principals also make reports on finances and attendance. They may be involved in fund-raising to get financial support for their schools.

Principals have significant decision-making authority in their schools, yet they must be aware of and sensitive to the concerns of parents, teachers, and community members when establishing school policies.

■ Working Conditions

Principals work more than 40 hours a week, 10 to 11 months a year in elementary, middle and high schools.

■ Training, Other Qualifications, and Advancement

To become a school principal you need a master's or doctoral degree in educational administration or leadership. Most states require principals to be licensed as school administrators. Most principals have previous experience as teachers or counselors.

■ Salary Range

Elementary school, $63,000; middle school, $67,000; high school, $72,000. Salaries vary with experience, size, and location of the school. Public school salaries are generally higher than those in private schools.

CRITICAL THINKING

What special attributes and skills should a principal have?

STANDARD &POOR'S

INDUSTRY OUTLOOK

Principals are often involved in choosing learning materials, such as textbooks, for use in schools. Textbooks represent a major investment for schools. Because of the time, research, and marketing involved, it can take three to five years to prepare texts. Only a few large companies publish textbooks.

BUSINESS MANAGEMENT *Online*

For more information on management careers, go to:

busmanagement.glencoe.com

ENTREPRENEURSHIP

WHAT YOU'LL LEARN

▶ What entrepreneurs do.
▶ The difference between managers and entrepreneurs.
▶ The need for entrepreneurship and innovation in large and medium-size companies.
▶ The importance of small businesses.

WHY IT'S IMPORTANT

Knowing what is involved in starting and running a business will help you decide whether you want to start your own company some day.

KEY TERMS

• professional manager
• entrepreneur
• small business

What Is an Entrepreneur?

Senior, middle, and supervisory managers are all **professional managers**. Professional managers are paid to perform management functions within a company. Like other employees, they receive salaries for the work they do. Professional managers work for businesses, but they do not own them.

Entrepreneurs are people who launch and run their own businesses. When they start out, they must perform many of the basic management functions that professional managers perform. As their companies grow, they sometimes hire professional managers.

Many large companies, including Estée Lauder, Kellogg, General Electric, Microsoft, and Dell were started by entrepreneurs. Gary Comer, for example, started a small mail-order company in 1963. Today his

▶ **ENTREPRENEURIAL CHALLENGES** Wally Amos created a cookie empire based on his gourmet chocolate chip cookie. *What kinds of business problems do you think he faced when he started his cookie company?*

company, Land's End, is a multimillion dollar company whose clothing is sold all over the world. The company has thousands of employees and many professional managers.

Being an entrepreneur is much riskier than being a professional manager. Without the right skills and a lot of hard work, entrepreneurs can go out of business and lose all the money invested in their company. Starting and owning a company can be more rewarding than working for a company, however. Successful entrepreneurs can create prosperous businesses that provide high incomes and a feeling of personal accomplishment.

Entrepreneurs and professional managers often have different personal characteristics. Entrepreneurs tend to be more independent than managers, and they may have less formal education. Some entrepreneurs jump from job to job before starting their own businesses.

Entrepreneurs start with an idea for creating or modifying a product or service that they believe in. Entrepreneurs like the idea of making decisions and being their own bosses. They often find tremendous satisfaction in their work, and their financial rewards can be great. Being an entrepreneur means working long hours and making decisions about every aspect of a business. It also means taking risks. Unlike professional managers, entrepreneurs invest money in their businesses and risk losing all of it if their business does not succeed. Without entrepreneurs, there would be no new businesses and fewer exciting developments, or innovations, in business and industry.

PREDICT

What do you think of when you hear the word *entrepreneur*?

◄ **ENTREPRENEURIAL CHARACTERISTICS** Bill Gates cofounded Microsoft as a small business with his high school friend, Paul Allen. *What special personal characteristics do you think entrepreneurs need in order to succeed?*

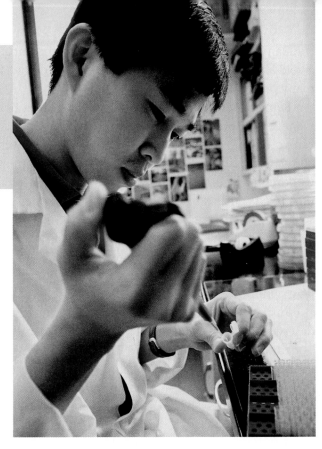

▶ **DEVELOPMENT** This pharmaceutical company spends hundreds of millions of dollars a year testing new drugs. *Why does it spend so much money developing new products?*

RESPOND

Would you like to be an entrepreneur? Explain.

Entrepreneurs own their businesses, but they can choose among several different types of ownership. Some entrepreneurs are *sole proprietors*, or people who run their businesses single handedly. Certain types of work are particularly well suited to this form of ownership—medicine, dentistry, and accounting, for example. Many store owners are also sole proprietors. Other entrepreneurs may form partnerships, especially when a large sum of money is involved. One or more partners may supply the money while another runs the business. Two or more people may also run a business together. Still other small businesses may choose to *incorporate*, or become a corporation, to avoid being held personally liable for financial losses. Some entrepreneurs choose to own franchises.

Entrepreneurs in Large and Medium-Sized Businesses

Many large and medium-sized organizations have begun to encourage their managers to become more innovative and to take more risks. At Dell Inc., for example, CEO and founder Michael Dell encourages his employees to take risks by allowing them to work independently, make mistakes, and learn from the process. He sets hard-to-meet targets and

BEBE STORES INC.

This Is No Fashion Victim

Who would have thought that skinny Capri pants would sell in January? Almost nobody. That's why skeptical buyers for bebe stores Inc. ordered a mere 1,000 pair—a clear bet that winter fashions wouldn't favor the cropped-leg look. But fashions did. And within a week, 800 pair were sold. For most chains, that unexpected popularity would have spelled disaster.

But for bebe (pronounced beebee), a "vertical" retailer that makes its own clothing, as Gap Inc. does, the fix was quick and decisive. Execs of the 100-store chain called the Los Angeles factory poised to make bebe suits and switched the order to Capri pants. More than 50,000 pairs of the pants sold.

It's that kind of quick-draw fashion sense and manufacturing savvy that has put bebe stores, managed by the husband and wife team of Manny and Neda Mashouf, on our list of fast-growing small companies. While many retailers catering to young women try to set fashions, bebe makes

a virtue of openly, and quickly, following someone else's lead. The stores' reputation for trendy clothing at mall prices has spawned a growing fan club among its target audience of women in their 20s and 30s.

The chain's numbers look as good as the dresses in its windows. Sales have grown an average of 31.1 percent annually over a three year period.

Continuing the company's breathtaking growth may prove more of a headache. Bebe's rise has been helped by the strong economy and consumer confidence. But demand for bebe's decidedly nonessential assortment of cocktail dresses and feather boas could quickly evaporate in less flush times.

Bebe's fashion status is also a risk. Successful chains such as Gap try to guard against the fickle nature of the fashion business by appealing to a wide range of customers, something bebe has yet to achieve.

To that end, Manny Mashouf is intent on building not just the bebe store but the bebe brand. An e-commerce Web site is up to give bebe wider name recognition. Plus, bebe has made its first steps toward going global, with stores in London and Vancouver.

Excerpted with permission from BusinessWeek, *May 31, 1999*

CRITICAL THINKING

What has been the key to bebe's success?

DECISION MAKING

As a manager, what steps would you take to ensure bebe's continued success?

▲ **SMALL BUSINESS** Being a part of a small business is hard work, but millions of Americans find that the rewards outweigh the drawbacks. *Why might someone leave a well-paying job in a large company to work in a small business?*

encourages his employees to stretch themselves to meet them. His approach has helped Dell become one of the most successful companies in the country.

Businesses that want to encourage managers to think more like entrepreneurs must find ways to support and encourage people who develop new products and services. Like Michael Dell, they must be willing to accept failure and to encourage people even after a new idea fails. Entrepreneurship within a large or medium-sized company is sometimes called *intrapreneurship*. Intrapreneurs take risks, but not with their own investments.

The Importance of Small Businesses

A **small business** is a company that is independently owned and operated. Some small businesses, such as neighborhood flower shops, restaurants, or dry cleaning stores, serve local areas. Other small businesses, such as mail-order and Internet companies, serve customers all over the world. Owners of small businesses often perform all management tasks.

QUESTION

Why are small businesses important?

The Small Business Administration (SBA), the government agency that lends money to small businesses, considers a business small if it has fewer than 100 employees. According to this definition, more than 99 percent of the businesses in the United States are small businesses. These small businesses play an important role in the U.S. economy. They employ millions of American workers and sell billions of dollars of products and services.

Small businesses tend to produce more innovations than larger businesses. Many of the most important high-technology companies in the country, including Intel, Apple, and Microsoft, began as small businesses. In 2003 Microsoft was one of the largest companies in the world, and its cofounders Bill Gates and Paul Allen were two of the world's richest people. Some of today's small companies may eventually become corporate giants.

Section 1.2 Assessment

FACT AND IDEA REVIEW

1. List three personal characteristics shared by many entrepreneurs.
2. Being an entrepreneur is easier than being a professional manager—true or false? Explain.
3. Describe two things companies can do to encourage their managers to think more like entrepreneurs.
4. Name two important roles small businesses play in the economy.

CRITICAL THINKING

1. **Predicting Consequences:** Why are entrepreneurs important to the economy? What would happen if no one wanted to be an entrepreneur?
2. **Analyzing Information:** How do companies benefit when managers think more like entrepreneurs?

ASSESSING WRITING SKILLS

Write a 250-word proposal for a type of business you would like to own. Include information on where you would locate your business, the types of products or services you would sell, and your plan for success.

CASE ANALYSIS

Craftings is a medium-size furniture distribution company specializing in children's bedroom sets. The firm has done well in the last ten years, but recently senior managers have noticed that sales have not been increasing. The managers believe that the problem boils down to too many firms selling the same kind of furniture.

Apply: What can Craftings do to increase sales?

CHAPTER 1 ASSESSMENT

CHAPTER SUMMARY

Section 1.1

▶ Businesses today operate in a world of constant change. Technology and society are changing more rapidly than ever before.

▶ Management is the process of deciding how best to use a business's resources to produce goods or provide services.

▶ Large companies generally have managers at three levels: senior, middle, and supervisory.

▶ Ways to examine how management works include: dividing the tasks managers perform into categories, looking at the roles different types of managers play in a company, and examining the skills required for management.

▶ Today, more and more women and minorities are working as managers.

Section 1.2

▶ Entrepreneurs are people who start and run their own businesses.

▶ A small business is a company that is independently owned and operated.

REVIEWING VOCABULARY

In groups of four or five, role-play a scenario for the class, using all of the terms and acting out examples of management skills.

management
senior management
middle management
supervisory management
role
conceptual skills
human relations skills

technical skills
principle
glass ceiling
professional
   manager
entrepreneur
small business

RECALLING KEY CONCEPTS

1. Name the three levels of management and describe the responsibilities of each.
2. Which of the management tasks listed on pages 12–13 best describes each of these activities:
   a. Setting a company goal
   b. Recruiting new staff
   c. Determining a financial plan
3. Management principles should be applied strictly at all times—true or false? Explain.
4. Why is being an entrepreneur riskier than being a professional manager?

THINKING CRITICALLY

1. Why do large businesses need management levels?
2. Why do all organizations, large and small, need management?
3. When might a manager change a principle?
4. Which managerial skills would an entrepreneur starting a new business need?
5. Consider businesses in your town. What advantages might small businesses have over larger ones?

CHAPTER 1 ASSESSMENT

ASSESSING ACADEMIC SKILLS

SOCIAL STUDIES Maria has a small home business designing flyers and brochures for other neighborhood businesses. Now she wants to buy a more powerful computer that will support the newest design software. Can Maria get a loan from the Small Business Administration, the federal agency that supports small U.S. businesses? Research the SBA at the library or on the Internet to learn whether it has a loan program for Maria. Share your findings with the class.

APPLYING MANAGEMENT PRINCIPLES

SOLVE THE PROBLEM You are the assistant manager of a large video store with many part-time employees. In the last few months, you

have noticed that many of these employees have been calling in sick. Part-time workers at your store earn the minimum wage, have no benefits, and are not involved in decision making. You believe these employees would be more responsible if they felt part of the business and had the chance to earn raises and perhaps some benefits.

Public Speaking Explain why you think part-time employees should be involved in the decision-making process and offered the chance to earn raises and receive benefits. Present the possible benefits of changing your store's policy to the class.

PREPARING FOR COMPETITIVE EVENTS

Which of the following is not one of the four responsibilities managers in an office environment generally have?

a. Planning

b. Organizing

c. Secret keeping

d. Leading

e. All are responsibilities of managers

BusinessWeek **ONLINE**

In this chapter you read the *BusinessWeek* Management Model about bebe. For more information, go to *BusinessWeek* online at: **www.businessweek.com**

Locate an article on a business that interests you. Write a summary of the article and present your findings to the class.

CHAPTER 2

THE MANAGEMENT MOVEMENT

LEARNING OBJECTIVES

When you have completed this chapter, you will be able to:

- Explain how the U.S. economy changed during the nineteenth and early twentieth century.
- Identify various theories of management.
- Explain the effects of Japanese business practices on management in the United States.

READING STRATEGIES

As you read

- **PREDICT** what the section will be about.
- **CONNECT** what you read with your own life.
- **QUESTION** as you read to make sure you understand the content.
- **RESPOND** to what you read.

UNITED
AIRLINES

WORKPLACE CONNECTIONS

Understanding Management

In December 2002, United Airlines succumbed to bankruptcy. However, management restructured the company to focus on its core advantages, meet its fiscal objectives, and eventually emerge from bankruptcy as a stronger, more efficient and competitive business.

Analyzing Management Skills

What are the benefits of a management philosophy that emphasizes teamwork? How might allowing employees to own shares increase their productivity?

Applying Management Skills

Recall or imagine a workplace task that you found inefficient or tedious. Imagine that your workplace supervisor asks you for suggestions to change the procedure for completing the task. How would being asked for your input make you feel about your workplace?

BusinessWeek ONLINE

For further reading on managers and management go to:
www.businessweek.com

THE EVOLUTION OF MANAGEMENT

WHAT YOU'LL LEARN

▶ How the Industrial Revolution created a new need for management.

▶ How the captains of industry of the last century created huge empires.

▶ The principles of scientific management.

▶ The results of the Hawthorne studies on worker productivity.

▶ Maslow's hierarchy of needs.

WHY IT'S IMPORTANT

To understand why businesses operate the way they do, you will need to understand how management systems evolved.

KEY TERMS

- monopoly
- trust
- scientific management
- hierarchy of needs

The Industrial Revolution

Some forms of management have existed since the beginning of time. Ever since one human tried to direct another, ideas about management have been developing. The challenges facing business managers have not always been the same, however. Those challenges changed dramatically more than a century ago, during the Industrial Revolution, and they continue to evolve.

As its name suggests, the Industrial Revolution refers to the period during which a country develops an industrial economy. In Europe, the Industrial Revolution began in the eighteenth century. In the United States, the Industrial Revolution began about 1860, just before the Civil War.

Before the Industrial Revolution, the U.S. economy was based on agriculture. Most people worked on small farms, using only simple

▲ **MANAGEMENT HISTORY** The new industrial enterprises that emerged in the nineteenth century demanded management skills that had not been necessary earlier. *Why was professional management less important when the U.S. economy was based on agriculture?*

technology, such as horse-drawn plows. Professional managers were not needed because most people worked for themselves.

By the late 1800s, the U.S. economy depended largely on industries such as oil, steel, railroads, and manufactured goods. Many people left their farms to take jobs in factories, where professional managers supervised their work.

Causes of the Industrial Revolution

Changes in technology, communication, and transportation made the Industrial Revolution possible. Advances in manufacturing processes allowed new products, such as steel, to be created. The growing use of steam power permitted more and more factories to operate. It also created a huge demand for coal.

Other factors also spurred the Industrial Revolution. Telegraph and cable lines in the United States were extended across the country after the Civil War, linking the country from coast to coast. The change made it possible for businesses to communicate with suppliers and customers. Communication became even more accessible after 1876, with the invention of the telephone.

Advances in transportation also improved opportunities for industry. By 1870 the United States had constructed 52,900 miles of railroad lines, including lines reaching the Pacific Ocean. Construction of canals and roads as well as improvements in the design of steamships made it easier for businesses to send and receive products and supplies.

Captains of Industry

Toward the end of the nineteenth century, powerful businesspeople who created enormous business empires dominated and shaped the U.S. economy. These captains of industry included John D. Rockefeller (oil), James B. Duke (tobacco), Andrew Carnegie (steel), J.P. Morgan (banking), and Cornelius Vanderbilt (steamships and railroads).

During this period entrepreneurs founded companies that later became industrial giants. One of these companies was Bethlehem Steel. In 1863 the company began producing the first iron railroad rails. It later became one of the largest shipbuilders in the world. By 1899 the company was selling almost $1 trillion worth of iron and steel products a year.

Most of the great entrepreneurs of the nineteenth and early twentieth centuries started with few resources. Andrew Carnegie, for example, was a poor immigrant

PREDICT

What are some advances in technology that have changed business practices from the 19th to the 20th centuries?

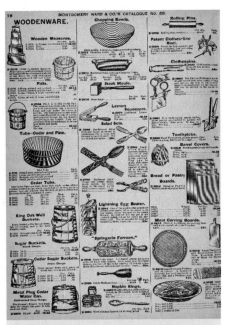

▲ **TECHNOLOGY AND MANAGEMENT** In 1872 Aaron Montgomery Ward created the first mail-order business in the United States. *What technological changes made creation of his company possible?*

from Scotland who worked in a cotton factory. At the age of 29 he entered the iron business, eventually creating one of the largest industrial enterprises in the United States.

Cornelius Vanderbilt began his empire at the age of 16, when he purchased a small vessel that sailed between Staten Island and New York. Eventually, he became the leading steamboat owner in the United States.

QUESTION

Why are large monopolies harmful to the consumer?

Creation of Monopolies

The captains of industry of the nineteenth century often pursued profit and self-interest above all else in order to create huge enterprises. They drove competitors out of business and created giant companies that maintained monopolies in their industries. A **monopoly** occurs when one party maintains total control over a type of industry.

John D. Rockefeller, for example, lowered the prices he charged for oil in order to force his competitors to sell out or join forces with him. He combined the dozens of companies he owned into a single **trust**, or giant industrial monopoly. Rockefeller's tactics were so successful that by 1879 he controlled more than 90 percent of the country's refining capacity and almost as large a share of its pipelines.

▲ BUSINESS LAW This 1884 cartoon portrays John D. Rockefeller's Standard Oil Company as an octopus whose tentacles choke small oil companies, the railroads, shipping companies, and banks. *How did legislators respond to the public sentiment captured in this cartoon?*

The Break-Up of the Trusts

By about 1870, many people became worried about the concentration of wealth in the hands of a few very rich business owners. They began to question the ways in which these businesses drove their competitors out of business. Legislators and the public alike began to voice growing concern that creation of monopolies was hurting consumers. In response to these concerns, the government decided to begin regulating business.

THE INTERSTATE COMMERCE ACT In 1887 Congress passed the Interstate Commerce Act, the first major piece of regulatory legislation. It passed the law in response to the widespread practice in which the railroads gave rebates to some customers but not others. The Interstate Commerce Act forced railroads to publish their rates and forbade them to change rates without notifying the public. The law also established the Interstate Commerce Commission (ICC) to supervise the railroads.

Hooked on Quality

For six generations, Norway's Mustad clan has manufactured a small but crucial product: the fishhook. Since fishermen are scrupulous in their evaluation of each and every hook they use, production of the tiny pieces of metal is deceptively specialized.

To get it right, sales representatives from O. Mustad & Son travel the globe investigating the sorts of hooks favored by anglers from Alaska to Asia and then report back to the outfit's factories around the world. The globetrotting pays off: Family-owned Mustad has been the world's No. 1 maker of fishhooks for 125 years.

WIRED. "Even though the fishhook is a very old product, you have to come to the market with new products so customers understand that you are not complacent," says Hans Mustad, the company's 45-year-old chairman.

In a country like Norway, the world's ninth-largest fish producer, hooks represent a key niche. Mustad mastered the craft early on, and in the late 1800s, it invented and perfected a machine that gave the

company a massive advantage over competitors, whose hooks were made by hand.

In addition, Mustad has its own wire mill, which gives it greater control over the end product. Having high-quality wire is a key part of producing superior hooks, according to Mustad. And making the hooks by machine helps to ensure that each is the same size. This consistency is a key factor in retaining customers, Mustad says. "Each fisherman has a very particular view on what kind of fishhook will make him catch the most fish," he says.

LOOKING EAST. Such a painstaking devotion to accuracy helps Mustad see $60 million to $70 million in total

sales each year. With production in Asia, Europe, and South America, Mustad's fishhooks are in 140 markets worldwide. The U.S., with some 45 million sport anglers, is now Mustad's biggest market.

In the months to come, the outfit is looking to expand even further, adding jobs in China and Singapore. Low labor costs and a fast-growing local market make Asia an attractive place to grow the business, and one of the most promising markets for introducing new, fishing-related products.

With such a strategy, Mustad's slogan—"So sharp even fish talk about us"—seems fitting.

Excerpted with permission from BusinessWeek, *January 21, 2004*

CRITICAL THINKING

What are some of the reasons that the Mustads have been so successful for so long?

DECISION MAKING

Imagine that you want to start a bakery. How might you apply the principles of the Mustads' success to your business?

THE SHERMAN ACT In 1890 Congress passed the Sherman Antitrust Act, which made it illegal for companies to create monopolies. The law was intended to restore competition at a time when monopolies had taken over many industries.

Under Presidents Theodore Roosevelt, William Howard Taft, and Woodrow Wilson, the government broke up many of the large trusts that had been established during the nineteenth century. The Standard Oil Company, for example, was broken up into smaller companies so that other oil companies could compete with the former giant.

New Challenges for Management

In the eighteenth century and early nineteenth century, when most Americans worked on farms, sophisticated management techniques were not necessary. However, by the end of the nineteenth century, giant companies employed thousands of people and distributed products all over the country. Workers performed specialized tasks that needed to be coordinated. These changes demanded new ideas about how to manage people working in large corporations.

▲ SCIENTIFIC MANAGEMENT
Frederick W. Taylor (1856–1915) was the father of scientific management. *What were his main ideas?*

Frederick W. Taylor and Scientific Management

In response to the need for management, many new ideas about productivity and motivation were developed in the late nineteenth century and early twentieth centuries. In 1874 Frederick Winslow Taylor (1856–1915) went to work as an apprentice at the Midvale Steel Company, where he soon became foreperson. Taylor quickly noticed that most workers did not work as hard as they could. He decided to find ways to motivate them to work harder.

To increase efficiency, Taylor tried to figure out the "one best way" to perform a particular task. To do so, he used a stopwatch to determine which work method was the most efficient. These studies, known as *time and motion studies*, enabled him to come up with scientific management principles. **Scientific management** seeks to increase productivity and make work easier by carefully studying work procedures and determining the best methods for performing particular tasks.

Taylor's scientific management was based on four main ideas:

1. Jobs should be designed according to scientific rules rather than rule-of-thumb methods. Employers should gather, classify, and tabulate data in order to determine the "one best way" of performing a task or series of tasks.

2. Employees should be selected and trained according to scientific methods. Employers should study worker strengths and weaknesses and match workers to jobs. Employers should also train employees in order to improve their performance.

3. The principles of scientific management should be explained to workers.

4. Management and workers should be interdependent so that they cooperate.

CONNECT

How would you design a scientific method for measuring the efficiency of a task at your workplace or school?

Companies today continue to use the principles of scientific management. The Marriott Corporation, for example, discovered that customer satisfaction with a hotel depends largely on how well a customer is treated during the first ten minutes. To make sure those first ten minutes exceeded customer expectations, Marriott changed the way it processed incoming guests. Every day the company makes a list of arriving guests, placing the names of guests expected earliest at the top of the list. The cleaning staff cleans the rooms of those guests first, so that they will not have to wait before checking in. Marriott also combined the jobs of doorperson, bellhop, and desk clerk by creating a new position, known as guest service agent. Under the new system, a guest service agent greets guests at the door, checks them in, and escorts them to their rooms.

All About
ATTITUDE

DO UNTO OTHERS
The Golden Rule may sound trite, but it's still true—you do benefit when you treat other people just the way you'd like to be treated. That goes for your attitude too. Your positive attitude should extend to your family and friends, as well as your employees. Expect the best from them—and for them.

The Hawthorne Studies of Productivity

Ideas on management continued to develop in the twentieth century. During the 1920s, researchers began to look at the relationship between working conditions and productivity. In 1924 researchers conducted a series of experiments at the Hawthorne plant of Western Electric in Cicero, Illinois. They lowered the lighting in the factory, expecting productivity to fall. Instead, to their astonishment, productivity increased. Over the next several months, the researchers repeated the experiment by testing many different levels of lighting as well as other factors. Whatever variable was changed, productivity increased.

Baffled by the results, the researchers called in a team of psychologists from Harvard University. For the next five years, these investigators conducted hundreds of experiments at the Hawthorne plant. They tested the effects of different wage payments, rest periods, work hours, and other variables. Regardless of the variable tested, the results were the same: productivity increased.

The researchers concluded that productivity rose because workers worked harder when they received attention. Even the attention paid to them by the researchers increased their productivity. This phenomenon, in which change of any kind increases productivity, has since been known as the "Hawthorne effect."

The Hawthorne studies also yielded other important results. The researchers concluded that factors other than the physical environment affected worker productivity. These included psychological and social conditions at work, such as informal group pressures, individual recognition, and participation in decision making. They also found that effective supervision significantly affected both productivity and employee morale.

Tips from Robert Half

When looking for a job, identify your ideal work environment. Do you want to work for a large or small company? Is pay or learning potential more important? Research companies at libraries, career centers, or through the Internet.

Abraham H. Maslow and the Hierarchy of Needs

Other important ideas about management came from the field of psychology. Abraham H. Maslow (1908–1970) was a psychologist who developed a theory of motivation. His ideas had a significant impact on management.

According to Maslow, all people have five basic types of needs, as shown in **Figure 2–1**:

- Physical needs (such as food, water, air, and sleep)
- Security needs (related to freedom from physical, psychological, or financial harm)
- Social needs (such as the need to talk to others, express feelings of friendship, and accept and be accepted by others)
- Status needs (self-esteem and the esteem in which one is held by others)
- Self-fulfillment needs (such as the need to realize one's own potential)

Maslow believed that individuals fulfill lower-level needs before seeking to fulfill higher-level needs. That is, people satisfy their need for food before they seek self-fulfillment. Because one set of needs must be met before another is sought, Maslow referred to a hierarchy of needs. The **hierarchy of needs** is Maslow's grouping and ordering of physical, security, social, status, and self-fulfillment needs.

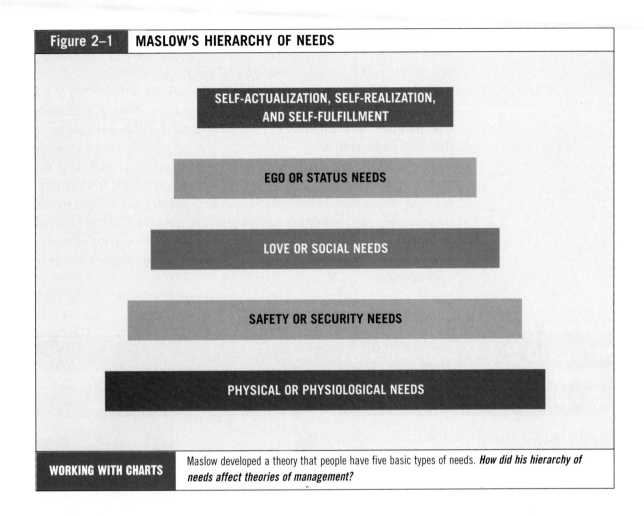

Figure 2–1 | MASLOW'S HIERARCHY OF NEEDS

SELF-ACTUALIZATION, SELF-REALIZATION, AND SELF-FULFILLMENT

EGO OR STATUS NEEDS

LOVE OR SOCIAL NEEDS

SAFETY OR SECURITY NEEDS

PHYSICAL OR PHYSIOLOGICAL NEEDS

WORKING WITH CHARTS Maslow developed a theory that people have five basic types of needs. *How did his hierarchy of needs affect theories of management?*

APPLYING MASLOW'S THEORY TO MANAGEMENT Maslow's hierarchy of needs has important implications for business managers. At the lowest level, according to this theory, workers are motivated by basic needs, such as the need for wages or salary. Basic needs also include the physical conditions in which a person works (for example, heating, lighting, and noise level).

Once these basic needs are met, employers can address the next level of needs—safety or security needs. It's important for employers to clearly communicate to their employees the benefits of working for their company. Some of these security needs can be met by providing employees with insurance, retirement benefits, and job security. Employees need to know that in their workplace, they are safe from physical, psychological, or financial harm.

Managers meet workers' social needs by providing work environments in which colleagues interact. They can also provide opportunities for co-workers to socialize with one another (by providing company lunch rooms or allowing employees to attend company retreats, for example).

RESPOND

What needs would you seek to have filled by a job? Do they correspond to Maslow's hierarchy of needs?

Status needs can be met by providing workers with signs of recognition that are visible to others. These include job titles, private offices, designated parking spaces, awards, and promotions.

Finally, employers can meet employees' need for self-fulfillment by providing them with opportunities to be creative at work. Managers who include their employees in decision making will help them meet this highest-level need.

Companies try to meet different needs in various ways. ITT, for example, has created a Ring of Quality Program, which honors outstanding employees. Employees who make a major contribution to the company receive gold rings or silver pins. The president or chairman of the corporation presents these awards at a formal dinner. Recognizing employees in this way fills a need that is not met by simply providing cash bonuses.

Section 2.1 Assessment

FACT AND IDEA REVIEW

1. How did the changes in the U.S. economy during the late nineteenth century increase the need for management?
2. What laws were passed in the nineteenth century to try to control the power of large companies?
3. How did Frederick W. Taylor change thinking about management?
4. What factors affect workers' productivity?

CRITICAL THINKING

1. **Analyzing Information:** Why is it difficult to apply the principles of scientific management to tasks such as writing a television script or creating a new computer game?
2. **Making Generalizations:** Which do you think is more important to employees, a high salary or a pleasant work environment? According to Maslow, which kind of workers would more likely prefer higher pay to better working conditions?

ASSESSING WRITING SKILLS

Many people influenced the development of effective management. Some of these people include Mary Parker Follett, James F. Lincoln, and Charles McCormick. Research and write a one-page paper about one of these important figures.

CASE ANALYSIS

In recent years, All-Steel, a manufacturer of metal fences, has had a serious problem retaining employees. Two years ago, in an effort to combat the problem, the company's president, Mark Esposito, raised wages by 10 percent. The move had almost no effect on turnover: last year almost 25 percent of the workforce quit. Mark's company pays higher wages than its competitors but they are still unable to retain a higher percentage of the workforce.

Apply: What factors explain the turnover rate at All-Steel? Explain your answer.

Management Careers in Focus

Farm Manager

◼ Nature of the Work

Farm managers help farmers manage day-to-day activities. They may oversee only one activity, such as livestock feeding, if the farm is large. Or they may take on all responsibilities from choosing crops to planting to harvesting. They may monitor production and marketing; hire, assign and supervise workers; and oversee maintenance of property and equipment. On very large corporate farms, they may oversee the tenant operators.

◼ Working Conditions

Full-time farm managers often work more than 60 hours a week. Time off is infrequent and the work is strenuous. Much of their work is outdoors in rural areas, where they work with plants and animals. However, they also spend time indoors working with computers, taking care of finances, and planning. Because they work with chemicals and large equipment, the work can be hazardous.

◼ Training, Other Qualifications, and Advancement

Farm managers often have a bachelor's degree in agriculture, or in business with a concentration in agriculture. Many have grown up on farms, but must have at least several years experience working on farms. They need a knowledge of business, manage-ment, bookkeeping, and accounting as well as agriculture.

◼ Salary Range

Full-time salaried farm managers earn $485 to $650 a week. They usually receive no benefits but may be provided with housing, in addition to food products.

CRITICAL THINKING:

Why do today's farm managers need computer skills? How can computers help farmers work more efficiently? What kind of challenges do you think farm managers face on their job?

STANDARD &POOR'S

INDUSTRY OUTLOOK

In 2000, approximately 1.5 million people were employed as farmers, ranchers, and agricultural managers. Although farm consolidation is expected to cause a decline in employment for farmers and ranchers through 2010, a modest growth in farm, ranch, and agricultural manager positions is expected over this time period.

BUSINESS MANAGEMENT *Online*

For more information on management careers, go to:
busmanagement.glencoe.com

THE DEVELOPMENT OF MODERN MANAGEMENT

WHAT YOU'LL LEARN

▶ The principles of total quality management.
▶ The principles of Theory X and Theory Y.
▶ Japanese management concepts and the ideas behind Theory Z.

WHY IT'S IMPORTANT

Becoming familiar with modern management principles will help you understand how businesses function in today's environment.

KEY TERMS

• Theory X
• Theory Y
• centralization
• decentralization
• total quality management (TQM)
• Theory Z

Empowering Employees

As organizations grew in size and complexity, new styles and methods of management began to emerge. Different philosophies developed on how best to manage people.

Theory X and Theory Y

In the 1960s, MIT Professor Douglas McGregor identified two types of management styles, which he called Theory X and Theory Y (see **Figure 2–2**). **Theory X** assumes that people are basically lazy and will avoid working if they can. To make sure that employees work, Theory X managers impose strict rules and make sure that all important decisions are made only by them.

Before it changed its approach to management, Preston Trucking was a typical Theory X company. "Management knew all the answers," according to the company's vice president. "If there was a question, management would make the judgment. No matter that the manager had 7 years' experience and the driver had 20. The feeling was 'I am the manager. I have the title.'"

Theory Y assumes that people find satisfaction in their work. Theory Y managers believe that people will work productively if put in the right environment. According to them, people are creative and will come up with good ideas if encouraged to do so. Theory Y managers tend to give their employees much more freedom than do Theory X managers. They also let their employees make mistakes. "In this company, you'll be fired for *not* making mistakes," said Steve Ross, the former chief executive officer of Time Warner.

TBWA/Chiat/Day, an advertising agency based in Los Angeles, has adopted a Theory Y approach to management. Job descriptions are intentionally ambiguous, and employees are given the freedom to make decisions on their own. "If you don't have the initiative or are scared or are waiting for your boss to say it's okay to try something, you're in trouble," says the company's director of administration. The company believes that its management approach sparks the creativity needed to succeed in the advertising business.

FIGURE 2-2

Theory X and Theory Y

Different managers make different assumptions about what motivates people to work. Their assumptions affect the way they manage their employees.

1 THEORY X

Theory X managers assume that workers will avoid working if they can. They impose strict rules and make sure that all important decisions are made only by them. Many traditional organizations, such as the U.S. Postal Service, are run by Theory X managers.

2 THEORY Y

Theory Y managers believe that people find satisfaction in their work. They have high expectations of their employees and grant them considerable freedom. They also let them make important decisions.

3 THEORIES X AND Y

Most companies combine elements of both theories of motivation. They allow employees freedom in some aspects of their professional lives and control their actions in others. Many companies, for example, set informal dress codes but strict guidelines on employee travel expenses.

RESPOND

Give an example of Theory X and Theory Y management. How do they differ?

Centralization versus Decentralization

QUESTION

Explain the difference between centralized and decentralized management systems.

In the early twentieth century, decisions at most large American companies were made by a small group of senior managers. These companies had centralized management systems. **Centralization** refers to the concentration of power among a few key decision makers.

Companies in which decisions were made by only a few key people often ran into problems. For example, Henry Ford, the inventor of the automobile, nearly destroyed the company he built by refusing to let his managers perform management tasks. Ford was so afraid of allowing anyone but himself to make decisions that he had secret police agents spy on his senior aides. Senior managers were limited to executing directives laid down by Ford himself.

▲ **CENTRALIZED MANAGEMENT** Henry Ford kept tight control over the company he founded. *How did his management style affect his company?*

To compete with Ford, General Motors decided to decentralize its operations. **Decentralization** is the process by which decisions are made by managers at various levels within an organization. In the 1920s, Alfred Sloan, GM's chair, broke the company up into five divisions: Chevrolet, Pontiac, Oldsmobile, Buick, and Cadillac. Breaking up the company allowed GM to better target different kinds of customers. It also allowed managers at each of the new divisions to make important decisions that central managers had once made. Decentralization was so effective at GM that by the end of World War II the company was selling more cars than Ford.

The Emphasis on Quality and Teamwork

Beginning about a half century ago, managers began to apply new management tools. Some of these new systems emphasized maintenance of flawless quality standards and teamwork.

Total Quality Management

In the 1950s, a new era of management began, as mathematical models were developed to quantify management. One important pioneer in this field was W. Edwards Deming, who used mathematics to help solve problems of quality control.

Deming began by studying how companies ensure that the products they produce are not defective. He came up with a mathematically based approach to quality control that became known as total quality management. **Total quality management (TQM)** is a system of management based on involving all employees in a constant process of improving quality and productivity by improving how they work. This approach, which has been widely adopted by American businesses, focuses on totally satisfying both customers and employees.

DEMING'S FOURTEEN POINTS Deming emphasized the maintenance of high quality standards. His overall philosophy for achieving high quality is contained in his 14 points:

1. Create consistent purpose for improving products and services in order to remain competitive.
2. Adopt a new philosophy. We are in a new economic age. We can no longer live with commonly accepted levels of delays, mistakes, defective materials, and defective workmanship.
3. Stop depending on mass inspection. Require instead statistical evidence that quality is built in to eliminate need for inspection on a mass basis.
4. Consider quality as well as price in awarding business.
5. Constantly improve the system of production and service. It is management's job to work continually on the system.
6. Institute a vigorous program of job training.
7. Adopt and implement leadership. The responsibility of supervision must change from focusing on sheer numbers to quality. Improvement of quality will automatically improve productivity.
8. Drive out fear so that everyone may work effectively for the company.
9. Break down barriers between departments. People in research, design, sales, and production must work as a team to foresee problems of production that may be encountered with various materials and specifications.

▲ **TOTAL QUALITY MANAGEMENT** Consumers must be happy with the price and quality of what a business produces. *What are some of the things managers can do to assure the quality of their products or services?*

10. Eliminate numerical goals, posters, and slogans for the work-force that ask for new levels of productivity without providing new methods.
11. Eliminate work standards that prescribe numerical quotas.
12. Remove barriers that stand between the hourly worker and his or her right to pride of workmanship.
13. Encourage education and self-improvement for everyone.
14. Create a structure in top management that will work every day to achieve the above 13 points.

CONNECT

Imagine a meeting between employees and supervisors at a manufacturer that stressed total quality management. What would the supervisors say to the workers?

APPLYING TOTAL QUALITY MANAGEMENT Companies in a variety of industries have adopted TQM programs. Most have found that the performance of their companies improved.

A large Silicon Valley computer company adopted TQM after facing growing customer dissatisfaction with its products. To improve quality, management involved every employee in the company. Hourly production workers and senior managers met regularly to discuss the company's production process. Together they worked out solutions to the problems that had cost the company business. Instituting TQM helped the company regain the confidence of its customers and reduce operating costs. Having managers work with production workers to solve problems affecting quality improved both profits and employee morale.

Other companies ensure that employees are committed to quality in different ways. For example, to constantly remind them of their commitment to quality, Motorola employees carry wallet-sized cards that state: "Our Fundamental Objective (Everyone's Overriding Responsibility): Total Customer Satisfaction." At General Electric, executives' bonuses depend on how well the company improves quality. At Burger King, no employee receives a bonus if the company fails to meet its quality goals.

International Management

THAILAND

The social culture of Thailand has given rise to highly centralized corporations with strict lines of authority. Self-managed teams would not be a viable management style because workers are used to taking direction from leaders whose authority is absolute and based on status.

BusinessWeek *ONLINE* For further reading about International Management go to: **www.businessweek.com**

Japanese Management Practices

The success of many Japanese companies in the decades following World War II drew worldwide attention to their management practices. To try to find out why Japanese companies were so successful, researchers tried to identify ways in which Japanese companies differed from American companies. They found, for example, that Japanese managers encouraged more employee participation in decision making than did American managers. Japanese managers also showed deeper concern for the personal well-being of their employees. Rather than presenting their workers with demands, Japanese managers tended to facilitate decision making by teams of workers. In contrast, Americans tended to work as individuals.

Japanese business practices have been successfully exported to the United States. At Honda's plant in Marysville, Ohio, for example, 5,500 American "associates" turn out one Honda Accord a minute. The high level of productivity at the plant is attributed to several innovative management practices.

▲ **DEMING'S FOURTEEN POINTS** Adopting Deming's ideas on quality helped Japan transform itself into one of the most successful economies in the world. *What are some of Deming's Fourteen Points?*

In a traditional assembly-line plant, workers are organized by functions. One worker might be responsible for installing seat belts, for example. Another might be responsible for checking headlights. In contrast, Honda workers are organized by teams rather than by functions. Workers are thus skilled in various aspects of production.

The Honda factory differs from traditional American factories in other ways as well. Unlike most American plants, where there is a clear distinction between workers and managers, all Honda employees are empowered to make decisions. As a result, Honda employees are energetic and committed to producing high-quality products.

Theory Z

In the 1980s, William Ouchi, a management researcher, developed a new theory of management, known as Theory Z. **Theory Z** is a business management theory that integrates Japanese and American business practices. As **Figure 2–3** shows, Theory Z incorporates the Japanese emphasis on collective decision making and concern for employees with the American emphasis on individual responsibility.

One company that increased its sales by adopting Japanese-style management practices is Johnsonville Foods, a Wisconsin sausage-making company. In 1978 a new chief executive officer, Ralph Stayer, took over the company. Sensing that the company's employees were unhappy, Stayer decided to institute some changes. He did away with front-line supervisors, replacing them with self-managing teams. The teams hire, evaluate, and fire their own employees. He also offered financial support to employees who wanted to take courses in the evenings, whether or not their courses were job-related. The results were impressive, with company sales rising from $7 million a year to $130 million in just ten years.

RESPOND

Which management philosophy do you think is best for running a business: Theory X, Y, or Z? Explain your answer.

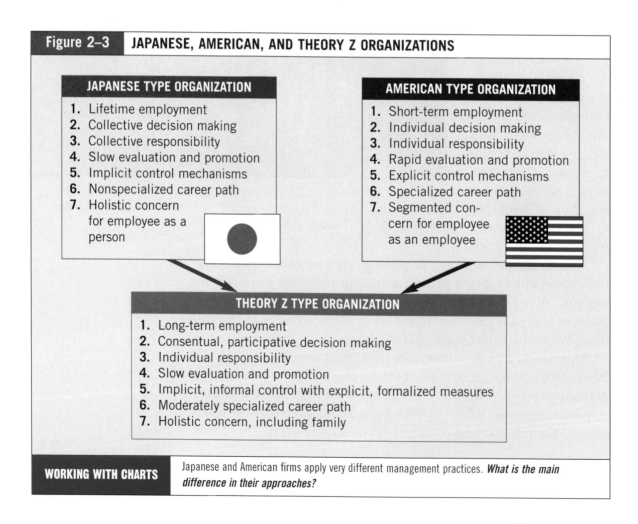

Figure 2–3	JAPANESE, AMERICAN, AND THEORY Z ORGANIZATIONS

JAPANESE TYPE ORGANIZATION
1. Lifetime employment
2. Collective decision making
3. Collective responsibility
4. Slow evaluation and promotion
5. Implicit control mechanisms
6. Nonspecialized career path
7. Holistic concern for employee as a person

AMERICAN TYPE ORGANIZATION
1. Short-term employment
2. Individual decision making
3. Individual responsibility
4. Rapid evaluation and promotion
5. Explicit control mechanisms
6. Specialized career path
7. Segmented concern for employee as an employee

THEORY Z TYPE ORGANIZATION
1. Long-term employment
2. Consentual, participative decision making
3. Individual responsibility
4. Slow evaluation and promotion
5. Implicit, informal control with explicit, formalized measures
6. Moderately specialized career path
7. Holistic concern, including family

WORKING WITH CHARTS   Japanese and American firms apply very different management practices. *What is the main difference in their approaches?*

◄ THEORY Z Many American companies now organize their workers into teams. *How was this development affected by Theory Z?*

Section 2.2 Assessment

 FACT AND IDEA REVIEW

1. Identify five of Deming's Fourteen Points.
2. Describe the difference between Theory X and Theory Y.
3. List three ways in which Japanese business practices differ from traditional American practices.

 CRITICAL THINKING

1. **Drawing Conclusions:** Why is total quality management (TQM) important? Explain.
2. **Evaluating Information:** How have Japanese business practices affected American corporations?

 ASSESSING MATH SKILLS

Three out of every 500 pairs of jeans your factory produces are defective and need to be thrown away. If the cost of each pair of discarded jeans is $9.00, how much money is your company losing on every 10,000 pairs of jeans it produces?

 CASE ANALYSIS

Over the past ten years, Peter Brown has built an automobile dealership that now has 15 branches in five states. Every day, Peter travels to another branch to supervise activities, order new vehicles, and observe the work of the service department. Recently, thousands of dollars in sales have been lost because the cars customers want have not been in stock at some dealerships. Peter's response to the decline in sales has been to keep closer tabs on activities at some of his branches.

Apply: Is Peter's approach to managing his company a sound one? What steps could Peter take to improve the operation of his company?

CHAPTER 2 ASSESSMENT

CHAPTER SUMMARY

Section 2.1

▶ By the end of the nineteenth century, the U.S. economy had become industrialized. The change created a new need for management.

▶ Frederick Taylor, Abraham Maslow, and others developed ideas that changed thinking about management.

Section 2.2

▶ Different kinds of managers make different assumptions about what motivates workers. Theory X managers believe that people do not like to work and need to be tightly controlled. Theory Y managers believe that people like to work and should be allowed freedom to be creative.

▶ W. Edwards Deming emphasized maintenance of high quality standards. His principles of total quality management are stated in his Fourteen Points.

▶ Japanese business practices differ from American practices. Theory Z incorporates practices from both business cultures.

REVIEWING VOCABULARY

Create a crossword puzzle using the following terms. Make sure the clues you write accurately define each term.

monopoly
trust
scientific management
hierarchy of needs
Theory X
Theory Y

centralization
decentralization
total quality
  management
  (TQM)
Theory Z

RECALLING KEY CONCEPTS

1. What legislation was passed in response to the unethical business practices of the nineteenth century?
2. What are the main principles of scientific management?
3. What did the Hawthorne studies show about worker motivation and productivity?
4. How do Theory X managers differ from Theory Y managers?
5. How do Japanese management practices differ from American management practices?
6. What is Theory Z?

THINKING CRITICALLY

1. How does business management today differ from business management in the nineteenth century?
2. How did Maslow's ideas affect thinking about management?
3. How would you apply the results of the Hawthorne studies to increase productivity?
4. Why do some companies centralize decision making and others decentralize it?
5. Why would American companies want to adopt Theory Z?

CHAPTER 2 ASSESSMENT

ASSESSING ACADEMIC SKILLS

SCIENCE Conduct an experiment in which you determine the fastest way to first test that ballpoint pens work and then package them into boxes. Use a stopwatch to time different methods. Write a brief report in which you identify the "one best way" of performing this task.

APPLYING MANAGEMENT PRINCIPLES

SOLVE THE PROBLEM The rules at your company are very strict. All employees must go to lunch between noon and 12:45 p.m. No personal phone calls are allowed, and employees are not allowed time off from work to take care of sick children. You believe that productivity at your company would actually increase if some of these rules were relaxed. Try to convince the manager of your company that relaxing the rules would increase productivity.

Public Speaking Prepare a short presentation in which you identify the benefits of a more relaxed work environment. Use examples of companies that do not impose strict rules.

PREPARING FOR COMPETITIVE EVENTS

The federal law that was enacted to establish the illegality of monopolistic practices is the:

a. Sherman Antitrust Act.

b. Federal Trade Commission Act.

c. National Labor Relations Act.

d. Interstate Commerce Act.

BusinessWeek ONLINE

In this chapter you read the *BusinessWeek* Management Model about the management approach of a family-owned fishhook manufacturer. For more information, go to *BusinessWeek* online at: **www.businessweek.com**

Locate an article on current approaches to management. Write a brief summary of what makes the approach successful. Present your findings to the class.

CHAPTER 3

CAREERS IN MANAGEMENT

LEARNING OBJECTIVES

When you have completed this chapter, you will be able to:

- Explain the difference between a job and a career.
- Discuss how personal characteristics, values, and lifestyle goals influence career decisions.
- Set career goals.
- Research the management job market.
- Write a résumé and cover letter for a job.

READING STRATEGIES

As you read

- **PREDICT** what the section will be about.
- **CONNECT** what you read with your own life.
- **QUESTION** as you read to make sure you understand the content.
- **RESPOND** to what you read.

WORKPLACE CONNECTIONS

Understanding Management

Charles O. Holliday, CEO of DuPont, suggests that a successful company must attract and retain the most talented employees. DuPont has built a reputation for recruiting high-quality employees with a wide variety of backgrounds and interests. Policies that encourage, train, and support employees help DuPont attract and keep excellent workers.

Analyzing Management Skills

Why is the quality of a company dependent on the quality of its employees? How can working in a business help an employee develop even greater skills?

Applying Management Skills

Describe a job that required you, a friend, or family member to learn new skills. How did learning that skill contribute to the success of the employer?

BusinessWeek *ONLINE*

For further reading on managers and management go to:
www.businessweek.com

53

EXPLORING CAREERS

WHAT YOU'LL LEARN

➤ Why your personal characteristics and strengths are important in deciding on a career.
➤ How to assess your abilities, personality, learning style, values, and lifestyle goals.
➤ How to match your personal strengths and characteristics with career options.
➤ How to research career fields and develop a plan to achieve your career goals.

WHY IT'S IMPORTANT

Understanding yourself is the first step to finding a career you'll enjoy.

KEY TERMS

• career
• personality
• learning styles
• values
• lifestyle
• trend
• professional association
• networking

How Do You Choose a Career?

Like many high school students, you may not have thought about what you want to do with your life. Maybe you've decided that college or a job after graduation will help you figure out what you want to do. Maybe wondering about what you'll do after high school makes you nervous. After all, you're still a teenager. Why should you worry about the future?

Consider this fact: when you start working full time, you'll spend as many as 2,000 hours a year on the job. (The only thing most people spend more time doing is sleeping!) That's a lot of time. You will probably want to spend it doing something you enjoy. How do you find out what you might enjoy doing? Ask people who like their work, and they will tell you that they knew what they wanted to do early on. They then got the training they needed to pursue a satisfying career.

▲ MAKING CAREER CHOICES Many teenagers work part time. *How might this job help you decide what kind of career you want?*

A career differs from a job. A **career** is a series of progressively more responsible jobs in one field or in related fields. People pursue careers based on interests, abilities, and education. A job is basically work for pay. It may be part of a career path—for instance, a job with a company that offers advancement. A job also can be a way to earn some money for a short period—serving fast food or packing items on an assembly line, for example.

You already may have had one or more jobs. You may have enjoyed the work and would think about doing it again. However, you may have had a job you disliked. Maybe you saw that it was a dead-end job with no challenges or opportunities for advancement. Whether you liked your job or not, it probably taught you something about what you want from your career.

PREDICT

How does someone begin a career in management?

Assessing Your Personal Strengths

The first step in determining what kind of work you'd like to do is to look closely at yourself. Understanding your personal strengths and values will help you decide which career fields interest you. Your career choice will be influenced by

- your interests and abilities
- your personality
- your learning style
- your personal values
- the kind of lifestyle you want to lead

YOUR INTERESTS AND ABILITIES Your interests are the things you enjoy doing. You may enjoy creating video games or acting in a local theater. If you aren't sure what your interests are, one way to find out is to try out new activities. You might want to take a drawing class or volunteer with a local hospital.

Do you already enjoy participating in a number of activities? Make a list of your ten favorite activities and rank them. Include activities you like to do in a group and by yourself—at home, at school, at work, or outdoors. Are you a computer whiz? Do you write well? Do you have good people skills? Identifying your interests and abilities can get you started on a great career.

Don based his career choice on the thing that interested him the most. Growing up in a small town, he loved to listen to the radio. When he was 13, he was already hanging around the local radio station begging for work. The staff gave him a job sweeping the floors. By

▲ DETERMINING PERSONAL STRENGTHS Eileen Collins is the first woman to command the Space Shuttle. *What kinds of abilities and personality does she need to do her job well?*

the time he left for college, Don had been hosting local radio shows for several years. After earning a degree in broadcasting, he began producing his own television shows. Today Don is a senior manager in the public affairs office of a government agency, working with the media to spread information about the agency around the country.

YOUR PERSONALITY Your **personality**—the combination of all the unique qualities that make you who you are—will determine whether you want to work with people or things, in a group, or by yourself. For example, the student in your class who is fascinated by scientific ideas may choose to be a manager of a biotechnology firm. A student who loves to entertain might want to open his own family-style restaurant.

What kind of a personality do you have? Would you rather read a book, or do you enjoy organizing activities with friends? Do you go out for the lead in the school play, or would you rather work behind the scenes? Are you especially funny or sympathetic? Be honest about yourself. Remember, there is no right or wrong kind of personality. There are only different kinds of people.

YOUR LEARNING STYLE An important part of your personality is the way you interact with the world around you to gather information and turn it into knowledge. The different ways people process information are called **learning styles**. Once you understand your learning style, you'll know the best approach to learning something new. You can also use the information to help you

OPEN YOUR EYES AND EARS

Look around and you'll more than likely find a book, article, television, or radio show that could help you improve your skills. Seek out seminars, workshops, and lectures that enable you to learn new skills and share information. Use your free time to better yourself.

QUESTION

What are the eight styles of learning?

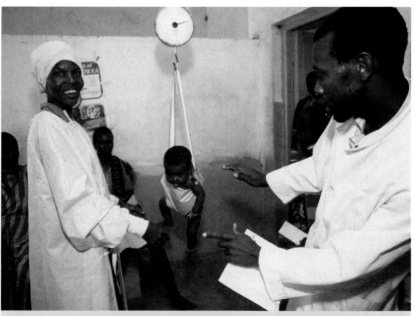

▲ **DETERMINING PERSONAL VALUES** Some people's values lead to a life of dedication to others. *What values do you think this doctor has?*

decide which career fields are best for you. Most people do well in a career that uses their strongest learning style.

Look at the learning styles in **Figure 3–1**. Decide which ones work best for you. Of these, the one you prefer and use most often is your

Figure 3–1	EIGHT STYLES OF LEARNING	
Type of Learner	**Likes**	**Best Ways to Learn**
Verbal/ Linguistic	*Likes* to read, write, and tell stories; good at memorizing names and dates	*Learns* best by saying, hearing, and seeing words
Logical/ Mathematical	*Likes* to do experiments, work with numbers, explore patterns and relationships; good at math, logic, and problem solving	*Learns* best by making categories, classifying, and working with patterns
Visual/Spatial	*Likes* to draw, build, design, and create things; good at imagining, doing puzzles and mazes, and reading maps and charts	*Learns* best by using the mind's eye and working with colors and pictures
Musical/ Rhythmic	*Likes* to sing, hum, play an instrument, and listen to music; good at remembering melodies, noticing pitches and rhythms, and keeping time	*Learns* best through rhythm and melody
Bodily/ Kinesthetic	*Likes* to touch and move around; good at hands-on activities and crafts	*Learns* best by interacting with people and objects in a real space
Interpersonal	*Likes* having lots of friends, talking to people, and joining groups; good at understanding people, leading, organizing, communicating, and mediating conflicts	*Learns* best by sharing, comparing, and cooperating
Intrapersonal	*Likes* to work alone and pursue interests at own pace; good at self-awareness, focusing on personal feelings, and following instincts to learn what needs to be known	*Learns* best through independent study
Naturalistic	*Likes* spending time outdoors and working with plants, animals, and other parts of the natural environment; good at identifying plants and animals and at hearing and seeing connections to nature	*Learns* best by observing, collecting, identifying, and organizing patterns

WORKING WITH CHARTS People learn in different ways and use different learning styles when necessary. *Which of your classes require you to use different learning styles?*

▲ **CHOICE OF LIFESTYLE** The New York Stock Exchange is a high-pressure environment where people devote themselves to making money. *What kind of lifestyle do you think interests people who work on the stock exchange?*

primary learning style. Most people do best in a career suited to their primary learning style.

YOUR VALUES In the 1960s hundreds of young Americans volunteered to work in poor countries in Africa and Asia. They were the first Peace Corps volunteers. Their goal was to help people in other countries have a better life. These volunteers were acting according to their **values**—beliefs that guide the way people live.

Just as people have different abilities and personalities, they also have different values. Your values will influence the kind of career you choose. You can identify your values by looking at the kinds of actions that are important to you. Are you a person who takes pride in doing what you say you'll do, is always on time, and can be counted on to make sure things get done? Then you value responsibility. Responsible people tend to make good managers and to work well without supervision.

Other important values include:

- *Achievement.* People who are willing to put in the extra effort to succeed value achievement. If you are an achiever, you can excel in any career but might enjoy one that presents many challenges, such as medicine, law, or aviation.
- *Recognition.* Some people want their work to be acknowledged and enjoy being in the public eye. If you want to be recognized, you might choose a career in writing, acting, or politics.
- *Relationships.* If interacting with friends and family members is especially important to you, then you value relationships. If you enjoy the interactions relationships offer, you may want to consider a career in psychology or education.
- *Compassion.* Like the early Peace Corps volunteers, compassionate people want to help others. If you are compassionate, you might enjoy being a nurse, veterinarian, social worker, community organizer, or counselor.
- *Courage.* People exhibit bravery in two ways. Some people are courageous when confronted with physical danger. They tend to make good soldiers, firefighters, and rescue workers. Other people exhibit courage by standing up for their beliefs. They may choose careers in politics or public service.

YOUR LIFESTYLE Your **lifestyle** is the way you spend your time, energy, and money. Lifestyles vary as much as personalities and values. What kind of lifestyle will you want in the future? Are you willing to work hard at a career in order to reach the top of your field? Do you want to have plenty of free time for your personal interests or families? Is becoming wealthy the most important consideration for you? The kind of lifestyle you want will help determine the kind of career you choose.

Now that you have an understanding of your interests and abilities, personality, learning style, and values, how can you tell whether they are suited to the career that interests you? A personal career profile like the one in **Figure 3–2** can help you decide if you and your career choice are a good match.

CONNECT

Imagine a typical day in your working life 20 years from now. What satisfies you about your chosen career?

Figure 3–2	PERSONAL CAREER PROFILE FOR HUMAN RESOURCES MANAGER
Personal Characteristics	**Compatible Career Choices**
Your Values: I am a responsible individual with a strong sense of compassion. I want to achieve my career goals.	*Career Values:* Human resources managers are responsible for helping workers deal with personal and job-related problems.
Your Interests: I volunteer as a mentor to two middle-school students and work with an agency that helps immigrant families. I enjoy participating in activities with my extended family.	*Career Duties and Responsibilities:* I will need to understand company benefits so I could explain them to others. I would also provide counseling programs to resolve disputes.
Your Personality and Learning Style: I am a friendly, outgoing person and don't mind being asked to organize activities or lead a discussion. The learning styles that work best for me are linguistic and interpersonal.	*Personality Type Needed:* A human resources manager must enjoy working with people. They must be compassionate but firm.
Skills and Aptitudes: I'm a good student, especially in English and math. I speak fluent Spanish. I communicate well with all kinds of people.	*Skills and Aptitudes Required:* This career requires strong people skills and organizational skills. I will need to learn new information quickly, explain it clearly, and motivate others.
Education/Training Acceptable: I am eager to attend college and graduate school. If I can't afford graduate school, I will find a job in human resources and attend school part time.	*Education/Training Required:* I will need at least a bachelor's degree in a business field. A graduate degree in human resources management will help me achieve my goals.

WORKING WITH CHARTS	A chart like this can help you decide whether your personal characteristics fit the career you've chosen. *Why is it so important to take personal characteristics into account?*

Manager of Computer Services

◼ Nature of the Work

Computer systems managers combine their knowledge of a company and their computer skills to solve computer-oriented problems throughout the company. They ensure that the company uses the correct software and hardware to meet the firm's needs. They may be involved in planning, developing, or purchasing new computer systems. They may help devise new ways to apply the existing systems to different operations. They oversee the implementation of new systems, and they see that existing systems run smoothly.

They may help develop training materials when new systems are installed. Computer systems managers are also responsible for seeing that a company's computer systems are secure.

◼ Working Conditions

Computer systems managers work 40 hours a week or longer, depending on when problems arise or new systems are installed. Because they work primarily with computers, they might suffer from eye strain, back discomfort, or wrist problems.

◼ Training, Other Qualifications, and Advancement

To become a computer systems manager, you need a bachelor's degree in computer science or business, and several years experience.

You also need to be familiar with a variety of hardware, software, services, and systems. You must also have excellent communication and project management skills.

◼ Salary Range

Computer systems managers earn $34,000 to $76,000 depending on degree, experience, and industry.

CRITICAL THINKING:

Name some reasons that computer services are the fastest growing fields.

STANDARD &POOR'S

INDUSTRY OUTLOOK

In the airline industry, preparing for a potential Year 2000 problem was vital. Addressing this problem and ensuring passenger safety cost hundreds of millions of dollars, but sound preparation and management resulted in no flight, accounting, baggage, or other errors and protected everyone from the possibility of more serious consequences.

BUSINESS MANAGEMENT Online

For more information on management careers, go to:
busmanagement.glencoe.com

Researching Career Options

The more career information you have, the easier it will be to decide which one is right for you. Research can provide you with a wealth of information on subjects such as salaries, working conditions, and prospects in your field.

Where can you look to find specific information on careers that interest you? Your school, the local library, or the Internet is a good place to start. Books, magazines, and Web sites can provide you with a wealth of information on types of careers, job prospects, and potential salaries. People in the business community have firsthand knowledge of the training their career field requires, working conditions, and employment possibilities.

OCCUPATIONAL OUTLOOK HANDBOOK A good place to start your research is the *Occupational Outlook Handbook* published by the U.S. Department of Labor. The handbook describes thousands of jobs that are available throughout the United States. It lists job responsibilities, working conditions, and salaries. It also outlines educational requirements and predicts future growth for many career fields.

The U.S. Department of Labor also keeps track of job trends in the United States. Trends show changes or movement in a certain area. A fashion trend is a style of clothing or accessories that become popular for a period of time. A job trend is an increase or decrease in the number of jobs in a particular field. **Figure 3–3** shows the estimated increases for some industries.

Figure 3–3	JOB OUTLOOK		
Industry	**Thousands of Jobs**		
		2000	*2010*
Total, all occupations		145,594	167,754
Management, business, and financial occupations		15,519	17,635
Professional and related occupations		26,758	33,709
Service occupations		26,075	31,163
Sales and related occupations		15,513	17,365
Office and administrative support occupations		23,882	26,053
Farming, fishing, and forestry occupations		1,429	1,480
Construction and extraction occupations		7,451	8,439
Installation, maintenance, and repair occupations		5,820	6,482
Production occupations		13,060	13,811
Transportation and material moving occupations		10,088	11,618

WORKING WITH CHARTS The government tracks both the percentage increase and the growth in the number of jobs that will be created. *Why is it important to know the number of jobs that will be created?*

Source: Bureau of Labor Statistics, *Monthly Labor Review* (November 2001)

MAGAZINES AND BOOKS Magazines are another good source of information. *Occupational Outlook Quarterly*, *Monthly Labor Review*, and *BusinessWeek* provide up-to-date information on job trends. You also can consult popular specialty books such as *What Color Is Your Parachute?* Books such as these can help you think further about your personal qualifications. Most also offer practical advice—for instance, how to find the best companies.

PROFESSIONAL ASSOCIATIONS You can find information on specific careers by contacting **professional associations** . A professional association is made up of people in the same field. It allows members to exchange information and ideas, promotes a positive image for the profession, and provides information to the public. The American Institute of Architects, for example, has many chapters around the country. Its

FIGURE 3–4

Planning for a Successful Career

Choosing a career is one of the most important decisions you'll ever make. Following these steps will help you get started.

1 ASSESS YOUR INTERESTS AND ABILITIES
The first step is figuring out what interests you and what you do best. Your abilities are more than the subjects you're good at in school. They also include musical and artistic talents, people skills, and organizing skills.

members often are involved in community work. Associations often publish their own magazines and maintain their own Web sites. The *Occupational Outlook Handbook* contains addresses for many of these associations.

NETWORKING Perhaps the best way to find out about a career that interests you is **networking**, or talking to people who may offer you job leads, contacts in your fields, or other information. One place to start is with your school guidance counselor. Your network can include family and friends as well as businesspeople. Many career professionals get to know a large number of people in their own field and related fields. They may use these contacts to find a new job for themselves or refer friends to jobs. Networking is so successful that some people believe it is the best way to learn about job opportunities.

Figure 3–4 reviews the steps that will help you plan for a successful career.

QUESTION

What are some ways to find out about job openings?

2 **CONSIDER PERSONALITY, LEARNING STYLE, VALUES, AND LIFESTYLE**
The second step is to consider your personality, learning style, values, and the kind of lifestyle you want to live. You want to spend your life doing what you enjoy. Understanding your personality and values will help you find out what that is.

3 **RESEARCH**
The third step is to find out all you can about the careers that interest you. Start at the library or on the Internet. Read books and magazines, contact professional associations, network, and visit with a school guidance counselor.

Achieving Your Career Goals

What do you do once you have a clear picture of your interests and the kinds of careers that interest you? At this point, you're ready to take action.

Develop a Plan

Suppose you now have information on several careers that seem interesting. A good first step is to try out the personal career profile for each of them (**Figure 3–2**). Your interests and personal characteristics will probably fit some fields better than others.

Decide which career interests you the most. Then ask your family members, friends, neighbors, teachers, and even your school counselors if they know of people who work in that career. See if you can meet one of those people to find more information about the career that appeals to you. Remember that reaching your ultimate career goal is going to take some time. There are some important things you'll have to do along the way.

RHI Robert Half International Inc.

Tips from Robert Half

Informational interviews help you learn about a field or profession. Before you go, learn about the company and the person you'll talk to. Contact that person and ask for a brief meeting to discuss his or her job or industry. Look your best, and have questions prepared.

EDUCATE YOURSELF Most employers want to hire people with some education beyond high school. In fact, almost every job requires some special training, and having an advanced education means more career opportunities for you to choose from. Therefore, how will you finance your education beyond high school? Investigate the alternatives using the research techniques you learned in this chapter. Consider also that some companies pay all or part of their employees' tuition for job-related courses.

GET EXPERIENCE Taking a part-time job in a field you think you'd like is a great way to get firsthand experience in a field. In fact, a part-time job will make it possible for you to observe a career from the inside. You'll gain valuable work experience and make personal contacts—and make some money doing it. If you like the world of finance, try a local bank, accounting firm, or the financial office of any local business.

In some cases volunteer work is the way to go. Although volunteers don't get paid, they are paid in valuable experience. It's another way to explore and find out about a career. Do you like the theater? Then volunteer to work behind the scenes at a community theater.

CONSIDER AN INTERNSHIP Internships are another good way of gaining career experience. Like volunteers, most interns are not paid, but they also gain valuable job skills. Businesses, government agencies, and arts organizations all offer internships to students. Some internships are only for the summer, while others may run longer. Some offer small stipends. Successful interns may be invited back summer after summer while they are in school and may ultimately be offered jobs. You can search for available internships on the Internet, talk to your guidance counsellor, or talk to professionals in your area of interest. You can contact businesses where you would like to serve as an intern. For example, if you want to get experience in the art field, you can call local museums and galleries to see if they have internship programs. Any work experience you can get will be beneficial to you in your search for a meaningful career.

Section 3.1 Assessment

FACT AND IDEA REVIEW

1. What is the difference between a career and a job?
2. Name three of the personal characteristics you need to consider before deciding on a career.
3. Which learning styles might be best suited to the following professions: accounting, architecture, teaching?
4. List three sources of information about careers and describe the kind of information each provides.
5. True or false: Before you make a plan of action, you should research the career fields you're interested in. Explain your answer.

CRITICAL THINKING

1. **Evaluating Information:** What kind of personality and values do you think a person needs to become a successful lawyer? A high school principal?
2. **Drawing Conclusions:** Why do you think that some people believe networking is the best way to find a job?

ASSESSING COMMUNICATIONS SKILLS

Prepare a three-minute speech that explains the importance of one of the following characteristics in choosing a career: personality, values, or lifestyle. Present your speech to the class.

CASE ANALYSIS

Kendra Taylor is just finishing her junior year in high school. Her mother is a middle school teacher, and Kendra (who loves children) always wanted to be a teacher. This year she took advanced biology and chemistry classes. She enjoyed them so much that she started to think about a career in medicine. Now she's beginning to panic. Her college applications are due in the fall. She can't decide whether to apply to schools with strong pre-med or teacher-education programs.

Apply: What steps can Kendra take over the summer to help her decide on a career?

A FUTURE IN MANAGEMENT

Types of Management Careers

All kinds of businesses need managers—construction firms, restaurants, rock bands, Internet companies, museums, and baseball teams, for example. In short, whatever field interests you has a need for managers.

Consider the television industry. Maybe you've thought only actors work in television. However, television is a business like any other—it needs many managers.

Every city has at least one television station. Depending on how big the station is, the general manager may oversee everything from advertising sales to budgeting. Many larger stations have lots of managers for separate areas. The sales manager makes sure the station has the advertising it needs to support its programming. The program manager buys programs from producers and sets schedules for airing them. The chief engineer makes sure the station has the equipment to air the programs and oversees the people who operate it. The human resources manager recruits candidates to run the station and works with employee benefit plans and payroll. The chief financial officer makes sure the station operates on budget.

Television networks need producers, or managers who

▶ MANANGEMENT RESPONSIBILITY This engineer has worked her way up to project manager in a construction firm. *What kind of responsibilities do you think she has?*

help create programs. The producer is responsible for everything that makes a show tick. This includes setting the budget, finding locations, getting people to the set, and organizing the equipment. Often a producer starts out as an assistant on a show, helping with the many detailed tasks that go into creating the final product.

Television is just one of the exciting businesses that need managers. Publishing companies need editorial managers who decide which books to publish and help get them to press. Software companies need computer-savvy managers to help develop and oversee the design of video games, "how-to" programs, and other innovative products.

▲ **MANAGEMENT CAREERS** America Online, a division of Time Warner, Inc. (TWX), is the country's biggest Internet service provider. *What kind of managers do you think AOL needs?*

In each chapter of this text, you'll find a "Careers in Management" feature. These features describe some of the many career opportunities available in management.

For-Profit Businesses

Businesses such as television stations, rock groups, publishing companies, and high-tech firms are **for-profit businesses** . For-profit businesses operate to earn money for their owners. These businesses include industry giants such as Microsoft, Coca-Cola, and General Electric as well as small neighborhood businesses such as grocery stores and dry cleaners.

If you're wondering what you can do in the for-profit world, the answer is "almost anything." Whether you're interested in becoming a stockbroker or an artist, you can find a career in a for-profit company.

Nonprofit Organizations

Nonprofit organizations include professional associations, environmental groups, arts groups, and many other special-interest organizations. A nonprofit organization operates to promote a special interest or cause. "Nonprofits" get their support from a number of sources, including members, other individuals, and companies. Some of these organizations are well known, such as United Way and Habitat for Humanity. Others may be small local groups dedicated to cleaning up a river or supporting a homeless shelter. Some nonprofits get their support from local, state, and federal tax dollars. Government agencies fall into this category, as do local schools.

Like for-profit businesses, nonprofits offer many managerial opportunities. Nonprofits need general managers, financial managers, and human resources managers. Public school systems need managers at their central offices and in the schools.

Small nonprofits also offer exciting opportunities. Janet, who has always loved music, found her career in a small nonprofit. In college she majored in vocal musical performance. However, she knew she didn't want to dedicate her life to performing. After graduating she worked in and managed a music store, produced and managed concerts, and managed a children's musical troupe. Today she is the conference manager for a professional association that promotes folk music.

As you can see, the possibilities for management careers are endless. **Figure 3–5** shows that jobs in many managerial fields are projected to increase in the coming years. That's more good news for up-and-coming managers.

Figure 3–5	ESTIMATED GROWTH IN SOME MANAGERIAL OCCUPATIONS	
	Thousands of Jobs	
Occupation	**Approximate 2000 Employment**	**Projected 2010 Employment Growth**
Administrative services managers	362	20.4%
Advertising, marketing, promotions, public relations, and sales managers	707	32.4%
Agricultural managers	1,462	−21.7%
Chief executives	547	17.2%
Computer and information systems managers	313	47.9%
Engineering managers	282	8.0%
Human resource managers	219	12.7%
Industrial production managers	255	6.2%
Purchasing managers	132	-5.5%
Social and community service managers	128	24.8%
Transportation, storage, and distribution managers	149	20.2%
Medical and health services managers	250	32.3%

WORKING WITH CHARTS Look at the growth for managers by the year 2010. *In which fields will managerial positions grow at the highest rate?*

Source: Bureau of Labor Statistics, *Monthly Labor Review* (November 2001)

BusinessWeek

Management Model

The Shape of Things to Come.Com?

Chan Suh, a 37-year old Korean native raised in New York and Paris, heads a Manhattan-based ad agency, but he couldn't be further from Madison Avenue. He has never shot a TV commercial or created a glossy magazine ad. Instead, his firm, Agency.com, specializes in the fast-growing world of online marketing.

Agency.com is one of the oldest of the online agencies. It had revenues of about $80 million in 1998, up from $15 million in 1997. Started in 1995 with two employees, it now boasts a staff of 750—with a median age of 28. Ranked No. 47 on Advertising Age's list of U.S. Agencies, its client roster includes Lipton, British Airways, and Texaco.

ZEN RETREAT. With a mix of marketing and technology services, Agency.com offers a decidedly '90s spin on advertising. About one-third of the firm's work is purely technical, such as coordinating a company's various computer functions and creating databases. On the marketing side,

Agency.com has handled everything from creating a corporate Web site for Metropolitan Life Insurance Co. to creating online promotions for the Almond Board of California.

Chan insists that technologists, strategists, and marketers work side by side—though they can retreat to private "zen" rooms for solitude. Teams collaborate throughout the process, from pitch to production to launch. "When they have to live together like that, they're more likely to come up with solutions that work in concert," he says.

NEW SHOPS VS. TRADITIONAL. Change at Agency.com is a way of life. The shared work spaces arrived in 1998. In the summer of 1999 the offices moved to a new space, complete with doors made of chalkboard for on-the-spot brainstorming and idea jotting. "When I don't change things, people say, 'Hey, what's going on around here?'" he says.

But Chan is not about to declare his type of agency the victor over the traditional shops. He does not envision the eclipse of Madison Avenue. At the same time that the Internet has been on the rise, other mediums such as newspapers and magazines have also shown great gains. "It does precipitate challenge for the previous generation. In 100 years, we'll run into the same issues." Until then, it's Chan's turn to be the brash young upstart.

Excerpted with permission from BusinessWeek, *July 26, 1999*

CRITICAL THINKING

How has Chan Suh used change to his advantage?

DECISION MAKING

If you were managing a company would you use shared work spaces or separate offices? Why?

Applying for a Job

RESPOND

What types of skills, work, and volunteer experiences do you think would be important to include in a résumé for a management position?

When you begin looking for the job that will start you on your career, how will you sell yourself to employers? Applying for a job is the process of convincing a potential employer to invest in a great new product—you. Every step of the way, you want to make the best possible impression.

Often the first piece of information a potential employer has about you arrives in the form of a résumé and cover letter, either by mail, fax, or the Internet. A **résumé** is a short document that provides potential employers with information about your specific qualifications for a job. Your résumé describes your education, experience, and achievements. Each time you send out a résumé, you should send a **cover letter** along with it. The cover letter serves as a brief introduction and emphasizes those accomplishments you feel are most relevant to the job.

The purpose of a résumé and cover letter is not to get you a job. The purpose is to convince potential employers that they want to ask you to come in for an interview.

Types of Résumés

There are two basic types of résumés, the **chronological résumé** and the **skills résumé** (also known as the *functional résumé*). You'll probably use both kinds of résumés during your career.

CHRONOLOGICAL RÉSUMÉ

The chronological résumé lists your work experience and education in reverse order. You

Figure 3–6	CHRONOLOGICAL RÉSUMÉ

Lisa Farulo
Tel: 503-555-4394
Fax: 503-555-4399

2031 East Long Branch Drive
Homewood, OR 97035
e-mail: lisafar@pacificnet.net

JOB OBJECTIVE: Seeking internship with Internet service provider.

WORK EXPERIENCE:

September 2002– present	Sales Clerk (part-time), Qwik Copy Shop, Homewood, Oregon. Assisted customers with in-store computers, troubleshooting software problems, making copies.
June 2002– August 2002	Camp Counselor, Homewood Community Center Computer Camp, Homewood, Oregon. Tutored third- and fourth-grade students in using computer software applications and Internet.
February 2002– May 2002	Server (part-time), McDonald's Restaurant, Homewood, Oregon. Took customers' orders, served food, helped clean restaurant area and kitchen.

EDUCATION: High school diploma, Homewood High School, Homewood, Oregon, 2003. Followed college preparatory course.

HONORS AND ACTIVITIES: Dean's Honor List, Student Council, Computer Club, Debating Club, Tennis Team.

SPECIAL SKILLS AND ABILITIES: Skilled on both MacIntosh and IBM-compatible computers. Proficient in HTML. Designed Web sites for school groups.

A chronological résumé presents your work experience in reverse order. *Why is it advantageous to use reverse chronological order?*

begin with your most recent job, then the one before it, until you've listed all your work experience. You list your education and other information the same way, beginning with your current schooling or degree and working backward. **Figure 3–6** gives an example of a chronological résumé.

The chronological résumé has the advantage of showing how you've grown in your jobs. If you have strong work experience, this type of résumé will allow you to display it to full advantage.

SKILLS RÉSUMÉ A skills résumé highlights your abilities and accomplishments rather than your work experience. You organize a skills résumé around your strengths. These can be things you studied in school, skills you developed on your own or with special training, and skills such as interpersonal communication. **Figure 3–7** gives an example of a skills résumé.

To prepare a skills résumé, you list the strengths and abilities you want to emphasize. After each heading on the résumé comes a brief description. The advantage of this type of résumé is that it showcases the abilities you want potential employers to see.

COMPUTERS AND RÉSUMÉS

Some companies have special Web sites that allow applicants to create and submit résumés online. You create the résumé by filling in a computer-generated form on the company's Web site.

Many companies now scan the résumés they receive and store them in a database. When positions open up, these companies search their databases using keywords that fit the job, such as the name of a type of

Figure 3–7	SKILLS RÉSUMÉ

Lisa Farulo
Tel: 503-555-4394
Fax: 503-555-4399

2031 East Long Branch Drive
Homewood, OR 97035
e-mail: lisafar@pacificnet.net

JOB OBJECTIVE: Seeking internship with Internet service provider.

SKILLS AND ABILITIES:

Computer skills: Skilled on both MacIntosh and IBM-compatible computers. Proficient in HTML. Designed Web sites for school groups.

Customer service: Experienced in serving members of the public. Have worked as food server and as sales clerk. Have also tutored students in computer applications. Deal with others respectfully and politely and work well as part of team.

Hardworking: Have had part-time jobs since I was 16. Began working as food server in local restaurant. Served as counselor at Homewood Computer Camp in the summer of 2002. Currently work part-time for Qwik Copy Shop, assisting customers with rental computers and troubleshooting software.

Communications: Excellent writing and speaking skills. Member of high school debate team. Had short story published in high school literary magazine.

EDUCATION: High school diploma, Homewood High School, Homewood, Oregon, 2003. Followed college preparatory course.

HONORS AND ACTIVITIES: Dean's Honor List, Student Council, Computer Club, Debating Club, Tennis Team.

A skills résumé emphasizes your abilities rather than your job experience. *Would you use a chronological or a skills résumé?*

software the employee needs to know. You can make your résumé easy to scan and search by following these guidelines:

- Use white paper and dark type.
- Avoid italics, underlining, and other fancy type.
- Leave plenty of white space.
- List all your specific skills—for example, the exact names of computer programs you can use.

These guidelines can help you create a résumé that's not only easy to scan and search but easy to read as well.

WORKPLACE DIVERSITY

FRANCE

Boasting is a sign of weakness in France, indicating self-satisfaction and immaturity. The French tend to shun questions about themselves to avoid showing self-centeredness. In conversations and presentations in France, managers need to avoid superlatives or focusing on "my team" or "I."

Preparing a Résumé

The first step in preparing your résumé is to think positively. Your goal is to make yourself look good on paper. Don't be shy about emphasizing your strong points. Carefully choose what you include and what you want to emphasize, leaving out any negative information.

Here are some hints to help you put your résumé together:

1. Showcase what you have to offer. Focus on what you have accomplished on the job or in school. Include any special activities you initiated and any decision-making responsibilities you were given.
2. Be honest. Don't try to pad your résumé with honors you didn't win and accomplishments that weren't your own. You can be terminated from a job if your employer finds out you included false information on your résumé.
3. Concentrate on your skills and education if you don't have much work experience. Include volunteer work that relates to the job you want.
4. Keep your résumé brief—no more than two pages. The format should be simple and attractive, with plenty of white space. If you can't do the formatting yourself, have a friend or a local copy shop do it.
5. Leave out any reference to your age, race, sex, marital status, height or weight, or overall health. The law forbids employers from taking such characteristics into account.

Once your résumé is organized, you can turn your attention to the cover letter.

QUESTION

What are keywords? Why are they important in a résumé?

Writing a Cover Letter

Your cover letter is your chance to introduce yourself to your potential employers and to convince them that they want to meet you. It does not go into the same detail as your résumé. Basically, it lets the company know how you heard about the job, why you're the right person for it, and how they can contact you.

You want your letter to stand out. You can make it sparkle by writing in plain, correct language. Keep it short (one page), polite, and to the point. **Figure 3–8** illustrates an effective cover letter.

Figure 3–8	**COVER LETTER**

Lisa Farulo
2031 East Long Branch Drive
Homewood, OR 97035

Yvonne Currin
Human Resources Manager
PacificNet, Inc.
17928 Research Boulevard
Tigard, OR 97729

March 4, 20--

Dear Ms. Currin:

Max Bardo, Homewood High School's Guidance Counselor, told me about PacificNet's internship program for high school graduates. Please consider me an applicant for the program. Enclosed please find my résumé.

I believe my background in computers, customer service experience, and interest in your company would make me a good intern. My interest in computers began in elementary school. I participated in advanced computer courses beginning in the fifth grade. My high school offered HTML and Web design programs, which I successfully completed. I belong to the school's computer club and designed its Web site on the school's Intranet.

Outside of school, I have worked as a computer camp counselor and assistant in a copy shop that rents computer time on in-store computers. At Homewood Computer Camp, I helped teach elementary school students to use the Internet and MicroSoft Office. At Qwik Copy Shop, I assist customers who rent computer time and troubleshoot problems with software packages.

PacificNet has been my Internet service provider for three years. I enjoy many of the features it offers and appreciate its excellent technical support. I am interested in a career with a company that treats is customers personally, as PacificNet does.

May I have an interview? You can reach me at 503-555-4394 or by e-mail at lisafar@pacificnet.net. Thank you for your time.

Sincerely,

Lisa Farulo
Encl:1

A cover letter gives a company a more personal glimpse of you than a résumé does. *How will you choose the information you want to emphasize in your letter?*

Dreams and goals are important. They can define your desires and provide your life with direction. However, taking action is how you achieve your objective. Now is the time and the place to start realizing your goals. Don't put off what you can do today until tomorrow.

Before you begin writing, make a short outline of your letter. Decide which of your strengths and what kinds of experience you want to highlight. Throughout your letter, use the "you approach," emphasizing what you can offer the firm. Then follow the one-two-three approach:

1. Tell the company why you are writing. In the first paragraph, give the full job title and say where you found out about the position—from a newspaper or web site, for instance. If someone referred you, give the name. You can also mention that you have enclosed your résumé.

2. Explain to the company why they should hire you. In the body of the letter (the second and possibly third paragraphs), state why you are right for the job. Point out details of your experience that relate directly to the job, such as special projects. If you're using a chronological résumé, you may want to summarize your experience in a few sentences.

▶ **SHARING YOUR RÉSUMÉ** It is a good idea to show your cover letter and résumé to a friend, family member, or career counselor before sending them out to a prospective employer. *Why should you show these documents to others?*

3. Ask for an interview in the closing paragraph. Give your telephone number and e-mail address here (even though they'll be elsewhere on the letter) so the reader doesn't have to search for them.

With a carefully composed résumé and cover letter, you've got a good shot at getting an interview for the job you want. Your cover letter and résumé highlight your best assets to potential employers by describing your skills, experience, and interests. The time and effort you put into preparing these documents also will draw attention to your good organization skills and eye for detail—traits that every employer looks for.

Section 3.2 Assessment

 FACT AND IDEA REVIEW

1. What is the difference between a for-profit firm and a nonprofit organization?
2. The purpose of a résumé and cover letter is to get you a job. True or false? Explain your answer.
3. List three things you should not include on your résumé and explain why you shouldn't list them.
4. Why do companies scan résumés and keep them in electronic databases?
5. What should you include in the first paragraph of your cover letter? The last?

 CRITICAL THINKING

1. **Making Comparisons:** Why is it important to know how to write both a chronological résumé and one that emphasizes your skills?
2. **Evaluating Information:** Why would you want to use the "you approach" when writing a cover letter?

 ASSESSING MATH SKILLS

The *Occupational Outlook Handbook* predicts that between 2000 and 2010, the number of jobs will increase by 22 million. The number of jobs in service industries is expected to account for 13.7 million of these jobs. What percent of jobs will be in the service industries?

 CASE ANALYSIS

Sanjay Muratpa owns AdCo, a small advertising agency. He is looking for an administrative/editorial assistant with excellent computer skills and experience in graphic design and writing. Although the pay is not high, Sanjay thinks the job is an interesting one. Apparently job seekers don't agree. He's hired two people with solid experience and good skills, but both quit after a few months. Now Sanjay is scanning his database of résumés again.

Apply: What kind of person should Sanjay be looking for if he wants someone who will stay on the job?

CHAPTER 3 ASSESSMENT

With one or two classmates, role-play a job interview. Prepare a script that includes all the vocabulary words from the chapter.

career
personality
learning style
values
lifestyle
trend
professional association
networking

for-profit business
nonprofit
    organization
résumé
cover letter
chronological
    résumé
skills résumé

CHAPTER SUMMARY

Section 3.1

▶ A career is more than a job. It's a series of progressively more responsible jobs in a field.

▶ Your career choice should be based on your interests and abilities, personality, learning style, values, and lifestyle goals.

▶ Researching in the library, on the Internet, and through networking can help you decide if a career is for you.

Section 3.2

▶ You'll find many management opportunities in both for-profit and nonprofit organizations.

▶ A résumé is a short document that presents your education and experience to a prospective employer.

▶ A cover letter that introduces you to a company always accompanies your résumé.

RECALLING KEY CONCEPTS

1. True or False: A job is always a stepping-stone in a career. Explain your answer.
2. List three occupations that would suit people with these values: achievement, relationships, compassion.
3. Which federal agency tracks information on job trends? What is its primary publication on careers?
4. Why is it so important for your résumé and cover letter to be well written?
5. Why should your résumé be formatted in a simple style without fancy typefaces?

THINKING CRITICALLY

1. Do you think skills are more important than personal characteristics, values, and lifestyle in choosing a career? Why or why not?
2. Why are learning styles important to career choice?
3. How important is projected job growth in a career that interests you?
4. Why do some people prefer to work for nonprofit organizations rather than for-profit businesses?
5. Why might a company ask job applicants to compose résumés online?

ASSESSING ACADEMIC SKILLS

SOCIAL STUDIES Research two professional associations in career fields that interest you. Search their Web sites for information on how to prepare for a career in their specialty or write to them requesting information. Remember that associations sometimes have local chapters. Once you have received the information, prepare a short presentation describing what you have learned.

APPLYING MANAGEMENT PRINCIPLES

SOLVE THE PROBLEM InTech is a growing software company headquartered in an outlying suburb of a large East Coast city. Competition for skilled employees in the area is stiff. InTech is having trouble finding the skilled programmers it needs to develop new products. Rich Miller, InTech's president, wants to recruit some bright young people who show potential but need more training. He wants to provide a training program customized to InTech's needs. He's asked several managers to help him draft a plan for training new employees.

Language Arts With several other students, research the different options for gaining experience that are discussed at the end of Section 3.1. Use library materials or the Internet. You may want to investigate several companies to see what options they prefer. Discuss the advantages of each option with other group members. On your own, write a 250-word report for Rich describing the options for InTech.

PREPARING FOR COMPETITIVE EVENTS

To find information about opportunities in a given occupation, which of the following sources would you consult?

a. *Occupational Outlook Handbook*

b. professional associations

c. people working in the field that interests you

d. Standard Industrial Classification

e. a, b, and c

In this chapter you read the *BusinessWeek* Management Model about a manager in an online agency. For more information, go to *BusinessWeek* online at:

www.businessweek.com

Locate an article about an online agency that interests you. Write a brief summary of the article and present it to the class.

CASE STUDY 1

Entrepreneurship and You—Anyone Can Be a Manager

OVERVIEW

In society today, there is a growing trend in which professionals are leaving their corporate lives and setting out on their own. According to the National Commission on Entrepreneurship, entrepreneurs create between 600,000 to 800,000 new businesses in the United States each year. This case study explores why people are leaving the corporate environment and what business-related skills are required of these entrepreneurs as they venture out to pursue their own businesses.

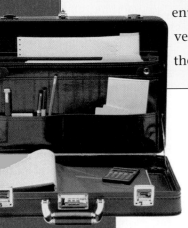

RESOURCES

- business periodicals
- word processor
- Internet (optional)
- college/university catalogs
- The Small Business Administration (SBA)

PROCEDURES

◆ STEP A ◆

Trends in the Global Arena

The environment in which businesses compete against one another has changed significantly during the past two decades. Such changes have resulted in challenges and opportunities that have led to an increasing number of people starting their own companies.

Identifying Information:

1. In groups of two to four students, identify five trends in society that have contributed to changes in the competitive arena. (Consider advances in technology and shifting demographics, for example.)

2. Illustrate how each of the factors provides a favorable business opportunity. Use examples to support your conclusions.

CASE STUDY 1

◆ STEP B ◆

What Skills Should an Entrepreneur Possess?

To succeed as an entrepreneur, a person must be trained in many areas. Unlike a larger company, with departments specializing in the different functional areas of business, a smaller business generally has to rely on the expertise of a single owner or a few owners. Such entrepreneurial efforts often fail when the owner or owners lack the business skills and training necessary to steer the company in the right direction.

Analyzing Information:

1. In your small groups, refer to business-related course listings in community college and state university catalogs. Also use business start-up information from the Small Business Administration or on its Web site.

2. Create a list of skills and training that an entrepreneur needs to succeed.

3. Analyze an entrepreneur's options if he or she lacks necessary business skills. How could the lack of certain skills affect his or her business financially? What can he or she do to gain skills?

◆ STEP C ◆

Management Report

Using a word processor, compose a 500-word essay that addresses how changes in society are reshaping the way business is done. In the essay, complete the following:

1. Highlight the importance of social change and how it leads many bright individuals to leave professional careers and run their own businesses.

2. Discuss skills that are necessary for an entrepreneur's business to succeed.

3. Focus on the potential problems that may be encountered when an entrepreneur lacks the prescribed knowledge needed to guide a company. Suggest how an entrepreneur can improve himself or herself.

4. Conclude by predicting the future of the entrepreneurial movement. Will more people find personal ownership to be attractive? If so, what impact does this have on the universities and colleges? What will happen to big business? What role does the U.S. government have in all of this?

5. Include a bibliography.

The Management Environment

Chapter 4
Ethics and Social Responsibility

Chapter 5
Business, Workers and the Law

Chapter 6
Economics

Chapter 7
International Business

IN THIS UNIT...

You will be introduced to the rights and responsibilities of managers and workers. Included in this unit are chapters covering ethics and social responsibility, the rights of businesses and workers, economics, and international business.

Journal Writing

In your journal, assess your knowledge of management by writing about the following:

1. What does the word *ethics* mean to you?
2. Name some of the rights that you think workers need to have protected.
3. Describe how supply and demand might determine the price of a new video game.
4. Make a list of items you own that are imported from another country. Why did you buy these items?

CHAPTER 4

ETHICS AND SOCIAL RESPONSIBILITY

LEARNING OBJECTIVES

When you have completed this chapter, you will be able to:

- Explain why ethics are important in business.
- Describe a code of ethics.
- Discuss ethical dilemmas.
- Describe laws that deal with ethical issues.
- Explain the change in corporations' views of social responsibility.
- Describe the ways in which businesses demonstrate their social responsibility.

READING STRATEGIES

As you read

- **PREDICT** what the section will be about.
- **CONNECT** what you read with your own life.
- **QUESTION** as you read to make sure you understand the content.
- **RESPOND** to what you read.

WORKPLACE CONNECTIONS

Understanding Management

Athletic apparel manufacturer Nike sells footwear that has been assembled in overseas factories where the minimum wage is much lower than it is in the United States. Maria Eitel, Vice President of Social Responsibility at Nike, oversees programs that prevent the abuse of poor workers abroad. As more consumers demand that companies produce products without harming workers or the environment, businesses like Nike learn to keep step.

Analyzing Management Skills

Why might it be challenging for a manager to balance the needs of the company with the needs of workers?

Applying Management Skills

Imagine that you are the "Vice President of Social Responsibility" at your workplace or school. What changes would you make to prevent unfair practices?

BusinessWeek ONLINE

For further reading on managers and management go to:
www.businessweek.com

83

ETHICS IN BUSINESS

WHAT YOU'LL LEARN

➤ Why business ethics are important.
➤ What ethical codes should include.
➤ How businesses solve ethical dilemmas.
➤ What laws relate to ethics in business.

WHY IT'S IMPORTANT

To succeed as a manager, you will need to understand the ethical issues that affect businesses.

KEY TERMS

• ethics
• code of ethics
• intellectual property

The Importance of Ethics

Individuals make personal decisions about what they believe is right and wrong. These decisions are based on their ethics. **Ethics** are a set of moral principles or values that govern behavior. All individuals develop their own set of ethical rules, which help them decide how to behave in different situations.

Like individuals, businesses develop ethics to help them determine how to behave. These ethics reflect a company's beliefs about what actions are appropriate and fair among people.

The role of ethics in management decisions is difficult. Management issues often are emotionally charged, and many types of ethical problems may arise in business situations. What should managers do if they are aware of unethical practices in their businesses? Should they

▲ CODE OF ETHICS Managers should write and enforce codes of ethics. *Why would it be important to cover product safety and quality in a code of ethics?*

blow the whistle and risk their jobs? Should they quit and allow unethical practices to continue? Should they ignore the practices? These are only a few of the difficult ethical decisions managers face.

CONNECT

Have you ever witnessed unethical behavior (cheating or stealing, for example) at your school or workplace? If so, how did you respond?

Codes of Ethics

To help managers know how to respond ethically to different business situations, many companies have developed codes of ethics. A **code of ethics** is a document that outlines the principles of conduct to be used in making decisions within the organization. Most corporations in the United States have codes of ethics.

Content of Ethical Codes

Codes of ethics are formal documents that are shared with all employees. Some of the areas they cover include the following:

- Honesty
- Adherence to the law
- Product safety and quality
- Health and safety in the workplace
- Conflicts of interest
- Employment practices
- Selling and marketing practices
- Financial reporting
- Pricing, billing, and contracting
- Trading in securities/ using confidential information
- Acquiring and using information about competitors
- Security
- Payments to obtain business
- Political activities
- Protection of the environment

International Management

THE NETHERLANDS

Companies in The Netherlands promote a culture of equality, encouraging individual autonomy and responsibility. Managers are not intimidated by their superiors and can directly comment on their bosses' performance. Work often bypasses organizational levels, and employees are given freedom to implement plans and perform tasks.

 For further reading about International Management go to: **www.businessweek.com**

Merely establishing a code of ethics does not prevent unethical behavior. To be effective, codes of ethics must be enforced. In fact, ethical codes that are not enforced probably do more harm than good. For this reason, it is very important that companies discipline employees who violate their codes of ethics.

Texas Instruments has developed a detailed code of ethics. As **Figure 4–1** shows, the company's code of ethics stresses honesty and respect for people.

Behaving Ethically

Businesspeople regularly make ethical decisions. These decisions have very important consequences for both individuals and their companies. Behaving unethically can hurt, or even end, a businessperson's

Figure 4–1	TEXAS INSTRUMENTS' CODE OF ETHICS
Honesty	**Respect for People**

Honesty	Respect for People
• Offer full disclosure and withdraw from discussions and decisions when our business judgment appears to be in conflict with a personal interest.	• Exercise the basic virtues of respect, dignity, kindness, courtesy, and manners in all work relationships.
• Respect the rights and property of others, including their intellectual property.	• Recognize and avoid behaviors that others may find offensive, including the manner in which we speak and relate to one another and the materials we bring into the workplace, both printed and electronically.
• Compete fairly without collaboration with competitors to divide markets, set prices, restrict production, allocate customers, or otherwise restrain competition.	• Respect the right and obligation of every employee to resolve concerns relating to ethics questions in the course of our duties without retribution and retaliation.
• Assure that no payments or favors are offered to influence others to do something wrong.	• Give all employees the same opportunity to have their questions, issues, and situations fairly considered while understanding that being treated fairly does not always mean that we will all be treated the same.
• Keep records that are accurate and include all payments and receipts.	• Trust one another to use sound judgment in our use of company business and information systems.
• Exercise good judgment in the exchange of business courtesies, meals, and entertainment by avoiding activities that could create even the appearance that our decisions could be compromised.	• Understand that even though Texas Instruments has the obligation to monitor its business information systems activity, we will respect privacy by prohibiting random searches of individual employees' communications.
• Refuse to speculate in company stock through frequent buying and selling or through other forms of speculative trading.	• Recognize that conduct socially and professionally acceptable in one culture and country may be viewed differently in another.

WORKING WITH CHARTS	Corporate ethics codes say much about a company's values. *What does Texas Instruments' code of ethics say about its values?*

career. It can cause a company to lose millions of dollars or even go out of business altogether. Behaving ethically helps employees gain the trust of the people with whom they work. It can also help businesses gain the trust of customers, suppliers, and others.

Behaving Honestly

In many situations, the ethical course of action is clear cut. Ethical employees never steal from their employers. They never lie about the hours they work. They never falsify documents. Employees who engage in any of these actions threaten their careers. They also risk causing severe damage to their employers.

SARBANES-OXLEY ACT OF 2002 In 2001, the Enron Corporation, one of the world's largest traders in gas, electricity, and related commodities, collapsed in scandal and declared bankruptcy. Enron was accused of crimes including deceiving investors, inflating profits, and hiding debts. Arthur Anderson, the company's accounting firm, was later convicted of obstructing justice by shredding documents related to its work on Enron's accounting. Finally, WorldCom, then the world's second largest long-distance provider, suffered the largest bankruptcy in American history after it was revealed that it had improperly booked over $7 billion in earnings.

As a result of these high-profile scandals and to shore up faith in the American economy, President Bush signed the Sarbanes-Oxley Act of 2002. The act contains important rules affecting the reporting and corporate governance of public companies and their directors and officers. Major provisions include requiring CEOs and CFOs to certify periodic reports filed with the SEC. It also prohibits most loans to directors and executive officers, and forces company insiders to report changes in beneficial ownership within two days after a transaction has been executed.

EMPLOYEE THEFT Employers trust their employees not to steal from them. Employees who behave ethically do not violate that trust.

Dishonest employees steal from their employers in a variety of ways. Some embezzle money or steal supplies or inventory from their employers. Some accept bribes from people who want to do business with their company. Others submit false expense accounts.

▲ **UNETHICAL BEHAVIOR** Some ethical violations are clear cut while others are not. *What are some examples of unethical behavior in business?*

LYING ABOUT HOURS WORKED Employees who behave ethically are honest about the hours they work. Employees who work at home, for example, accurately report how long they work. They do not take advantage of the fact that their managers cannot check to see if they are actually at their desks.

Ethical employees also show up at work unless they are ill or need to be away from their jobs for a legitimate reason. They do not pretend to be sick in order to stay home when they should be at work.

FALSIFYING RECORDS One of the worst ethical lapses an employee can commit is falsifying records. This can cause very grave damage to a company's reputation. It can even cause people to become ill or die. A manager at a pharmaceutical company, for example, who falsifies records documenting the side effects of the drugs the company produces can cause people who take the drug to die. Years of excellent corporate performance can be wiped out by these kinds of unethical actions.

Figure 4–2	SOLVING ETHICAL DILEMMAS

1. Have you defined the problem accurately?

2. How would you define the problem if you stood on the other side of the fence?

3. Whom could your decision or action injure? Can you discuss the problem with the affected parties before you make your decision?

4. Are you confident that your position will be as valid over a long period of time as it seems now?

5. Could you disclose without qualm your decision or action to your boss, your CEO, the board of directors, your family, and society as a whole?

Guidelines can help managers decide how to respond when confronted with ethical dilemmas.
Why is it important for managers to consider how others may view their behavior?

Excerpted from Nash, L. (1981). Ethics without the Sermon. *Harvard Business Review* (59).

Dealing with Ethical Dilemmas

Ethical dilemmas are situations in which the ethical course of action is not clear. Such situations arise regularly in the business world. Consider the following examples:

1. Your boss informs you confidentially that one of your friends is going to be fired. Your friend is about to buy a house. Should you warn your friend that he is about to be fired, even though you promised your boss that you would not?

2. Your colleague has been violating your company's code of ethics by accepting expensive gifts from a salesperson who does business with your company. Should you notify your supervisor?

3. One of your employees has been having serious personal problems, and you have tried to be understanding. However, your entire staff is suffering because of poor performance by this key team member. What should you do?

One way of approaching ethical dilemmas like these is to answer the series of questions shown in **Figure 4–2**. Talking to people you trust can also help you develop solutions to ethical problems.

Some companies help their employees solve ethical dilemmas. Aerospace giant Boeing, for example, employs a full-time Corporate Director of Business Practices. Employees who are unsure of how to behave in an ethical situation can call the director for advice.

FIGURE 4–3

Ethical Problems in the Business World

Having a code of ethics and a personal sense of what is right and wrong can help business managers choose the right course of action.

1 NORMAL INTERACTIONS BETWEEN BUSINESS ACQUAINTANCES
Many interactions between people doing business together are considered a normal part of doing business. Managers often take clients out to lunch or invite them to play golf, for example. These kinds of interactions help businesspeople get to know each other.

2 QUESTIONABLE INTERACTIONS BETWEEN BUSINESS ACQUAINTANCES
Some interactions between business acquaintances are questionable. A manager who sends a client a very expensive gift, for example, could be seen as trying to bribe the client into doing business with his or her company. Businesses often provide their employees with guidelines on the types of gifts they consider acceptable.

3 ILLEGAL INTERACTIONS BETWEEN BUSINESS ACQUAINTANCES
Paying bribes to attract business is unethical and illegal. Managers who engage in this kind of activity could face legal action and go to jail.

RESPOND

Suppose a supplier who wants to do business with your company offers to take you out for a meal. What factors would help you decide whether to accept or not?

Laws Relating to Ethics in Business

Over the years, various laws have been enacted that directly relate to the issue of ethics in business. These laws apply to competitive behavior, consumer protection, product safety, and environmental protection.

Competitive Behavior

Since the late nineteenth century the federal government has regulated companies to make sure that they do not engage in anticompetitive behavior. All companies operating in the United States must abide by these laws. Enforcement of these laws is handled by the Antitrust Division of the Justice Department and by the Federal Trade Commission.

THE SHERMAN ACT As you learned in Chapter 2, the Sherman Antitrust Act of 1890 makes it illegal for companies to monopolize trade. Under the law, mergers can be prohibited if the new company that results from the merger will control too large a share of the market. The purpose of the law is to ensure that companies remain able to compete fairly.

THE CLAYTON ACT The Clayton Act of 1914 makes it illegal to charge different prices to different wholesale customers. This means that a manufacturer of steel, for example, cannot charge one price to General Motors and another price to Chrysler.

The Clayton Act also bans the practice of requiring a customer to purchase a second good. Manufacturers of computer hardware, for example, cannot require customers to purchase software as well.

THE WHEELER-LEA ACT The Wheeler-Lea Act of 1938 bans unfair or deceptive acts or practices, including false advertising. Under the Act, businesses must inform consumers of possible negative consequences of using their products. Labeling of cigarette packages is an example of the kind of disclosure required by the Wheeler-Lea Act.

▲ **BUSINESS LAWS** Truth in labeling requires that drug manufacturers identify possible side effects of their products. *What law requires them to do so?*

Consumer Protection

Several laws protect consumers in the United States against unethical and unsafe business practices. These laws cover food and drugs, other manufactured products, and loans.

FOOD AND DRUGS The Federal Food, Drug, and Cosmetic Act of 1938 bans the sale of impure, improperly labeled, falsely guaranteed, and unhealthful foods, drugs, and cosmetics. The law is enforced by the Food and Drug Administration (FDA), which has the power to force manufacturers to stop selling products it considers unsafe.

CONSUMER PRODUCTS The Consumer Product Safety Commission (CPSC) was established in 1972. It establishes minimum product safety standards on consumer products. If a product is found to be defective, the Consumer Product Safety Commission has the authority to force the manufacturer to recall the product. For example, in 1999 the CPSC recalled a quarter of a million Nike water bottles. The bottles were recalled because the cap was not attached properly, possibly causing users to choke.

LOANS A series of laws protects U.S. consumers against unfair lending practices. Under the Truth in Lending Act of 1968, creditors are required to let consumers know how much they are paying in finance charges and interest. The Equal Credit Opportunity Act of 1975 prohibits creditors from making credit decisions on the basis of discriminatory practices.

L EADING THE W AY

INTERNAL AND EXTERNAL CUSTOMERS
The way you deal with a customer can make or break a company. Be considerate and treat customers with respect. Next, think of your co-workers as internal customers. Treat them exactly as you would an external customer. They may become more receptive to you and your ideas with this new approach.

QUESTION
List four laws that protect consumers and keep business competition fair.

▲ **CONSUMER PROTECTION** Many laws protect consumers against unsafe business practices. *How are laws enforced by the FDA important to consumers?*

Environmental Protection

Since the late 1960s environmental protection has been an important social and economic issue in the United States. This concern has been reflected in the many laws designed to protect the environment.

THE NATIONAL ENVIRONMENTAL POLICY ACT OF 1969 The key piece of legislation in environmental protection is the National Environmental Policy Act of 1969. This law created the Environmental Protection Agency (EPA), whose mission is to protect human health and safeguard the air, water, and land.

Since 1969 many environmental laws affecting businesses have been passed. These laws include the Clean Air Act, the Toxic Substances Control Act, and the Clean Water Act. All of these laws are enforced by the EPA.

THE CLEAN AIR ACT OF 1970 The Clean Air Act of 1970 is the comprehensive federal law that regulates air emissions. The original Act set maximum air pollution standards for each of the 50 states. In 1990 the Act was amended to deal with problems of acid rain, ground-level ozone, stratospheric ozone depletion, and toxic substances in the air.

THE TOXIC SUBSTANCES CONTROL ACT OF 1976 The Toxic Substances Control Act of 1976 was enacted to give the EPA the ability to track the 75,000 industrial chemicals currently produced in or imported into the United States. The EPA screens these chemicals and can require reporting or testing of those that may pose an environmental or human health hazard.

THE CLEAN WATER ACT OF 1977 The Clean Water Act of 1977 gives the EPA the authority to set standards on the type and quantity of pollutants that industries can put into bodies of water. The law makes it illegal to discharge any pollutant into navigable waters unless a permit is obtained.

◀ **ENVIRONMENTAL PROTECTION LAWS**
Many corporations are making efforts to reduce the amount of pollution they produce. *What laws govern the environment?*

Property Manager

■ Nature of the Work

Industrial or commercial property owners often hire a property manager to manage their real-estate investments. Property managers negotiate contracts for services (such as janitorial, security, groundskeeping, and trash removal), arrange for property repairs, and purchase supplies and equipment. They see that financial obligations, such as mortgages, taxes, and insurance premiums are met. Property managers investigate and resolve complaints from tenants. When space becomes available, they advertise the space and set the rental rate.

Some commercial property managers help with long-term planning. They consider local property values, taxes, zoning, population growth, and traffic. They then negotiate the purchase, development, and sale of the property.

■ Working Conditions

Property managers spend much of their time away from their desks, visiting the properties, and overseeing work.

■ Training, Other Qualifications, and Advancement

To become a property manager, you need a bachelor's or master's degree in business administration, finance, public administration, or related fields. You must have good communication and financial skills.

■ Salary Range

Property managers earn $39,800 to $60,700, depending on experience and the size of property managed. The job may include a company car if involved in land development. Property managers may also receive a small percentage of ownership in projects they develop.

CRITICAL THINKING

What are some of the environmental concerns that property managers handle?

STANDARD &POOR'S

INDUSTRY OUTLOOK

The U.S. population is expected to reach nearly 350 million people by 2025. As the demands on water supply and treatment grow, so will environmental regulations. Cities that upgrade their treatment systems to keep pace with federal regulations will place tighter restrictions on commercial and industrial properties.

BUSINESS MANAGEMENT *Online*

For more information on management careers, go to:
busmanagement.glencoe.com

Robert Half International Inc.

Tips from Robert Half

Good management skills are not enough to succeed. Global business requires people of various backgrounds to work together in person, online, and on the phone. Work to improve your willingness to cooperate. Be flexible and sensitive.

RESPOND

What is intellectual property and why do you think it is important to protect it?

Ethical Standards and Culture

Standards of business ethics differ around the world. This means that business practices that are acceptable in one country may be considered unethical in others.

Business managers working in foreign countries must be aware of these different ethical standards. They must set guidelines for their companies on how to operate both within their own culture and in other cultures.

Corporate Gift Giving

Gift-giving customs differ around the world. In some cultures, gifts are expected; failure to present them is considered an insult. In Japan, for example, lavish gift giving is an important part of doing business. Gifts are usually exchanged at the first meeting.

In the United States, government officials are not allowed to accept expensive gifts from businesses. Regardless of local practices, American managers operating abroad must abide by the standards set in the United States.

▲ **CORPORATE GIFT GIVING** Managers are sometimes offered expensive gifts, such as paid vacations, from people who want to do business with them. *Why might accepting such gifts be considered unethical?*

Intellectual Property

Intellectual property refers to ownership of ideas, such as inventions, books, movies, and computer programs. In many countries, including the United States, creators of intellectual property have the exclusive right to market and sell their work. These rights are guaranteed through patent, trademark, and copyright laws. These types of protection ensure that only the creators of intellectual property profit from their work. These laws will be explored further in Chapter 5.

Intellectual property protection is very important to business. Without such laws, a computer company could market a best-selling game created by another computer company. A pharmaceutical company could manufacture and sell drugs developed by another drug company.

Although the United States has tough laws governing intellectual property, enforcing those laws is a problem, particularly in the software industry. In 1999 the Justice Department, the FBI, and the Customs Service began cracking down on piracy and counterfeiting of computer software and other products in the United States.

Rules concerning intellectual property rights differ in some countries. In China and India, for example, the government does not enforce such rights. As a result, some Chinese companies copy and sell foreign computer programs. Some publishers in India reprint foreign textbooks, selling them as if they had published them themselves. In the United States, someone who engages in this practice is guilty of plagiarism and can be sued in a court of law. Intellectual property must be respected in the American workplace.

All About _____
ATTITUDE

HONESTY *IS* THE BEST POLICY

You want to do your best in understanding complicated issues. If you're having trouble getting up to speed grasping a difficult concept, just say, "I don't get it." It's always less costly to admit your concerns at the start of something new rather than in the middle of it.

Section 4.1 Assessment

 FACT AND IDEA REVIEW

1. Why is it important for businesses to act ethically?
2. List five areas a code of ethics should cover.
3. Explain one way businesses solve ethical dilemmas.
4. Identify three laws that affect the way companies do business.

 CRITICAL THINKING

1. **Evaluating Information:** What do you think the most important elements of a corporate code of ethics are? Why?
2. **Predicting Consequences:** How might the differences in ethical standards in different cultures create problems for an American businessperson working abroad?

 ASSESSING COMPUTER SKILLS

Using a computer or your local library, research codes of ethics. Try to find ethical codes for two different corporations.

CASE ANALYSIS

For the past several weeks, Jan Morrison has been arriving late for her factory job. Rather than lose wages, she has asked her co-workers to punch her time card for her before she arrives each morning. Last week Jan asked you to punch her in.

Apply: You are aware of your company's policy prohibiting employees from punching other workers in. Explain how you would respond.

SOCIAL RESPONSIBILITY

Changing Views of Social Responsibility

Social responsibility refers to the obligation that individuals or businesses have to help solve social problems. Most companies in the United States feel some sense of social responsibility.

Businesses' concept of their role in society has changed dramatically over the past century. Views toward social responsibility evolved through three distinct schools of thought: profit maximization, trusteeship management, and social involvement.

PREDICT

What are some ways that businesses demonstrate their social responsibility?

◄ **CHANGING VIEWS** Most business owners in the nineteenth century were not concerned about the quality of life of their employees. *How has corporate thinking changed since then?*

Profit Maximization

In the nineteenth and early twentieth centuries, business owners in the United States believed that their role was simply to maximize the profits their companies earned. Dealing with social problems was not considered a legitimate business activity.

Trusteeship Management

Thinking about the role of business changed in the 1920s and 1930s, when a philosophy known as *trusteeship management* became popular. This philosophy recognized that owners of businesses had obligations to do more than just earn profits. They also had obligations to their employees, their customers, and their creditors. Most businesspeople continued to hold this view until the 1960s.

Social Involvement

During the 1960s many people began to believe that corporations should use their influence and financial resources to address social problems. They believed corporations should help solve problems such as poverty, crime, environmental destruction, and illiteracy.

According to this view, businesses should be responsible corporate citizens, not just maximizers of profit. Businesses have obligations to all of the people affected by their actions, known as stakeholders. **Stakeholders** include a company's employees, customers, suppliers, and the community.

Since the 1960s corporations have increasingly demonstrated their commitment to social change. One example of this commitment is the increased diversity in the workplace. Over the past 35 years, most corporations have made efforts to diversify their workforces by hiring and promoting more women and minorities. Many businesses also have established workshops to help their employees understand people from different backgrounds.

> **CONNECT**
>
> Imagine a situation where a business, motivated solely by profits, ignores a sense of social responsibility. What are some examples you can think of?

▶ **DIVERSITY** The workplace is much more diverse today than it was in 1960. *What is one of the reasons for the change?*

**LAUNDERING IMAGES OF SOILED COMPANIES
IS TURNING INTO BIG BUSINESS**

Ethics for Hire

It's a familiar routine. A scandal erupts at a large corporation. Bowing to public pressure, the board vows to get to the bottom of the mess, hiring a retired government big shot or blue-chip law firm to conduct an "independent" investigation.

Name a major company that's been in trouble recently, and it has probably gone through the drill. Mitsubishi Motor Manufacturing of America Ltd. in May asked former Labor Secretary Lynn M. Martin to examine its workplace policies. Her preliminary prescription for combating sexual harassment is due in mid-July. Swedish drugmaker Astra responded to its own sexual harassment scandal two months ago by commissioning a probe by New York law firm Winthrop, Stimson, Putnam & Roberts.

A BILLION-DOLLAR INDUSTRY. The business of helping companies clean up their acts—a sort of Ethics Inc.—is booming. Competitors range from management consultants to law firms and private eye outfits to nonprofits. "When you add it all together, you've probably got a billion-dollar industry,"

says Carole Basri, a Deloitte & Touche ethics consultant.

One reason: Ethics overhauls can be hugely expensive. Orange & Rockland Utilities in Pearl River, N.Y., found that out. In 1993, after running afoul of regulators for widespread financial improprieties, the small utility hired Price Waterhouse and the New Jersey law firm Stier, Anderson & Malone to do an independent investigation. A team of nearly 50 produced a 1,200-page report at a cost of some $7 million. But Orange & Rockland President Larry S. Brodsky says the investment has paid off: "There's no question that we have regained the confidence of the regulators."

The drill that ethics mavens put companies through varies little. First, the investigation. Then a new corporate code of ethics is drafted. Ethics training is beefed up, and a toll-free whistle-blower hot line installed. Then ethics officers are frequently brought aboard to manage the training programs and investigate complaints.

DOES IT WORK? Critics contend that companies are simply looking for window dressing. "They'll have a code of ethics, but there's no effort by senior management to assure middle management that they really mean it," says Swenson of KPMG Peat Marwick.

Excerpted with permission from BusinessWeek, *July 15, 1996*

CRITICAL THINKING

Why do companies hire consultants to review their workplace policies?

DECISION MAKING

As a manager, what would be the pros and cons of hiring a consulting company to conduct an ethics overhaul on your company?

Measuring Social Responsibility

To measure how socially responsible a company is, some managers perform social audits. A **social audit** is a review of a business's social responsiveness.

Corporations demonstrate their sense of social responsibility in various ways. Performance in each of these areas is measured as part of a social audit.

RESPOND

Would you feel happier working for a company that demonstrated a strong sense of social responsibility? Why or why not?

Philanthropy and Volunteerism

One way a company demonstrates its sense of social responsibility is by contributing time and money to charitable, cultural, and civic organizations. Corporate philanthropy, or efforts to improve human welfare, can take many forms. Computer giant Hewlett-Packard, for example, provides technology, product, and cash contributions to organizations throughout the United States. It also has planted seedlings in Australia, supported an institute for people with disabilities in India, and refurbished a school in Brazil. All of these activities reflect the company's sense of social responsibility.

Some companies grant employees paid time off to participate in charitable activities. Many high-tech companies, for example, allow their employees to volunteer for the U.S. Tech Corps, which sends employees from technology companies to work in public schools. Other corporations allow employees time off to donate blood, participate in food and clothing drives, or raise money for such causes as the United Way.

Many corporations also donate money by matching charitable donations made by their employees. In this way companies both encourage employee giving and make their own contributions to philanthropic causes.

▲ **CORPORATE VOLUNTEERISM** Many corporations allow their employees time off to volunteer in underprivileged areas. *Why do corporations support such activities?*

Environmental Awareness

Another way companies demonstrate their sense of social responsibility is by limiting the damage their operations cause to the environment. They do so by creating production processes that are as environmentally friendly as possible.

Businesses also can affect the environment by establishing policies that reduce pollution. Encouraging employees to carpool, for example, reduces toxic emissions and conserves gasoline. Using biodegradable products also helps protect the environment.

One company well known for its commitment to preserving the environment is The Body Shop. The company's founder, Anita Roddick, has demonstrated her commitment to the environment by using only biodegradable products and refillable containers. She also has promoted environmental causes, such as preserving the rain forest.

Sensitivity to Diversity and Quality of Work Life

One of the most important ways a company can demonstrate its sense of social responsibility is through its workforce. Socially responsible businesses maintain ethnically diverse workforces that reflect the societies in which they operate. More than 37 percent of all McDonald's U.S. owner/operators are women and minorities, and women and minorities make up more than 40 percent of the company's officers.

▲ **ENVIRONMENTAL AWARENESS** Companies such as The Body Shop have established reputations as being environmentally responsible. *How can companies demonstrate their commitment to the environment?*

Companies also can demonstrate their social responsibility by adopting policies that contribute to the quality of life of their workers. Flexible work hours, for example, allow workers to better meet their families' needs. On-site day care centers make life easier for employees with young children. For example, Jessica Longman is a physician with demanding hours. The hospital she works at offers a day care center where her six-month-old baby can be cared for. This service helps Jessica—as well as other hospital employees with young children—perform her job better.

▲ **EMPLOYEE WORK LIFE** Some companies provide on-site day care centers for their employees. *What other ways can businesses help employees better manage their lives?*

Section 4.2 Assessment

● FACT AND IDEA REVIEW

1. What are the three schools of thought about the role of the corporation? How is the workplace different today than it was in the nineteenth and early twentieth century?
2. What are three ways in which corporations can demonstrate a sense of social responsibility? Give an example for each.

● CRITICAL THINKING

1. **Making Generalizations:** How does hiring women and minorities demonstrate a business's sense of social responsibility?
2. **Evaluating Information:** Why do you think companies have obligations to their stakeholders?
3. **Drawing Conclusions:** What purpose does a social audit serve?

● ASSESSING SOCIAL STUDIES SKILLS

Select a large company operating in the United States. Using the resources at your local library, research how that company demonstrates its sense of social responsibility. Prepare a one- to two-page report summarizing what you find.

● CASE ANALYSIS

Mark Smith owns a growing Internet company, ReThink. Last year his company earned more than $45 million, and he hired 20 new employees.

Mark would like to use his new wealth to help people in the poor community in which he grew up. He has asked you to prepare a memo for him, identifying various options for providing aid.

Apply: How would you recommend that ReThink help a poor community?

CHAPTER 4 ASSESSMENT

Write a dialogue between two businesspeople using the following vocabulary words:

ethics	stakeholder
code of ethics	social audit
intellectual property	social responsibility

CHAPTER SUMMARY

Section 4.1

▶ Ethics are a set of moral principles or values that govern individuals' and businesses' behavior.

▶ Most companies in the United States have codes of ethics that outline their basic ethical principles.

▶ Ethical standards differ across cultures. American businesspeople doing business abroad need to be aware of differences in these standards.

▶ Certain laws, including the Sherman Act, the Clayton Act, the Wheeler-Lea Act, consumer laws, and environmental laws, govern business practices.

Section 4.2

▶ Most businesses today have a sense of social responsibility. They demonstrate their commitment in various ways, such as giving money to charitable causes, trying to protect the environment, and creating diverse workforces.

▶ Social audits are used to measure a company's social responsiveness.

RECALLING KEY CONCEPTS

1. What purpose does an ethical code serve?
2. What items should be included in an ethical code?
3. What are some examples of ethical dilemmas that arise in businesses?
4. Cite three laws that affect how companies conduct business.
5. Explain how thinking about social responsibility has changed since the nineteenth century.
6. Describe three ways businesses can demonstrate their sense of social responsibility.

THINKING CRITICALLY

1. Why are ethical codes more common today than they were 50 years ago?
2. How might people from other cultures find fault with American business practices?
3. Why does the government regulate business?
4. Why is it important for businesses to behave in a socially responsible manner?
5. Why might it make good business sense for companies to play a role in solving social problems? In your opinion, are profits and social responsibility compatible?

ASSESSING ACADEMIC SKILLS

MATH Last year your company earned $2.5 million in profits. Your charitable donations totaled $37,000. This year you expect profits to reach $3 million. If you donate the same percentage of your profits that you did last year, how much money will you give away this year?

APPLYING MANAGEMENT PRINCIPLES

SOLVE THE PROBLEM The company you work for, a mid-sized real estate agency, has recently faced a series of ethical problems. In response to the problem, the agency's owner has decided to create a code of ethics so that all employees will know the kind of behavior that is expected of them. You have been asked to create a draft of the document. Identify what issues the code should address and prepare a draft.

Public Speaking Present your draft to your colleagues, explaining why you included the items you did.

PREPARING FOR COMPETITIVE EVENTS

Answer True or False for the following statements.

1. A code of ethics is a statement of values and rules that guide the behavior of employees or members of an organization.

2. In the 1960s profit maximization was the prevalent school of thought for managers.

BusinessWeek ONLINE

In this chapter you read the *BusinessWeek* Management Model about business ethics. For more information, go to *BusinessWeek* online at: **www.businessweek.com**

Locate an article that deals with business ethics. Write a brief summary of what the ethical issue is about and how the business solved its problem. Present your findings to the class.

CHAPTER 5

BUSINESSES, WORKERS, AND THE LAW

LEARNING OBJECTIVES

When you have completed this chapter, you will be able to:

- Identify the different kinds of laws that affect businesses.
- Describe the different kinds of laws that protect workers on the job.
- Explain how tax laws affect business profits.
- Explain the differences between copyrights, patents, and trademarks.
- Describe the different laws that protect workers on the job.
- Explain the importance of the National Labor Relations Act.

READING STRATEGIES

As you read

- **PREDICT** what the section will be about.
- **CONNECT** what you read with your own life.
- **QUESTION** as you read to make sure you understand the content.
- **RESPOND** to what you read.

> **❝MANAGEMENT TALK❞**
>
> ❝Sun's first responsibility as stewards of the Java technology is to preserve the significant investments that Sun and hundreds of companies have made. We are required to take this action on behalf of our licensees, the Java industry and Sun's shareholders.❞
>
> —Alan Baratz,
> Former President of
> Sun Microsystems'
> JavaSoft division

Understanding Management

In 2002, Sun Microsystems brought a lawsuit against Microsoft Corporation for allegedly using its operating system monopoly to damage Sun's Java-based businesses. The lawsuit also aimed at forcing Microsoft to distribute Sun's Java plug-ins with Microsoft's Windows XP® operating system. Sun argued that Microsoft created an illegal barrier to competition by hindering the distribution of Sun's Java platform.

Analyzing Management Skills

Why is it important to protect products with legal contracts?

Applying Management Skills

Imagine that you own a pizzeria. You have come up with a method for delivering pizzas twice as fast as your competitors. How will you keep your competitors from copying your method?

BusinessWeek *ONLINE*

For further reading on managers and management go to:
www.businessweek.com

LAWS THAT REGULATE BUSINESSES

Government Regulation of Business

Congress and state and local legislatures pass many laws that regulate businesses. The federal, state, and local governments enforce these laws. If businesses do not comply with these laws, they may be subject to legal sanctions, such as fines, penalties, loss of license, or even jail. Many companies hire a government affairs manager, who makes sure that the company knows the laws that regulate its activities. The government affairs manager also makes sure that the company keeps up with new laws and does not become liable for their actions.

Regulations are rules that government agencies issue to implement laws. Businesses spend a lot of time and money making sure they comply with laws and regulations and do not face unwanted liability.

There are six important areas of law that affect business operations:

1. *Corporate law.* Corporate law regulates how businesses can set themselves up to operate as companies.
2. *Tax law.* Tax law regulates how much money businesses must pay the government to help provide services for the public.
3. *Intellectual property law.* Intellectual property law regulates how businesses can protect inventions and new products.
4. *Consumer law.* Consumer law protects individuals against business activities that might be harmful to them.
5. *Commercial law.* Commercial law regulates how businesses enter into contracts with other businesses and with consumers.
6. *Licensing and zoning law.* Licensing laws regulate who can go into certain businesses. Zoning laws regulate where they can establish operations.

▲ **TAX LAWS** It is Congress's responsibility to pass legislation that regulates businesses in many areas, including taxes and intellectual property. *Why should businesses have to pay taxes?*

Corporate Law

Not all businesses are alike. Some companies are enormous, with more than 10,000 employees and offices in many states and even in other countries. Some are small, with only a couple of partners working together in a single office. Still others are run by just one person. There are laws regulating three kinds of business entities or ownership: sole proprietorships, partnerships, and corporations.

Sole Proprietorships

The simplest kind of business is a **sole proprietorship**. A sole proprietorship is a business owned by a single individual, or proprietor. Small businesses often are sole proprietorships, and entrepreneurs often are sole proprietors.

Sole proprietorships are easy to start. In most cases, a person can become a sole proprietor simply by beginning to do business. Sandy Kleppinger, a Virginia homemaker, became a sole proprietor by selling discounted computer software on eBay, an Internet auction house. Within a year, she had developed a successful business with profits of nearly $42,000.

Other people become sole proprietors by setting up small businesses such as restaurants and grocery stores. Sole proprietors set up businesses

PREDICT

In what situations would it be better to form a sole proprietorship? A partnership? A corporation?

▲ **SOLE PROPRIETORSHIP** Many small businesses operate as sole proprietorships. *What are some advantages of this type of ownership?*

after checking with state and local officials about licenses, zoning regulations, and other requirements. Sole proprietors have many advantages. First, they control the entire business and keep all the profits. Second, sole proprietors can make decisions quickly. Additionally, sole proprietors usually pay fewer taxes than other kinds of businesses.

There are several disadvantages of sole proprietorship, however. Sole proprietors have full responsibility for the business. If the business runs into financial trouble, for instance, the owner has full liability for all debts. A sole proprietor may have to use personal savings or even sell a house or car to pay debts from a business. In addition, sole proprietorships can fail entirely if, for example, the owner becomes ill or disabled. Despite these disadvantages, sole proprietorships are popular in the United States.

Partnerships

A **partnership** is an association of two or more persons who jointly own a for-profit business. The Uniform Partnership Act, which governs general partnerships, requires them to meet two requirements. First, a partnership must be owned by two or more persons. Under the law, a "person" can be a corporation or another organization as well as an individual. Second, partners must share the profits from their business.

A partnership allows partners to combine their talents and their financial resources. Partners share responsibility for making decisions, and a partnership pays less in taxes than a corporation. With two people rather than one, a partnership may have an easier time getting a loan than a sole proprietorship.

The biggest disadvantage of a partnership is that the partners, like sole proprietors, have unlimited liability for business debts. Even if only one partner is responsible for a business's debts, all the partners are responsible for paying them. A second disadvantage is that partners may disagree on how the business should be run or how profits should be shared. Such disagreements can hurt the business.

Corporations

A **corporation** is a business formed under state or federal statutes that is authorized to act as a legal person. A corporation exists apart from its owners and can be taxed and sued like an individual. Corporate owners have limited liability. This means they cannot lose their personal resources if the corporation fails. Only the corporation loses.

Corporations have many advantages. Like partnerships, they offer stockholders limited liability and a share of the profits. Stockholders have no management responsibilities. Corporations can raise money by selling stock. They generally have an easier time getting credit than any other type of business.

Corporations have two major disadvantages, however. First, they must comply with many more federal and state laws than either sole proprietorships or partnerships. Corporations must register with a state government agency to begin a business, while a sole proprietor can begin a business at any time. Second, corporations pay more taxes than any other type of business. They pay special taxes to the state and federal governments as well as a tax on profits.

Tax Law

The type of ownership managers choose for their businesses often depends on the types of taxes involved. Taxes are monies paid by corporations and individuals and are used to fund government programs and services, such as highways and schools.

Income Tax

Businesses pay several different types of taxes, but the most important tax is called an income tax. An **income tax** is a tax levied against a business's profits. For example, if a business earns $100,000 in profits this year, and the income tax rate is 30 percent, the business will pay the government $30,000 in taxes.

▲ **ASSESSED VALUATION** Property in New York City is assessed at a higher value than in many other parts of the country. *What does this mean for businesses there?*

Property Tax

Businesses also must pay property taxes. **Property taxes** are taxes levied against the property, buildings, or land owned by a business. Property taxes are based on an assessed valuation of the building or land. An *assessed valuation* is the amount that a piece of property is worth, according to a tax assessor. For example, the assessed valuation of land and buildings in the heart of Manhattan in New York City is extremely high because there is very little space to construct new buildings. The business owners of property and land in New York City would pay more in taxes than business owners in many other parts of the country.

Taxes may hurt businesses by taking away part of their profits. To make up for these losses, businesses often pass on costs by charging consumers more money for products.

Withholding Federal Taxes

Businesses also collect taxes from workers. The government requires businesses to withhold income taxes from employees' earnings and send them to the federal government. Without the help of business, it would be very difficult for the federal government to collect taxes from working people.

Managers make important decisions because of taxes. For example, a manager may decide to relocate the business's operations because of more favorable taxes in another state. In the late 1990s, for example, the Caterpillar Corporation, a major equipment manufacturer, moved its operations from Illinois to Texas because the taxes were more favorable in the state of Texas. When managers develop strategic plans for making profits, they always need to take the effect of taxes into account.

Intellectual Property Laws

Taxes can cut into a company's profits, but there are also laws that protect business profit. For example, as you learned in Chapter 4, businesses are protected by intellectual property laws. Intellectual property laws protect the inventions and new ideas of businesses.

Our society could not survive without new inventions. Inventions lead to advances in fields such as medicine that improve our quality of life. In the business world, inventions lead to new products. The three kinds of intellectual property protections are patents, trademarks, and copyrights.

Patents

Inventors and companies come up with thousands of inventions every year. Just think about it—television, CDs,

▲ **PATENTS** Howard Head invented the metal ski. Before the invention of the Head ski, skiers used wooden skis. Now, skiers often use fiberglass. At the time of his invention, Head received a patent. *How long was his patent good for?*

cellular phones, bar codes at grocery stores—our world is full of new technological devices made possible by creative inventors.

Some inventors work on their own, while others work for companies. A company can protect its inventions by applying for a patent. A **patent** is the document the federal government issues to inventors and companies that gives them the exclusive right to make, use, and sell their inventions for 17 years. When the 17 years are up, other companies can begin selling that invention. The inventor of each type of new product must apply for another patent.

Trademarks

The Nike "swoosh" is one of the most famous trademarks in the world. A **trademark** is a word, name, symbol, or slogan a business uses to identify its own goods and set them apart from others. Companies apply to the federal government's patents and trademark office when they want to establish a new trademark. Once a company owns its trademark, no other company can use it. Registered trademarks are good for 10 years, and companies can renew them every additional 10 years.

▲ TRADEMARKS Some trademarks, like Nike's, have become status symbols. *Why else might people look for a favorite trademark when buying something?*

Trademarks are powerful selling tools. Nike puts its trademark on every item of athletic wear it makes, from shoes to underwear. In many countries of the world, wearing Nike goods is a status symbol. The Nike swoosh shows people the item is genuine.

Copyrights

John Grisham's novels are widely read in the United States and abroad. When Grisham writes the novel, he copyrights the manuscript so that no one else can publish his work without his permission. A **copyright** is the protection provided to a creative work. It can be used to protect literary works, musical compositions, plays, dances, paintings, movies, maps, and computer programs. The owner of the copyright, usually the person who creates the work, is the only one with the legal right to reproduce the work, sell it, or allow others to use it. Under copyright law, photocopying pages of a book can be illegal without the author's or publisher's permission.

▲ **COPYRIGHTS** Copyright laws protect authors from people illegally copying or selling their work. *Why is that so important to authors?*

The U.S. Copyright Office grants copyrights, which last for the holder's life plus 70 years. After that time, the work becomes part of what is called the "public domain."

Consumer Law

Some laws, such as intellectual property laws, protect businesses. Other laws are designed to protect consumers. *Consumers* are individuals who buy goods and services for their own use. You and the members of your family are consumers every time you buy food, clothing, drugs, or any other item from a business. To protect consumers from unfair business practices, the federal and state governments have established consumer protection laws.

Consumers should understand consumer laws so they know their rights when dealing with businesses. For example, many consumers who buy used cars from dealerships may not know that the law requires dealers to tell buyers certain things about that car, including how many miles it has been driven. Knowing what a car dealer must tell you about buying a car protects both you and the dealer.

QUESTION

What are two laws that protect consumers?

The Federal Trade Commission

If you think that someone in business has treated you unfairly, you can write a letter of complaint to the Federal Trade Commission (FTC).

▲ **CONSUMER PROTECTION** Many people today expect to see nutritional labels on all food packages. *Why is it important for consumers to know what is in food products?*

The FTC, an agency of the federal government, will take action against a company if it receives enough consumer complaints to establish a "pattern of wrongdoing." For example, if a large number of people complain that a catalog company is making false promises about its merchandise, the FTC will investigate the complaint.

The FTC has many rules governing all kinds of sales. For instance, the Used Car Rule requires dealers to tell customers important information about a used car. The Telemarketing Sales Rule helps protect consumers from being bombarded with unwanted telemarketing calls by placing limitations on companies that sell or promote by telephone. Some of the FTC rules have been very successful. For example, many consumers would be surprised to find an article of clothing without a care label that tells you how to wash and dry the clothing.

Other Rules that Protect Consumers

There are other laws and agencies that protect consumers as well. You learned about some of these in Chapter 4. For example, the Food and Drug Administration (FDA) protects consumers against problems with mislabeled and impure foods, drugs, cosmetics, and medical devices. The FDA approves all new drugs before they are sold. The Fair Packaging and Labeling Act requires manufacturers of foods, drugs, cosmetics, and medical devices to clearly label products with the name of the manufacturer, the contents, and the amount the package contains. Labels on packaged foods must provide complete nutritional information as well.

Commercial Law

In addition to complying with laws regulating their dealings with consumers, businesses must comply with commercial laws that regulate their contracts and dealings with other businesses. The basic commercial law document is called the Uniform Commercial Code.

Contracts

Businesses must follow laws governing how they can enter into contracts. A **contract** is an agreement between two parties to carry out a transaction, such as the sale of goods from a seller to buyer. Contracts create an obligation between the parties, or those agreeing to the contract, that can be enforced in a court of law. For example, when McDonald's agrees to purchase orange juice from Minute Maid to sell in their restaurants, they enter into a contract that is legally enforceable.

◀ LEGAL CONTRACTS A contract to buy a house is a long, complicated document. *What kinds of things do you think you would need to know before signing such a contract?*

Most of us enter into different kinds of contracts during our lives. When we buy cars, expensive pieces of furniture, computers, and houses, we generally sign a contract. The contract describes the item being sold, sets out the terms of payment, and states whether the item can be returned.

Businesses enter into contracts daily. Like individuals, they buy things, such as office supplies and computer equipment. They also may lease items, such as furniture or even temporary employees. In each instance, they become a party to a contract.

Contracts must follow very specific rules if they are to stand up in a court of law. Anyone signing a contract—an individual, a representative of a group, the manager of a company—must know exactly what is in the contract and make sure the contract is properly prepared.

Contracts are often difficult to break. If you sign a contract and do not live up to your end of the bargain, the other party can take you to court. You have the same option if the other party does not complete the contract. It's always best to review contracts carefully beforehand. Knowing what you are signing is the best way to avoid problems with a contract later on.

Because most businesses deal in amounts of goods worth more than $500, most business sales contracts are written contracts. To satisfy the Uniform Commercial Code, written contracts must contain certain information. They must state that the parties involved have agreed to the sale and must give the quantity of the goods involved. The exact quantity is important because courts will enforce a contract only for the amount of the goods listed in the contract.

WORK SMART
Many people confuse working long hours with working hard. Long hours may sometimes be necessary, but not if the same work can be done in a shorter amount of time. Help your employees look for quicker ways to do things by involving technology or reevaluating the current process.

Business Sales Contracts

Business sales contracts are often short, simple documents that meet the requirements of the Uniform Commercial Code. When businesses write a contract for a very large quantity of goods, however, the contract often is many pages long. Suppose the National Aeronautic and Space Administration (NASA), a branch of the Federal Government, orders parts to build a new shuttle from the Boeing Corporation. A space shuttle is a complicated machine that must be extremely safe. The contract must describe the parts using exact measurements that may be tiny fractions of an inch. It must list everything used to make the parts. Because the parts may have more than one component, the contract must provide details for each component. It must break down the costs so that NASA can see what it is paying for each item, no matter how small.

Managers are involved at every stage of assembling and reviewing a contract. Managers in several departments at Boeing make sure the

▲ **BUSINESS SALES CONTRACTS** A sales contract must contain a complete listing of everything you've bought. *Why is it important to make sure a sales contract is correct?*

right information gets to the people who write the contracts. The manager of the financial department makes sure the costs are listed correctly. The manager of the contracts department makes sure the contract is complete. When the contract reaches NASA, the process starts all over again, with managers reviewing the contract to make sure it satisfies the agency's requirements.

Licensing and Zoning Law

Government passes rules on commercial law to make sure that businesses follow rigid standards when they make deals with other businesses. In addition, state and local governments pass licensing and zoning laws that regulate who can operate a business and where owners can set up shop.

State and local governments use licensing as a way to limit and control people who plan to enter certain types of businesses. For example, if you wanted to start a restaurant, you would need to apply for a license from the local department of food and beverage control. The government may deny your application if it thinks there already are more than enough restaurants in the area.

Government officials can take away a license from a business that is not complying with laws and regulations. For example, the department of sanitation inspects local restaurants to make sure that they are complying with health codes, such as storing foods properly and keeping

RESPOND

Why do you think local governments pass zoning laws?

bathrooms sanitary. If the restaurant is not complying with the rules, the department of sanitation will issue a warning or possibly suspend the restaurant's license to operate. A government agency also has the power to completely revoke a restaurant's license, which means that the restaurant would have to close and go out of business altogether.

Local governments also may regulate businesses through building codes, which regulate physical features or structures of buildings. Building codes may regulate the maximum height, minimum square feet of space, and the types of materials that can be used in constructing an office. Finally, local governments regulate where a building can be built through zoning ordinances and regulations. For example, businesses can operate in commercially zoned areas but not residential areas.

Section 5.1 Assessment

 FACT AND IDEA REVIEW

1. How can the government enforce its regulations against businesses?
2. List three types of business ownership.
3. Why should businesses be concerned about taxes?
4. What kind of intellectual property law protects an invention? a soft drink's logo? a hit movie?
5. True or False: Consumer protection laws apply to both individuals and businesses.
6. Why does a manager need to know exactly what is contained in a business contract?

 CRITICAL THINKING

1. **Drawing Conclusions:** If there is disagreement between two businesses about what certain provisions in a contract really mean, how should they resolve their dispute?
2. **Evaluating Information:** What kinds of business activities do you think should and should not be regulated? Explain your answer.

 ASSESSING SOCIAL STUDIES SKILLS

Research one of the federal agencies responsible for protecting consumers, such as the Consumer Product Safety Commission or the Food and Drug Administration. Write a one-page summary of the agency's primary responsibilities.

 CASE ANALYSIS

Ted Chang is the government affairs manager for Emerging Inc., a software firm in California. He just found out that California has passed two new laws. One law raises income taxes from 30 to 35 percent on company profits. The other law restricts companies from selling software to consumers without including instructional guides in the packages. Ted's boss asks him to write a memo about the effects the laws may have on the company.

Apply: Prepare a memo answering these questions: If Emerging makes $100,000 in profit, how much more in taxes will it have to pay? What kind of law is the "how-to" guide restriction?

Management Dietitian

■ Nature of the Work

Management dietitians work in places such as health-care facilities, company cafeterias, prisons, and schools. They plan large-scale meals and nutritional programs, and supervise the preparation and serving of food. They may evaluate diets (especially in hospitals) and suggest diet modifications, such as reduced fat and sugar intake for those who are overweight.

They hire, train, and supervise other dietitians and food-service workers. Management dietitians budget for and purchase food, equipment, and supplies, and prepare records and reports. They see that sanitary and safety regulations are observed.

■ Working Conditions

Management dietitians work in clean, well-lighted, and well-ventilated areas, although kitchens may be hot and steamy. They may be on their feet most of a workday. Most dietitians work 40 hours per week, although some may work on the weekends.

■ Training, Other Qualifications, and Advancement

To become a management dietitian, you need a bachelor's or master's degree in dietetics, food and nutrition, food-service systems management, or related area. Many states require licensing and certification or registration.

■ Salary Range

Management dietitians earn $34,000 to $43,000. Their salaries vary by responsibility, experience, educational level, and size and location of the facility.

CRITICAL THINKING:

Why do some states require licensing of management dietitians? What skills are necessary to become a management dietician?

STANDARD &POOR'S

INDUSTRY OUTLOOK

Management dietitians work with a variety of food suppliers. Most small food companies produce a limited product line, such as baked goods or snack foods. The top national firms focus on multimillion-dollar products that can be sold nationwide. These companies tend to ignore regional products and preferences.

BUSINESS MANAGEMENT *Online*

For more information on management careers, go to:
busmanagement.glencoe.com

WORKERS AND THE LAW

The Importance of Employment Laws

In the early part of the twentieth century, companies had tremendous power over employees. Companies could pay workers as little money in salary as they wanted and could make employees work under dangerous conditions. Companies could refuse to hire minorities and could pay women less than men for doing the same job.

Beginning in the 1930s, Congress and state legislatures wanted to do something to help the average worker and create a better power balance between companies and workers. They therefore passed employment laws that protect and provide benefits to employees. **Employment laws** regulate the relationship between companies and their workers and give workers significant rights and benefits, including the right to work in a safe environment. There are strict penalties for companies who violate these laws, including fines and loss of government contracts.

Companies must comply with five major kinds of employment laws:

1. *Equal Employment Opportunity (EEO) laws:* EEO laws prohibit companies from discriminating against workers.
2. *Occupational safety and health laws:* Occupational safety and health laws require employers and employees to comply with safety and health standards established by federal, state, and local governments.
3. *Wage-hour laws:* Wage-hour laws establish minimum wage, overtime, and child labor standards for employees.
4. *Benefits laws:* Benefits laws guarantee that workers will receive certain benefits regardless of what happens to them on the job.
5. *Labor relations laws:* Labor relations laws protect the right of employees to organize into unions to bargain collectively for better wages and working conditions.

PREDICT
What kinds of laws regulate employment practices?

▲ EMPLOYMENT LAWS Conditions were not always safe for workers in the United States. *What kinds of laws help protect the safety of American workers?*

Equal Employment Opportunity Laws

In the early 1960s the civil rights movement in the United States was at its height. Civil rights leaders helped educate Americans about discrimination against African Americans and other minorities in and out of the workplace. Congress listened to the civil rights leaders and other influential policymakers and passed three major federal equal employment opportunity laws that protect workers from discrimination by companies: Title VII of the Civil Rights Act of 1964, the Age Discrimination in Employment Act, and the Americans with Disabilities Act.

Title VII of the Civil Rights Act of 1964

Under Title VII of the Civil Rights Act of 1964, companies cannot discriminate against an employee because of race, color, religion, sex, or national origin. The Equal Employment Opportunity Commission (EEOC) can sue a company that discriminates against an employee. The employee also can take a company to court for discriminating in the workplace. Employees bring thousands of lawsuits against companies for discrimination every year. In 1999, for example, the California Superior Court awarded a supervisor at a public transit company $5.7 million because the company had discriminated against him on the basis of his national origin.

Age Discrimination in Employment Act

Under the Age Discrimination in Employment Act, companies cannot discriminate against employees because of their age. Workers between the ages of 40 and 70 can sue employers for discrimination. Companies cannot discriminate against workers because of age in hiring, promotions, or retirement. For example, in 1998, a 61-year-old senior manager at Goodyear Tire & Rubber Company successfully sued the company for age discrimination when it tried to force him to accept early retirement.

Americans with Disabilities Act

Under the Americans with Disabilities Act, companies cannot discriminate against persons with disabilities. Companies cannot fire or refuse to hire people because of certain disabilities and illnesses, such as blindness or diabetes. Companies also must accommodate a worker's disabilities. For example, a court ruled in 1998 that a supermarket could not make a worker with a bad back lift or carry heavy boxes and had to find him less strenuous work.

Occupational Safety and Health Laws

The Occupational Safety and Health Act, enforced by the U.S. Department of Labor's Occupational Safety and Health Administration (OSHA) sets standards for keeping workplaces clean and free of hazards, such as unsafe machinery and dangerous chemicals. Businesses must keep records of employee illnesses, injuries, and deaths and submit them to the U.S. Department of Labor.

OSHA inspectors visit many workplaces every year to make sure they comply with regulations. Employees can ask OSHA inspectors to visit their workplace if they suspect their company is violating OSHA regulations. For example, in 1999, utility workers in Florida bombarded OSHA with complaints following an explosion at Tampa

Electric Company. OSHA responded by investigating these complaints. Companies are not allowed to retaliate against workers who ask OSHA inspectors to visit their workplaces.

OSHA issues citations, or written warnings, to companies who violate OSHA laws and regulations. OSHA also fines companies for violating the law. For example, Helena Laboratories in Beaumont, Texas agreed to pay $137,100 in 1999 for exposing workers to blood-related products without adequate protection.

Wage-Hour Laws

Salaries and hours of work are very important to workers. Until 1938 many workers toiled under oppressive conditions, including substandard wages and excessive hours. In that year, Congress passed the Fair Labor Standards Act (FLSA), also known as the Wage-Hour Law. The Fair Labor Standards Act protects workers in three ways. It sets the minimum wage companies can pay their workers; it sets the number of hours employees can work in a week without receiving overtime pay; and it prohibits companies from employing children under the age of 14.

CONNECT

Have you ever held a job that paid minimum wage? What is the current minimum wage in your state?

▲ **WAGE-HOUR LAWS** In the nineteenth and early twentieth century, it was not unusual to find children working in factories. *What law now protects against child labor?*

Benefits Laws

In addition to wages and hours, workers are concerned with the benefits their companies give them. Benefits include vacation and sick leave, pensions, and tuition assistance. Companies must comply with five different benefits laws:

RESPOND

How would you feel if the Social Security system did not exist?

1. *Social Security Act.* The government designed the Social Security Act of 1935 to provide workers and their families with income after retirement. Social Security funds also support disabled workers and the federal Medicare program, which provides health insurance for senior citizens.

   Employers and employees share the cost of Social Security taxes while the worker is employed. Self-employed workers pay the full tax. When workers retire, they receive a pension based on their lifetime earnings. The spouse, children, and other dependents of a worker who dies can receive a portion of the worker's benefits.

2. *Employee Retirement Income Security Act (ERISA).* ERISA protects the money put into an employee's retirement fund by companies and workers. Every employee and employer must pay Social Security, but not every company establishes an ERISA program.

3. *Unemployment Insurance Laws.* Both the Social Security Act and the Federal Unemployment Tax Act provide workers with financial assistance during periods of unemployment. To be eligible for unemployment insurance, workers must meet two requirements. They must have lost their jobs through no fault of their own, and they must have worked a certain length of time.

   Employers must pay a certain amount into the unemployment fund for each worker. The amount a worker receives depends on the length of employment and the salary. In some areas with a very large number of unemployed workers, state governments extend the length of time workers can receive benefits.

4. *Workers' Compensation Laws.* All states have laws that insure workers against injury, illness, or death because of job conditions. In some states, employers pay into a special fund. In others, they buy insurance from private companies. Employers are

WORKPLACE DIVERSITY

SINGAPORE

The word *no* is rarely heard in Singapore. The polite but evasive *yes* is considered a valid technique to avoid giving offense. A true yes is usually followed by paperwork and documentation. Successful managers never openly contradict anyone but learn the subtle methods of expressing agreement and disagreement.

liable for an employee's on-the-job injury no matter how the illness or injury occurs. Workers' compensation covers accidents even if they are the fault of the worker.

5. *Family and Medical Leave Act (FMLA).* The Family and Medical Leave Act requires companies to give employees up to 12 weeks of leave to care for a child, spouse, or parent. The law only affects companies with 50 or more employees. Companies do not need to pay employees while they are on leave but must give them their jobs back with no penalties. Employers must also maintain health insurance for employees who take leave.

Companies may have to pay damages to employees who are victims of FMLA discrimination. For example, in 1998 a court in Pennsylvania awarded more than $8,000 in damages to a woman who was not allowed to reduce her 60-hour workweek to recuperate from radiation treatments.

Labor Relations Laws

Many laws protect individual employees. Congress also has enacted labor relations laws that protect groups of employees. The most important labor relations law is the National Labor Relations Act

(NLRA), which gives employees the right to organize into unions. **Unions** are groups of workers who collectively bargain for rights such as higher wages and better working conditions. Under the NLRA, companies must at least listen to what unions say they want for their members in terms of wages, hours, and conditions of employment, such as safety in the workplace. Managers must bargain with unions over such matters as sick leave, work rules, drug testing, layoffs, overtime, seniority, holiday bonuses, and disciplinary procedures.

Unions are effective in getting what they want for their members because businesses know that, under the NLRA, they must bargain in "good faith." Businesses do not have to agree to everything the union

FIGURE 5–1

Labor Relations Law

Under the National Labor Relations Act, workers can organize into unions in order to protect their rights as employees. They also work to achieve better wages and working conditions from their employers.

1 ORGANIZING
Employees who want to form a union petition the National Labor Relations Board for permission to hold an election. Then all company employees vote to join a union.

wants, but they cannot dismiss union demands without at least making a counteroffer.

Unions also can be effective because they have the right to strike, or to stop working. Unions decide to strike as a last resort when they think that companies will not agree to their demands and they see no other alternative.

Strikes are a union's ultimate weapon. When unions strike, companies don't have employees to do work. Unions hope that by striking, they will force companies to agree to their terms because the companies will want their members to go back to work. **Figure 5–1** shows the steps employees can take to reach acceptable working conditions.

CONNECT

Imagine that you and a number of fellow students want to ask the school board to change a policy. Would it be better to approach the board individually, or in a group? If you think a group would be better, how would you organize it?

3 STRIKING
When workers feel that management is treating them unfairly and there is no other alternative, unions may decide to strike. The stoppage of work may force management to reconsider the requests of union workers.

2 COLLECTIVE BARGAINING
Employees appoint representatives to negotiate for higher wages and better working conditions. These representatives bargain with managers in order to set out policies that are acceptable both to workers and management.

MAKE WAY FOR JAPANESE WOMEN WITH WELDING GUNS

Japanese Women Are Winning More Rights— and Factory Jobs

Madoka Matsumae, 24, doesn't want to be treated like a man, just to earn as much as one. For six years, she has snapped rings onto pistons at Mazda Motor Corp.'s engine plant in Hiroshima. Yet unlike her male colleagues, Matsumae leaves work every day at 5:30 p.m. Japanese factory workers can earn up to 30% more than their regular pay by doing night shifts. But women have been banned from working after 10 p.m. or putting in more than six hours of overtime a week.

REVISED LAW. That is starting to change. On Apr. 1, 1999 Japan revised its Equal Employment Opportunity Law to end overly protective restrictions on women's work. The most immediate impact will be felt in factories. Thanks to the greater flexibility, Japanese manufacturers are likely to hire many more women for manual jobs. An aging population means fewer young men are entering the workforce. So companies must rely more on women to keep factories humming.

Factories are even starting to refit assembly lines with

lighter tools and equipment to accommodate female workers. Toyota Motor Corp. spent $424,000 to retool two assembly lines staffed by 650 women in 1999—up from 440 in 1998.

The gender gap in Japan is still wide compared to the West. Even with 60 new female hires this year, only 8 of every 1,000 Mazda factory workers will be women, compared with 158 per 1,000 at the North American factories of Mazda's largest shareholder, Ford Motor Co.

Female executives are rare at Japan's elite corporations, and few experts expect dramatic improvement. "The good jobs are still restricted to men," contends Mizuho Fukushima, a leading women's rights activist and a House of Councillors member. "Women are so low on the totem pole that they cannot see what is happening at the top."

WOMEN'S WORK. Women still suffer because most were hired and trained as clerical workers. Men are more likely to be put on a management track.

The revised labor law, however, is an important step forward. Big corporations such as Toyota, Mitsui, and NEC now want to put women as well as men on the same management track.

Excerpted with permission from BusinessWeek, *April 19, 1999*

CRITICAL THINKING

Why did Japan revise its Equal Employment Opportunity Law?

DECISION MAKING

What would you do as a Japanese manager to ensure women are put on the same management track as men?

The Teamsters, the National Education Association, and the AFL-CIO are three of the most powerful and well-organized unions, but any group of employees can unionize. For example, in the mid-1990s, the baseball players union went on strike for higher salaries, and the baseball season stopped. The strike even forced the cancellation of the World Series. The strike ended when the players and owners of major league baseball teams compromised on player salaries.

Managers need to be aware of the rights of unions. They should balance the demands and needs of their employees with the needs of their companies. Union members should communicate with management regularly. Unions and managers can work together to foster a productive work environment.

Tips from Robert Half

Large firms are not for everyone. Working in smaller companies gives managers more hands-on involvement. You have more direct impact on the company's future, and there is less bureaucracy. However, smaller staffs can mean longer hours.

Section 5.2 Assessment

 FACT AND IDEA REVIEW

1. Which kind of employment law protects workers against discrimination based on race?
2. True or False: A 30-year-old man can sue for age discrimination. Explain.
3. Why would a company receive an OSHA citation?
4. Why did Congress pass the FLSA?
5. Will workers' compensation laws help employees who are blind? Explain.
6. Why would a union decide to strike?

 CRITICAL THINKING

1. **Analyzing Information:** In what ways are workers protected after they retire?
2. **Making Generalizations:** Under what kinds of situations would workers ask for FMLA leave?

 ASSESSING ENGLISH SKILLS

There have been several books written about the horrible conditions faced by many workers in the early 1900s. Take out a book from your local library and prepare a two-page book report. Here are three suggestions: *The Jungle* by Upton Sinclair, *Cannery Row* by John Steinbeck, and *Children in Bondage* by Edward Markham.

CASE ANALYSIS

You are an attorney representing an insurance company. The president of the company asks you for advice on what kinds of EEO laws regulate the company.

Apply: Write a one-page memo advising the president.

CHAPTER 5 ASSESSMENT

CHAPTER SUMMARY

Section 5.1

▶ The six important areas of law that affect business operations are corporate law, tax law, intellectual property law, consumer law, commercial law, and licensing and zoning law.

▶ The three different kinds of business entities include sole proprietorships, partnerships, and corporations.

Section 5.2

▶ The five major kinds of employment laws that protect workers are equal employment opportunity, occupational safety and health, wage-hour, benefits, and labor relations.

▶ Under the National Labor Relations Act, workers have the right to join unions and strike.

REVIEWING VOCABULARY

Write a dialogue between a government affairs manager and the president of a company using the following vocabulary words:

regulations	patent
sole proprietorship	trademark
partnership	copyright
corporation	contract
income tax	employment laws
property tax	unions

RECALLING KEY CONCEPTS

1. Identify the six different kinds of laws that affect businesses. Which kinds of laws protect business inventions and new products?
2. How do income and property taxes affect businesses? What can businesses do to lessen the effects of those taxes?
3. Why do businesses need to be concerned with employment laws? What kinds of laws protect employees from discrimination?
4. What is the Family and Medical Leave Act?

THINKING CRITICALLY

1. Think about businesses in your community. What difficulties do they face in complying with laws that affect them?
2. Do you think that managers and workers always see eye-to-eye on employment law issues? Explain your answer.
3. Imagine you just bought a computer from a company. You think that the computer is defective. Identify several ways you could try to get your money back from the company, using your knowledge of consumer and commercial law.
4. Why are unions important?

CHAPTER 5 ASSESSMENT

ASSESSING ACADEMIC SKILLS

SOCIAL STUDIES Find out who represents your district in Congress. Send your representative an e-mail with questions about the laws affecting businesses in your community. Share the responses with your class.

APPLYING MANAGEMENT PRINCIPLES

SOLVE THE PROBLEM You are a manager for a carpet manufacturer. One of your employees, Renee Watson, has just developed asthma problems. She wants to be transferred to another department in your company where she will not be exposed to harmful allergens.

Language Arts Do you have to transfer Watson? Explain your answer in a one or two-paragraph memo.

PREPARING FOR COMPETITIVE EVENTS

Answer True or False to the following statements.

1. Owners of corporations are personally liable for any business debts.

2. Unions were designed to protect individual employees against discrimination.

BusinessWeek ONLINE

In this chapter you read the *BusinessWeek* Management Model about Japan revising its Equal Employment Opportunity Law. For more information, go to *BusinessWeek* online at: **www.businessweek.com**

Using the Internet, research articles on the Equal Employment Opportunity Law in the United States. Write a two-page summary of your findings and present it to the class.

CHAPTER 6
ECONOMICS

LEARNING OBJECTIVES

When you have completed this chapter, you will be able to:

- Explain the concepts of scarcity and opportunity cost.
- Recognize how supply and demand work to determine price.
- Understand why businesses contract and expand during different phases of the business cycle.

READING STRATEGIES

As you read

- **PREDICT** what the section will be about.
- **CONNECT** what you read with your own life.
- **QUESTION** as you read to make sure you understand the content.
- **RESPOND** to what you read.

Understanding Management

Big-league sports are a big business. In the 1980s and 1990s average ticket prices to professional sporting events skyrocketed, making it difficult for middle-income fans to attend games. In the meantime, salaries for players increased. When setting ticket prices, managers such as Harry Hutt of the Portland Trail Blazers have to balance what fans are willing to pay with the costs of running a team. If there are too many empty seats in the stands, even a winning team will lose money.

Analyzing Management Skills

For what reasons would a manager lower prices for a service or good?

Applying Management Skills

How would you determine ticket prices for a sports team in your area? What factors would you consider?

BusinessWeek ONLINE

For further reading on managers and management go to:
www.businessweek.com

"MANAGEMENT TALK"

"We've created a new, fan-friendly ticket pricing structure that will give a greater cross-section of fans throughout Oregon and Southwest Washington accessibility to our games. By creating more affordable price points, a greater number of families will have the opportunity to see, in person, Blazers basketball."

—Harry Hutt, Portland Trail Blazers, Senior Vice President of Marketing Operations

MAKING DECISIONS IN A MARKET ECONOMY

WHAT YOU'LL LEARN

▶ How businesses in a market economy make decisions about what to produce.
▶ How a market economy differs from a command economy.
▶ How the law of supply and demand determines the equilibrium price of a good or service.
▶ How businesses determine how much profit they earn.

WHY IT'S IMPORTANT

Understanding the basic concepts of economics helps managers make good decisions.

KEY TERMS

• economics
• scarcity
• opportunity cost
• command economy
• market economy
• equilibrium price
• breakeven analysis
• breakeven point

Allocating Resources

All societies have resources. Some societies have rich natural resources, such as fertile land or vast mineral deposits. Other societies have well-developed resources, such as sophisticated machinery and educated workforces. Whatever their resources, all societies try to figure out how best to use them to produce goods and services. **Economics** is the study of how societies decide what to produce, how to produce it, and how to distribute what they produce.

If all consumers throughout the world could consume everything they wanted, economic decisions would not need to be made. Such decisions are necessary because all goods and services are scarce. **Scarcity** refers to the fact that too few resources are available for everyone in the world to consume as much as he or she would like.

▲ **OPPORTUNITY COST** The opportunity cost to this woman of buying a new car is the cost of the next best way she could have spent her money. *What might this cost have been?*

The Concept of Opportunity Cost

Because goods and services are scarce, producing one good means not producing another. The **opportunity cost** of taking an action refers to the loss associated with the best opportunity that is passed up. A greeting card company that spends $2 million producing birthday cards, for example, will have $2 million less to spend on other kinds of cards. By choosing to produce birthday cards, the greeting card company passes up the opportunity to earn profits on other kinds of cards. This lost opportunity represents the opportunity cost of producing birthday cards.

Businesses and individuals must consider opportunity cost whenever they choose one option over another. A manager who is considering quitting her job in order to go back to school to get a Master of Business Administration (M.B.A.) degree must weigh the opportunity cost of leaving her job against the benefits of getting a degree. This manager has a scarce resource—time—which she must decide how best to allocate. If she chooses not to go back to school, she will remain at her job, where she earns $55,000 a year. The opportunity cost of returning to school is thus $55,000 a year plus the cost of tuition. The manager must consider this entire cost, not just the cost of tuition, in deciding whether to remain at work or return to school.

QUESTION

What factors might make the opportunity cost of going back to school for an M.B.A. worth the expense?

Types of Economic Systems

All societies make decisions about how to allocate resources. Different types of economies make these decisions in different ways.

THE COMMAND ECONOMY In some countries, the government decides what goods and services are produced. This kind of economy is called a **command economy**. In a command economy, government planners decide how many tons of steel factories produce. They decide the kinds of shoes shoe manufacturers produce and how many loaves of bread bakeries bake. Decisions are made by command, not in response to consumer tastes.

Until the 1990s, many countries in Eastern Europe had command economies. Product quality was poor, and

▲ **COMMAND ECONOMY** The command economy failed to allocate resources effectively. As a result, many people in the former Soviet Union spent hours standing in line to buy food. *Why are consumer goods more plentiful in a market economy?*

consumers often had difficulty finding the products they wanted. Market shelves were often empty and clothing stores carried few styles of clothes.

THE MARKET ECONOMY In a **market economy**, private companies and individuals decide what to produce and what to consume. The government plays only a minor role in a market economy, regulating businesses to make sure that they compete fairly (see Chapter 4). Most countries in the world today, including the United States, have market economies.

The market economy is based on competition. Private companies compete with one another to attract consumers, in the hope of earning profits from a successful product or service. No one tells companies what or how to produce. Instead, each company makes its own decisions. Companies that make the right decisions earn profits and succeed. Companies that make the wrong decisions lose money and may eventually go out of business.

One case of misjudging what consumers wanted is Sony's video recorder. In the 1980s, Sony introduced the video recorder using a technology known as beta-max. The Sony technology produced a better picture than the VHS video recorder, which was introduced later. However, beta-max was priced higher than its VHS competitors. Despite its superior quality, sales of the product declined, and Sony eventually stopped producing it. Consumers, not business managers or the government, determined which video technology won.

The Law of Supply and Demand

It is easy to understand how companies produce goods in a command economy: a government planner simply gives an order. It is more difficult to understand how companies make decisions in a market economy. How do producers in such an economy know what to produce? How do they know how much to produce? How do they know how much to charge for their products? In a market economy, supply and demand determine the prices and quantities of the goods and services that are produced.

PREDICT

How do you think the laws of supply and demand work?

THE LAW OF DEMAND Economists use the term *demand* to refer to the quantity of a good or service individuals are willing to purchase at various prices. Demand depends on individuals' needs and wants. It also depends on their incomes. Demand for high-priced stereo equipment, for example, will be lower among low-income people than among high-income people because low-income people cannot always afford to purchase expensive luxury goods.

According to the law of demand, as the price of a good increases, the quantity of the good demanded falls. At a price of $4.00 a gallon, for example, gasoline consumption will be much lower than it will be at $0.50 a gallon. At this high a price, more people may carpool, and some people will avoid long trips. These measures will reduce the quantity of gasoline demanded.

If the price of gasoline falls to $0.50 a gallon, the quantity of gasoline demanded will rise. Many people are likely to use their cars more. They may also purchase larger cars, which consume more gasoline. These actions will increase the quantity of gasoline demanded. A demand curve, shown in **Figure 6–1**, describes this relationship between demand and price.

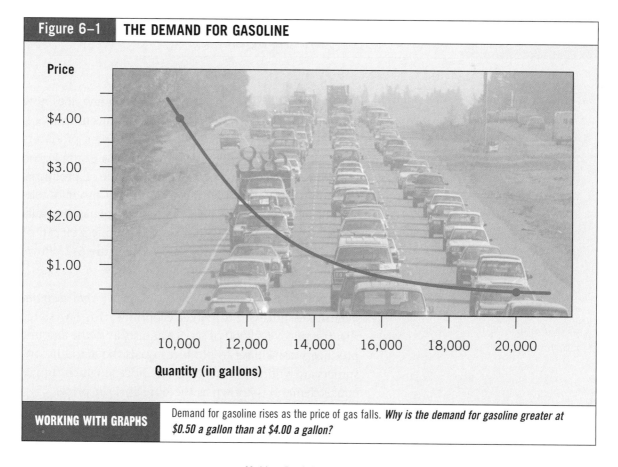

Figure 6–1 | **THE DEMAND FOR GASOLINE**

Price: $4.00, $3.00, $2.00, $1.00

Quantity (in gallons): 10,000 12,000 14,000 16,000 18,000 20,000

WORKING WITH GRAPHS Demand for gasoline rises as the price of gas falls. *Why is the demand for gasoline greater at $0.50 a gallon than at $4.00 a gallon?*

Figure 6–2   THE SUPPLY OF GASOLINE

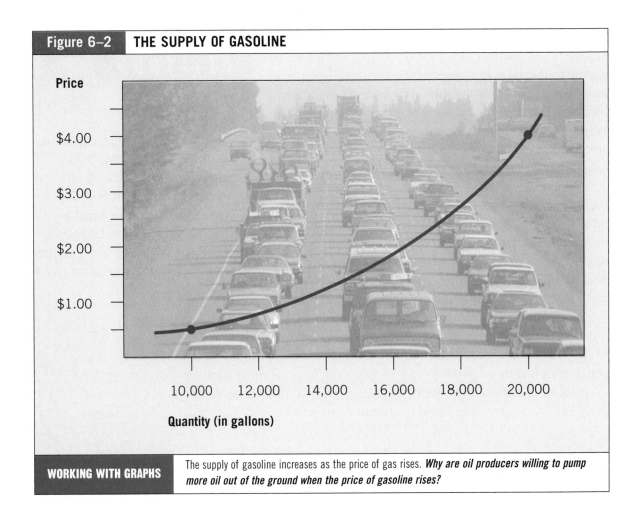

Price

$4.00

$3.00

$2.00

$1.00

10,000   12,000   14,000   16,000   18,000   20,000

Quantity (in gallons)

WORKING WITH GRAPHS   The supply of gasoline increases as the price of gas rises. *Why are oil producers willing to pump more oil out of the ground when the price of gasoline rises?*

RHI Robert Half International Inc.

Tips from Robert Half

Keep your own "personnel file." Make notes of contributions you make to the company, speeches you've given, and papers you've written as well as letters of commendation. When it's time to ask for a raise or look for a new job, you'll be well prepared.

THE LAW OF SUPPLY The law of supply describes how price affects the amount of a good producers produce. According to this law, as the price of a good rises, producers are willing to supply more of the good. If, for example, the price of gasoline rises to $4.00 a gallon, crude oil producers will pump more oil out of the ground. They also may consider developing new oil fields. If the price of gasoline falls to just $0.50 a gallon, producers will pump less oil out of the ground. The supply curve, shown in **Figure 6–2**, shows this relationship between price and quantity.

DETERMINING PRICE The *law of supply and demand* determines prices in a market economy. This law states that the price of a good or service adjusts until the amount producers are willing to produce equals the amount consumers are willing to consume. The price at which supply equals demand is known as the **equilibrium price**.

At $0.50 a gallon, consumers in a certain community are interested in purchasing 20,000 gallons of gasoline a week, as **Figure 6–3** shows. At this price, however, producers are willing to produce only 10,000 gallons. Demand exceeds supply, and there is a shortage of gasoline.

At $4.00 a gallon, producers produce 20,000 gallons of gasoline, but consumers are interested in purchasing only 10,000 gallons. Supply exceeds demand, and some gas goes unsold.

Only at the equilibrium price of $1.25 a gallon does the amount producers produce equal the amount consumers want to purchase. At this price there is exactly enough gasoline to meet consumer demand.

Because supply and demand are constantly shifting, the equilibrium price also changes. For example, an increase in demand for gasoline during the summer months will cause the equilibrium price to rise, as the demand curve shifts to the right. A decline in demand for gasoline as a result of more fuel-efficient automobiles will cause the equilibrium price to fall, as the demand curve shifts to the left.

CONNECT

You are starting a small business selling chocolate chip cookies. What factors should you take into account when setting the price for your cookies?

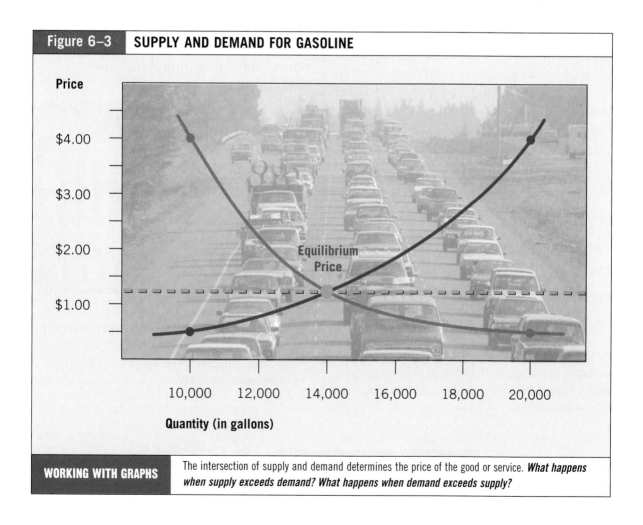

| Figure 6–3 | SUPPLY AND DEMAND FOR GASOLINE |

WORKING WITH GRAPHS   The intersection of supply and demand determines the price of the good or service. *What happens when supply exceeds demand? What happens when demand exceeds supply?*

Marketing Manager

■ Nature of the Work

All firms need marketing expertise. Marketing managers (in large firms, often a vice-president) are responsible for fully developing a company's marketing strategy. This includes devising a pricing strategy that gives the company the largest market share and highest profits, yet ensures that customers are satisfied. Marketing managers work with sales and product managers and other managers to monitor trends that can indicate the need for new products. They oversee product development as well. When advertising and promotion are in separate departments, marketing managers work with those managers to see that advertising and promotional strategies accurately target and attract potential customers.

■ Working Conditions

Marketing managers work in comfortable offices close to top managers. High wages are often offset by frequent travel and long hours. They work 50 hours or more per week, and are often under pressure.

■ Training, Other Qualifications, and Advancement

To become a marketing manager, you need a bachelor's or master's degree in liberal arts, or suitable experience in the field. There are several industry-sponsored certification programs available. They must be creative, self-motivated, resistant to stress, flexible, decisive, and have excellent communication skills.

■ Salary Range

Marketing managers earn $23,000 to $97,000 or more. Vice-president of marketing earns $133,000, plus bonuses. Salaries vary with responsibilities, experience, education, size and location of firm, and the industry.

CRITICAL THINKING

Why is marketing important to all companies?

STANDARD & POOR'S

INDUSTRY OUTLOOK

Marketing professionals are essential in the retail industry, where companies must appeal to dynamic changes in style, trends, and customer demands. Retail is the second largest industry in the United States, employs over 23 million Americans, and generates more than $3 trillion in retail sales annually.

BUSINESS MANAGEMENT *Online*

For more information on management careers, go to:
busmanagement.glencoe.com

Determining Profits

Understanding supply and demand is important because it helps managers determine the prices they should charge. Setting prices correctly affects how much profit a business earns. *Profit* is the difference between what a business earns (revenue) and what it spends (costs). To determine profits, businesses need to estimate their expected revenue and costs.

Estimating Revenue

Managers estimate their sales in order to determine whether a product appears likely to earn a profit. To forecast how many units of a good they will sell, they try to gauge consumer demand.

For example, before it introduces a new cleanser, Procter and Gamble tests the product in a few cities. Based on customer interest in those

International Management

RUSSIA

As Russia moves from a bureaucracy to responsive entrepreneurial enterprise, Russian managers can no longer follow procedures and structures to control outcomes. Yet, they do not have the experience to judge the degree of risk involved in a deal. As they cope with the challenges of uncertainty, they are learning to develop management creativity.

BusinessWeek ONLINE For further reading about International Management go to: **www.businessweek.com**

◀ **FIXED COSTS** This shipping company must make payments on its fleet of trucks whether or not the trucks are being used. These payments represent fixed costs. *Why do companies try to keep fixed costs to a minimum?*

Figure 6–4 | BREAKEVEN ANALYSIS

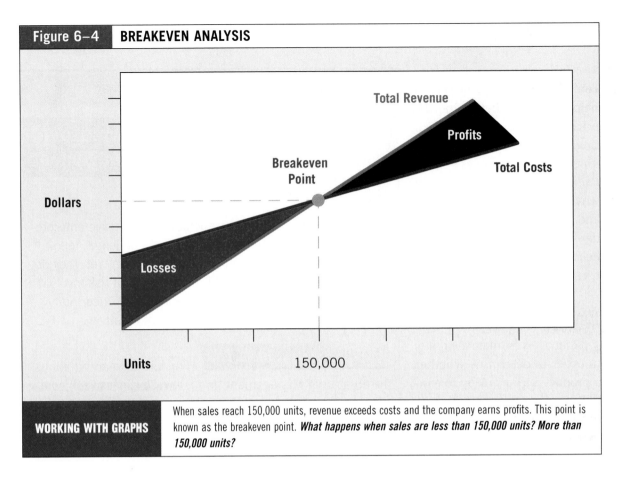

When sales reach 150,000 units, revenue exceeds costs and the company earns profits. This point is known as the breakeven point. *What happens when sales are less than 150,000 units? More than 150,000 units?*

cities, the company estimates how many units of the product it expects to sell nationwide. To calculate its revenue, it multiplies the number of units it expects to sell by the price it plans to charge.

Estimating Costs

Managers also need to estimate their costs before they launch a new product. Businesses incur two kinds of costs, fixed costs and variable costs.

FIXED COSTS Costs that a business absorbs regardless of the number of units it produces are called *fixed costs*. These costs include rent, management salaries, and property taxes.

As long as they remain in business, businesses face fixed costs. These costs are incurred even if the business produces no goods at all. Boeing Corporation, for example, pays property taxes on the factories and office buildings it owns, even if it has no orders for airplanes and its factories sit idle.

VARIABLE COSTS Costs that rise or fall depending on how much of a good or service is produced are called *variable costs*. These costs include the cost of labor and materials.

Variable costs rise with the level of production. For example, the more airplanes Boeing produces, the more it will spend on labor, titanium, and glass.

QUESTION

Why are labor costs considered variable costs?

Performing Breakeven Analysis

Managers make decisions about production by analyzing revenue and costs. One of the ways they do so is by performing breakeven analysis. **Breakeven analysis** reveals how many units of a good or service a business needs to sell before it begins earning a profit.

An electronics company must sell 60,000 units just to cover its fixed costs. These costs include the rent on its factories and offices and the salaries it pays to its managers. To cover both variable costs and fixed costs, it must sell 150,000 units. The point at which revenue is sufficient to cover all costs is called the **breakeven point**, as shown in Figure 6–4.

Section 6.1 Assessment

FACT AND IDEA REVIEW

1. Define scarcity.
2. What do you need to calculate the opportunity cost of a particular course of action?
3. What is a command economy?
4. What is a market economy?
5. How is the equilibrium price of a good or service determined?
6. Indicate which of the following types of costs are fixed costs and which are variable costs: overtime expenses, carpeting at the office, salary of the public relations director, rent, income tax.
7. How is the breakeven point calculated?

CRITICAL THINKING

1. **Making Comparisons:** Compare a market economy with a command economy. Which system allocates resources better?
2. **Making Generalizations:** Name three factors that affect consumer demand.

ASSESSING MATH SKILLS

ast year, your company sold 250,000 spiral notebooks at $1.89 each. If demand for your product rises by 12 percent this year, how many dollars worth of notebooks will your company sell?

CASE ANALYSIS

As the marketing manager of a mid-sized clothing manufacturer, you must come up with prices for the eight different kinds of blouses and three kinds of pants your company produces.

Apply: What kind of information about consumer demand would help you set prices? What are some ways you could obtain that information?

THE BUSINESS CYCLE

WHAT YOU'LL LEARN

▶ What the business cycle is.
▶ What happens during economic expansions and contractions.
▶ What business cycles have occurred in the past 80 years.
▶ How economic indicators are used to forecast business cycles.

WHY IT'S IMPORTANT

Business cycles can cause sales in an industry to rise or fall.

KEY TERMS

• business cycle
• recession
• depression
• economic indicators

CONNECT

When do you feel most likely to purchase new items for yourself?

Phases of the Business Cycle

Almost all businesses experience periods during which they grow and periods during which they contract. A series of good business decisions may allow a business to expand. A series of miscalculations may force a business to contract. Tastes or technology may change, making winners of some businesses and losers of others. These kinds of ups and downs are normal for every business.

Sometimes businesses in many industries simultaneously expand or contract. Expansion and contraction by many industries at once is known as the **business cycle**. It is called a cycle because it consists of several phases, which occur every few years. Most business cycles consist of two major phases, the expansionary phase and the contractionary phase, as shown in **Figure 6–5**.

Figure 6–5	THE BUSINESS CYCLE

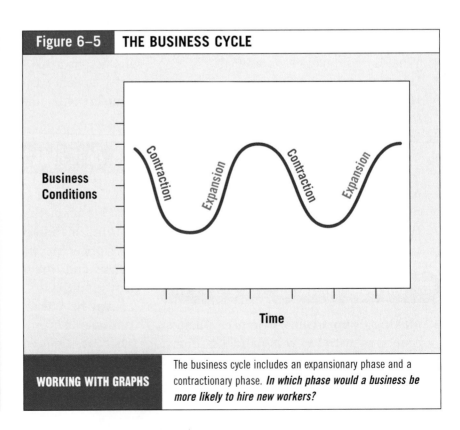

WORKING WITH GRAPHS

The business cycle includes an expansionary phase and a contractionary phase. *In which phase would a business be more likely to hire new workers?*

Retired—to a New Job

Forget leisure. Retirement is increasingly regarded as a transition to another work life, although at a more relaxed pace. In 2000, 37% of men and 31% of women age 55 to 64 were employed full- or part-time while receiving pension income, according to investment giant TIAA-CREF. Those proportions are likely to go higher. And 8 out of 10 baby boomers say they plan to work in retirement, according to the AARP, the lobbyist for the over-50 crowd.

The movement toward embracing work during the last third of life calls for a much broader definition of investing for retirement. The typical retirement worksheet deals with financial assets such as equities, bonds, cash, and real estate. But investing for the long-term should also encompass education, training, and networking—what economists call human capital. Economists estimate that human capital is the most important form of wealth in the U.S., worth three to four times as much as all other assets, including stocks, bonds, and real estate.

STAYING SHARP. The return on investment? Working longer can make a huge difference in retirement living standards. Pocketing even a slim income often allows retirement portfolios to compound over a longer period of time. For example, a $400,000 portfolio at age 55 compounding annually at a 5% rate with a $1,000 contribution a month is worth around $579,000 at age 60. But if earning an income means the portfolio is left alone to compound at a 5% rate until age 65—even with no new contributions—it will grow to around $738,000.

HIGHER CALLING. Many retirees are eager to work by volunteering or taking a job at a local nonprofit. But good intentions and a willing spirit aren't enough to get a fulfilling job. A smart investment of your time is to network at the nonprofit long before you retire. Otherwise, you might get stuck with boring tasks that don't take advantage of your talents.

So, while struggling to put money aside for your later years, dream about what you would like to do in the next stage of life. Once you're drawn to an idea, invest in the skills and contacts you'll need to bring that dream to life.

Excerpted with permission from BusinessWeek, *July 17, 2003*

CRITICAL THINKING

What are some of the rewards for remaining in the workforce after retirement?

DECISION MAKING

Do you intend to work full- or part-time in your retirement years? Why or why not? What factors influence your decision?

The Expansionary Phase of the Business Cycle

Economic expansion occurs when consumer spending is strong and companies invest in new factories and equipment. During a period of expansion, unemployment usually declines, as people who were unemployed find jobs with new or expanded businesses. Wages, prices, and interest rates usually rise during an expansion because people generally have more money to spend.

Eventually, unemployment drops to such a low level that companies are unable to find workers to hire. In Minnesota, for example, workers were so hard to find in the late 1990s that some businesses there were unable to expand. A large chain of convenience stores considered closing several branches because it was unable to find cashiers. Large manufacturing companies also left the state because they were unable to hire enough employees.

As expansion continues, prices rise so much that both businesses and consumers cut back on their purchases. Companies stop expanding, and the next phase of the business cycle begins.

QUESTION

What factors cause a recession or depression?

The Contractionary Phase of the Business Cycle

In the next phase of the business cycle, consumers reduce their purchases and business investment slows (see **Figure 6–6**). Unemployment rises, as companies lay off workers they no longer need. As more and more people lose their jobs, consumer spending falls, causing companies to reduce production and employment even further.

During a contraction, both businesses and consumers are pessimistic about the future. Companies produce less and banks provide fewer loans than they would during an expansion. As a result, economic growth declines.

When growth falls for two three-month periods in a row, the economy is said to be in a **recession**. When business activity remains far below normal for years, the economy is said to be in a **depression**.

▲ BUSINESS CYCLE One out of every three Americans was unemployed during the Great Depression. *What event eventually brought prosperity back?*

The Business Cycle in U.S. History

The United States has always experienced business cycles. In the 1920s, for example, the economy expanded, as a new era of prosperity

FIGURE 6-6

The Business Cycle

Businesses expand and consumers increase their purchasing during the expansionary phase of the business cycle. During the contractionary phase of the cycle, businesses lay off workers and consumers cut back on their spending.

1 EXPANSION
During an expansion, businesses may build new plants and hire new workers. Unemployment is low, and companies have to pay competitive salaries to attract new workers. The stock market often booms, adding to many people's sense of economic well-being.

2 CONTRACTION
As the expansion slows down, consumers begin to spend less. The drop in consumer spending forces businesses to cut back on production. Businesses may lay off some workers, causing consumer spending to fall even more.

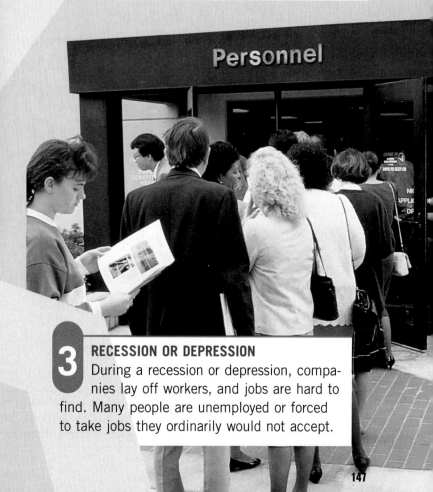

3 RECESSION OR DEPRESSION
During a recession or depression, companies lay off workers, and jobs are hard to find. Many people are unemployed or forced to take jobs they ordinarily would not accept.

RESPOND

If you managed a small business
and leading economic indicators
predicted a recession, what would
you do?

began following World War I. This boom period ended abruptly
in 1929, when the stock market crashed.

The period that followed, known as the Great Depression, was
the longest and most severe period of economic stagnation the
United States has ever known. During the Depression, 25 percent
of the workforce was unemployed, and many people lost everything they owned.

The Depression ended in the 1940s, when the United States
entered World War II. The need to increase production for the
war effort caused the economy to expand. Factories began to
increase production, hiring workers who previously had been
unemployed.

Economic Indicators

Business managers would find it useful to be able to predict when
changes in the business cycle might occur. If, for example, a company
knew that the economy was about to expand, it would increase production. It might even begin developing new products. If a company knew
that a recession was likely to occur, it might put off plans to expand its
operations. It might also try to sell off its current inventory quickly.

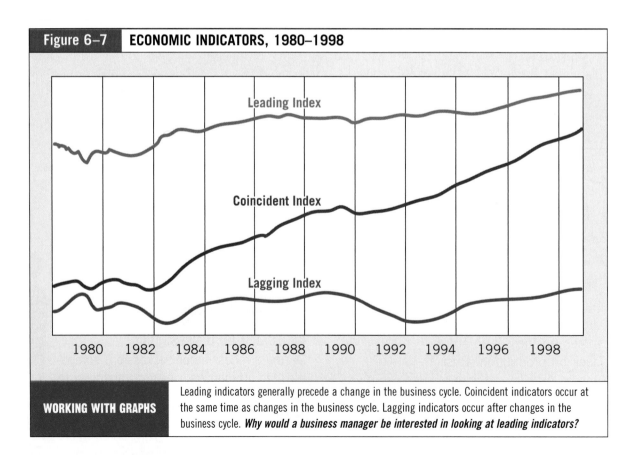

Figure 6–7 **ECONOMIC INDICATORS, 1980–1998**

WORKING WITH GRAPHS Leading indicators generally precede a change in the business cycle. Coincident indicators occur at the same time as changes in the business cycle. Lagging indicators occur after changes in the business cycle. *Why would a business manager be interested in looking at leading indicators?*

The economy is affected by so many factors that no one can predict with certainty when an expansion or contraction will occur. Economists and business managers can only try to forecast these events. One way of doing so is by examining economic indicators.

Economic indicators are data that show how the economy is performing. Data on housing loans and bankruptcies, for example, provide valuable information on the performance of the economy. Figure 6–7 illustrates economic indicators for 1980–1998. Economic measures that rise or fall before other measures are known as *leading economic indicators*. These measures are important to business managers because they show which way the economy is likely to move.

One leading economic indicator is new orders of consumer goods and materials by manufacturers. Business managers like to see increased orders by manufacturers, because such orders suggest that other businesses are optimistic about the future. An increase in manufacturers' orders may indicate that the economy is likely to expand.

Section 6.2 Assessment

FACT AND IDEA REVIEW

1. What are the two phases of the business cycle?
2. What happens to prices and wages during an expansion?
3. In which phase of the business cycle does unemployment rise?
4. What was the longest contraction in U.S. history?
5. What is a leading economic indicator?

CRITICAL THINKING

1. **Making Generalizations:** Why do business managers need to understand the business cycle?
2. **Drawing Conclusions:** How did the United States' entry into World War II pull the economy out of the Great Depression?

ASSESSING COMPUTER SCIENCE SKILLS

Use the World Wide Web or the library to find out the current phase of the U.S. economy's business cycle. Justify your answer by providing statistics on unemployment, growth, consumer spending, and interest rates.

CASE ANALYSIS

American Lighting and Fixtures has seen sales decline for four months in a row. Managers at the company are concerned about the decline, which they are unable to explain.

Apply: If the company's competitors also are experiencing a drop in sales, what may be happening? What kind of evidence would you collect to support your explanation of why the company's sales are falling?

CHAPTER 6 ASSESSMENT

CHAPTER SUMMARY

Section 6.1

▶ Economics is the study of how societies decide what to produce, how to produce it, and how to distribute what they produce.

▶ The opportunity cost refers to the loss associated with the best opportunity that is passed up.

▶ In a command economy, the government decides what goods and services are produced. In a market economy, individuals and private businesses make these decisions.

▶ Fixed costs do not vary with the level of production.

▶ Variable costs vary with the quantity of the good produced.

▶ The breakeven point indicates how many units a company needs to sell before it begins to earn a profit.

Section 6.2

▶ Business cycles consist of two phases, a contractionary phase and an expansionary phase.

▶ Economic indicators show how the economy is performing.

 REVIEWING VOCABULARY

Divide into groups of four or five. Have each group member explain four of the following vocabulary words to the rest of the group:

economics
scarcity
opportunity cost
command economy
market economy
equilibrium price
breakeven analysis

breakeven point
business cycle
recession
depression
economic
   indicators

 RECALLING KEY CONCEPTS

1. In a command economy, who decides how much to produce? Who makes these decisions in a market economy?
2. How does a manager calculate profit?
3. How do fixed costs differ from variable costs?
4. What does calculating the breakeven point show?
5. What are the two phases of the business cycle?

 THINKING CRITICALLY

1. Why would economic decisions be unnecessary if scarcity did not exist?
2. Why is it important to consider the opportunity cost of an action?
3. What is the difference between the concepts of scarcity and shortage? When does scarcity exist? When do shortages exist?
4. Why is the concept of supply and demand so important in a market economy?
5. Why are companies more likely to lay off workers in the contractionary phase of the business cycle than in the expansionary phase?

ASSESSING ACADEMIC SKILLS

HISTORY Interview someone you know who lived through the Great Depression, or research the topic in your local library. Find out what life was like then. What was life like during the Great Depression? How severe was the economic stagnation? How long did it last? Include answers to these questions in your report and share your findings to the class.

APPLYING MANAGEMENT PRINCIPLES

SOLVE THE PROBLEM In the past few years, your company has earned a lot of money producing turtle stuffed animals. You suspect that the turtle craze may be coming to an end. How should your company prepare for the possibility that demand for turtle toys may fall? How might you determine whether the fall in sales your company has experienced in the past few months is temporary or permanent? How might you determine whether the decline represents a drop in demand for turtle toys or a drop in demand for all toys?

Writing Prepare a short report explaining why you think the demand for your company's products is falling. Write a step-by-step plan on what your company should do next.

PREPARING FOR COMPETITIVE EVENTS

The point at which the total cost equals the total revenue is the

a. breakeven point.

b. equalized profit margin.

c. equalized supply vs. demand point.

d. fixed cost point.

BusinessWeek ONLINE

In this chapter you read the *BusinessWeek* Management Model about working during your retirement years. For more information, go to *BusinessWeek* online at: **www.businessweek.com**

Using the Internet or your local library, find a current article about economic trends in the United States. Write a two-page summary of the article and share it with the class.

CHAPTER 7

INTERNATIONAL BUSINESS

Learning Objectives

When you have completed this chapter, you will be able to:

- Explain why countries trade.
- Explain why companies export and import.
- Explain how and why countries restrict international trade.
- Describe the strategies organizations use to compete in the global economy.

READING STRATEGIES

As you read

- **PREDICT** what the section will be about.
- **CONNECT** what you read with your own life.
- **QUESTION** as you read to make sure you understand the content.
- **RESPOND** to what you read.

MANAGEMENT TALK

"Our confidence in the international marketplace is exemplified by our continued profitable expansion.... Our strategy of extending our leadership position in the global marketplace continues as we concentrate on providing customers quality, value, and convenience as we capitalize on our global infrastructure."

—James R. Cantalupo,
Former McDonald's Chairman and CEO

Understanding Management

The Golden Arches of McDonald's are a familiar sight in 119 countries around the world. The fast-food restaurant's international expansion is a good example of business practices that will become more prevalent in the global economy of the 21st century. McDonald's is able to operate successfully in foreign countries by offering consistent standards for "quality, value, and convenience."

Analyzing Management Skills

Why would a successful American company like McDonald's want to open new restaurants in foreign countries? What are the risks involved?

Applying Management Skills

Choose one of your favorite American-made products or services. Explain how you would sell it in a foreign country. What are the risks and benefits?

BusinessWeek ONLINE

For further reading on managers and management go to:
www.businessweek.com

INTERNATIONAL TRADE

What Is International Trade?

International trade consists of the exchange of goods and services by different countries. It includes the purchase of American blue jeans in China and the purchase of Belgian chocolate in the United States.

Most of the world today depends on international trade to maintain its standard of living. American manufacturers sell automobiles, heavy machinery, clothing, and electronic goods abroad. Argentine cattle ranchers ship beef to consumers in dozens of foreign countries. Saudi Arabian oil producers supply much of the world with oil. In return, they purchase food, cars, and electronic goods from other countries.

Countries trade for several different reasons. One country may not be able to produce a good it wants. France, for example, cannot

▲ **INTERNATIONAL TRADE** International trade allows people in one country to enjoy products made in other countries. *Without international trade, what kinds of products would these people consume?*

produce oil because it has no oil fields. If it wants to consume oil, it must trade with oil-producing countries. Countries also may trade because they have an advantage over other countries in producing particular goods or services.

CONNECT

Make a quick mental list of some of your favorite personal possessions such as clothes, electronic equipment, and sporting goods. Which items come from foreign countries?

Absolute Advantage

Different countries are endowed with different resources. Honduras, for example, has fertile land, a warm and sunny climate, and inexpensive labor. Compared with Honduras, Great Britain has less fertile soil, a colder and rainier climate, and more expensive labor. Given the same combination of inputs (land, labor, and capital), Honduras would produce much more coffee than Great Britain. It has an absolute advantage in the production of coffee. An **absolute advantage** is the ability to produce more of a good than another producer with the same quantity of inputs.

Comparative Advantage

Countries need not have an absolute advantage in the production of a good to trade. Some countries may be less efficient at producing *all* goods than other countries. Even countries that are not very efficient producers are more efficient at producing some goods than others, however. The **law of comparative advantage** states that producers should produce the goods they are most efficient at producing and purchase from others the goods they are less efficient at producing.

According to the law of comparative advantage, individuals, companies, and countries should specialize in what they do best. Jennifer

Thompson applies this principle to her job as the head of the marketing department at a large pharmaceutical company. Jennifer, who used to work in advertising, is a better copywriter than the people who work for her. She lets the copywriters write the advertising copy, however, because her time is too valuable to spend on copywriting. Her *comparative advantage* is in managing her department.

Just as Jennifer devotes her time to managing rather than copywriting, countries allocate their resources to producing what they produce most efficiently. The United States, for example, imports many simple manufactured goods so that it can devote its resources to other activities, such as the production of sophisticated high-tech products.

QUESTION

What is the difference between comparative advantage and absolute advantage?

Exporting and Importing

International trade takes place when companies sell the goods they produce in a foreign country or purchase goods produced abroad. Goods and services that are sold abroad are called **exports**. Goods and services that are purchased abroad are called **imports**.

The United States is the largest exporter in the world, exporting about $700 billion worth of goods and services a year. It also is the world's largest importer, purchasing about $900 billion worth of foreign goods and services annually.

All About

ATTITUDE

THINK POSITIVE

A negative attitude is not only unproductive, but will often turn people off. If you act more positive, you'll begin to feel that way too. Consider yourself a happy and intelligent individual. Soon, others will begin to see you the same way. Outside perceptions often start from the inside.

Exports

Exports represent an important source of revenue for many companies. Northwest Airlines, for example, earns about a third of its revenues outside the United States. IBM earns almost 40 percent of its revenues abroad.

WHY DO COMPANIES EXPORT? About 95 percent of the world's consumers live outside the United States. Companies that sell their products exclusively within the United States miss out on the opportunity to reach most of the world's consumers.

To increase their sales, companies like Procter and Gamble spend millions of dollars trying to identify what customers in foreign countries want. "In more than 140 countries around the world, we work to understand what consumers want and need. Then we develop innovative brands to serve those needs—creating new products, new categories and new growth opportunities for our company," reports the company's chief executive officer.

Companies also seek out export markets in order to diversify their sources of revenue. *Diversification* is engaging in a variety of operations. Businesses like to diversify their sales so that sluggish sales in one market can be offset by stronger sales elsewhere. In the first half of 1999, for example, sales of Hewlett-Packard's computer products rose just 2 percent in the United States. The company's overall sales rose by much more, however, thanks to strong sales performance outside the United States.

HOW DO COMPANIES IDENTIFY EXPORT MARKETS? To determine if there is sufficient demand for their products or services overseas, companies analyze demographic figures, economic data, country reports, consumer tastes, and competition in the markets they are considering. Business managers contact the International Trade Administration of the U.S. Department of Commerce, foreign consulates and embassies, and foreign and international trade organizations. They also visit the countries they are considering and conduct surveys in order to assess consumer demand.

Businesses also need to find out what restrictions they may face as exporters. All countries require exporters to complete certain kinds of documents. Some countries also insist that foreign companies meet specific requirements on packaging, labeling, and product safety. Some also limit the ability of exporters to take money they earn from their exports out of the country.

Tips from Robert Half

When you look for a job, your contacts may be critical. They might be able to offer you a job, introduce you to someone who is hiring, or give information about a company. Make business contacts even when you are not looking for a job.

Imports

American companies import billions of dollars worth of goods and services every year. They import consumer goods, such as television sets and automobiles, and industrial goods, such as machines and parts. They import raw materials, such as petroleum, and food products, such as fruits and vegetables. They import these goods in order to use them to produce other goods or to sell them to customers.

PREDICT

For what reasons would a country choose to import goods from a foreign country?

IMPORTS OF MATERIALS Many companies import some or all of the materials they use in order to reduce their production costs. Manufacturers of appliances, for example, import steel from Japan because it is less expensive than steel manufactured in the United States.

Some companies use imported inputs because domestically made inputs are not available or their quality is not as good as that of imported goods. Jewelry designers import diamonds and

emeralds, which are not produced in the United States. Fashion designers use imported cashmere wool, which is softer than domestic wool.

IMPORTS OF CONSUMER GOODS Companies also import products that they can resell in their own countries. Automobile dealers import cars and trucks from Europe and Asia. Wholesalers and retailers import clothing from Thailand, electronic goods from Japan, and cheese from France.

Companies import these goods because consumers want to purchase them. Some of these goods, such as garments from Asia, are less expensive than domestically manufactured products. Others, such as Saabs and Volvos, are popular despite costing more than domestically produced goods.

The Trade Balance

The **balance of trade** is the difference between the value of the goods a country exports and the value of the goods it imports. A country that exports more than it imports runs a *trade surplus*. A country that imports more than it exports runs a *trade deficit*.

For many years the United States has run a trade deficit. This means that the value of the goods and services it buys from other countries exceeds the value of the goods and services it sells to other countries. Other countries, such as Japan, have run huge trade surpluses. In these countries, the value of exports exceeds the value of imports.

▲ **IMPORTS** American consumers are sometimes willing to pay more for imported products than they are for domestically produced goods. *What explains their interest in imports?*

▲ **FOREIGN EXCHANGE** Exchange rates may rise and fall daily. *How does a rise in the value of the dollar affect American companies that do business abroad?*

Foreign Exchange

Companies that purchase goods or services from foreign countries must pay for them with foreign currency. If a U.S. company purchases goods from Japan, for example, it must pay for them in yen. If it purchases goods from Switzerland, it must pay for them in Swiss francs.

Companies purchase foreign currency from banks, which convert each currency into dollars. The value of one currency in terms of another is the foreign exchange rate.

Exchange rates can be quoted in dollars per unit of foreign currency or units of foreign currency per dollar. The exchange rate for the Swiss franc, for example, might be 1.5 to the dollar. This means that one dollar is worth 1.5 Swiss francs and one Swiss franc is worth 1/1.5 dollars, or $0.67.

Most exchange rates fluctuate from day to day. Managers involved in international trade must follow these fluctuations closely, because they can have a dramatic effect on profits. Consider, for example, an American electronics store that wants to purchase 10 million yen worth of Japanese stereos, camcorders, and cameras. If the exchange rate of the yen is 115 to the dollar, the U.S. company must pay $86,956 to purchase 10 million yen worth of Japanese equipment (10 million yen/115 yen per dollar). If the value of the yen rises so that a dollar is worth only 100 yen, the company would have to spend $100,000 dollars to purchase the same value of Japanese goods (10 million yen/100 yen per dollar).

LISTEN BEYOND THE WORDS
The way an employee relates information to you goes beyond the sentences he or she is saying. Listen to his or her voice. You may be able to hear unspoken concerns through his or her tone or emphasis of certain words. Ask questions to understand the situation more clearly.

Protectionism

International trade can benefit all trading partners. It also may hurt some domestic producers, however. A U.S. manufacturer of watches may find it difficult to compete with a Taiwanese producer, who pays his workers a fraction of what workers in the United States earn. Competition from the Taiwanese producer may force the U.S. company out of business.

To help domestic manufacturers compete against foreign companies, governments sometimes impose protectionist measures, such as tariffs, quotas, and other types of restrictions. All of these measures reduce the volume of international trade.

Tariffs

A **tariff** is a tax on imports. The purpose of a tariff is to raise the price of foreign goods in order to allow domestic manufacturers to compete. The United States imposes tariffs on many goods, including most textiles and apparel. This means that a Korean company that sells men's shirts in the United States must pay an import tax on every one of its shirts that enters the country. The purpose of this tax is to make it more difficult for foreign manufacturers of textiles and apparel to compete with American companies in the United States.

QUESTION

How does a country's economy benefit from trade protectionism? How is it harmed? Do you think the benefits outweigh the harms, or vice versa?

▲ **PROTECTIONISM** The quota on sugar raises the price consumers pay for a variety of products, including candy bars and breakfast cereal. *Why does the United States impose a quota on sugar imports?*

Quotas

Quotas are restrictions on the quantity of a good that can enter a country. The United States imposes quotas on many kinds of goods. In 2002, the Bush administration announced new trade measures aimed at protecting the flagging U.S. steel industry, including a 5.4 million ton import quota on unfinished steel. As a result, the European Union, South Korea, and other steel producing countries have lodged complaints with the World Trade Organization, alleging that such protections violate international free trade rules.

Embargoes

An **embargo** is a total ban on the import of a good from a particular country. Embargoes usually are imposed for political rather than economic reasons. Since 1961, for example, the United States has imposed an embargo on Cuba, whose regime it opposes. This embargo bans the importation of goods from Cuba and the export of U.S. goods to Cuba.

Section 7.1 Assessment

 FACT AND IDEA REVIEW

1. What does it mean if one country has an absolute advantage over another country?
2. Why do U.S. companies import goods from other countries?
3. What does it mean for a country to have a trade deficit or surplus?
4. Name three trade protection measures countries impose.

 ASSESSING MATH SKILLS

Your company imports 3 million pounds of chocolate from Switzerland a year at a cost of 3 Swiss francs a pound. Last year the value of the Swiss franc was 1.5 francs per dollar. How much did your imports cost in dollars? If the value of the Swiss franc goes to 1.2 francs per dollar next year, how much will your imports cost?

 CRITICAL THINKING

1. **Evaluating Information:** Should a country that is better at producing all goods than another country trade with that country? Why or why not?
2. **Distinguishing Fact from Opinion:** Is trade protection good or bad? Explain your answer.

 CASE ANALYSIS

Your company, which sells organic fruit juice, has decided to expand its operations abroad.

Apply: Make a list of the information you would need to decide which countries to target for exports. Use the Internet or your public library to find the information you need.

THE GLOBAL ECONOMY

WHY IT'S IMPORTANT

Business managers must understand how to function in the global economy.

KEY TERMS

• global economy
• free trade area
• multinational corporation

The Rise of the Global Economy

Over the past 50 years, companies from all over the world have begun operating globally. Nike operates factories in Vietnam and Indonesia. The Gap owns stores in Canada, France, Germany, Great Britain, and Japan. Perrier and Evian sell bottled water in dozens of countries outside of France. Nokia, a Finnish company, dominates the cellular phone market. Consumers everywhere own products made in other countries.

Many factors have led to the rise of the **global economy**, an economy in which companies compete actively with businesses from all over the world. These factors include improvements in communications technology, the rise in democracy in much of the world, and the elimination of trade restrictions.

Improvements in Telecommunications Technology

Improvements in telecommunications technology have had an enormous impact on international trade. Exchanges of information

▲ **GLOBAL ECONOMY** Companies like Dell make a significant percentage of their sales over the Internet. *How has the Internet made it easier to market products?*

that once took weeks now take seconds, as a result of the development of fax machines and e-mail.

Development of the Internet also has led to *e-commerce,* or sales made over the World Wide Web. E-commerce has enabled even small companies to reach consumers in foreign countries by marketing their products on web sites.

CONNECT

Have you ever shopped for an item over the Internet? What goods and services are available?

Political Changes

The political changes that have taken place since the late 1980s have dramatically increased opportunities for businesses. As a result of the end of the cold war with Russia and the thawing of relations with China, American companies have earned billions of dollars selling products and services in markets from which they were once excluded. Holiday Inn, for example, now runs a hotel in Warsaw. Colgate-Palmolive has a facility in Huangpu, China. Both of these companies, and thousands of others, have benefited from the spread of capitalism.

Free Trade Areas

To promote international trade and limit protectionism, countries create free trade areas. A **free trade area** is a region within which trade restrictions are reduced or eliminated.

The largest free trade area in the world is in North America. Under the terms of the North American Free Trade Agreement (NAFTA) of 1994, businesses in the United States, Mexico, and Canada can sell their products anywhere in North America without facing major trade restrictions.

Consumers in all three countries have benefited from lower prices on North American imports. The price of a blouse imported from Canada or a pair of shoes imported from Mexico, for example, is lower than it used to be because the price no longer includes a tariff.

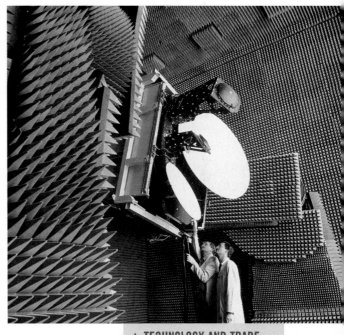

▲ **TECHNOLOGY AND TRADE**
Companies like this telecommunications company have seen their sales to Mexico increase since NAFTA came into effect. *How did NAFTA increase the attractiveness of products manufactured in the United States?*

Many producers have also benefited from NAFTA by increasing their exports within North America. American grain farmers, for example, have increased their sales to Mexico as a result of NAFTA. U.S. automobile sales to Mexico also have risen.

NAFTA has forced some American workers to lose their jobs, however. Sara Lee laid off more than a thousand American workers after it moved some of its operations to Mexico. Many other companies have also reduced their workforces in this country to take advantage of lower labor costs south of the border.

BusinessWeek

Management Model

Women-Owned Businesses: In the Pink

In a perfect world, it wouldn't matter if a business owner was male or female. But for now, the differences are both intriguing and surprising, according to the results of a 100-question survey of 1,400 family-business owners conducted by MassMutual Financial Group and Babson College.

LESS DEBT. When researchers controlled for the size of the business and its industry (women and men tend to own family businesses in the same fields—manufacturing, wholesale, retail, service, and construction), women-owned firms were 1.7 times as productive as their male-owned counterparts.

"We think the reason for this is that women-owned family businesses are younger" by 10 years on average, says I. Elaine Allen, Babson's associate professor of statistics and entrepreneurship. "Therefore, they are able to change and adapt more quickly. They don't have to teach the elephant to dance."

Women-owned family businesses also tend to carry less debt than male-owned ones, notes Allen, who says this may

be due either to less access to capital or an inherent fiscal conservatism. While a lower debt level protects businesses in a downturn, an unwillingness to take on debt can also prevent them from growing as quickly, she points out.

The number of women-owned outfits is growing, the survey found, now comprising 15.6% of all U.S. family businesses—up 37% on five years ago. And that number seems destined to keep on growing, with the survey's findings noting that women are just as likely as men to take over second- and third-generation family businesses. Notes Allen: "We no longer have male primogeniture."

ALL IN THE FAMILY. Another reason the percentage of female-owned family businesses should continue to rise: Women owners say they are more interested in keeping the business in the family. In the 20% of cases where the female owner was not the chief executive, they were far more likely than men to hire a woman as CEO. They also employ more women family members.

Sums up Allen: "The emergence and growing presence of women in U.S. family-owned businesses is having an enormous favorable impact on family business—from productivity to leadership and involvement."

Excerpted with permission from BusinessWeek, *September 9, 2003*

CRITICAL THINKING

If a male-owned business is twice as large as a woman-owned business, is it also twice as productive?

DECISION MAKING

What advantages might a woman-owned firm have during an economic downturn?

Doing Business Globally

Thousands of U.S. businesses, large and small, participate in the global marketplace. Some companies, such as Benneton, build factories in foreign countries or set up retail outlets overseas. Others, such as Harley-Davidson, export their products throughout the world and import materials from other countries.

QUESTION

Why are international trade agreements necessary?

Forms of International Operations

Companies can sell their products or services in foreign countries in various ways. Small companies often work through local companies, which are familiar with local markets. Large companies often establish sales, manufacturing, and distribution facilities in foreign countries.

WORKING THROUGH A FOREIGN INTERMEDIARY Companies that are not willing or able to invest millions of dollars in operations abroad often export their products through foreign intermediaries. A *foreign intermediary* is a wholesaler or agent who markets products for companies that want to do business abroad. In return for a commission, the agent markets the foreign company's product.

Working through a foreign intermediary saves a company the expense of setting up facilities in a foreign country. It also ensures that the company is represented by someone familiar with local conditions. Foreign intermediaries usually work for many foreign companies at a time, however. Thus they are not likely to devote as much time to a single company's products as the company's own sales force would.

SIGNING A LICENSING AGREEMENT WITH A FOREIGN COMPANY Another way companies can reach foreign consumers is by licensing a foreign company to sell their products or services abroad. A *licensing agreement* is an agreement that permits one company to sell another company's products abroad in return for a percentage of the company's revenues.

TGI Friday's, a Dallas-based restaurant company, has used licensing agreements to expand its operations overseas. Signing such agreements enabled it to open branches in Singapore, Indonesia, Malaysia, Thailand, Australia, and New Zealand. Without such agreements, it might not have been able to penetrate those markets.

▲ **LICENSING AGREEMENT** Licensing agreements can help companies expand their operations abroad. *What do you think were the advantages and disadvantages of TGI Friday's signing of foreign licensing agreements?*

FORMING A STRATEGIC ALLIANCE Some companies can expand into foreign markets by forming *strategic alliances* with foreign companies. A strategic alliance involves pooling resources and skills in order to achieve common goals. Companies usually form strategic alliances to gain access to new markets, share research, broaden their product lines, learn new skills, and expand cross-cultural knowledge of management groups.

One of the largest strategic alliances in recent years was the 1998 merger between two of the world's largest automakers, Daimler-Benz, which produces Mercedes-Benz vehicles, and Chrysler. The American automaker benefited from the merger by gaining access to the European market—something it had been unable to do on its own. The German partner benefited by improving access to U.S. consumers, thus increasing sales.

BECOMING A MULTINATIONAL CORPORATION Companies willing to make a significant financial commitment often establish manufacturing and distribution facilities in foreign countries. Businesses with such facilities are known as **multinational corporations**. (See **Figure 7–1**).

▶ **GLOBAL EXPANSION** Paris DisneyWorld and DisneyWorld Tokyo are important tourist attractions in France and Japan. *Give one reason why the Disney Corporation might have decided to expand abroad.*

Advertising Manager

◼ Nature of the Work

Advertising managers work in domestic and international industries—sports, printing and publishing, department stores, computer and data processing services. They are often vice-presidents. They work with other managers to determine advertising needs, and oversee the development, presentation, and dissemination of the ads. They coordinate advertising with the plans of the marketing and public relations departments. In small companies, advertising managers are the liaison with an independent advertising firm. In advertising companies, they oversee the account services department, the creative department, and the media department.

◼ Working Conditions

Advertising managers work 50 hours or more per week. Work is stressful as schedules change, problems arise, and deadlines approach.

◼ Training, Other Qualifications, and Advancement

To become an advertising manager, you need a bachelor's degree in advertising, journalism, or related studies in marketing, consumer behavior, market research, sales, communication, and visual arts. Word processing skills, data base applications, and Internet skills are vital. An internship in high school is recommended.

◼ Salary Range

Advertising managers earn $23,000 to $97,000; vice-presidents earn $79,00 to $133,000. Salaries vary with responsibility, experience, education, industry, and company size and location.

CRITICAL THINKING:

What skills and characteristics would be useful to an advertising manager?

STANDARD &POOR'S

INDUSTRY OUTLOOK

The advertising market includes television, cable, radio, newspapers, magazines, the Internet, yellow pages, and billboard advertising, among others. In 2002, total advertising spending was $305.6 billion. Advertising expenditures are expected to grow at an annual rate of 6.3 percent from 2002 to 2007.

BUSINESS MANAGEMENT Online

For more information on management careers, go to:
busmanagement.glencoe.com

Businesses become multinational corporations for several reasons. Some do so in order to sell their products or services in other countries. McDonald's, for example, maintains restaurants in 119 countries. Sales to customers in foreign countries represent half of the company's total revenue.

Companies also expand abroad in order to take advantage of inexpensive labor costs. For example, Tarrant Apparel, a U.S. manufacturer of blue jeans, weaves most of its fabric in Mexico. It also has most of its jeans sewn in Mexico, where labor is cheaper than in the United

FIGURE 7–1

Multinational Companies

There are many ways for companies to do business globally. Multinational corporations often purchase their materials abroad or manufacture or assemble their products abroad. They also sell their products in foreign countries.

1 IMPORTED MATERIALS
Multinational corporations may import materials used to manufacture their products. General Motors (GM), the largest automobile producer in the United States, works with thousands of suppliers worldwide. Many of these suppliers are overseas.

States. The company's chief executive, Gerard Guez, believes manufacturing his products in Mexico will allow him to increase his profits significantly.

Challenges of Working in an International Environment

Working for a multinational corporation presents many challenges. Managers must learn to deal with customers, producers,

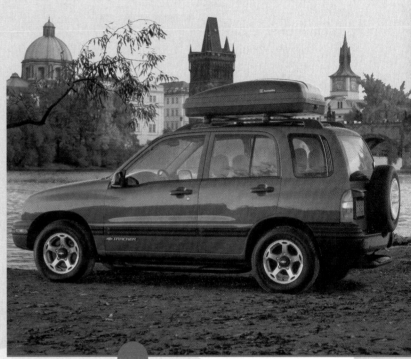

2 INTERNATIONAL PRODUCTION
Multinational companies may produce their products in other countries. GM has manufacturing operations in 32 countries. It operates abroad to improve service or reduce costs.

3 INTERNATIONAL SALES
Multinational companies sell their products in other countries. GM cars and trucks are sold in Africa, Asia and the Pacific, Europe, the Middle East, and North America. Foreign sales represent a significant share of the company's total sales.

suppliers, and employees from different countries. They must become familiar with local laws and learn to respect local customs. They must try to understand what customers and employees want in countries that may be very different from the United States.

Understanding Foreign Cultures

Business managers from different countries see the world differently. Japanese managers, for example, tend to be more sensitive to job lay-offs than American managers. Asian and African managers often have different views about the role of women in the workplace than American managers do.

Managers who work in foreign countries need to be aware of different cultural attitudes. They also need to understand business customs in different countries (see **Figure 7–2**). Not knowing how to act in a foreign country can cause managers

RESPOND

How would you prepare yourself if you were sent overseas to do business in a foreign country such as Japan or Saudi Arabia?

Figure 7–2	EXAMPLES OF FOREIGN BUSINESS PRACTICES
Country	**Business Practice**
China	Food is extremely important. All business transactions require at least one and usually two evening banquets. The first banquet is given by the host, the second by the guest.
Indonesia	Even foreigners are expected to arrive late to social occasions. It is generally appropriate to arrive about 30 minutes after the scheduled time.
Singapore	Businesspeople exchange business cards in a formal manner, receiving the card with both hands and studying it for a few moments before putting it away.
Saudi Arabia	Businesspeople greet foreigners by clasping their hand, but they do not shake hands.
Switzerland	Business is conducted very formally. Humor and informality are inappropriate.

Why is it important for businesspeople to respect local customs?

Source: *Doing Business Around the World*, Morrison, Conaway, and Douress, Prentice-Hall, 1997

◄ **FOREIGN CULTURES**
In China, all business transactions require at least one banquet. *Why would it be important for a manager to know this before conducting business in China?*

embarrassment, and it can cause them to miss out on business opportunities. Showing up for a business meeting without a tie might be acceptable in Israel, for example, but it would be completely out of place in Switzerland. Demonstrating great respect to a superior would be appreciated in Indonesia, but it would send the wrong signal in the Netherlands, where equality among individuals is valued.

Section 7.2 Assessment

 FACT AND IDEA REVIEW

1. What is NAFTA?
2. What is a multinational corporation?
3. What are some of the challenges business managers who work in foreign countries face?
4. Give two examples of foreign business customs that differ from customs in the United States.

 CRITICAL THINKING

1. **Making Comparisons:** What factors do you think might make an American businessperson support or oppose NAFTA? What factors might make a Mexican businessperson support or oppose NAFTA?
2. **Drawing Conclusions:** Why might an American business manager seek out a strategic alliance with a Korean company?

 ASSESSING HISTORY SKILLS

Your company, which manufactures window frames, is considering exporting its products to Mexico. Prepare a two-page report describing political and economic events that occurred in Mexico in the past decade that might have had an effect on your company.

 CASE ANALYSIS

You have just been asked to move to Singapore to take over the East Asian office of your company, a manufacturer of kitchen cabinets. Your new staff will include two Americans, three Malays, and four Chinese.

Apply: What are some of things you would do to prepare for your new assignment?

CHAPTER 7 ASSESSMENT

REVIEWING VOCABULARY

Working in groups of three, create a word-find puzzle that uses each of the following vocabulary words.

international trade	tariff
absolute advantage	quota
law of comparative	embargo
advantage	global economy
exports	free trade area
imports	multinational
balance of trade	corporation

RECALLING KEY CONCEPTS

1. List three reasons a country might import goods.
2. Explain the purpose and give an example of a free trade area.
3. How do countries restrict international trade?
4. What are some ways a company can become a multinational corporation?

THINKING CRITICALLY

1. Use the concept of comparative advantage to explain why managers hire assistants even if they could do the work better themselves.
2. Explain how changes in the exchange rate affect importers, exporters, and consumers.
3. Who benefits from trade protection? Who suffers from trade protection? Why?
4. What are some of the challenges facing business managers who work in foreign countries?

CHAPTER SUMMARY

Section 7.1

▶ International trade consists of the exchange of goods and services by different countries.

▶ Exports are goods and services sold abroad; imports are goods and services purchased abroad.

▶ A country that exports more than it imports runs a trade surplus. A country that imports more than it exports runs a trade deficit.

▶ Countries often restrict trade by imposing tariffs, quotas, and other measures. These measures reduce the volume of trade and hurt consumers.

Section 7.2

▶ Businesses become global companies by working through foreign intermediaries, entering into licensing agreements or strategic alliances with foreign companies, or by becoming multinational corporations.

▶ Business managers working in foreign countries need to be familiar with local laws and business customs.

ASSESSING ACADEMIC SKILLS

GEOGRAPHY Create a map of the world on which you show the United States' major trading partners. Identify the four countries that account for the greatest share of exports of U.S. goods and the four countries that are the leading exporters of goods to the United States.

 ## APPLYING MANAGEMENT PRINCIPLES

SOLVE THE PROBLEM Blockbuster Video is considering expanding into ten new countries. The company's chief executive officer has asked you to analyze which countries might represent good choices.

Writing Use the World Wide Web or the resources at your public library to find out where Blockbuster has already expanded. Then prepare a one-page report in which you identify all of the issues you think the company should consider. Be sure to discuss the importance of international trade agreements, economic factors, and cultural and political issues.

 ## PREPARING FOR COMPETITIVE EVENTS

Answer True or False to the following statements.

a. Countries impose tariffs in order to restrict international trade.

b. The easiest way for a company to expand abroad is by becoming a multinational corporation.

BusinessWeek ONLINE

In this chapter you read the *BusinessWeek* Management Model about women-owned businesses. For more information, go to *BusinessWeek* online at: **www.businessweek.com**

Using the Internet or your local library, find two articles on the impact of e-commerce in Asia. Write brief summaries of each article and present them to the class.

CASE STUDY 2

Profit Maximization and Social Responsibility

OVERVIEW

During the past decade, society has challenged many American businesses to be socially responsible. Some businesses have been alleged to care only about profit maximization, to demonstrate unethical practices, and to have little concern for the consumer and society. Public debate has left many people confused. Should all businesses be socially responsible? If so, what should businesses do? This case study explores the issue of social responsibility that businesses in the United States face today.

RESOURCES

- word processor
- poster board or flip chart
- colored markers
- Internet (optional)
- public library
- economics texts

PROCEDURES

◆ STEP A ◆

Profit Maximization vs. Social Responsibility

A primary objective for every business is to profit economically and to be financially successful. According to Milton Friedman, businesses should increase profits and leave social problems for the government to control. Opponents of Friedman believe that if a company is not responsible to society in its actions, society will naturally correct the situation through the normal interactions of the marketplace.

Identifying and Analyzing Information:

1. In groups of two to four students, research Friedman's viewpoints and identify the arguments that are made by the opponents to social responsibility.

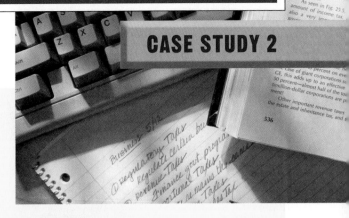

2. Research Keith Davis and Robert Blomstrom's *Iron Law of Responsibility*. List the arguments that support social responsibility.

3. Research Adam Smith's theory of the *Invisible Hand* and its role in businesses responding to societal interests.

◆ STEP B ◆

The Responsibilities of a Company

Research today indicates that businesses have responsibilities in four areas: economics, legal, ethical, and voluntary. Successful businesses understand the importance of each of the responsibilities and incorporate them within their strategic plans.

Evaluating Information:

1. In your small groups, brainstorm ideas that illustrate how a company can fulfill the responsibilities in each of the four areas.

2. Individually or in your group, visit three businesses and interview a manager or assistant manager. Ask the manager to identify the strategies that the company uses to meet the four responsibilities described above. Have the manager rank each responsibility in order of importance to his or her company.

3. Analyze and evaluate the impact of a company's size on its ability to meet the four responsibilities. Is it easier for a multinational corporation to meet the responsibilities than it is for a local sole proprietorship?

◆ STEP C ◆

Management Report

Using a word processor and poster boards or flip charts, create a 10-minute presentation that addresses the impact that social responsibility has on the U.S. marketplace. The presentation should include the following:

1. An introduction that focuses on the pros and cons of a market economy.

2. Explain society's increased demands for American businesses to be socially responsible.

3. Discuss the works of Friedman, Davis and Blomstrom, and their historical viewpoints of social responsibility.

4. Illustrate how Adam Smith's *Invisible Hand* supports Davis and Blomstrom's *Iron Law of Responsibility*.

5. Address the responsibilities that all businesses share and indicate how they can achieve them.

6. Use real world examples to support your conclusions.

UNIT 3

Foundation Skills

Chapter 8
Decision-Making Skills

Chapter 9
Communication Skills

IN THIS UNIT...

You will see how success depends on good decisions and the ability to communicate these ideas, both verbally and in writing. Included in this unit are chapters covering decision-making skills and communication skills.

Journal Writing

In your journal, assess your knowledge of
management by writing about the following:

1. How do you make important decisions?
2. List five examples of how *values* might
   affect a manager's decisions.
3. If you have to present a speech at your
   school's honor society induction, what
   are some ways you would prepare?

CHAPTER 8

DECISION-MAKING SKILLS

LEARNING OBJECTIVES

When you have completed this chapter, you will be able to:

- Explain the differences between intuitive and rational decision making.
- List various factors, conditions, risks, and values affecting decision making.
- Describe the advantages and disadvantages of group decision making.
- Name the different ways managers go about making decisions.
- Discuss how to make creative and effective decisions.

READING STRATEGIES

As you read

- **PREDICT** what the section will be about.
- **CONNECT** what you read with your own life.
- **QUESTION** as you read to make sure you understand the content.
- **RESPOND** to what you read.

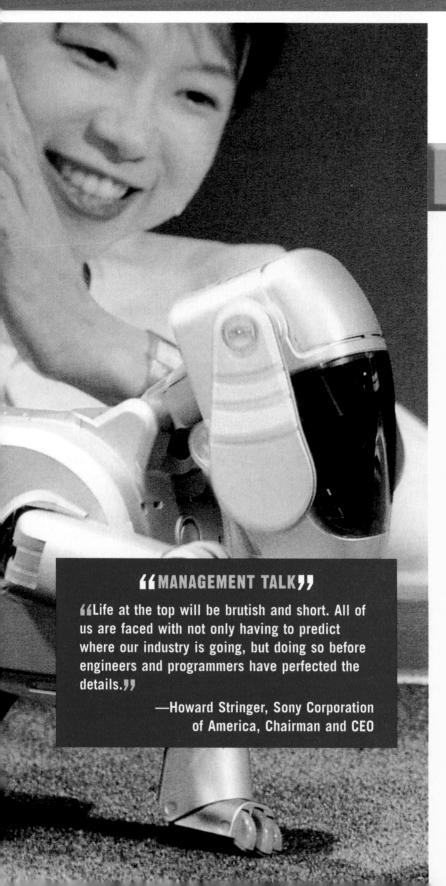

Understanding Management

All managers make tough decisions about how best to use their companies' resources. "Life at the top will be brutish and short," says Sony Corporation of America's Chairman and CEO, Howard Stringer. The rapid pace of technological improvement will test managers' ability to think quickly in an era that is "dazzling but unpredictable and unsettling" as well.

Analyzing Management Skills

What trends will managers have to predict in the upcoming decade? Why must managers keep up with changing technology?

Applying Management Skills

Imagine that you are in charge of purchasing a new computer system for your workplace or school. What type of research would you do? What factors would you consider before making your purchase?

BusinessWeek ONLINE

For further reading on managers and management go to:
www.businessweek.com

"MANAGEMENT TALK"

"Life at the top will be brutish and short. All of us are faced with not only having to predict where our industry is going, but doing so before engineers and programmers have perfected the details."

—Howard Stringer, Sony Corporation of America, Chairman and CEO

WHAT IS DECISION MAKING?

WHAT YOU'LL LEARN

▶ The two basic ways to make decisions.
▶ The six steps to rational decision making.
▶ How corporate culture influences decision making.
▶ Two value systems that play a part in decision making.
▶ The principles of team decision making.
▶ The five types of management decision styles.

WHY IT'S IMPORTANT

To understand why some businesses succeed and others fail, you will need to understand how management makes decisions.

KEY TERMS

• intuitive decision making
• rational decision making
• team decision making

The Importance of Decision Making

Managers constantly make decisions that affect the futures of their companies. Managers must make decisions so that their companies can adapt to the latest changes in society, technology, and the marketplace. Companies whose managers do not know how to make decisions properly will lose out to the competition. Decision making is part of all the basic management functions: planning, organizing, staffing, leading, and controlling. Each of these functions requires different types of decisions.

Not all decisions are equally important. For example, sometimes managers have to decide whether to let an employee take a day off. That decision might be important to the worker, but it probably would not affect the company as a whole. On the other hand, a manager may need to decide whether to produce an entirely new product. This decision could potentially bring in millions of dollars, or could cost the company millions of dollars. It would have an enormous effect on the future of the company.

Some decisions are easy to make, while others are extremely difficult. If managers have company handbooks or policy manuals to follow, they often can make decisions quickly by following guidelines. However, sometimes managers face situations about which they know very little. To make decisions in these situations, managers may need to consult other people. For example, when Virginia-based health-care publisher St. Anthony Publishing needed to decide whether to sell stock to the public, the chief financial officer consulted with outside financial experts, including the brokerage firm of Morgan, Stanley, for advice.

Different Ways to Make Decisions

There are two basic ways to make decisions: intuitively and rationally. Managers can use either approach. They also can combine both the intuitive and rational approaches when they make decisions.

INTUITIVE DECISION MAKING Making decisions based on intuition or hunches is **intuitive decision making**. For example, managers at a

▲ **GROUP DECISION MAKING** Managers often need to speak with co-workers and outside consultants to help make difficult decisions. *Why would managers need others' help in the decision-making process?*

toy company may decide to raise the price of a new computer game because they *think* customers will be willing to pay more money for the game. The managers are making their decision based on their feelings rather than the facts. They may have failed to ask some important questions, such as whether customers would in fact be willing to pay more for the toy or if the competition is selling the toy at a lower price.

Intuitive decision making holds great potential. However, it also offers the risk of regret if the "facts" turn out differently than one might have thought. Managers make the most successful intuitive decisions when they have considerable experience in a particular area. For example, it would make sense for toy managers to rely on intuition if they had made dozens of similar decisions about raising toy prices in the last 15 years.

Stephen Gordon, Chairman and founder of Restoration Hardware Inc., in California, decided in 1999 to spend $1 million to advertise a special sale. It was a successful decision. For the most part, Gordon made that decision intuitively, based on his experience in the furniture business. Gordon said: "I believed the sales would spur consumer interest in the first quarter. It did. I assumed it would draw an increase in customer traffic. It did."

Managers also make intuitive decisions when there is no time to conduct research or to do further study on a particular situation. For example, when Exxon decided in the mid 1990s to lower gas prices in

▶ **DECISION-MAKING PROCESS** A managerial decision, such as lowering product prices, is made intuitively. *What does it mean to make an intuitive decision?*

certain areas of the country, Amoco had to decide quickly whether to lower its prices as well. Amoco managers knew that customers generally would not buy Amoco gas at a higher price if they could get the same gas at Exxon for a lower price. Amoco managers made an intuitive decision to lower their prices so they didn't lose business to Exxon.

Intuition plays a critical role in decision making. Managers who make intuitive decisions, however, must not ignore facts when they are available.

PREDICT

What steps would a manager have to take in order to make a rational decision?

RATIONAL DECISION MAKING Making decisions based on factual information and logical reasoning is **rational decision making**. There are six basic steps to rational decision making:

1. *Recognizing the need for a decision.* Managers must first understand that there is a decision that needs to be made.
2. *Determining how to go about making a decision.* Managers can make some decisions quickly, without developing a plan. At other times, however, managers must make systematic research efforts.
3. *Gathering information to help make a decision.* Decision makers try to collect as much data as possible so that they can make well-informed decisions.

4. *Identifying possible alternatives.* Managers usually can identify several possible decision options.
5. *Evaluating each alternative.* Managers should evaluate each option independently.
6. *Selecting the best alternative.* Making a decision ultimately involves choosing among competing options.

Although both methods of decision making are valid, rational decision making is more scientific than intuitive decision making. It has a systematic process and is based on evaluating factual information and data. Rational decision making, however, is only effective if the decision maker can gather the best available information.

To help get information to make the best rational decisions, managers may seek help by surfing the Internet. For example, in 1994 Jay Bloom, cofounder of Pet Assure Inc., a fast growing discount club for pet owners, needed to decide whether to offer pet insurance services to pet owners. He surfed the Internet to find out more about the competition. When he found only one well-known pet-insurance carrier, he rationally decided to offer insurance services. Managers also may decide to contact outside experts, called consultants, to help them solve these problems.

CONNECT

Imagine you are trying to decide what college to attend. How would you use the six basic steps of rational decision making to choose your college?

Factors Influencing Decisions

A manager's ability to make decisions may depend on the manager's position in the company. In general, higher-level managers have more flexibility to make decisions than lower-level managers. Lower-level supervisors often must receive approval from higher-level managers before making final decisions.

In addition, a company's corporate culture influences decision making. For example, 3M's corporate culture encourages creativity and independent decision making. Management trainers at 3M tell managers to try to make their own decisions, without always consulting their bosses. The 3M manager who invented Post-It Notes credits the company's corporate culture for encouraging creativity and independent decision making.

3M and many other companies believe that managers need to learn how to make decisions themselves. They encourage supervisors to be independent and to learn from their own mistakes. However, some companies have more rigid, hierarchical organizational structures. Managers in those companies must follow established procedures whenever they make decisions.

A manager's ability to make decisions also depends on the employees the manager supervises. Managers usually want their employees to support their decisions. Thus, most managers consult

LEADING THE WAY

SOLUTION-ORIENTED
Difficult situations arise every day in a business setting. Don't get bogged down with the complexities of an issue. Get yourself and your employees to be solution-oriented. Be positive and focus on ways to fix a problem. Dwelling on the negativity won't resolve anything.

▲ **COMMUNICATION** Managers often discuss their decisions with their employees. *Why would managers do this?*

with their workers before making important decisions. Not all employees will like the decisions made by managers, but they usually appreciate managers who discuss decisions with them beforehand.

Risk in Decision Making

Companies often must make decisions without all the facts. For example, when Disney decided to acquire ABC, it did not know whether the television shows ABC executives had selected for the fall schedule would be successful or not. Disney decision makers did not want to wait an entire year before purchasing ABC, so they bought the company without knowing all the facts. As it turned out, some shows were hits, while others were not. The decision was ultimately worth the risk.

Like the Disney decision makers, all managers face risk when making decisions. They can, however, try to minimize risk. For example, it is often risky for a business to hire large numbers of new employees at one time due to the increased payroll costs. To minimize risk, companies often decide to hire new employees over a long time period, rather than all at once.

Companies also can minimize risk by using dynamic growth strategies. For example, Starbucks' managers had to make important decisions about how to expand their business in areas where they were not well known. They decided to minimize their risk by creating minifranchises in nontraditional outlets, such as bookstores.

Magazine Editor

■ Nature of the Work

Magazine editors plan each magazine edition by deciding what articles and information will appeal to readers and assigning stories to writers. Editors oversee the publication's production, including layout, art, and printing. They may negotiate contracts with writers, review finished stories for errors in grammar, punctuation and spelling. They also consider the story's readability and may ask the writer to rewrite or revise a story. When necessary, they may rewrite a story themselves. Editors work with writers to check information, asking questions to see that the information is as accurate as possible. Magazine editors who work for trade or technical journals may need special knowledge of their particular field, although that may be learned with experience.

■ Working Conditions

Magazine editors work in offices with desktop publishing equipment and computers. They work 35 to 40 hours a week. Deadlines and late changes can create stress.

■ Training, Other Qualifications, and Advancement

To become a magazine editor, you need a bachelor's degree in liberal arts, communications, journalism or English. Excellent writing, language, word processing, and organizational skills are vital, as well as creativity and a broad range of knowledge. Experience on a high school or college publication, or an internship program is recommended.

■ Salary Range

Magazine editors earn $25,000 to $70,000, depending on experience, and the size and type of publication.

CRITICAL THINKING

When determining whether a story was readable or not, what qualities might an editor look for?

STANDARD &POOR'S

INDUSTRY OUTLOOK

The U.S. market for magazines totaled $29.4 billion in 2002. Consumer magazines were the largest segment of this market, with $25.6 billion in sales, or 87 percent of the total market. The U.S. magazine market is forecast to grow by 8 percent between 2003 and 2007, when sales are estimated to be approximately $32.2 billion.

BUSINESS MANAGEMENT *Online*

For more information on management careers, go to:
busmanagement.glencoe.com

The Importance of Timing

Managers need to make decisions at the right time. This is not as easy as it sounds. The manager may not be able to get all the information needed to make a sound decision. Sometimes managers take too much time to make a decision, even on the simplest matters. They may be afraid that they will make the wrong decision, or even that they will be fired for making that decision. These managers often listen to problems, promise to act, but never do. These managers also are usually afraid to make decisions without consulting their bosses.

RESPOND

What do you think would cause a manager to take too much time to make a decision?

Other managers always seem to make decisions on the spot. Those managers sometimes run the risk of making bad decisions. They often fail to gather and evaluate information, consider other people's feelings, or fully anticipate the effect of their decision.

Knowing when to make a decision often is complicated because different decisions have different time frames. For example, a manager generally has more time to decide on an appointment to a committee than to decide what to do when three employees call in sick at the same time. In making decisions, managers must first recognize the importance of timing and not make decisions that are either too hasty or too delayed. **Figure 8–1** shows how timing can affect decision making.

▲ **VALUES** Managers face tough decisions when deciding whether to let workers go if the business isn't doing well. *What values determine how quickly a manager decides to lay off workers?*

The Role of Values

Values play an important role in the decision-making process. Every manager and employee brings a certain set of values to the workplace.

Economic and social values most affect decision making. Economic values involve placing emphasis on making money for a company. Social values involve making the lives of consumer, workers, or the community better. A manager's values have an impact on the way performance is measured. For example, a manager concerned primarily with economic values probably would measure performance differently than a manager concerned mainly with social values. The "economic" manager might look only at the profit that someone made for the company. The "social" manager might measure performance by the number of customer complaints received.

FIGURE 8–1

Timing for Hiring Decisions

When hiring new employees, managers sometimes have no choice but to make timely decisions. If they don't call top job candidates back within 72 hours, they "probably shouldn't even bother," says Barry Deutsch, a Los Angeles executive recruiter for CJA-Adler Group Inc.

1 MAKING A HIRING DECISION TOO QUICKLY
Managers who make the decision to hire a person for a job after interviewing only one candidate might be acting too hastily. Managers need to evaluate more than one option before making such a decision.

2 MAKING A HIRING DECISION TOO SLOWLY
Managers who interview hundreds of candidates for an important job are probably taking too long.

3 MAKING A HIRING DECISION IN A TIMELY MANNER
Managers should interview enough candidates to make a rational decision. Managers should check references of top candidates and make a decision in a reasonable time period so that they do not lose a potential "best hire."

Sometimes companies are forced to lay off workers because they are experiencing difficult economic times. The managers with predominantly economic values probably would decide to lay off workers more quickly than managers with predominantly social values. Managers should be aware of both their own values and those of their employees. They also should maintain a balance between economic and social values.

Participation in Decision Making

Do groups make better decisions than individuals? Some say that "two heads are better than one." In general, that's true. Managers make better decisions when they solicit more information and receive different points of view. Many companies now believe that team decision making works best. **Team decision making** is the process of resolving problems and issues by assigning several people with different backgrounds (accounting, administration, manufacturing, research) to a group.

FedEx has boosted productivity by 40 percent by adopting self-managed work teams. Corporate officials at FedEx say that they can make better decisions because they receive more input from their employees. They say their employees feel more positive about decisions because they have been empowered to make them.

Employees in 65 percent of the Fortune 1,000 companies now work in teams. The most common types of teams are work teams and problem-solving teams.

▲ **TEAMWORK** Many businesses use teams to make important decisions. *Why would teams be effective in the decision-making process?*

Teams can be useful as long as the company plans how to use its people and does not assume that more is always better. **Figure 8–2** shows the positive and negative aspects of group decision making.

Types of Management Decision Styles

A manager's personality will be reflected in his or her style of decision making. There are five types of management decision styles.

1. *Autocratic.* The manager makes the decision alone, with little or no input from subordinates. George Steinbrenner, the president of the New York Yankees, is often described as an autocratic

Figure 8–2

POSITIVE AND NEGATIVE ASPECTS OF GROUP DECISION MAKING

Positive Aspects	Negative Aspects
1. The sum total of the group's knowledge is greater.	1. One individual may dominate and/or control the group.
2. The group possesses a wider range of alternatives in the decision process.	2. Social pressures to conform can inhibit group members.
3. Participation in the decision-making process increases the acceptance of the decision by group members.	3. Competition can develop to such an extent that winning becomes more important than the issue itself.
4. Group members better understand the decision and the alternatives considered.	4. Groups have a tendency to accept the first potentially positive solution while giving little attention to other possible solutions.

WORKING WITH CHARTS Many companies use group decision-making processes. *Do you think that the positive aspects of group decision making outweigh the negative aspects?*

manager, because he makes staffing decisions quickly, with little or no input from subordinates.

2. *Semi-autocratic.* The manager asks subordinates for information needed to make the decision, but still makes the decision alone. Subordinates may or may not be informed of the decision. The role played by subordinates is one of providing information as opposed to generating or evaluating alternative solutions. Ross Perot, the president of IDS, is sometimes described as a semi-autocratic manager, because he often makes strategic decisions by himself.

3. *Leading.* The manager shares the situation with a few selected subordinates and asks them individually for information and advice. The manager still makes the final decision, which may or may not reflect the subordinates' influence. President Franklin D. Roosevelt made decisions through leadership. Before he decided to implement his New Deal program, he asked for advice from his Cabinet officers, heeding some and ignoring others.

4. *Collaborative.* The manager meets with all subordinates as a group to discuss the situation. Information is freely shared, although the manager still makes the final decision. Michael Dell and Kevin Rollins of Dell Inc. have adopted desktop props to remind them of the importance of teamwork. Dell has a plastic bulldozer cautioning him not to drive ideas through without consulting with others on his management team, and Rollins has a Curious George doll to encourage him to listen to his team before deciding on a course of action.

QUESTION

What is the difference between a "leading" decision-making style and a "collaborative" decision-making style?

5. *Accommodating.* The manager and subordinates meet as a group and freely share information. The entire group makes the decision. The senior sales manager at DuBois Chemicals in Cincinnati, Ohio, sometimes makes decisions through accommodation. He instituted a system where all of the management positions are equal.

There is no correct decision style. In general, most managers prefer either the leading or collaborative style. The autocratic style ignores the input of stakeholders, those supervisors, workers, or groups most affected by the decision. The accommodating style places too much authority in the hands of a group. This makes it difficult for a manager to lead or make timely decisions. Managers should use a decision style that fits their personality and helps the organization to succeed.

Section 8.1 Assessment

 FACT AND IDEA REVIEW

1. Why is it important for company managers to make good decisions?
2. What are the six basic steps in rational decision making?
3. How does corporate culture influence decision making?
4. What kind of value system does a manager who makes decisions on the basis of customer complaints have?
5. True or False: Team decision making is always preferred to individual decision making. Explain.
6. What are the five types of management decision styles?

 CRITICAL THINKING

1. **Draw Conclusions:** Would a manager who always consulted his or her boss be a good decision maker? Why or why not?
2. **Making Comparisons:** Would a manager with a collaborative decision-making style work well under a structure of team decision making? Why or why not?

 ASSESSING SOCIAL STUDIES SKILLS

How have teams helped to increase productivity at companies? Go to the library or search the Internet to find examples of successful teamwork at Fortune 1000 companies. Present your findings to the class.

 CASE ANALYSIS

XYZ Banking, a mid-sized financial services firm, has formed problem-solving teams. The information technology team cannot figure out whether to hire additional personnel to fix the bank's computer problems or whether to let an outside company handle the problem. The team leader, Joann Williams, has tried unsuccessfully to get the team to reach a decision. She now must report to the vice president for operations that her team has failed to reach a consensus. She goes to the vice president for advice.

Apply: What advice should the vice president give Joann? Explain your answer.

BusinessWeek

Management Model

FLIGHT SIMULATORS FOR MANAGEMENT

Computer Models May Give Execs Previews of How Decisions Pan Out

Thor Sigvaldason is late. As part of a novel consulting cluster at Pricewaterhouse-Coopers, he is supposed to be at an important client meeting at 10 A.M. But he has overslept for the session with a top executive of Macy's East.

Sigvaldason finally arrives 20 minutes late. He eases quietly into the room, watched only by his boss, K. Winslow Farrell Jr., 45, whose face doesn't hide his displeasure.

SCI-FI? Soon, though, Thor brings up on a computer screen what has taken the team 1,800 hours to construct. It shows awkward blocklike figures roaming about a crude layout of a department store. The idea is to simulate how real shoppers actually operate in a store. But the little figures bounce off the blue walls. Explains Farrell: "We haven't built certain rules into their brains yet, and they have primitive vision."

TESTING DECISIONS. The client, Macy's group vice-president William M. Connell can see that the team is making some progress toward an incredibly ambitious goal: to harness the emerging science

of complexity, the notion that complicated behavior emerges from the interaction of many components, and create a powerful new tool for top executives. Farrell's team is creating artificial worlds of evolving, reactive software creatures. If all goes well, the actions of those "adaptive agents" will so closely mimic human behavior that managers for the first time will be able to use them to test the impact of their decisions before implementing them.

THE STUFF OF SCIENCE FICTION? Well, it may seem a bit far out and abstract. But Farrell sees it as the ultimate "flight

simulator" for management—and his firm appears to be the furthest along of several consultants vying to take the concept out of the laboratory and turn it into a commercial business. If Farrell succeeds, Price-waterhouseCoopers expects the tool could be used in a broad range of consulting assignments, generating millions in revenues over the next three to five years.

Farrell is trying to create a virtual world where executives could safely test hunches, run scenarios, and preview the impact of big and small decisions—all without major investments, public embarrassments, and competitive backfires.

Excerpted with permission from BusinessWeek, *September 21, 1998*

CRITICAL THINKING

What is the significance of Farrel's "flight simulator" to management?

DECISION MAKING

Determine one management decision you might make in which you could employ the flight simulator.

MAKING EFFECTIVE DECISIONS

WHAT YOU'LL LEARN

➤ How managers make creative decisions.
➤ How to encourage creativity through brainstorming, brainwriting, and wish lists.
➤ The six stages of the Meyers model of creative decision making.
➤ The four barriers to effective decision making.

WHY IT'S IMPORTANT

The most successful companies have managers who know how to make effective decisions.

KEY TERMS

• brainstorming
• brainwriting

Making Creative Decisions

The most successful companies have creative managers. To make creative decisions, managers follow these five basic steps:

1. *Preparation.* The manager investigates thoroughly to make sure all parts of the problem are understood and that all the facts are known.
2. *Concentration.* The manager sets a timetable for solving the problem.
3. *Incubation.* The manager looks at various options for solving the problem.
4. *Illumination.* The manager finds an acceptable solution for the problem.
5. *Verification.* The manager tests the solution for the problem.

◀ CREATIVE DECISION MAKING There are five steps to creative decision making. *Which step is this manager following? Why is this step important?*

▲ BRAINSTORMING One way to encourage creative decisions is brainstorming. *What are some of the advantages of brainstorming?*

Even the most creative managers might find it difficult to be effective if their bosses are too controlling. Upper-level managers need to set an example for other managers by being creative themselves. Otherwise, middle managers will not try anything new, and the company will not be as successful as it could be.

Encouraging Creativity

Good managers know how to encourage creativity. Making creative decisions involves trust. Managers should reward employees for creativity and not punish them if creative ideas do not work out as planned. Some ways to encourage employees include recognizing employees' creativity at company luncheons or dinners, or in company newsletters. This emphasizes that coming up with new ideas is an important goal. Managers also can use several processes to encourage creative decision making.

BRAINSTORMING Managers often use a technique called brainstorming. In **brainstorming** a group of people come up with as many different ideas as possible to help solve a problem, without making judgments about those ideas. A brainstorming session should have a leader who is responsible for running the meeting. The leader presents

All About

ATTITUDE

SUPERHUMAN POWER

You can't take on the world by yourself, so don't attempt to. Do what you're supposed to do and concentrate on getting it right. It's much better to be consistently accurate, rather than being successful once every so often.

RESPOND

Under what conditions would you feel comfortable enough to make a creative decision?

the problem to a group of people and tells the group to present any ideas that come into their heads.

Brainstorming sessions begin with three basic rules:

- Members of the group cannot criticize any idea.
- Members of the group cannot praise any idea.
- Members of the group cannot question or discuss ideas.

The leader of the brainstorming session writes all the ideas on a blackboard or chart and then asks the group to comment on them. During this process, the ideas that won't work are eliminated. The leader leaves only the best ideas on the board for discussion. The group then discusses these ideas and selects the best solution to the problem.

BRAINWRITING Another way to encourage creativity is by using a technique called **brainwriting**. In the brainwriting approach, a leader presents group members with a problem situation, just like in brainstorming. However, unlike brainstorming, the leader asks the group to write down their ideas rather than say them aloud. The papers are not signed. Members share their papers with others in the group, who then add their own comments. The leader then collects the papers and presents the best ideas to the group.

WISH LISTS A third way to come up with creative ideas is through wish lists. A leader tells the group to make believe they have the power to solve any problem because there are no physical or financial constraints. For example, when creating a wish list, if a company's problem was a shortage of trained computer experts, the company could hire as many computer experts as it wanted because money would be no problem. Lack of sufficient office space also would not be a problem.

The leader encourages the group to come up with creative ideas. The leader does not want the group to rule out any ideas at the beginning because some of the best suggestions eventually come from "ideal" solutions. The leader instructs the group to take the ideas and make them as practical as possible. Finally, the leader and the group together select the most practical solutions. Instead of hiring as many new computer experts as it wanted, the group might recommend hiring several new employees on a permanent basis and several others on a temporary basis.

Managers should use all these techniques—brainstorming, brainwriting, and wish lists—to encourage creativity. While these techniques help provide managers with lots of ideas for solving problems, managers still have the final responsibility for making the best decisions for their companies.

RHI **Robert Half International Inc.**

Tips from Robert Half

Business people waste about five weeks a year looking for misplaced files, addresses, memos, and reports. To reduce lost time, purge files regularly by keeping only what you need. It's also a good idea to clear your desk each evening.

QUESTION

In what situations would making a wish list be more helpful than brainstorming?

The Meyers Model for Creative Decision Making

Successful managers often use practical models to make their jobs easier. A model is a framework for doing a particular task. There are models that can lead to better and more creative decisions, such as the Meyers model, named after its originator, Bruce Meyers, a professor at Western Illinois University. Meyers developed his model in 1987.

A manager can use the Meyers model to come up with creative decisions to solve a problem. The Meyers model has six stages, which are defined below.

Stage 1: Recognition. If a manager faces a problem or decision, he or she should first describe it in writing. Managers should also describe any events that may occur that could affect the problem.

Stage 2: Fact Finding. Managers should systematically gather additional information about the problem. Managers should ask questions that begin with *who, what, where, when, how many,* or *how much* to find out as much information as possible.

Stage 3: Problem Finding. Managers revisit the problem to encourage more creative solutions or a broader range of solutions.

Stage 4: Idea Finding. Managers use brainstorming to come up with alternative solutions to the problem. As in all brainstorming sessions, all ideas are considered and no idea is rejected.

▲ **CREATIVE DECISIONS** Managers can use the Meyers model to make creative decisions. *Which stage do you think would be the most difficult?*

Stage 5: Solution Finding. Managers evaluate the ideas and solutions reached in Stage 4. The first step is to make a list of the problems on one side of the paper and all the possible solutions on other side of the paper. The managers then try to match problems and solutions, aiming for the most practical solutions.

Stage 6: Acceptance Finding. In this stage, managers try to figure out what needs to be done to carry out or implement a solution. In this stage, managers also should try to anticipate potential objections to the decision.

Barriers to Effective Decision Making

No matter what model they use to make decisions, managers face many possible barriers when trying to make decisions. The four basic barriers to effective decision making are discussed below.

1. *Complacency.* The manager thinks the decision is easier than it really is. For example, a manager may think there will be no problem manufacturing a new product for the business. However, the manager may not understand how difficult it will be to find the right material to manufacture the product.

2. *Avoidance.* The manager denies the importance of a problem. For example, the manager realizes the difficulties of finding the right material to manufacture a new product, but chooses to ignore those difficulties.

3. *Panic.* The manager becomes frantic trying to make a decision. For example, the manager may rush into a decision to produce a new product because of fear that some other company will manufacture it first.

4. *Indecisiveness.* The manager becomes unable to make a final decision. For example, the manager may never reach a decision to produce a new product until it is too late.

Managers cannot make effective decisions until they know how to deal with these barriers. When hiring a manager for a job, companies try to find someone who understands the barriers to effective

CONNECT

Have you ever experienced complacency, avoidance, panic, or indecisiveness when faced with a tough decision? How did you deal with the barrier?

decision making and who has demonstrated an ability to make sound decisions in previous jobs.

Dynamic companies and the managers who run them need to make good decisions at precisely the right time. Successful companies have several decision-making characteristics in common. These include:

- accepting change
- listening to customers
- decentralizing authority
- hiring carefully
- training employees continuously
- controlling costs

Decision making can be one of the most difficult tasks a manager makes. With good decision-making tools, experience, and a calm, positive attitude, managers will learn to make sound decisions.

Section 8.2 Assessment

 FACT AND IDEA REVIEW

1. What are the five basic steps to creative decision making?
2. What is the difference between brainstorming and brainwriting?
3. What are the six stages of decision making in the Meyers model?
4. What are the four basic barriers to effective decision making?

 CRITICAL THINKING

1. **Analyzing Information:** What problems are best addressed by brainstorming? Explain.
2. **Making Comparisons:** What are the advantages and disadvantages of brainwriting compared to brainstorming? Explain.

 ASSESSING SOCIAL STUDIES SKILLS

Select a large, successful company operating in the United States. Using the resources at your local library or on the Internet, research how the company found creative solutions to difficult problems. Prepare a two-page report summarizing what you find.

 CASE ANALYSIS

You work for a popular toy manufacturer. Your major competitor has just come out with a new toy aimed at six-year-old boys. The toy is a truck that makes different noises, such as screeching tires and blowing horns. Your boss asks you to come up with an idea for a similar kind of product that would appeal to this market.

Apply: Your boss asks you to prepare a memo on how you would go about coming up with creative solutions to this problem.

CHAPTER 8 ASSESSMENT

REVIEWING VOCABULARY

Write a dialogue between two managers using the following vocabulary words:

intuitive decision making
rational decision making
team decision making
brainstorming
brainwriting

RECALLING KEY CONCEPTS

1. Name the two basic ways to make decisions and explain the differences.
2. How do values affect the decision-making process? Give two examples.
3. What are the five management decision styles?
4. What are the three basic rules of brainstorming? Why are they important?

THINKING CRITICALLY

1. Should you always take a long time before you reach a decision? In what kinds of situations would you want to decide an issue quickly?
2. Think about decision makers in your family or your community. Are they intuitive or rational decision makers?
3. Would you rather work for a boss with economic or social values? Why?
4. How could teachers use brainstorming to solve problems in the classroom?

CHAPTER SUMMARY

Section 8.1

▶ Managers constantly make decisions that affect the future of their companies.

▶ Intuitive decision making is based on hunches, and rational decision making is a more scientific process.

▶ Decisions are affected by corporate culture, degree of risk, timing, and economic and social values.

▶ Today, many top companies use teams to make key decisions.

Section 8.2

▶ Creativity is an important element in decision making. The most successful companies have creative managers.

▶ Brainstorming, brainwriting, and wish lists allow managers to get creative ideas from employees.

▶ The Meyers model can help managers make creative decisions.

▶ The four barriers to effective decision making are: complacency, avoidance, panic, and indecisiveness.

CHAPTER 8 ASSESSMENT

ASSESSING ACADEMIC SKILLS

SOCIAL STUDIES What kinds of management decision styles do business leaders in your community have? Contact your local Chamber of Commerce to get in touch with three business leaders in your community. Interview them about their management styles and share your findings with your class.

APPLYING MANAGEMENT PRINCIPLES

DECISION MAKING You supervise six employees in the accounting department of a publishing firm. In the last several months, you've noticed a decline in productivity among two of these employees. You call these two workers into your office and they blame each other for the decline in productivity. The workers say they just don't get along with each other. Your boss tells you to make a decision to solve the problem quickly.

Writing Write a one-page memo to your boss explaining how you will go about solving this problem.

PREPARING FOR COMPETITIVE EVENTS

Which of the following is *not* a barrier to effective decision making?

a. panic

b. complacency

c. intuition

d. indecisiveness

e. avoidance

BusinessWeek ONLINE

In this chapter you read the *BusinessWeek* Management Model about flight simulations for management. For more information, go to *BusinessWeek* online at: **www.businessweek.com**

Research the Pricewaterhouse-Coopers Web site to find more information about the significance of the flight simulator to management. Discuss your research with the class.

CHAPTER 9

COMMUNICATION SKILLS

LEARNING OBJECTIVES

When you have completed this chapter, you will be able to:

- Understand why business managers need effective communication skills.
- List the skills needed to listen actively.
- Name five ways that business managers can improve their writing.
- Name four ways that business managers can improve their oral communication skills.
- Identify which form of communication is appropriate in different business situations.

READING STRATEGIES

As you read

- PREDICT what the section will be about.
- CONNECT what you read with your own life.
- QUESTION as you read to make sure you understand the content.
- RESPOND to what you read.

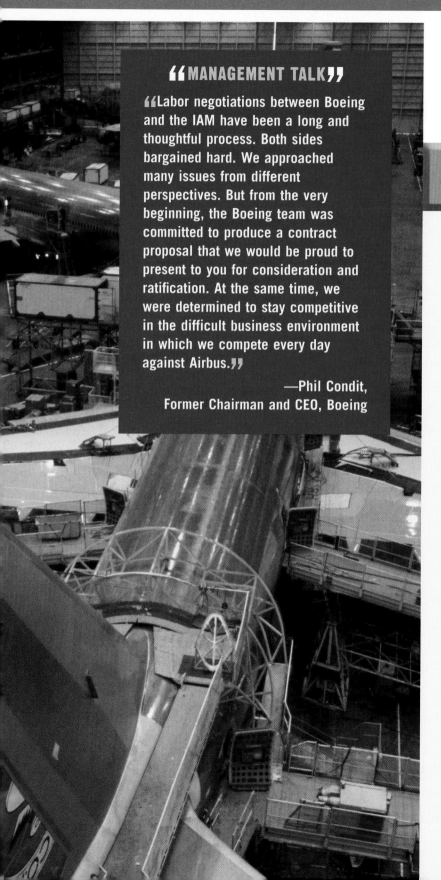

WORKPLACE CONNECTIONS

Understanding Management

In 1999, aircraft manufacturer Boeing negotiated a contract with its workers, represented by the International Association of Machinists and Aerospace Workers. After IAM leaders and Boeing management agreed on a contract, Boeing workers were asked to vote on the contract. The majority of workers voted "yes." The contract was ratified with the help of good business communication skills.

Analyzing Management Skills

What should managers do in order to communicate effectively with employees?

Applying Management Skills

Recall a time that you, a friend, or family member successfully worked through a disagreement with a supervisor or co-worker. How was the dispute resolved?

BusinessWeek *ONLINE*

For further reading on managers and management go to:
www.businessweek.com

DEVELOPING COMMUNICATION SKILLS

What Is Communication?

Communication is the act of exchanging information. It can be used to inform, command, instruct, assess, influence, and persuade other people. Communication skills are important in all aspects of life, including business.

Managers use communication every day. In fact, they spend as much as three-quarters of their time communicating (see **Figure 9–1**). Good managers develop effective communication skills. They use these skills to absorb information, motivate employees, and deal effectively with customers and co-workers. Good communication can significantly affect a manager's success.

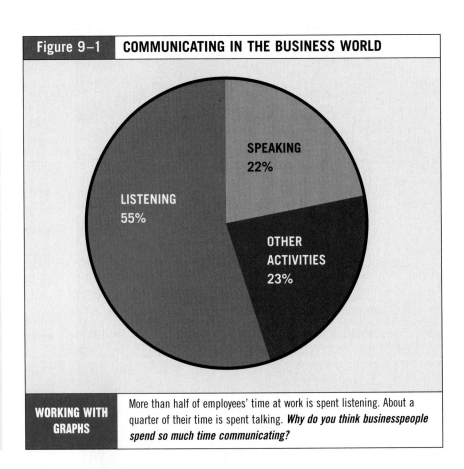

Figure 9–1   COMMUNICATING IN THE BUSINESS WORLD

SPEAKING 22%

LISTENING 55%

OTHER ACTIVITIES 23%

WORKING WITH GRAPHS More than half of employees' time at work is spent listening. About a quarter of their time is spent talking. *Why do you think businesspeople spend so much time communicating?*

Communication as a Management Skill

Communicating effectively is an important management skill for several reasons:

PREDICT

Why is it important for managers to be able to communicate persuasively?

- *Managers must give direction to the people who work for them.* Managers who fail to give clear guidance often find that employees perform their jobs poorly because they do not understand what is expected of them.
- *Managers must be able to motivate people.* Good managers use their ability to communicate to get other people excited about their jobs.
- *Managers must be able to convince customers that they should do business with them.* Effective communication is the key to convincing a customer to purchase a product or service. Without good communication skills, managers will find it difficult to attract customers, even if their companies' products or services meet the customer's needs.
- *Managers must be able to absorb the ideas of others.* Business managers interact with many people, including co-workers, customers, and suppliers. To be effective, they must be able to understand and accept other people's viewpoints.
- *Managers must be able to persuade other people.* Managers often have ideas that others oppose. To persuade other people to accept their ideas, managers must be able to communicate effectively.

▶ **COMMUNICATION APPLICATIONS** Good managers have excellent communication skills. *What are some of the ways they use these skills?*

Learning to Communicate

Managers communicate in writing and verbally. Before they can master either form of communication, they must be able to identify the audience, develop good listening skills, and understand the importance of nonverbal communication.

Understanding the Audience

Business managers communicate with many different kinds of people. Hotel managers, for example, communicate with hotel guests, food and beverage managers, housekeepers, maintenance people, architects, travel agents, furniture salespeople, and many other types of people. They also may deal with senior management from the hotel's corporate office. Each of these groups of people represents a different audience.

To communicate effectively, managers need to determine their audience. Specifically, they need to be able to answer the following questions:

1. What does the audience already know?
2. What does it want to know?
3. What is its capacity for absorbing information?
4. What does it hope to gain by listening? Is it hoping to be motivated? Informed? Convinced?
5. Is the audience friendly or hostile?

▼ COMMUNICATION PREPARATION Before communicating, a speaker must size up the audience. *What kind of information about the audience should this manager gather before making her presentation?*

Hotel managers communicate with the hotel's housekeeping staff about complaints by guests. In doing so they must inform the staff of the problem and motivate them to work harder to prevent complaints in the future. They would not need to provide background material on the nature of the housekeeper's role. The audience already understands what that role includes.

If a lawsuit is filed against the hotel, managers must inform management about the situation. In communicating with the hotel's corporate management, they would describe what was being done to deal with the situation. They would also provide detailed background information that would allow the corporate officers to fully understand the situation.

CONNECT

Imagine that you are the manager of a rental car business. What audiences might you expect to address?

Developing Good Listening Skills

One of the most important skills a manager can develop is the ability to listen (see **Figure 9–2**). Good listening skills enable managers to absorb the information they need, recognize problems, and understand other people's viewpoints.

Managers need to learn to listen actively. **Active listening** involves absorbing what another person is saying and responding to

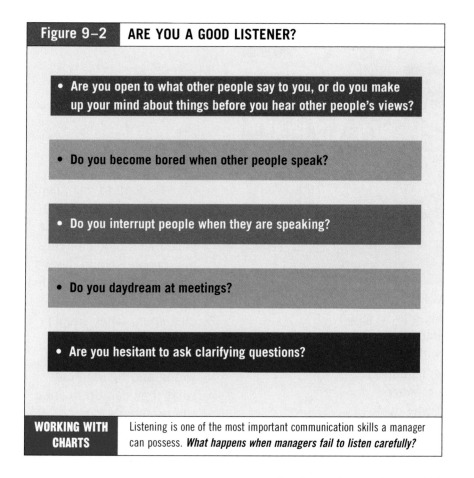

Figure 9–2	ARE YOU A GOOD LISTENER?

- Are you open to what other people say to you, or do you make up your mind about things before you hear other people's views?

- Do you become bored when other people speak?

- Do you interrupt people when they are speaking?

- Do you daydream at meetings?

- Are you hesitant to ask clarifying questions?

WORKING WITH CHARTS Listening is one of the most important communication skills a manager can possess. *What happens when managers fail to listen carefully?*

the person's concerns (see **Figure 9–3**). Learning to listen actively is the key to becoming a good communicator.

Most people do not listen actively. Tests indicate that immediately after listening to a ten-minute oral presentation, the average listener has heard, comprehended, accurately evaluated, and retained about half of what was said. Within 48 hours, the effectiveness level drops to just 25 percent. By the end of a week, listeners recall only about 10 percent or less of what they heard.

Managers need to work at being active listeners. Many people daydream or think about an unrelated topic when someone else is talking. Some people become angry by a speaker's remarks and fail to fully

---

FIGURE 9–3

Using Active Listening to Handle Customer Complaints

1 LISTENING
Knowing how to listen is an important part of dealing with customers. Using active listening skills helps managers understand why customers are dissatisfied.

2 RESPONDING
The way managers respond to complaints can be just as important as the way they solve the customer's problem. Businesspeople should always be courteous and friendly when dealing with customers. They should demonstrate interest in determining what went wrong and figuring out what they can do to solve the problem.

absorb what the person is saying. Others become impatient and interrupt, preferring to talk rather than listen.

Learning to listen actively involves the following steps:

1. *Identify the speaker's purpose.* What is the speaker trying to achieve? Why is the speaker speaking?
2. *Identify the speaker's main ideas.* Which of the points are the key points? Which points need to be addressed by the listener?
3. *Note the speaker's tone as well as his or her body language.* Is the speaker angry? Nervous? Confident?
4. *Respond to the speaker with appropriate comments, questions, and body language.* Use facial expressions and body language to

QUESTION

Why is it important to "listen" to a speaker's body language?

3 MAKING SURE THE CUSTOMER IS SATISFIED Managers need to determine whether they have satisfied the customers' needs. To do so, they must interpret the feedback they receive from the customer.

express the emotions you want to express. Establish eye contact, sit up straight, and lean toward the speaker to show interest. Ask a question or make a comment from time to time to show that you are listening attentively.

Managers who listen actively incorporate the feedback they obtain. In the 1990s, Whirlpool adopted a policy of "When consumers talk, Whirlpool listens." The company mailed surveys to about 180,000 customers, asking them to rate Whirlpools products. The surveys revealed that customers claimed to want kitchen ranges with touch-pad controls similar to those used on microwave ovens. When it came time to purchase a range, however, the same customers who indicated a desire for touch-pad stoves purchased traditional stovetops equipped with knobs they could push, turn, or adjust. By listening carefully to consumers' survey responses, Whirlpool figured out that consumer reluctance to purchase touch-pad stovetops had to do with the fact that such units were not as simple to operate as the control knob stovetops. Using this feedback, Whirlpool engineers designed a stovetop with touch-pads that was so easy to operate it needed no instruction manual. The unit became one of Whirlpool's hottest models.

Understanding the Importance of Nonverbal Communication

People communicate in many subtle ways. They do so by establishing eye contact, using facial expressions, and raising or lowering their voices. The way they dress and the way they walk also communicate information that other people use.

▶ **NONVERBAL COMMUNICATION** Nonverbal cues help managers evaluate people. *What nonverbal cues should this manager be looking for during this job interview?*

Business managers must learn to use nonverbal means of communication effectively. They must also learn to read the nonverbal cues of others. **Nonverbal cues** are pieces of information acquired by observing rather than listening to other people. Nonverbal cues sometimes provide more information than verbal cues.

Sara Fielding, a marketing manager, uses nonverbal communication when she conducts job interviews. To put job candidates at ease, Sara greets them with a warm smile and a firm handshake. These nonverbal cues reinforce Sara's verbal message: "I'm so happy you could come in this morning. I've been looking forward to meeting you."

Sara also uses her knowledge of nonverbal communication to evaluate the candidates' performance during their interviews. She is put off by candidates who fidget in their chairs or fail to maintain eye contact with her during the interview. She is impressed by candidates who dress professionally and appear to be listening thoughtfully. These cues give valuable information about how candidates might perform if given the job.

Section 9.1 Assessment

 FACT AND IDEA REVIEW

1. About how much of their time do managers typically spend communicating?
2. Name two reasons why it is important for managers to be able to communicate effectively.
3. Name three things a speaker or writer needs to know before addressing an audience.
4. Define active listening.

 CRITICAL THINKING

1. **Drawing Conclusions:** Why is it important for business managers to listen actively?
2. **Predicting Consequences:** What may happen if a manager fails to identify the audience correctly?
3. **Cause and Effect:** Why would nonverbal communication be a factor in a manager's marketing presentation?

 ASSESSING SPEAKING SKILLS

Together with a partner, role-play a customer complaint situation. One student should play the role of the customer. The other should play the role of the manager. The student playing the customer should try to persuade the manager to provide a refund and $500 in compensation for damages suffered as a result of the defective product. The student playing the manager should listen actively to the customer and try to resolve the situation as effectively as possible.

 CASE ANALYSIS

You have been asked to present a 15-minute talk at a regional conference of computer engineers.

Apply: Make a list of the information you would like to know about the conference attendees and conference program before preparing your speech.

TYPES OF COMMUNICATION

Written Communication

Managers communicate in writing every day. They send e-mails, write letters, and draft reports. To communicate effectively, managers must be able to write clearly, concisely, and persuasively.

Before actually writing a business document, managers need to think about what they want to achieve. They must identify the purpose of the document, the audience, and the main point they want to convey. Using a form like that shown in **Figure 9–4** can help them work through this stage of the writing process.

Figure 9–4	IDENTIFYING THE PURPOSE, AUDIENCE, AND MAIN POINT OF A DOCUMENT

PURPOSE

• Why am I writing this document?
• What action do I want the reader to take after reading it?

AUDIENCE

• Who will read this document?
• How much does the reader already know about the topic?
• How will the reader use the document?
• Are there any special sensitivities I should be aware of?

MAIN MESSAGE

• What is the main message I want to convey in this document?
• How will I support that message?

Managers need to think carefully about what they want a report to say before they prepare it. *What are some of the kinds of documents managers write?*

Figure 9–5   TIPS ON IMPROVING WRITTEN COMMUNICATION

Tips	Examples	
	Weak Writing	*Strong Writing*
Use language that is easy to understand. Avoid using jargon or bureaucratic language.	Interfacing with foreign counterparts is likely to continue in the future at an accelerated pace.	We plan to work closely with foreign partners.
Use short, simple sentences.	After three years of declining sales, corporate management decided to adopt a quality-improvement program, which was instituted in all production units last month, with plans for expansion throughout the company by early April.	Sales fell for three consecutive years. In response, corporate management put a quality-improvement program in place in all production units. By April, it hopes to expand the program throughout the company.
Use restrained, moderate language that is not overly emotional.	Sales were terrible this year!	Sales were weaker than management had expected.
Avoid the passive voice in favor of the active voice.	The decision was made to create two new brochures.	The marketing department decided to create two new brochures.
Use gender-neutral language. Avoid sexist language.	Every man in this company does his best to increase company profits.	Everyone in our company does his or her best to increase company profits.

WORKING WITH CHARTS — Being able to write well is an important skill for business managers. *Why do you think managers need to be able to write clearly and persuasively?*

Principles of Good Writing

Many business managers have difficulty writing well. To improve their writing, managers can apply several basic principles:

1. *Write as simply and clearly as possible.* Avoid writing in a way that is difficult to understand (see **Figure 9–5**).
2. *Be sure that the content and tone of the document are appropriate for the audience.* Do not waste readers' time communicating information they already know. However, do not assume they are as familiar with the topic as you are. Always use a polite tone, especially when writing to customers.

3. *Proofread the document.* If you are using a computer, use the spell-check function. If you are not using a computer, use a dictionary to check the spelling of words you do not know. Always read the document for incorrect grammar or usage.

Types of Business Documents

Most managers engage in some kind of writing every day. Each form of communication serves a different purpose and requires slightly different skills.

MEMOS The most common form of business communication is the office memorandum, or memo. **Memos** are used to communicate with people within the same company. They can be used to announce staff changes or changes in company policy. They also can be used to share new ideas or report on developments that are of interest to others.

All memos must include certain basic information. They must include the name of the sender and recipient of the memo, the date, and the subject of the memo (see **Figure 9–6**).

Many companies use e-mail to send memos. Sending memos via e-mail is less expensive than distributing hard copies and saves time and paper. Using e-mail also means that employees all over the world receive the same information at the same time.

Figure 9–6	SAMPLE OFFICE MEMO

OFFICE MEMORANDUM

To: Marketing Department Staff

From: James Wilson

Date: December 20, 20--

Subject: Theresa Donnelly

I am very pleased to announce that Theresa Donnelly will be joining the Marketing Department next Monday as a Marketing Assistant. Theresa is a 2003 graduate of Notre Dame College, where she majored in marketing. She is an avid backpacker and enjoys cross-country running. I look forward to having her join our team and hope that you will welcome her to the department.

Memos are used to communicate with people within a company. *What information must be included in a memo?*

Controller

■ Nature of the Work

Controllers are responsible for the preparation of all a company's financial reports, income statements, balance sheets, and special reports, such as depreciation schedules. They may oversee accounts payable and accounts receivable, audit, or budget departments.

In publicly traded companies, controllers make sure all reports meet federal guidelines. They monitor the flow of cash receipts and payments, and determine whether the company needs a loan to meet financial obligations. They decide when to invest extra money in interest-bearing instruments.

Controllers work in all profit-making industries and non-profit organizations. With the demand for qualified accounting professionals, experienced controllers can choose where they will work.

■ Working Conditions

Controllers work in comfortable, well lighted offices with a support staff. They may work long hours and sometimes work under pressure.

■ Training, Other Qualifications, and Advancement

To become a controller, you need a bachelor's or master's degree in finance or accounting. The CPA exam can also be helpful. Strong analytical and organizational skills are necessary, as are computer skills in spreadsheet and word processing software.

■ Salary Range

Assistant controllers earn $41,000 to $81,000; controllers earn $47,000 to $138,000. Salaries vary with responsibility, experience, industry, and size and location of firm.

CRITICAL THINKING

Why are word processing skills necessary to a high-level accountant such as a controller? Why are spreadsheet skills necessary? What kind of person do you think would make a good controller?

STANDARD & POOR'S

INDUSTRY OUTLOOK

Controllers monitor the loans a company obtains from banks or other financial services companies. Like banks, financial service companies lend money at interest, charge interest, and offer many lending products that suit business needs. They are less regulated than banks and are not insured by the Federal Deposit Insurance Corporation (FDIC).

BUSINESS MANAGEMENT *Online*

For more information on management careers, go to:
busmanagement.glencoe.com

Figure 9–7 | SAMPLE BUSINESS LETTER

Sylvan Instruments
200 Lancaster Avenue
Bryn Mawr, Pennsylvania 19010
610-585-9399

July 18, 20--

Ms. Juanita Marquez
District Sales Manager
ABC Products
465 York Road
Timonium, Maryland 21245

Dear Ms. Marquez:

Thank you for coming by last week to discuss ABC's new line of products. I plan to review the material you left me and make a decision about a new supplier within the next two weeks.

Sincerely yours,

John Williams

John Williams
Purchasing Director

Businesses generally correspond with people outside the company through the postal service, rather than through e-mail. *What elements must a business letter include?*

LETTERS While businesses use e-mail for internal communications, most contact customers and suppliers by sending formal business letters. **Business letters** should include the date, the recipient's name and address, the purpose of the letter, and the name and job title of the sender (see **Figure 9–7**). Letters should be neatly typed on company letterhead. Senders of business letters should make copies of the letter to keep for their own records.

REPORTS **Reports** are documents that provide a lot of information on a particular topic. They are used to provide managers with the information they need to make decisions. For example, regional sales managers may write quarterly reports documenting sales and identifying strengths and weakness during the period. Their reports help them and higher-level managers to develop strategies for increasing sales.

QUESTION

What are the main differences between a memo and a letter?

Writing reports requires much more thought and organization than writing memos or letters. To help organize their ideas, business managers often use the following checklist:

- ☐ Analyze the purpose of and audience for the report (see **Figure 9–4**).
- ☐ Brainstorm ideas and determine what kind of information to include in the report.
- ☐ Group ideas under headings.
- ☐ Make an outline of the headings.
- ☐ Check to make sure the order of the headings makes sense.
- ☐ Create a first draft.
- ☐ Edit the draft for grammar, spelling, clarity, and style.
- ☐ Make the report look as attractive as possible by using bullets, numbered lists, headings, short paragraphs, and charts.
- ☐ Proofread the final version of the report.

WORKPLACE DIVERSITY

INDIA

In India, it is common to ask personal questions of potential business partners and to be very hospitable. Indian culture values interpersonal understanding, sharing, and friendship because these things often bond people together and allow them to understand each other better. The formality typical of many business relations in the United States is less common in business relationships in India.

Oral Communication

Not all business communication is done in writing. In fact, most business communication is done orally.

Some oral communication is formal and takes place at meetings or interviews. Most oral communication is informal. It takes place in offices and hallways, next to the water fountain, in the cafeteria, and over the telephone.

◀ **VERBAL COMMUNICATION** Oral communication takes place constantly in the business world. *Why is it important for business managers to be able to communicate well verbally?*

The Mess Made for Business by Junk E-Mail

As the art of letter writing goes the way of the 32-cent stamp, more and more of what pops up in our mailboxes at home is nothing but garbage. So is it asking too much to want our e-mail boxes, especially those at work, to be junk-free?

Don't count on it. A study from Internet security consultant Worldtalk Corp. says that almost one-third, or 31%, of corporate e-mail is junk. And unlike the innocuous supermarket sales fliers that jam up the mail slot at home, this junk mail is causing financial loss and service interruption. "Internet e-mail abuse is worse than we expected," says Simon Khalaf, who oversaw the study at Worldtalk, based in Santa Clara, California. The

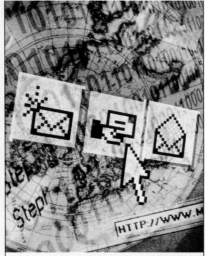

study was compiled from network surveillance of more than 31 million messages in systems worldwide.

OTHER FINDINGS: Employees spend, on average, 30 minutes a day sifting through their deluge of e-mail. Spam-mail—unsolicited messages from unknown senders—can cost a 5,000-person organization more than $12,000 per day to process. That's 50 cents per employee, to check and delete junk-mail messages.

And incidents of e-mail leaks aren't all that uncommon. According to the study, some 9% of all corporate e-mail messages include some form of proprietary or confidential information, such as product plans, and are sent out maliciously or without the company's permission. More and more, "you've got mail" is likely to mean you've got a problem.

Excerpted with permission from BusinessWeek, April 19, 1999

CRITICAL THINKING

How does junk e-mail affect a company financially?

DECISION MAKING

As a manager of a company, write a one-page policy for e-mail use in your company. Set standards for personal use and for downloading junk mail and attachments.

BITS & BYTES

What's in the corporate e-mail box?

Business & Personal	69%
Spam	10%
Confidential Information	9%
Profanities	4%
Jokes	2%
Viruses	2%

DATA: Worldtalk Corporation

The Importance of Oral Communication

Communicating well verbally is important for managers. Successful managers use their oral communication skills to give clear instructions, motivate their staffs, and persuade other people.

Being able to communicate effectively also is important because it can set the tone within a department or company. In some departments, managers say "good morning" to as many co-workers as they can. They invite their employees to discuss problems with them. In other departments, managers isolate themselves from lower-level employees and make no effort to communicate. These small differences can have a big effect on employee morale.

Developing Oral Communication Skills

All businesspeople need to be able to speak effectively (see **Figure 9–8**). Whether they are talking to a colleague or presenting a keynote address before thousands of people, they need to follow the same rules of thumb:

1. *Make emotional contact with listeners by addressing them by name where possible.* When talking face-to-face, establish eye contact.
2. *Avoid speaking in a monotone.* Use your voice to emphasize important words within a sentence.

CONNECT

Have you ever been in a work or school situation where poor communication led to low morale? How could communication have improved in order to boost morale?

All About

ATTITUDE

THE K.I.S. PRINCIPLE

The K.I.S. Principle ("Keep It Simple") holds that rather than trying to impress your group with dynamic charts and complex formulas, you should present concepts in a clear and concise manner. Being able to explain your premise in 30 seconds or less can help you focus on what is truly important.

Figure 9–8	TECHNIQUES FOR SPEAKING EFFECTIVELY
Technique	**Example**
Enumeration (listing key points)	Our department is looking for people with excellent technical ability, outstanding communication skills, and the desire to contribute to a team.
Generalization followed by examples	We continue to demonstrate our commitment to staff education. Last year we sent almost half of our employees to seminars and training sessions. This year, we expect to include up to 75 percent of all employees in staff education.
Cause and effect	We increased our sales force by 25 percent in the Northeast region in 2000. As a result, sales rose by more than $2 million.
Comparison and contrast	Our newest portable computer is as light as our competitors' and has as much computing power. It is $400 less expensive than our competitors' product, however.
WORKING WITH CHARTS	Managers use these techniques in both speaking and writing. *Why do you think these techniques help managers make their point?*

3. *Be enthusiastic and project a positive outlook.* Focus on what is going right, rather than what is going wrong.
4. *Avoid interrupting others.* Even if you know what the other person is going to say, avoid cutting other people off or finishing their sentences for them.
5. *Always be courteous.* Avoid getting angry when other people are talking, even if you disagree with what they are saying.
6. *Avoid empty sounds or words, such as "uh," "um," "like," and "you know."* Sprinkling your speech with empty fillers will make you sound unprofessional.

RESPOND

What speaking practices distract or annoy you when you are listening to someone?

Choosing the Best Method of Communication

Managers need to master both written and verbal communication skills. They also need to understand when to use each kind of skill (see **Figure 9–9**). In general, verbal communication is most appropriate for

Figure 9–9	CHOOSING THE BEST METHOD OF COMMUNICATION
Method of Communication	**Most Appropriate Method of Communication**
Oral communication alone	• Reprimanding employees • Resolving disputes within the company
Written communication alone	• Communicating information requiring future action • Communicating information of a general nature
Oral communication followed by written communication	• Communicating information requiring immediate action • Communicating directives or orders • Communicating information about an important policy change • Communicating with one's immediate superior about a work-related problem • Praising an employee for outstanding performance
WORKING WITH CHARTS	Different communication methods are appropriate in different situations. *What method would you use to let an employee know that he or she had been promoted?*

QUESTION

Which method of communication would you choose to respond to a customer's complaint?

◄ **METHOD OF COMMUNICATION** Managers need to know when to use written or verbal communication. *Why has this manager chosen to use verbal communication?*

sensitive communications, such as reprimanding or dismissing an employee. Written communication is most appropriate for communicating routine information, such as changes in company policies or staff. Choosing the best method of communication will help you relay information in an appropriate and professional manner.

Section 9.2 Assessment

FACT AND IDEA REVIEW

1. Name two techniques managers can use to improve their writing.
2. Name three kinds of documents managers need to know how to write.
3. Name two techniques managers can use to improve their oral communication skills.
4. Explain when managers would use written communication and when they would use oral communication.

CRITICAL THINKING

1. **Cause and Effect:** What conclusions might a customer draw after receiving a badly written letter from a manager?
2. **Making Generalizations:** Why do you think it is important for managers to connect emotionally with listeners when they speak?
3. **Drawing Conclusions:** Which do you think is more important for a manager: written or verbal communication skills? Why?

ASSESSING WRITING SKILLS

rite a short letter to a customer letting her know why you think she should do business with your company. Be sure to use all of the writing tips you learned in this section. Also check that your letter includes all of the standard elements a business letter must include, such as the date and the recipient's address.

CASE ANALYSIS

s the manager of the marketing department of a wholesale food distributor, you supervise 45 people. Last week you terminated one of your workers, announced a new vacation policy, resolved an argument between two employees, and promoted two junior staff members to more senior positions.

Apply: Explain what method of communication you used for each type of communication.

CHAPTER 9 ASSESSMENT

REVIEWING VOCABULARY

In pairs, discuss the idea of **communication** and explain the different ways in which managers communicate. Also discuss the difference between a **memo**, **business letter**, and **report**. Finally, demonstrate **active listening** and **nonverbal cues**.

CHAPTER SUMMARY

Section 9.1

▶ Communication is the act of exchanging information. Business managers use communication to inform, command, instruct, assess, influence, and persuade other people.

▶ To communicate effectively, business managers must understand the audience, develop good listening skills, and understand the importance of nonverbal communication.

Section 9.2

▶ Most business managers communicate in writing every day. To be effective, they must be able to write clearly, concisely, and persuasively.

▶ Oral communication takes place constantly in the business world. Managers must be able to communicate well verbally in order to give clear instructions, motivate their staffs, persuade other people, and set the proper tone in their departments.

RECALLING KEY CONCEPTS

1. Explain what it means to understand an audience.
2. What is involved in active listening?
3. Give three examples of nonverbal cues.
4. Name three techniques that can improve the quality of your writing.
5. What is the purpose of an office memo? An e-mail? A report?
6. What method of communication would a manager use to let an employee know that his or her performance was inadequate?

THINKING CRITICALLY

1. Explain why business managers need to be able to communicate effectively.
2. Explain why active listening is an important communication skill.
3. How would a manager use communication skills to deal with a customer complaint?
4. Why is writing a report more complicated than writing a letter or a memo? What steps do managers need to take before writing a report?
5. What would it be like to work for a manager who was unable to communicate verbally?

CHAPTER 9 ASSESSMENT

ASSESSING ACADEMIC SKILLS

WRITING Write a memo to your staff explaining why raises will average just 2 percent this year. Use the format shown in **Figure 9–6**. Also try to apply all of the writing techniques you used in this chapter.

APPLYING MANAGEMENT PRINCIPLES

SOLVE THE PROBLEM Shaniqa Johnson manages a large department store. In recent months, the store's sales have been falling, and customers have complained about poor service. Shaniqa needs to communicate with her employees to try to improve her store's performance.

Language Arts Write a short essay explaining what you would do if you held Shaniqa's job. Indicate how you would use your communication skills to try to inform and motivate the store's staff.

PREPARING FOR COMPETITIVE EVENTS

Which of the following rules does *not* help a manager write effectively?

a. Use short, simple sentences.

b. Avoid the passive voice.

c. Use jargon and complex language.

d. Use gender-neutral language.

In this chapter you read the *BusinessWeek* Management Model about Internet e-mail abuse in corporations. For more information, go to *BusinessWeek* online at: **www.businessweek.com**

Using the Internet or your local library, find articles about how junk e-mail affects corporations. What standards do businesses have regarding the use of company e-mail?

CASE STUDY 3

Creative Decision Making

OVERVIEW

Today's workplace requires managers to make decisions on a daily basis. Some situations require managers to solve problems by implementing a new policy. This type of decision making is used when the work is fairly routine. But in highly specialized situations, managers make decisions on a case-by-case basis. This type of decision making is more difficult than carrying out a predetermined policy. This case study illustrates a creative approach that uses brainstorming to help managers make a final decision.

RESOURCES

- poster board or flip chart
- colored markers

PROCEDURES

◆ STEP A ◆

The Rewards of Creative Intelligence

Businesses spend thousands of dollars each year on new product research and development. Only those businesses that dedicate themselves to new and better products will continue to exist in the future. Therefore, a manager's decision regarding these products could dramatically impact a business.

Identifying Information:

1. In groups of three to five students, identify five new products that have been introduced to the market in the past year. List the manufacturer responsible for the development of each product.

2. Next, identify the problems and benefits these new products provide to the customer.

3. For each of the products listed, identify two products that compete directly against the new products. List the manufacturers of these products.

CASE STUDY 3

◆ STEP B ◆

Strategic Webs

When developing a new product, it's a good idea to use techniques that will effectively evaluate the product. One such technique is a "Strategic Web." The primary advantage of the web is that a problem can be broken down into a series of isolated questions. Once the questions are answered, these thoughts can then be used to develop new ideas, or to make a final decision.

Problem Solving:

1. In your small groups, determine a product that everyone would like to produce.

2. Place your *Product Name* in a bubble in the middle of a sheet of paper and draw five short lines originating out of it. At the end of each of these lines, draw five more bubbles.

3. Within each new bubble, place an *Attribute* of your product (for example, the shape, color, size, material, etc.). From these five bubbles, draw five more lines with bubbles connecting at the ends.

4. Within each of the final bubbles, place an *Example of the Attribute*. (For instance, if "shape" is an attribute, five examples would include: oval, square, rectangle, triangle, and circular.)

5. Using the web, make connections between the possibilities. As a group, choose the best combination to come up with a new product.

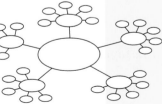

◆ STEP C ◆

Management Report

Using poster boards or flip charts, illustrate the importance of brainstorming and team decision making. Prepare a 5- to 10-minute presentation that includes the following:

1. Address the importance of creative decision making and present the team's "Strategic Web."

2. Analyze the web that the group developed to solve its problem.

3. Focus on the decisions the group had to make during the activity.

4. Discuss the final product that was selected, addressing the key features incorporated into the product idea.

5. Provide a picture of what the finished product would look like.

6. Identify the targeted customer, the problems solved by the product, and the benefits that would be provided to the customer.

Chapter 10
Planning and Strategic Management

Chapter 11
Operations Management and Planning

IN THIS UNIT...

You will see how strategic planning helps managers set goals and how operations planning helps a business run efficiently. Included in this unit are chapters on planning, strategic management, and operations management.

Journal Writing

In your journal, assess your knowledge of management by writing about the following:

1. Why is planning necessary to stay organized and successful?

2. What does the word *strategy* mean to you?

3. What must a manager consider when planning for the physical work environment of a company?

225

CHAPTER 10

PLANNING AND STRATEGIC MANAGEMENT

LEARNING OBJECTIVES

When you have completed this chapter, you will be able to:

- Explain the differences between formal and functional plans.
- Recognize the differences between strategic planning and operational planning.
- Discuss the differences among missions, goals, policies, procedures, and rules.
- Understand the role of SWOT analysis in planning and strategic management.
- Discuss the organizational factors that need evaluation in implementing strategic plans.

READING STRATEGIES

As you read

- **PREDICT** what the section will be about.
- **CONNECT** what you read with your own life.
- **QUESTION** as you read to make sure you understand the content.
- **RESPOND** to what you read.

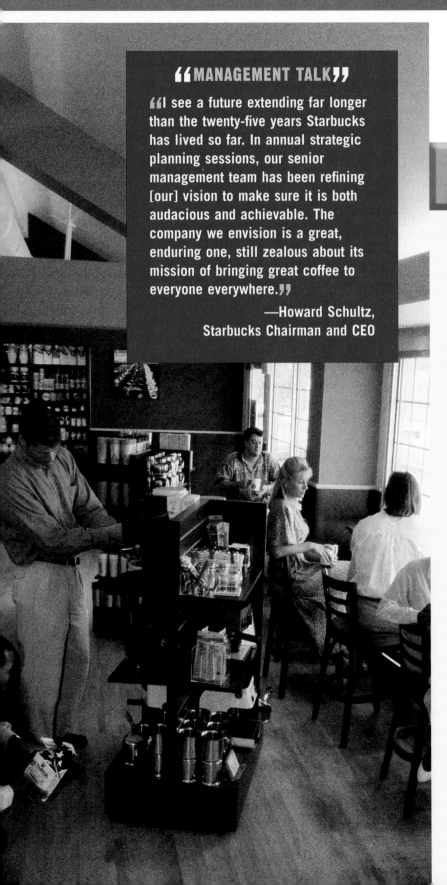

WORKPLACE CONNECTIONS

Understanding Management

In the early 1980s, Howard Schultz predicted that consumers would support a new type of "coffee bar," serving specialty coffee and espresso products. Under his leadership, Starbucks grew from a homey little coffee shop in Seattle to a multi-million dollar corporation. Today, Schultz still centers the company's growth strategy on introducing customers to great coffee.

Analyzing Management Skills

Why do you think it is important for a company like Starbucks to refine its vision? What other functions might annual strategic planning sessions serve?

Applying Management Skills

What trends do you think will influence businesses in the next 10 years? If you opened a business today, what things would you do to plan for its future success?

BusinessWeek *ONLINE*

For further reading on managers and management go to:
www.businessweek.com

WHAT IS THE PLANNING PROCESS?

Why Plan?

While leaving the movies with your friends on Saturday afternoon, everyone is talking about the big football game tomorrow. You had hoped to go, but realize that you still have to prepare for your English presentation and Calculus test on Monday. You can't do the work tonight because you are baby-sitting. Now you will have to miss out on the game. Effective planning could have avoided all of these problems.

Key executives in every company spend a considerable amount of time planning. This process is important to the success of any business. Planning is the process that businesses use to decide the company's goals for the future and ways to achieve those goals.

▲ TIME MANAGEMENT Effective planning is necessary to maintain a balance between school and social activities. *What kind of plans do you consider to balance your workload?*

Planning prepares managers and businesses to meet the challenges of economic, social, technological, and political changes. Plans also allow businesses to prepare for the future. Without plans, companies would not know how to handle crisis situations. They also would be unable to deal with new developments, such as changes in technology or increased competition.

Failing to implement a business plan forced Pittsburgh's Sutersville Lumber Inc. to shut down. The 51-year-old company was forced to close its doors when the lumber giant, Home Depot, opened three enormous stores in the area—one just three miles away. The majority of Sutersville's owners refused to allow the chief financial officer to finish her plan of reducing costly inventory and complete the company's five-store expansion. As a result, Sutersville ran out of cash and was forced to file for bankruptcy.

Effective Planning

Everything that an effective manager does involves planning. For example, managers who attempt to hire employees without a plan find that they waste company resources constantly hiring and firing workers. Effective planners encourage employees from all areas of the company to participate in plan development. This active participation benefits the organization in several ways:

▲ **COMMUNICATION** When making changes in company policies or procedures, effective managers may hold meetings with employees. *Why do companies need input from many employees to develop a plan?*

- Good suggestions can come from any level of management.
- Employees have a better understanding of the company's overall direction.
- Employees feel they are part of the process and become committed to the plan.
- Positive participation and pro-company attitudes improve morale and loyalty to the organization.

Effective planning also gives managers experience and knowledge in understanding the forces that affect a company's operations. These forces range from new technologies to changes in tax laws. A manager also must keep current with what is happening in the firm's industry and with current law.

There are several ways to plan effectively. The best managers use combinations of formal and informal planning. They develop plans that look months ahead, as well as those designed to meet changes five years in the future.

Formal Planning

Formal planning is the systematic studying of an issue and the preparation of a written document to deal with the problem. Some formal plans are simple, but others can be very complicated. A plan to give long-time employees a gold watch is fairly simple. However, a plan to make company stock available to the public, as Amazon.com did in the late 1990s, is complicated.

In general, larger companies must prepare more complicated plans than smaller companies. There are three basic ranges, or time spans, for developing business plans:

- *Short-range plans* cover a one-year period of time.
- *Long-range plans* cover a three-to-five-year period of time, but some cover as far as 20 years into the future.
- *Intermediate plans* cover the time span between short-range and long-range, generally from one to three or one to five years.

Operational Versus Strategic Plans

CONNECT

Strategic and operational plans are great ways to zero in on your goals. How might you use these plans to assist with your studies?

Plans cover not only different time spans, but also different kinds of tasks in the workplace. There are two basic types of business plans: operational and strategic. **Operational planning** is short-range planning. It focuses on forming ideas for dealing with specific functions in the company, such as the production of new products. **Strategic planning** is long-range planning done by the highest management levels in the company, including the president, vice president, and chief operating officer. Different types of planning are illustrated in **Figure 10–1.**

Strategy

In order to develop a plan, you need a course of action or strategy. A *strategy* is an outline of the basic steps management is going to take to achieve a goal. Strategies exist at three primary levels in a company—grand or corporate, business, and functional.

Grand Strategies

PREDICT

What do you think is the difference between a grand or corporate plan and a business plan?

Grand or **corporate strategies** provide overall direction for the company. These plans deal with the most important aspects of the company's operations. These include products the company will manufacture and services it will provide; the number of employees it has;

FIGURE 10–1

Implementing Planning Decisions

Different levels of management are responsible for different kinds of planning. No matter who does the planning, it is important to communicate planning decisions effectively to those implementing the plans.

1 SENIOR MANAGE-MENT PLANNING Disney's strategic plan to open theme parks in other countries was the result of a meeting attended by the company's top officers.

2 MIDDLE MANAGE-MENT PLANNING However, Disney's operational plan to put certain toys in the stores at DisneyWorld was developed by middle- and lower-level managers.

3 SUPERVISORY MANAGEMENT PLANNING In an organization where there are many levels of management, like Disney, decisions will be made by many different people. While top executives may decide what kind of restaurants will be placed in the park, lower level managers and restaurant workers may decide on the daily food specials and menu items.

how much money the company will spend on salaries and benefits; and how the company will market its products to consumers and other businesses. These long-range plans are developed at the highest levels of the company, usually the president or chief operating officer. There are four basic grand strategy types: growth, stability, retrenchment, and combination.

QUESTION

Why would a company pursue a stability strategy instead of a growth strategy?

GROWTH STRATEGY Plans developed when a company tries to expand sales, products, or number of employees are called **growth strategies**. Under a growth strategy, a company can expand in the following ways:

- *Concentration strategy* extends the sale of current products or services to a company's current market.
- *Vertical integration* moves a company into a market it previously served either as a supplier or as a customer.
- *Diversification* moves a company into a similar kind of business with new or different products or services.

Tips from Robert Half

Ninety-six percent of executives say that communication skills are essential to their work. Learn what it takes to put your ideas into writing, and practice speaking to large groups of people.

STABILITY STRATEGY Sometimes a company does not want to, or cannot, expand because it lacks necessary financial resources. In those cases, a company may adopt a stability strategy. A **stability strategy** is a plan to keep the company operating at the same level that it has for several years. If a company is satisfied with its profits and not seeking growth, this is a good option. Management does not initiate any broad-sweeping actions that could dramatically affect the entire company.

Stability strategies will most likely succeed in slowly changing, work environments. Company growth is possible under a stability strategy, but it will be very slow. The owner of Peet's Coffee and Tea, a group of coffeehouses in the San Francisco Bay area, refused to franchise the business for many years. Owner Gerald Baldwin was concerned that the quality of the coffee would suffer if the company tried to grow too quickly. Instead, Baldwin pursued a stability strategy, and the company experienced steady, but slow growth.

RETRENCHMENT STRATEGY Sometimes a company is losing money or wants to reduce its costs. Under these circumstances, the company would adopt a defensive or retrenchment strategy. A **defensive** or **retrenchment strategy** is a plan to reverse negative trends in a company, such as losses in sales. Retrenchment strategies became popular in the 1990s, when businesses sought to reverse the excesses of the 1980s and focus on new directions for corporate growth.

This type of strategy also is used to overcome a crisis or problem, such as competition that undercuts a company's main product. The three most popular types of defensive strategies are:

- *Turnaround* is used to regain success.
- *Divestiture* is when a company sells some part of its business, often an unprofitable part or a unit that is not in the firm's major line of business.
- *Liquidation* is when the entire company is sold or dissolved.

COMBINATION STRATEGY Sometimes companies are not sure whether to pursue a growth, stability, or retrenchment strategy. It is possible that all issues cannot be addressed by implementing just one strategy. A company may decide to adopt what is called a combination strategy. A **combination strategy** is a plan that employs several different strategies at once.

Most multiple business companies use some type of combination strategy. Coca Cola, for example, pursued a combination strategy in 1989 when it divested its Columbia Pictures division while expanding its soft drink and orange juice businesses. Companies usually cannot afford to use all of the strategies that might benefit them because they have limited resources and talents. Managers must establish priorities, or the competition will gain an advantage.

Business Strategies

While grand or corporate plans affect the entire corporation, business strategies affect only one or two departments. **Business strategies** are plans that pertain to single departments or units within a company. For example, strategies may deal with marketing issues such as how to reach new customers or how to develop a new product. Business strategies are most effective when they consider the creative input of all employees. They can be classified as overall cost leadership, differentiation, and focus strategies.

▶ **DEFENSIVE STRATEGIES** Chrysler corporation was on the verge of bankruptcy when it hired Lee Iacocca as their new CEO. Iacocca let go of a large number of employees and closed 20 plants. Remaining workers agreed to give up part of their salaries and benefits to save the company and by 1982 Chrysler began to show profit. *What kind of strategy did Iacocca implement?*

OVERALL COST LEADERSHIP An **overall cost leadership** strategy is designed to produce and deliver a product or service for a lower cost than the competition. This strategy can be tremendously effective when there are many buyers who are price-sensitive. Wal-Mart, BIC, and McDonald's all have adopted this strategy with great success.

DIFFERENTIATION A strategy that strives to make the product or service unique is called **differentiation**. Customers are willing to pay average to high prices for these particular items. Because customers are price-insensitive, companies tend to emphasize quality. Differentiation can be achieved through a superior product (Gillette), a quality image (Jaguar), or a brand image (Adidas sportswear).

RESPOND

What are some examples of products that have become popular through differentiation?

FOCUS A *focus* strategy directs marketing and sales towards a small segment of the market. The company can serve a well-defined market better than competitors that serve a broader market. Some examples of companies that pursue a focus strategy include Colgate-Palmolive, Red Lobster, Federal Express, and Midas.

Functional Strategies

The final primary level of strategy is a functional strategy. **Functional strategies** are short-range operational plans that support business strategies by emphasizing practical implementation. Function or use often defines plans. The most common functional plans are:

- *Sales and marketing:* developing new products or services and selling them
- *Production:* producing products or services on time
- *Financial:* dealing with the company's expenses
- *Research and development:* developing new products, improving on product quality, or improving manufacturing processes to reduce costs
- *Personnel:* managing human resource needs

◀ **BUSINESS STRATEGIES** Colgate-Palmolive has a 70 percent market share of toothpaste sold to Hispanics. This is attributed to an understanding that three-quarters of Hispanics who watch TV or listen to the radio do so with Spanish-language stations. *What kind of business strategy does this illustrate?*

Many functional plans are interrelated. A personnel plan is directly tied to a financial and production plan. The number of employees a company hires, and how much they are paid, depends on company's finances and the amount of work needed. A production schedule will account for deadlines and seasonal needs, for example, more snow shovels in the winter months.

Boeing is an example of a company that learned from past functional planning mistakes. The airline manufacturer was experiencing massive interruptions with its production, human resource, and marketing functions in the manufacture and delivery of its 747-400 airplane. When designing its new 777 airplane, Boeing used a different approach. The company used teams of marketing, engineering, manufacturing, finance, and service representatives so that each functional area knew what the other was doing. The success of this project depended on the interrelationship of functional plans and strategies.

Section 10.1 Assessment

FACTS AND IDEA REVIEW

1. What is planning and what questions does it answer?
2. What is the difference between strategic planning and operational planning? Between long-range and short-range planning?
3. What is the difference between vertical integration and diversification?
4. Under what circumstances would a business adopt a retrenchment strategy?
5. List the three classifications of business strategies.

CRITICAL THINKING

1. **Analyzing Information:** Why is it necessary to plan? What are the benefits of planning? Give an example of how you plan at home.
2. **Making Comparisons:** This year a company might employ a stability strategy. However, next year it might use a retrenchment strategy. How could this happen? What would the company be like to work for this year? Next year?

ASSESSING SOCIAL STUDIES SKILLS

Go to the school library and find a recent magazine article that focuses on strategic planning. Write a two-page summary of the article. Include your comments and personal reaction. Exchange papers with your classmates and discuss.

CASE ANALYSIS

You are the president of a major sportswear company. Sales have bottomed-out in your footwear line, but your brand new headband is selling like crazy. You have more orders for headbands than you can fill from your inventory. You also hear about a company up for sale that manufactures sports watches. Your board of directors would like to discuss what planning options are under consideration.

Apply: Discuss what options are available to you. Include a thorough discussion of the different strategies discussed in this section.

STRATEGIC MANAGEMENT PROCESS

What Is Strategic Management?

Business changes so rapidly today that it is difficult for managers to maintain current plans. It is the responsibility of upper management to develop corporate plans for the future and to engage in strategic management. **Strategic management** is the application of the basic planning process at the highest levels of the company. Through the strategic management process, top management sets goals for the performance of the company. This is done by carefully formulating, implementing, and evaluating plans and strategies.

The most important part of strategic management is developing strategic plans. These plans must remain current as changes occur within and outside of the company. It is possible for a plan to become outdated because of changes occurring inside a company (a new line of products), or outside of the company (new government regulations).

▲ **SHARING RESPONSIBILITY** Top-level managers often ask middle- and lower-level managers for their input when making top-level plans. *Why would the president of the company do this?*

Practicing strategic management doesn't guarantee that a company will successfully meet all changes, but it does increase the chances of that happening.

Successful strategic management involves many levels of management. Top-level management formally develops basic plans. But once top-level plans are finalized, different departments of the company may be asked to develop plans for their own areas. A solid strategic management process guarantees that plans are coordinated and are supported by everyone at the company.

International Management

SWEDEN

In Sweden, work does not interfere with private life. Managers can expect all tasks to be completed within working hours and need to schedule all meetings and special projects accordingly. They do not expect late hours and working on weekends.

BusinessWeek *ONLINE* For further reading about International Management go to: **www.businessweek.com**

Strategic Management Approach

Although different companies use different approaches to the strategic management process, most companies use an approach that is made up of these three phases:

- Formulation, or developing the strategic plan
- Implementation, or putting the formulated plan to work
- Evaluation, or continuously evaluating and updating the strategic plan

Each of these phases is critical to the success of the strategic management process. If any phase breaks down, it can cause the entire process to fail.

Formulating Strategy

All strategic management begins with the development of the strategic plan or formulating strategy. **Formulating strategy** is developing the grand- and business-level strategies to be used by the company. The company's internal strengths and weaknesses, as well as threats and opportunities outside of the company, shape the strategies.

The first part of the formulation phase is to obtain a clear understanding of the current position of the company. This includes identifying the mission, identifying past and present strategies, diagnosing the company's past and present performance, and setting objectives for the company's operation.

IDENTIFYING THE MISSION STATEMENT A company always has a mission, or reason for being, when it is created. A **mission statement** outlines why the company exists. It describes the company's basic products and/or services and defines markets and sources of revenue. It is designed to accomplish several goals and ensures a common purpose within the company (see **Figure 10–2**).

Every company's mission statement will be a little different, but most are short and refer to lofty corporate goals (See **Figure 10–3**).

Figure 10–2	OBJECTIVES OF THE COMPANY MISSION

A mission statement is designed to accomplish the following objectives:

- To ensure a common purpose within the company.

- To provide a basis for motivating the use of the company's resources.

- To develop a standard for allocating the company's resources.

- To establish a general tone or company climate.

- To serve as a focal point for those who can identify with the company's purpose and direction and to deter those who cannot do so from participating further in its activities.

- To facilitate the translation of goals into a work structure involving the assignment of tasks to responsible elements within the company.

- To specify company purposes and the transfer of those purposes into goals in such a way that cost, time, and performance can be assessed and controlled.

Companies work hard to develop a mission statement that defines the purpose of the company. *What are some other goals of a mission statement?*

Adapted from King and Cleland, *Strategic Planning and Policy* (New York: Van Nostrand Reinhold 1978).

Figure 10–3	EXAMPLES OF MISSION STATEMENTS

Pfizer Inc.'s Mission Statement

Over the next five years we will achieve and sustain our place as the world's premier research-based health care company. Our continuing success as a business will benefit patients and our customers, our shareholders, our families, and the communities in which we operate around the world.

AT&T's Mission Statement

We are dedicated to being the world's best at bringing people together—giving them easy access to each other and to the information and services they want—anytime, anywhere.

Harley-Davidson's Mission Statement

We fulfill dreams through the experience of motorcycling, by providing to motorcyclists and to the general public an expanding line of motorcycles and branded products and services in selected market segments.

There are many different kinds of mission statements that a company might choose to employ. *Based on these mission statements, can you identify some elements of a good mission statement?*

Hospital Administrator

Nature of the Work

Hospital administrators plan, organize, coordinate, supervise the delivery of health care, and set the direction of the hospital. In addition, they are involved in marketing, human resources, and finance. They determine the hospital's need for services, staff, facilities, and equipment. They see that the hospital complies with government regulations.

Administrators often speak to community groups and encourage people to participate in health programs. They must keep up with a variety of developments in medicine as well as in business and management.

Working Conditions

Hospital administrators work in comfortable surroundings. However, hours are often long and the work is stressful. They may be called in at any time to solve problems.

Training, Other Qualifications, and Advancement

To become a hospital administrator, you need a master's degree or Ph.D in health services administration, nursing administration, public health, or business administration. The job also requires leadership ability, analytical skills, and the ability to understand and interpret complex data. Hospital administrators are responsible for millions of dollars of facilities and equipment, and hundreds of employees.

Salary Range

Hospital administrators earn about $190,500 or more, depending on responsibilities, experience, location, and the type and size of the hospital.

CRITICAL THINKING

In what situations might hospital administrators have to weigh the financial needs of the hospital against the health care needs of the community? Why is it important to have a balanced understanding of business knowledge and new medical developments? What kinds of challenges do you think hospital administrators face?

STANDARD &POOR'S

INDUSTRY OUTLOOK

Hospital administrators must understand healthcare information technologies. The market for IT in healthcare could reach $56 billion by 2004, and U.S. hospitals and clinics could spend up to $748 million on electronic medical record systems, up more than 40 percent from 2000.

BUSINESS MANAGEMENT *Online*

For more information on management careers, go to:
busmanagement.glencoe.com

IDENTIFYING PAST AND PRESENT STRATEGIES To plan for the future, companies need to understand and appreciate their corporate history. Before a strategic change can be developed and implemented, the past and present strategies must be clarified. Strategic managers should ask these general questions:

- Has past strategy been developed?
- If not, can past history of the company be analyzed to identify the strategy that has evolved?
- If yes, has the strategy been recorded in writing?

DIAGNOSING PAST AND PRESENT PERFORMANCE To evaluate how past strategies have worked and to determine if strategic changes are needed, a corporate planner must examine the company's performance record, asking these questions:

- How is the company currently performing?
- How has it performed during the past few years?
- Is the performance trend moving up or down?

Good managers must address all of these questions before attempting to develop any type of future strategy. Once management has an accurate picture of the current status of the company, the next step is to establish goals.

Figure 10–4	AREAS FOR ESTABLISHING GOALS IN MOST COMPANIES
Profitability	Measures the degree to which the company is reaching an acceptable level of profits
Markets	Reflects the company's position in its marketplace
Productivity	Measures the efficiency of internal operations
Products	Describes the introduction or elimination of products or services
Financial resources	Reflects goals relating to the funding needs of the company
Physical facilities	Describes the physical facilities of the company
Research and innovation	Reflects the research, development, and/or innovation objectives
Organization structure	Describes objectives relating to changes in the company's structure and related activities
Human resources	Describes the human resource assets of the company
Social responsibility	Refers to the commitments of the firm regarding society and the environment

WORKING WITH CHARTS	In addition to financial performance, goals are established in many other areas of a company, including marketing and human resources. *What are some goals that these two departments might establish?*

◄ STANDARDS AND RULES
Companies depend on rules to set standards and implement strategy within an organization. *What are some ways that rules are used in your school?*

SETTING GOALS Goals are concise statements that provide direction for employees and set standards for achieving the company's strategic plan. Often goals are set in terms of financial performance, but goals are established in many other areas of the company (see **Figure 10–4**). To be effective, goals must be reevaluated as the environment and opportunities change. Long-range goals look beyond the current year, while short-range goals come from an in-depth evaluation of these long-range goals.

Normally, multiple goals are used to reflect the desired performance. A problem with giving only one goal is that it is often achieved at the expense of other desired goals. For example, if production is the only goal, quality may suffer in attempts to realize maximum production.

POLICIES, PROCEDURES, AND RULES To help in the goal-setting and strategy-formulation processes, the manager can rely on company policies and procedures. *Policies* are broad general guides to action that establish boundaries within which employees must operate. For example, a policy of "answering all written customer complaints in writing within 10 days" does not tell a manager exactly how to respond, but it does say it must be done within 10 days.

Procedures and rules may be thought of as low-level policies. A *procedure* is a detailed series of related steps or tasks written to implement a policy. Procedures define the methods through which policies are achieved. For example, a company's procedure on handling customer complaints might state that "the customer service representative must note the complaint on Form 622 and forward the yellow copy of the form to the customer complaint supervisor within six hours after receipt of the complaint."

Because procedures do not tell employees what to do in every situation, companies develop rules. *Rules* detail specific and definite corporate actions that employees must follow. Rules leave little doubt about what is to be done. They permit no flexibility or deviation. For example, "no smoking in the conference room" is a rule.

SWOT ANALYSIS Companies must develop a process that allows them to evaluate overall health. The most utilized process for determining a company's overall health is called **SWOT analysis**. SWOT is an acronym for **s**trengths, **w**eaknesses, **o**pportunities, and **t**hreats. A SWOT analysis is a technique that evaluates a company's internal strengths and weaknesses and its external opportunities and threats.

An internal analysis of the company can identify strengths and weaknesses. Assessing the external environment can identify threats and opportunities. This stresses the fact that companies do not operate all by themselves—they are affected by their surroundings.

St. Anthony Publishing in Reston, Virginia was having problems with one of its newsletters. The company was losing money because subscribers were not renewing subscriptions at the same rate they had in the previous 5 years. St. Anthony Publishing conducted a SWOT analysis. As a result, the company determined that the newsletter was not reporting on technological changes in the industry.

▲ SWOT ANALYSIS Companies conduct SWOT analyses to revise their strategic plans. *Why are these analyses important?*

RESPOND

How might you benefit from a SWOT analysis of your preparation for the job market?

BusinessWeek

Management Model

Yahoo! Act Two

When Terry S. Semel walked into the Sunnyvale (Calif.) headquarters of Yahoo! Inc. for his first day as chief executive on May 1, 2001, he faced an unenviable task. Ad sales at the Internet icon were plummeting, and the new CEO was replacing the well-liked Timothy Koogle, who had been pushed aside by the company's board. Worse, leery employees quickly saw that Semel, a retired Hollywood exec, didn't know Internet technology and looked stiffly out of place at Yahoo's playful, egalitarian headquarters.

Two years after taking control as chairman and CEO, Semel has silenced the doubters. By imposing his buttoned-down management approach on Yahoo, the 60-year-old has engineered one of the most remarkable revivals of a beleaguered dot-com.

Semel has done nothing less than remake the culture of the quintessential Internet company. The new Yahoo is grounded by a host of Old Economy principles that Semel lugged up the coast from Los Angeles. The contrast with Yahoo's go-go days is stark. At

Terry Semel's Yahoo, spontaneity is out. Order is in. New initiatives used to roll ahead following free-form brainstorming and a gut check. Now, they wind their way through a rugged gauntlet of tests and analysis.

Semel's not kidding about the homework. In the old days, Yahoo execs would brainstorm for hours, often following hunches with new initiatives. Those days are long gone. Under Semel, managers must prepare exhaustively before bringing up a new idea if it's to have a chance to survive.

It's a Darwinian drama that takes place in near-weekly meetings of a group called the Product Council. Dreamed up by a couple of vice-presidents and championed by Semel and his

chief operating officer, Daniel Rosensweig, a former president of CNET Networks Inc., the group typically includes nine managers from all corners of the company. The group sizes up business plans to make sure all new projects bring benefits to Yahoo's existing businesses.

It's all part of the growing buzz at Yahoo. Using his mix of discipline, sales, and deal-making, Terry Semel has pulled off a stunning revival. But can he pull off Act Two and build Yahoo into the digital theme park of his dreams? The fact that Yahoo shares are banging on the ceiling and not the floor is a vivid sign that Semel's turnaround may be just getting started.

Excerpted with permission from BusinessWeek, *June 2, 2003*

CRITICAL THINKING

What are some differences between the old and new management styles at Yahoo?

DECISION MAKING

What are the advantages and disadvantages of Semel's management style? Which style do you prefer?

As a result, St. Anthony Publishing developed a strategic plan to increase coverage of technological developments in that newsletter as well as other newsletters the company published. The most important result of a SWOT analysis is the ability to draw conclusions about the attractiveness of the company's situation and the need for strategic action.

Implementing Strategy

QUESTION

Why is implementing strategy often considered one of the most difficult phases of strategic management?

Once a company has formulated a strategy, it turns to the implementation phase of strategic management. **Implementing strategy** is the action stage of strategic management. Managers need to determine and implement the most appropriate company structure, motivate employees, develop short-range goals, and establish functional strategies. This can be the most difficult stage of strategic management.

Not only does a company have a strategic history, but it also has existing structures, policies, and systems. Although each of these factors can change, each must be dealt with as part of the implementation process. Structure can be changed, but the costs may be very high. For example, reorganization may result in substantial hiring and training costs for newly structured jobs. A company's current structure places certain restrictions on strategy implementation.

The strategy must fit with current company policies, or the conflicting policies must be changed. Sometimes past

▲ **STRATEGY EVALUATION** Managers must continuously evaluate and monitor the company's strategic plan. *Why is it necessary to evaluate the strategic plan?*

company policies heavily influence the extent to which future policies can be changed. For example, A.T. Cross Company, the manufacturer of world-class pens and pencils, has a policy of unconditionally guaranteeing its products for life. Because customers have come to expect this policy, Cross would find this policy difficult to discontinue.

Evaluating and Controlling the Strategic Plan

After the company's strategic plan is put into action, the next challenge is to evaluate strategy. **Evaluating strategy** is the process of continuously monitoring the company's progress toward its long-range goals and mission. Managers should ask:

- Does the grand strategy need revising?
- Where are problems likely to occur?

The three basic strategy evaluation activities are:

- Reviewing external and internal factors that are the bases for current strategies
- Measuring performance
- Taking corrective action

The emphasis on evaluating strategy is on making the company's managers aware of the problems that are likely to occur and of the actions to take if they do arise. Continuously evaluating and responding to internal and environmental changes is what strategic management is all about. This allows companies to plan ahead and avoid disaster.

Sometimes companies forget the importance of strategic planning and strategic evaluation. Those companies often find they have lost their "competitive edge." Strategic planning and evaluation should be done not just on a predetermined schedule, but as frequently as necessary, as determined by both internal and environmental factors.

Section 10.2 Assessment

 FACT AND IDEA REVIEW

1. What is the most important part of strategic management?
2. What are the three phases of the strategic management approach?
3. What is the difference between a policy, a procedure and a rule?
4. What are the four components of a SWOT analysis?
5. What are three basic evaluation activities?

 CRITICAL THINKING

1. **Evaluating Information:** Give an example of a company policy, procedure and rule.
2. **Drawing Conclusions:** Comment on the following statement, "Most companies succeed or fail based on their ability to react to environmental changes." What does this statement have to do with strategic management?

 ASSESSING SOCIAL STUDIES SKILLS

Use the Internet or the telephone directory to find a local company that does interesting strategic planning. Either visit or invite the owner to class, and ask the following questions:

1. What type of strategic planning does your company use?
2. Who is involved?
3. Do you have a mission statement?
4. Is there a downside to strategic planning?

 CASE ANALYSIS

You are the head of human resources at a bank. Last year, you created a strategy that gave every employee one additional week of paid vacation to retain more employees. Your boss asks you to evaluate the effectiveness of that strategy.

Apply: Write a memo explaining how you will evaluate the success of the strategy.

CHAPTER 10 ASSESSMENT

REVIEWING VOCABULARY

Give a definition and example for each of the following:

formal planning
operational planning
strategic planning
grand or corporate
 strategies
growth strategy
stability strategy
defensive or
 retrenchment strategy
combination strategy
business strategies
overall cost leadership
differentiation

functional
 strategies
strategic
 management
formulating
 strategy
mission statement
goals
SWOT analysis
implementing
 strategy
evaluating strategy

CHAPTER SUMMARY

Section 10.1

▶ Planning defines future objectives.

▶ Strategic planning is long range, while operational planning is short range.

▶ Grand strategies provide direction.

▶ Business strategies concentrate on how to compete in a given industry.

▶ Functional strategies deal with the activities of the different functional areas of the business.

Section 10.2

▶ Strategic management determines a company's direction and performance.

▶ Mission statements define purpose.

▶ Objectives or goals are statements that outline desired achievements.

▶ Policies are general guides to action that establish boundaries. Procedures are a series of related steps for a specific purpose. Rules are inflexible guidelines for employees.

▶ A SWOT analysis is a technique for evaluating a company's internal strengths and weaknesses and external opportunities and threats.

RECALLING KEY CONCEPTS

1. How does strategic planning differ from operational planning?
2. Define strategic management and explain the strategic management process.
3. What organizational factors need to be evaluated in implementing a strategic plan?
4. Explain the purpose of SWOT analysis. Why should it precede strategy selection?
5. What are the three retrenchment strategies?

THINKING CRITICALLY

1. Are mission statements necessary, or have they become obsolete?
2. How could you conduct a SWOT analysis in your personal life?

CHAPTER 10 ASSESSMENT

 ASSESSING ACADEMIC SKILLS

SOCIAL STUDIES Using the Internet, find a company that is strong in social responsibility. Make a list of what the company has done for the local community. Think of a local company that has made similar commitments to the community.

 APPLYING MANAGEMENT PRINCIPLES

SOLVE THE PROBLEM You work in the admissions office at a local university. The president of the school is developing a mission statement. She has asked you to research the mission statements of two other schools and evaluate them. Then she would like for you to present the material and discuss what you think needs to be addressed in the new mission statement.

Public Speaking Select two universities/colleges that have a written mission statement. Evaluate the mission statement based on length, explanation of academic opportunities, and discussion of student life.

What should you highlight in your school's mission statement? How can you distinguish your school from other colleges and universities? Prepare an oral report by clearly presenting your new ideas based on your findings.

 PREPARING FOR COMPETITIVE EVENTS

Indicate whether the following statements are true or false.

   a. A SWOT analysis looks mostly at a company's strengths.

   b. Strategic planning is long range and includes the formulation of goals.

   c. Rules are flexible guidelines for employees.

BusinessWeek ONLINE

In this chapter you read the *BusinessWeek* Management Model about Yahoo. For more information, go to *BusinessWeek* online at: **www.businessweek.com**

Using the Internet, find a current article on companies like Yahoo, such as Excite, Infoseek, or Lycos. What business strategies do these companies use? Write a two-page summary of the article and share it with the class.

CHAPTER 11

OPERATIONS MANAGEMENT AND PLANNING

PEPSICO

LEARNING OBJECTIVES

When you complete this chapter, you will be able to:

- Explain what operations managers do.
- Explain the differences between a continuous-flow and an intermittent-flow operating system.
- Name four ways businesses use computers to help them design, engineer, and manufacture products.
- Describe the factors managers must consider in choosing a site for their facilities.
- Describe the three kinds of facilities layouts.

READING STRATEGIES

As you read

- **PREDICT** what the section will be about.
- **CONNECT** what you read with your own life.
- **QUESTION** as you read to make sure you understand the content.
- **RESPOND** to what you read.

"Today size drives success. The bigger the better. Because that's how you achieve true economies of scale in manufacturing and distribution. Equally important, size enables a bottler to provide the service that large, geographically diverse retailers need—whether it's a single invoice or unified marketing support over a large area. So we've been aggressively consolidating more of our bottling volume among a handful of large, well-capitalized 'anchor bottlers' that are closely aligned with PepsiCo. . . ."

—Roger A. Enrico, PepsiCo, Chairman and CEO

WORKPLACE CONNECTIONS

Understanding Management

PepsiCo owns a number of snack-food and beverage brands. Several smaller bottling companies pay for the right to bottle and distribute Pepsi Cola to local vendors, such as supermarkets. By the late 1990s, many of the larger supermarket chains in the United States merged, creating huge corporations. PepsiCo, led by CEO Roger Enrico, responded to this change by consolidating its own bottling operations and by giving more business to larger bottling companies.

Analyzing Management Skills

Why would a large company like PepsiCo benefit from using local bottling companies to distribute its products?

Applying Management Skills

Have you, a friend, or family member ever worked for a company that reorganized its way of doing business?

BusinessWeek /ONLINE/

For further reading on managers and management go to:
www.businessweek.com

OPERATIONS MANAGEMENT

The Role of the Operations Manager

Ronald Crenshaw is responsible for marketing the inflatable pool toys his company produces. Vanessa Cheng handles all of the financial planning for a large data-processing company. Rick O'Brien oversees the production department at a 500-employee assembly plant. All of these people are managers. Each handles different kinds of issues. Each has a different set of responsibilities. Some of these responsibilities include ensuring that products are produced efficiently, that products and services are marketed to maximize sales, and that the company is earning a profit.

▲ **PRODUCTION OPERATIONS** The production manager is responsible for all of the activities involved in producing a company's products. *What are some of these activities?*

Product Manager

■ Nature of the Work

In industries that depend on staying ahead of technological developments, product managers are invaluable. They keep abreast of consumer demand for the products and services offered by their company as well as their competitors. Considering factors such as region, age, income, and lifestyle, product managers constantly reevaluate and identify the market for their products.

In addition to current and future market analysis and establishing prices for the product, product managers work with the marketing department to develop the advertising and promotional materials. They develop sales tools and train the sales team.

■ Working Conditions

Product managers work in comfortable offices, often near top management. They may work long hours, 40 to 50 hours per week, and may work under pressure.

■ Training, Other Qualifications, and Advancement

To become a product manager, you need a bachelor's or master's degree in liberal arts, or suitable experience in the field. You must have excellent research, presentation, and communication skills. Computer skills are also important for product managers in the technology industry.

■ Salary Range

Product managers earn $23,000 to $85,000. A vice-president of product development earns $105,000+. Salaries vary depending on responsibilities, education, and the size and location of the firm and the industry.

CRITICAL THINKING

What kind of pressures might a product manager face? Why do you think product managers need good research and communication skills? What other skills do you think would be helpful for this job?

STANDARD &POOR'S

INDUSTRY OUTLOOK

Experienced product managers will be invaluable in the world of the Internet. There will be demands for new equipment and software to link businesses and their employees with the Internet. Personal use will increase, too. About 59 percent of American households now own a PC, a result of less expensive computers.

BUSINESS MANAGEMENT Online

For more information on management careers, go to:

busmanagement.glencoe.com

Managers that are responsible for the activities involved in producing the goods or services for a company are called **operations managers.** Their activities include the following:

- choosing a process for producing the company's goods or services
- selecting a production site
- laying out the production facility
- designing production workers' jobs
- planning day-to-day production operations

FIGURE 11–1

What Is an Operating System?

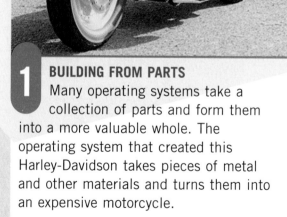

Operating systems transform labor and raw materials into goods or services. Different production processes require different kinds of operating systems.

1 BUILDING FROM PARTS
Many operating systems take a collection of parts and form them into a more valuable whole. The operating system that created this Harley-Davidson takes pieces of metal and other materials and turns them into an expensive motorcycle.

- controlling costs (see Chapter 20)
- monitoring inventories (see Chapter 20)

Operating Systems and Activities

An **operating system** consists of the processes and activities needed to produce goods or services. All organizations use some kind of operating systems, as **Figure 11–1** shows.

CONNECT

You're in charge of creating souvenirs for your school's 50th anniversary. Proceeds from the sale go to much-needed repairs for the school gym and auditorium. How would you design the product and assembly process in order to maximize profits?

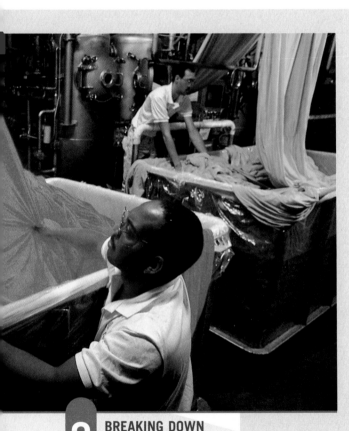

2 **BREAKING DOWN OF PARTS**
Some operating systems break down something large into smaller quantities of greater per-unit value. Fabric stores, for example, cut large bolts of fabric into smaller pieces that they sell for a higher price per yard.

3 **USING SKILL OR ARTISTRY**
A third type of operating system transforms simple materials into more valuable ones, usually as a result of labor. This potter, for example, uses her artistic skills to turn a simple piece of clay into a valuable bowl.

Operating systems are made up of people, materials, facilities, and information. As **Figure 11–2** shows, managers combine these inputs to produce the company's goods or services.

Businesses use two types of operating systems—continuous-flow systems and intermittent-flow systems. **Continuous-flow systems** are operating systems that function all the time, regardless of customer orders. **Intermittent-flow systems** are operating systems that operate only when an order needs to be filled.

To understand the difference between the two types of operating systems, consider the difference between McDonald's and Taco Bell. McDonald's uses a continuous-flow operating system. It makes a certain number of products, based on sales history, and hopes people will buy them. Taco Bell uses an intermittent-flow operating system. It does not produce anything until a customer places an order.

Continuous-Flow Systems

Continuous-flow operating systems are used to produce standardized products that a business keeps in stock. Production at the 3M

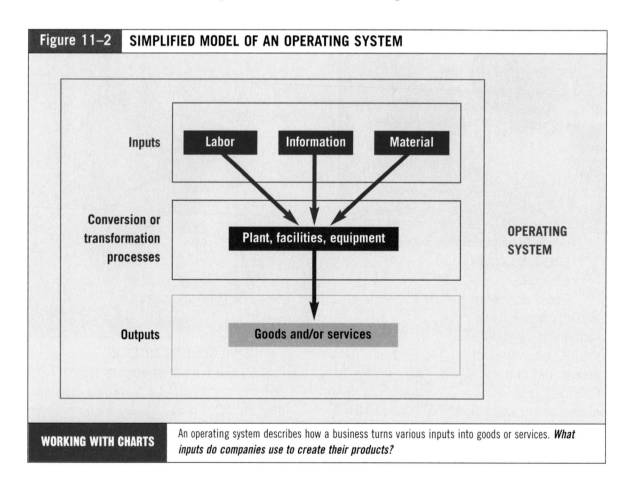

| Figure 11–2 | SIMPLIFIED MODEL OF AN OPERATING SYSTEM |

Inputs: Labor, Information, Material

Conversion or transformation processes: Plant, facilities, equipment

Outputs: Goods and/or services

OPERATING SYSTEM

WORKING WITH CHARTS An operating system describes how a business turns various inputs into goods or services. *What inputs do companies use to create their products?*

company, for example, occurs continuously throughout the year, allowing the company to turn out millions of rolls of Scotch™ tape. The company ships products to customers and stores the remainder in inventory.

Most large manufacturing companies use continuous-flow operations systems. These systems allow them to keep their assembly lines running all the time. This helps an assembly line achieve maximum efficiency and high profits.

Intermittent-Flow Systems

An intermittent-flow system is used to produce customized products and services. Shutters Unlimited, for example, makes custom wooden blinds. Each set of blinds is made to meet a particular set of customer specifications. The company maintains no finished-goods inventory because all products are immediately shipped to the customers who ordered them.

Most service companies use intermittent-flow systems. An advertising agency, for example, cannot use exactly the same production process for all of its clients, because each client has different needs. A construction company cannot use the same workers on every job, because every construction project is different. These kinds of businesses operate only in response to specific requests by customers.

▲ **OPERATING SYSTEM** Construction jobs vary greatly from project to project. *Which type of operating system is most suitable to this kind of business?*

Computer Technology for Operations Management

If you were to visit most large factories today, you would see something you would not have seen 50 years ago—computers. In many industries, computers have revolutionized the way businesses produce their products.

Four processes—computer-aided design, computer-aided engineering, computer-aided manufacturing, and computer-integrated manufacturing—have helped businesses streamline their operations. Managers need to be familiar with each of these processes.

QUESTION

What is the difference between an intermittent-flow operating system and a continuous-flow operating system?

Computer-Aided Design

Many companies use computer technology to design their products. Designing products with the help of computers is known as *computer-aided design,* or *CAD.* CAD helps companies create better products because it allows them to try various product designs without actually manufacturing the product. Computer simulation helps businesses identify defects or problems at the design stage, before they spend millions of dollars on production.

CAD has significantly reduced the time it takes companies to design new products. General Motors, for example, cut the time it takes to redesign a new model from 24 months to 14 months as a result of CAD.

Computer-Aided Engineering

Businesses also use computers to engineer products, a process known as *computer-aided engineering,* or *CAE.* Businesses use CAE to analyze the performance of a product under different conditions. A business interested in manufacturing a new bicycle helmet, for example, might use CAE to design several types of helmets. To determine which helmet provides the best protection, it would use CAE to test each helmet under various simulated conditions.

PREDICT

How can computers make the design and manufacturing processes more efficient?

▲ **TECHNOLOGY** Computers help companies design better products by identifying problems before the products go into production. *What is the process of using computers to design products called?*

◄ COMPUTER-INTEGRATED MANUFACTURING Many factories today use computers to design, engineer, and manufacture their products. *What are some of the benefits of using computer-integrated manufacturing?*

Computer-Aided Manufacturing

Companies sometimes use computers to actually produce the products they make. In *computer-aided manufacturing,* or *CAM,* computers provide instructions to automated production equipment, such as robots. To use CAM, businesses collect and store data on how a process should be performed. The computer then programs equipment to perform particular tasks. Automobile manufacturers, for example, use CAM extensively. Many of the tasks once performed by workers are now done by robots.

Computer-Integrated Manufacturing

Using computers to integrate all manufacturing operations into a single, smoothly operating manufacturing system is known as *computer-integrated manufacturing,* or *CIM.* Every aspect of manufacturing a product is aided by computers, including

- conception
- design and development
- production
- marketing
- product support

Businesses use CIM because it lowers manufacturing costs and reduces production time. CIM also improves product quality.

Tips from Robert Half

Higher positions do not mean shorter hours. Among executives surveyed, 76 percent said they spend more time in the office than they did five years ago. Employees who want to advance as a company expands will often work additional hours at home.

Figure 11–3

FACTORS TO CONSIDER IN SELECTING EQUIPMENT

- Availability of production workers able to operate equipment

- Training required to be able to operate equipment

- Availability of parts and services

- Availability of supplier assistance in installation and debugging

- Compatibility of equipment with existing equipment

- Maintenance record

- Flexibility of equipment in handling changes to product

- Safety

- Expected delivery date

- Warranty coverage

- Price

Choosing equipment for a company can be a difficult process. *How important a factor do you think the availability of parts and services is?*

Process Selection

The selection of an operating system is known as *process selection*. Process selection involves a wide range of decisions about the specific processes to use, the sequences in which to perform the processes, and the equipment to use. Once managers select the overall type of operations process, they need to make specific decisions about such issues as which type of equipment to use, which components to use, and which functions to automate.

All operating processes require equipment. Managers make decisions about purchasing or leasing equipment based on several factors, as **Figure 11–3** shows.

Site Selection

Entrepreneurs may come up with excellent ideas for a business but locate the business in the wrong place. A restaurant or retail store located in an area that few people visit is not likely to succeed. A factory located in an area where few people live may have difficulty finding workers. Choosing a location that meets the needs of a

▶ SITE SELECTION Saturn chose Spring Hill, Tennessee, as the site for its U.S. operations. *What was the main reason Saturn located there?*

business is a very important management decision. The process of selecting a location for a business is known as **site selection.**

Managers consider many factors in choosing a site for their businesses, as **Figure 11–4** shows. One of the most important factors is wage rate. Many manufacturing companies, including Guess! Jeans and Hewlett-Packard, operate manufacturing plants in Mexico, where labor costs are lower than those in the United States. Many clothing and shoe manufacturers, including Calvin Klein and Nike, also operate factories abroad to take advantage of low hourly wage rates.

Managers at the Saturn Corporation looked at many sites before choosing Spring Hill, Tennessee, in 1985. They wanted to attract and retain the workers they needed. They realized the attractiveness of location (climate, terrain, beauty), business atmosphere, community interest, and proximity to quality education. Saturn's recent plant development in 1998 in Wilmington, Delaware, also exhibits this concern for both employee and community.

When a company outgrows its facilities, managers face three options for obtaining more space. They can

- expand the site
- move the entire operation to another site
- add another facility elsewhere

Many businesses first try to expand their current facilities in order to avoid the expense of moving or the inconvenience of operating more than one facility.

Figure 11–4	FACTORS TO CONSIDER IN CHOOSING A SITE

- Cost of land
- Cost of plant construction
- Location of competitors
- Location of customers
- Transportation costs
- Cost of materials
- Labor costs
- Taxes
- Availability of materials, supplies, and workers
- Strength of labor unions
- Community attitudes
- Political situation
- Laws
- Climate
- Living conditions

Businesses consider a range of factors in selecting a site. *Why do you think it is important for a business to consider a community's attitudes toward business?*

Facilities Layout

After selecting a site, a company must design its facilities. **Facilities layout** is the process of planning the physical arrangement of a facility. It includes identifying where office space, meeting rooms, customer service areas, eating areas, production areas, equipment, storage space, bathrooms, hallways, and other areas will be located.

QUESTION

Why is site selection important to a company?

Materials Handling

Managers must closely coordinate the design and layout of their facilities with the design of the materials-handling system. A **materials-handling system** is the network that receives, stores, and moves materials between processing points within a factory.

Many factors, including the size, shape, weight, density, and flexibility of materials, affect a facility's layout. Some materials require special handling and storage. Computer chips, for example, should not be exposed to humidity, light, or extreme temperatures. In designing the facilities layout, computer manufacturers must take these special factors into account.

Operations managers also need to consider the equipment that will be needed to transport products. Companies that use forklifts, for example, must create wide aisles to accommodate them.

Types of Layouts

Most companies use one of three types of layouts: product layout, process layout, or fixed-position layout. The kind of layout a business chooses depends on the type of product or service it produces.

PRODUCT LAYOUT A *product layout* groups equipment and staff based on the various steps involved in producing a product. Such layouts are often set up as assembly lines. For example, a commercial bakery uses a product layout to produce cakes. In the first stage of production, workers combine ingredients to form a batter. In the second stage, workers fill cake pans. In the next stage, workers put pans into the oven and take them out. In the fourth stage, workers ice the cakes. In the final stage, workers box the cakes.

A product layout is efficient because it simplifies production planning. It also allows workers to specialize in a small number of simple tasks. This kind of layout may cause problems. First, workers who perform a limited number of repetitive tasks often grow bored. Second, an assembly line can move only as fast as the slowest link in the chain.

In the case of the bakery, for example, the batter mixers, cake bakers, and boxers could perform their tasks very quickly. If, however, the cake icers fall behind, the entire assembly line will have to slow down to accommodate them.

PROCESS LAYOUT A *process layout* groups together equipment and staff that perform similar functions. To see how this kind of layout works, think about how a newspaper is produced. First, the various editorial departments write the articles.

▲ **FACILITY LAYOUT** Many kinds of businesses cannot use assembly lines to produce their goods or services. *What kind of layout does this tree service use?*

Second, the typesetting department typesets the articles. Third, the printing department prints the papers. Once the papers are printed, a fourth department assembles the various sections of the paper and ties the completed papers together.

The main advantage of the process layout is that employees perform a wider variety of tasks than do people working on assembly lines. As a result, they are less likely to become bored at their jobs and more likely to perform well. A disadvantage of the process layout is that it requires highly skilled workers.

FIXED-POSITION LAYOUT The third kind of layout is the *fixed-position layout*. In this kind of layout, the product is too large to move and remains in one place. Manufacturing of very large products, such as ships or airplanes, and construction of most houses and buildings use the fixed-position layout. A disadvantage of fixed-position layout is that it is not always as efficient as a product layout or a process layout.

Section 11.1 Assessment

 FACT AND IDEA REVIEW

1. What is the role of the operations manager?
2. What are the two types of operating systems? How do they differ?
3. Name four ways that businesses use computers to produce the goods they sell.
4. Name five factors to be considered when choosing equipment.

 CRITICAL THINKING

1. **Drawing Conclusions:** What kind of operating system would a large candy manufacturer most likely use? Why?
2. **Predicting Outcomes:** What kind of production process would you select if your workforce consisted entirely of unskilled workers? Explain your answer.

 ASSESSING ART SKILLS

Choose one of the three types of layouts described in the chapter. Then prepare a scale drawing of a plant based on the layout type you chose.

 CASE ANALYSIS

Your company, a multinational footwear manufacturer, has decided to expand its production. You have been asked to prepare a list of possible locations for a new factory that will employ 400 unskilled workers.

Apply: Think about the factors you should consider in making your recommendations. Then write a one-page memo that describes the advantages to your company of building a new factory in the location you chose.

JOB DESIGN AND PLANNING

WHAT YOU'LL LEARN

▶ How managers design jobs.
▶ Factors affecting the physical work environment.
▶ The role of the Occupational Safety and Health Administration.
▶ How managers plan aggregate production.

WHY IT'S IMPORTANT

Careful planning of a business's day-to-day operations is necessary if companies are to use their resources efficiently.

KEY TERMS

• job design
• aggregate production planning
• activity scheduling

Job Design

Lisa Bryan just took over as the manager of a 75-employee insurance company. To perform her job, she needs to understand exactly what each of the 75 people in the company does. She needs to become familiar with the job designs of the people who work for her. A **job design** describes the work an individual or group of individuals is supposed to perform.

Job Characteristics

Job designs can be described in terms of five key characteristics:

• skill variety
• task identify
• task significance
• autonomy
• feedback

Skill variety refers to the number of different skills a worker needs to perform a job. Security officers who only check people's bags as they enter a building have little skill variety in their jobs. People whose jobs demand little skill variety often become bored at work.

Task identity refers to the degree to which a job allows a worker to complete an entire task rather than just part of the task. Mechanics who work at small garages have a high degree of task identity because they are responsible for every aspect of the job of repairing cars. In contrast, mechanics on assembly lines that do nothing but check transmissions have a lower degree of task identity.

Task significance refers to the level of impact a job has on the whole organization. Workers who feel that their work affects the organization generally have high job satisfaction. Workers who feel that their jobs do not affect others rarely share this feeling.

Autonomy refers to the independence workers have to make decisions about how to perform their jobs. Check-out clerks in supermarkets have almost no job autonomy. In contrast, supermarket store managers are able to decide how they spend their time. They evaluate the tasks they need to accomplish during the day and perform them in the order they choose. Most people prefer to have some autonomy in their jobs.

Feedback involves the extent to which managers let workers know how they are performing. Feedback can be presented in a formal or informal manner (see Chapter 15). People who receive feedback are generally happier at work than people who do not.

People who hold jobs that rank high in these five characteristics are more motivated than other workers are. They also produce better-quality work (see **Figure 11–5**). Finally, they are more satisfied with their jobs and have lower rates of absenteeism and turnover.

The Physical Work Environment

To attract and retain good workers, managers need to provide a satisfactory and pleasant physical work environment. Poor work environments may prevent employees from working efficiently. Examples of negative environments are those that are too hot or cold, poorly ventilated, noisy, poorly lit, or crowded.

▲ **SKILL VARIETY** A ticket-taker's job requires very few skills. *How might skill variety affect job performance?*

CONNECT

Describe the job characteristics of your current job or one that you would like to hold.

Figure 11–5	THE IMPORTANCE OF JOB DESIGN

Core Job Characteristics	**Work Outcomes**
Skill variety	High level of work motivation
Task identity	High quality work performance
Task significance	
Autonomy	High satisfaction with work
Feedback	Low absenteeism and turnover

WORKING WITH CHARTS

Managers need to design jobs that motivate their employees. *Why do you think workers whose jobs allow them some autonomy are more satisfied with their jobs than workers whose jobs do not?*

Managers must ensure that the work environment is safe. The Occupational Safety and Health Act of 1970 established specific safety guidelines governing most workplaces. The law is enforced by the *Occupational Safety and Health Administration (OSHA),* a federal government agency that inspects workplaces to ensure that they comply with OSHA regulations. Businesses that violate OSHA standards are subject to fines and closure.

RESPOND

How important are workplace safety standards to you in considering a job? Explain the reasons for your answer.

In general, the work area should allow for normal lighting, ventilation, and humidity. Exposure to less than ideal conditions should be limited to short periods. Managers should minimize potential physical or psychological damage to employees.

Day-To-Day Operations Planning

Designing an effective operating system does not ensure that the system will operate efficiently. Managers need to carefully plan day-to-day operations to ensure that production proceeds smoothly and that costs are low. This process of planning a business's production needs is known as *production planning*.

Production planning involves three components:

- aggregate production planning
- resource allocation
- activity scheduling

WORKPLACE DIVERSITY

TAIWAN
Traditional Taiwanese office workers—and even high-level executives—take a short nap after lunch, between 1:00 and 1:30 P.M. The office management cooperates by dimming the lights and keeping activity to a minimum. Obviously, this is not a good time for an appointment.

Aggregate Production Planning

Roberto Nunez is the production manager of a South Carolina company that manufactures towels. As part of his job, he needs to estimate what resources his company will need in the next 6 to 18 months to produce enough towels to meet demand. This part of Roberto's job is aggregate production planning.

A Cutting-Edge Strategy Called Sharing

Thousands of small manufacturers are skating on thin ice. Most earn their keep by producing parts for large suppliers who serve masters such as the Big Three or the Pentagon. But the Boeings, Chryslers, and TRWs of the world no longer want to bother buying parts from a score of suppliers. To assure quality and to speed products to market quickly, they want one company to take responsibility for the whole thing. For a company with 10 or 15 employees, that can be asking for the moon.

So independent small manufacturers are learning a new skill: electronic data interchange.

EDI involves linking companies together electronically so their computers can automatically handle many business chores, from dealing with purchase orders to exchanging blueprints. The system is critical today, when all facets of product development, from design to final assembly planning, happen simultaneously and in different locations.

TALENT POOL. Hundreds of small manufacturers in the U.S. and abroad are learning to think

as one by joining flexible manufacturing networks. The members of these mini-consortiums pool talents for jobs too big for any one of them to tackle.

Going digital would reap many benefits. Small companies could then connect to a shared database and instantly coordinate production schedules and blueprint revisions. The flexible manufacturing alliances can organize smaller teams for contracts that last only as long as it takes to get a specific job done.

While such a concept may seem foreign to most executives in the job-shop business, others are quick to spot a parallel. "We thought we were a flexible

manufacturing group until someone told us we were really a virtual corporation," says Robert E. Steele, chief operating officer of PosiTech Manufacturing Group, an alliance of nine small companies in West Virginia. "We've become a virtually large company. But instead of farming out work to internal departments, we farm it to our member companies."

Considering the benefits, EDI is not expensive. Setting up a system—including a computer, modem, software, and certification of compliance with EDI standards—can cost $3,000 to $5,000.

Excerpted with permission from BusinessWeek, *November 20, 1995*

CRITICAL THINKING

Why are companies demanding that all phases of product development be integrated?

DECISION MAKING

As a manager for a small manufacturing company, decide if you would use an EDI system. Explain your reasoning.

CONNECT

If the demand for your company's product suddenly increased, how would you plan to meet that demand?

Aggregate production planning uses an organization's resources to produce enough goods or services to meet demand. Roberto relies on his company's demand forecasts to make decisions about production planning. Last month's forecast indicated that the company expects to ship 20,000 towels a month for six months. Based on this forecast, Roberto calculates the workers and supplies necessary to meet this goal. His aggregate production plan establishes production rates, workforce needs, and inventory levels for the operating system for the next six months.

Resource Allocation

Roberto must make decisions about resource allocation to produce 20,000 towels a month. *Resource allocation* is the allocation of people, materials, and equipment to meet the operating system requirements.

Roberto can spend $18,000 on production. He must allocate these resources to labor, textile purchases, shipping expenses, and equipment maintenance. Allocating these resources efficiently will keep company costs low

All About

ATTITUDE

DIRECTIONS TO CARNEGIE HALL—PRACTICE!

Professional athletes and entertainers rehearse their moves over and over again. This repetition leads to greater accuracy. The more accurate you become at something, the more likely you are to be confident at your abilities. Practice makes perfect.

▶ **ACTIVITY SCHEDULING** To make the most efficient use of expensive machinery, production managers create detailed activity schedules that indicate when each machine will be used. *What would happen if these schedules were not made?*

while producing quality goods. Inefficient allocation of resources may prevent Roberto's company from competing in its market.

Activity Scheduling

Activity scheduling involves creating a detailed production timetable. It involves *loading* and *dispatching*. *Loading* is the term production managers use for assigning a job to a factory or department. *Dispatching* refers to the scheduling of each task that is performed in the factory.

To schedule work at his company, Roberto first decides which towels will be produced by each of his company's two factories. He then prepares a detailed schedule that indicates when the towels will be cut, sewn, dyed, and boxed. His schedule identifies which workers and equipment will be involved. This increases efficiency and ensures that all workers understand their role in the production process.

Section 11.2 Assessment

 FACT AND IDEA REVIEW

1. List the five job characteristics managers need to consider in designing jobs.
2. Explain the concept of task identity.
3. Which federal government agency inspects workplaces to ensure that they are safe?
4. What is resource allocation?
5. How do production managers schedule production activity?

 CRITICAL THINKING

1. **Analyzing Information:** How does a production manager use forecasts of demand for the company's products?
2. **Making Comparisons:** Using the five job characteristics identified in the chapter, create a table comparing a police officer's job with that of a telemarketer.

 ASSESSING MATH SKILLS

Ronald Lewis, the production manager of a factory that produces metal lunch boxes, needs to produce 1,800 units a week for the next nine months. To do so, he plans to schedule 22 workers a day, 8 hours a day, 5 days a week. If the average wage in the factory is $8.02 per hour, how much will weekly labor costs run? If total production costs run $17,000 a week, what percent of these costs does labor represent?

CASE ANALYSIS

As the production manager of a small glassware factory, you are responsible for designing jobs and planning production.

Apply: Write a one-page essay describing specific features that you would build into the job designs at your company in order to create jobs that motivate workers.

CHAPTER 11 ASSESSMENT

CHAPTER SUMMARY

Section 11.1

▶ Operations managers are responsible for activities involved in producing company goods or services.

▶ Two types of operating systems are continuous-flow and intermittent-flow.

▶ Businesses use computer-aided design, computer-aided engineering, computer-aided manufacturing, and computer-integrated manufacturing to help design, engineer, and manufacture products.

▶ There are many factors to consider in site selection.

▶ The three types of facilities layouts are product layout, process layout, and fixed position layout.

Section 11.2

▶ Job design describes the work an individual or group is supposed to perform.

▶ Production planning includes aggregate production planning, resource allocation, and activity scheduling.

REVIEWING VOCABULARY

Together with a partner, discuss the meaning of each of the following terms:

operations manager
operating system
continuous-flow system
intermittent-flow system
site selection
facilities layout

materials-handling system
job design
aggregate production planning
activity scheduling

RECALLING KEY CONCEPTS

1. What are the two types of operating systems?
2. Describe the three types of facility layouts.
3. What is a materials-handling system?
4. List five important characteristics of well-designed jobs.
5. What are the three main components of production planning?

THINKING CRITICALLY

1. How much control do you think operations managers have over the job satisfaction of their employees?
2. What kinds of companies use continuous-flow operating systems? Intermittent-flow systems? Why do you think different types of companies use different operating systems?
3. What can computers do to help with modern assembly line planning?
4. Give an example of how resource allocation works at your school.

CHAPTER 11 ASSESSMENT

 ## ASSESSING ACADEMIC SKILLS

COMPUTER SKILLS Use the Internet or the resources at your public library to research how businesses use computers to design, engineer, and manufacture products. Prepare a two-page paper that discusses what you have learned. Be sure to identify your sources, including the addresses of any Web sites.

 ## APPLYING MANAGEMENT PRINCIPLES

SOLVE THE PROBLEM Three of your friends are thinking of starting their own businesses and have asked you for advice. One friend plans to start a landscaping company. A second plans to start a manufacturing company that will produce calendars and greeting cards. A third plans to start his own catering company.

Language Arts Write a short memo to each of your friends. In each memo, identify which type of operating system and facility layout you believe is appropriate. Explain each of your recommendations.

PREPARING FOR COMPETITIVE EVENTS

Answer true or false to the following statements.

a. A continuous-flow system operates only when there is an order that needs to be filled.

b. The OSHA inspects workplaces to ensure that safety guidelines are being met.

BusinessWeek ONLINE

In this chapter you read the *BusinessWeek* Management Model about electronic data interchange (EDI) systems. Using the Internet or your school library, find additional articles about EDI systems and share your findings with the class. For more information, go to *BusinessWeek* online at: **www.businessweek.com**

CASE STUDY 4

Capacity Planning

OVERVIEW

Have you ever waited in a long line? Were you frustrated? What was holding it up? While these questions might seem trivial, the answers are important to operations managers. Customers want quality products and prompt services. Therefore, businesses must continuously analyze their processes. This case study illustrates a technique that helps managers determine the capacity of their facilities. *Capacity* is defined as the highest rate of output possible for a facility. Capacity planning allows managers to adapt to both short-term and long-term changes in demand.

RESOURCES

- poster board or flip chart
- colored markers

PROCEDURES

◆ STEP A ◆

The Bottleneck

Every business has a process made up of stages that transform inputs into finished goods or services. The stage that takes the longest time to complete is called the *bottleneck*.

Apply your understanding of capacity (maximum output rate) in this case study:

Jim Thomas owns *Formula One Quick Lube*. Recently his company has been unable to keep up with demand for his services. Long lines are starting to form. Jim's facility has two bays for servicing cars. A time-motion study showed that the work is broken down into five stages:

Stage 1	Greet the customer	45 seconds
Stage 2	Vacuum/clean windows	240 seconds
Stage 3	Drain oil/replace oil filter	510 seconds
Stage 4	Fill new oil	195 seconds
Stage 5	Pay the cashier	80 seconds

Jim has five full-time employees. One employee works at each stage.

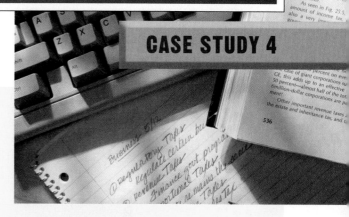

CASE STUDY 4

Analyzing and Evaluating Information:

1. In small groups, identify the bottleneck for *Formula One Quick Lube*. What is the current rate of output? (Hint: Divide one hour by the bottleneck time.)

2. How many cars can be serviced daily from 8:00 AM to 6:00 PM? What is the maximum number of cars that can be serviced seven days a week?

3. If the average price per customer is $19.99, what are Jim's maximum potential gross revenues per month? Per year?

◆ STEP B ◆

The Economy and Production

Businesses are confronted with economic challenges that pertain to the business cycle. During expansionary periods, businesses are pressured to increase the number of variable inputs (such as employees and raw materials) to meet short-term demand. At some point, however, a company must consider expanding other factors of production (such as equipment). Managers can use capacity planning to meet economic challenges during the business cycle.

Drawing Conclusions:

1. In your groups, examine the contractionary and expansionary phases of the business cycle. Under each phase, identify three operational (short-term) challenges that Jim will need to plan for, and three responses that Jim could make.

2. Describe three strategic (long-term) decisions that Jim could make to increase the rate of output during a prolonged expansionary period.

◆ STEP C ◆

Management Report

In your small groups, brainstorm and use creativity to demonstrate the importance of capacity planning. Using poster boards or flip charts, prepare a 15-minute presentation that includes the following:

1. Introduce Jim's current rate of output for *Formula One Quick Lube*.

2. Develop a new operating system that increases the rate of output in the short run without altering the current physical facilities.

3. Address the short-term challenges and the responses that Jim could make under different economic climates.

4. Analyze the impact of capacity on a company's pricing strategy by focusing on a firm's breakeven analysis. Why are both numbers important? How do the numbers aid Jim in his planning efforts?

5. Discuss two grand strategies that Jim could implement to grow *Formula One Quick Lube* in the future.

Organizing Skills

IN THIS UNIT...

You will be introduced to the value of organization for any well-run business. Introduced in this unit are chapters on organizing work, organizational structure, understanding work groups, and working with employees.

Journal Writing

In your journal, assess your knowledge of management by writing about the following:

1. What is the difference between *power* and *authority*?

2. Why do you think most organizations divide their employees into departments?

3. What kind of group norms does your group of friends set for each other?

CHAPTER 12

ORGANIZING AND WORK

LEARNING OBJECTIVES

When you have completed this chapter, you will be able to:

- Recognize the reasons for organizing work.
- Understand how businesses prevent their workers from losing interest in their jobs.
- Explain why managers need to delegate authority and responsibility.

READING STRATEGIES

As you read

- **PREDICT** what the section will be about.
- **CONNECT** what you read with your own life.
- **QUESTION** as you read to make sure you understand the content.
- **RESPOND** to what you read.

SATURN

Understanding Management

The Saturn company began in the mid-1980s as the brainchild of a group of 99 General Motors employees. Working conditions at the company's Spring Hill, Tennessee, plant are different from the typical assembly line factory. Saturn "team members" have the freedom to improve the production process. Within a few years, Saturn won awards for the quality of its vehicles. Other companies now look to Saturn for new and effective ways to manage workers.

Analyzing Management Skills

How might involving employees in making decisions help factory operations run more smoothly?

Applying Management Skills

You are in charge of building your school's homecoming float with ten volunteers. How would you organize them?

BusinessWeek *ONLINE*

For further reading on managers and management go to:
www.businessweek.com

"MANAGEMENT TALK"

"We believe that all people want to be involved in decisions that affect them, care about their jobs and each other, take pride in themselves and in their contributions, and want to share in the success of their efforts."

—the Saturn Team, in concert with the UAW and General Motors

DESIGNING ORGANIZATIONS

WHAT YOU'LL LEARN

➤ How organizing helps groups of people achieve results they could not achieve individually.
➤ Three reasons why businesses organize workforces.
➤ Nine characteristics of successful organizations.
➤ How businesses prevent workers from losing interest in highly specialized jobs.
➤ Why businesses decentralize their operations.

WHY IT'S IMPORTANT

Without a well-defined organization, no business can be successful.

KEY TERMS

• organization
• authority
• chain of command
• division of labor
• job rotation
• job scope
• job depth

What Is an Organization?

A team of enthusiastic preschoolers shows up for its first soccer meet. The team takes the field, but none of the players know where to stand. The children on the team run madly every time the ball is kicked, but no one passes the ball or sets up a play. The lack of organization results in chaos.

On the next field, a group of high-school students competes. The teams are well organized, with all team members playing their positions well. The competition is fierce, and plays are well executed.

What distinguishes these two scenarios is the organization of the teams. The preschool team is a disorganized group of individuals. It has no plan for how to work together to achieve its goals. The high-school team takes the field with a clear-cut plan on how to work together to beat its opponents.

▲ **ORGANIZATION** Without organization, this team of soccer players would not be able to work together to score goals. *What role does organization play in a business?*

The high-school students' team represents an **organization**, a group of people working together in a coordinated effort to reach certain goals. Organizations are formed to help groups of individuals work together as efficiently and effectively as possible. In business, as in soccer, organizations help people achieve better results than they could working individually.

All organizations need managers, people who direct the activity of others. Without managers, some people in the organization might not act in ways that help the organization meet its goals. The manager's job is to make sure that everyone in the organization works together in a coordinated manner.

Why Do Businesses Organize Their Workforces?

Organizations are formed for three basic reasons: to create clear lines of authority, to improve productivity, and to make it easier for people within a company to communicate with each other. In addition to increasing profit, workers feel a sense of stability and belonging when working for an effective organization.

Establishing Lines of Authority

One of the main reasons businesses organize is to establish authority within a group. **Authority** is power based on the rights that come with a position. The President of the United States, for example, has the authority to order U.S. troops into battle. Likewise, chief executive officers have the authority to make important decisions about the companies that they run. Store managers have the authority to approve returns or offer discounts on damaged merchandise.

Establishing authority is important in an organization. Without lines of authority, decisions could be made by people not qualified to make them. Salesclerks, for example, could change the prices of the products they sell. Bank tellers

International Management

LATIN AMERICA

Latin American management styles tend to be multi-focused on many simultaneous issues. Tasks are completed through the strength of relationships. It may be challenging for a manager who is single-focused to be constantly interrupted or asked to wait while something more pressing takes precedence.

BusinessWeek ONLINE For further reading about International Management go to: **www.businessweek.com**

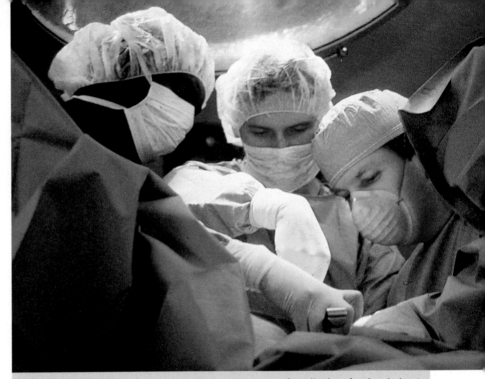

▲ **CHAIN OF COMMAND** The surgeon leading this team of medical professionals is at the top of the chain of command. *How does the chain of command in an operating room compare to that in a business organization?*

PREDICT

What are some of the advantages of a chain of command?

could make loan decisions. Establishing lines of authority means that decisions are made only at the appropriate level.

The line of authority within an organization is known as the **chain of command**. In the business world, the chain of command begins with the chief executive officer. Beneath the chief executive officer are other senior managers, who in turn supervise mid-level managers. Mid-level managers supervise lower-level managers, who in turn supervise their own workers.

ADVANTAGES OF A WELL-DEFINED CHAIN OF COMMAND A well-defined chain of command makes it easy for all members of an organization to understand who is in charge. A counter person in the deli department of a supermarket, for example, understands that he or she reports to the deli manager. The deli manager understands that he or she reports to the store manager. Store managers know that they report to the regional manager, who in turn reports to the corporate office.

This kind of organization means that problems are addressed at the lowest possible level. Only problems that cannot be handled by an immediate supervisor are brought to the attention of higher-level managers. For example, at the media store, all returns will be handled by sales associates, except for those damaged items returned without a receipt. The store manager will tend to these special returns.

Convention Services Manager

■ Nature of the Work

Convention services managers may work for hotels, all kinds of professional organizations, and other businesses. They coordinate all the activities and services necessary to host large meetings, conventions, and special events. They meet with the organization representatives, plan lodging requirements, make reservations, arrange entertainment and speakers, choose the number of meeting rooms, and coordinate food services. During the event, they resolve unexpected problems and see that hotel operations conform to the expectations of the group.

■ Working Conditions

Convention service managers work in pleasant surroundings, either in their offices or at convention sites. They often deal with stressful situations and deadlines. They may work more than 40 hours a week, evenings or weekends, and may travel to convention sites.

■ Training, Other Qualifications, and Advancement

To become a convention services manager, you need a bachelor's degree in liberal arts, plus hotel experience; or a bachelor's degree in hotel or food management. Internships, work study programs, or part-time work in hotels or food service are useful and are recommended. You must be able to work with people under stressful conditions and tight deadlines. Communication skills are essential, as are the abilities to problem-solve, concentrate on details, organize, and direct the work of others.

■ Salary Range

The average salary for a convention services manager is $43,000. This varies with location, size and type of company or organization, as well as responsibilities and experience.

CRITICAL THINKING

Name three problems that could arise during the course of a large convention. Come up with possible solutions.

STANDARD &POOR'S

INDUSTRY OUTLOOK

In 2002, the U.S. lodging industry occupancy rate was 59.2 percent and revenue per available room (REVPAR) was $83.15. The lodging industry increased total room supply by 1.8 percent, while demand for rooms increased 0.8 percent. Full year room revenue for the industry was down a modest 0.7 percent from 2001 to $77.5 billion.

BUSINESS MANAGEMENT *Online*

For more information on management careers, go to:
busmanagement.glencoe.com

DISADVANTAGES OF A WELL-DEFINED CHAIN OF COMMAND Establishing a chain of command can create problems if the structure is too rigid or too complicated. Too many layers of management make assigning responsibility difficult. It also means that decisions are made slowly, often by people with only a limited understanding of the issues involved.

During the past few decades, many companies with complicated bureaucracies saw profits tumble. In response, many tried to simplify their organizational structures. The Ford Motor Company reduced the number of levels of management from 15 to nine during the 1990s. It recognized that the large number of management levels slowed decision making, thus preventing quick response to customer needs. The company's reorganization increased Ford's ability to respond rapidly to market changes. This is a crucial advantage in a highly competitive industry.

Improving Productivity

Organizing involves the **division of labor**, or the assignment of specific tasks to individuals or groups. In 1776, Adam Smith, a Scottish philosopher, showed that individuals and economies could increase their wealth by dividing labor by tasks. In *The Wealth of Nations* Smith illustrated his idea with a simple example of a pin factory.

Each worker in a pin factory could perform each step of the production process—forming the metal, sharpening the point, creating the pin head, and so forth. Smith showed that the factory could increase the number of pins it produced if each worker specialized in a particular function. The factory, Smith argued, could produce more pins if it assigned some workers to sharpen pins and others to work on pin heads. Businesses apply this principle today by organizing their workforces into groups of people that perform specialized functions (**Figure 12–1**).

SPECIALIZATION In many companies, groups of workers perform very specific tasks or sets of tasks. Electronics companies, for example, have workers who do nothing but check electrical connections. Banks have employees who do nothing but process checks. Such workers are easy to train, because they only need to master a limited set of skills.

Some specialization can increase the productivity of a business. Too much specialization, however, can cause boredom. Managers prevent this by taking steps to make specialized jobs more interesting.

JOB ROTATION **Job rotation** involves periodically moving workers from one job to another. By rotating workers through different positions, managers prevent workers from becoming bored. They also create a multiskilled workforce.

CONNECT

Imagine your ideal "dream job." What levels of job depth and job scope would it have?

FIGURE 12–1

The Division of Labor

The division of labor helps managers increase productivity by organizing their workforces efficiently.

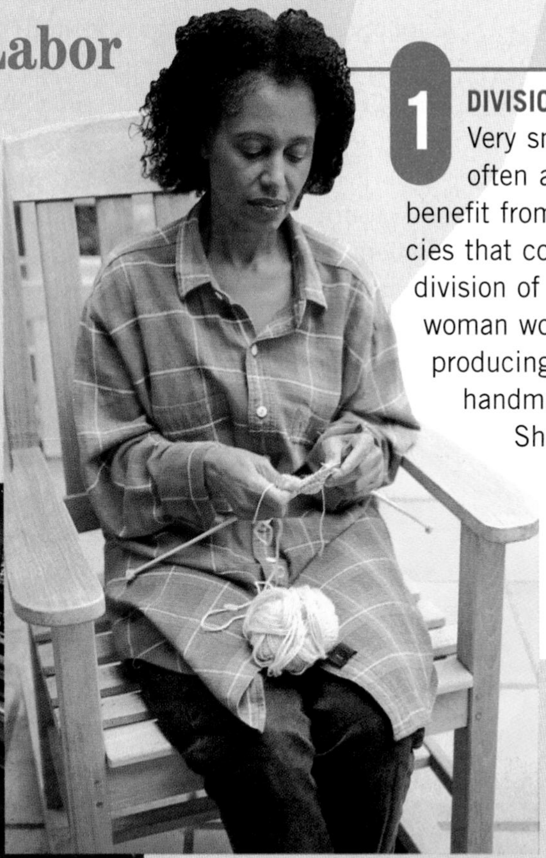

1 DIVISION OF LABOR
Very small businesses often are unable to benefit from the efficiencies that come with the division of labor. This woman works alone producing and selling handmade sweaters. She handles all functions herself, from purchasing wool to billing customers.

2 SPECIALIZATION
This factory is large enough to enable workers to specialize in specific tasks. Some workers spend all of their time sewing seams. Workers in another part of the factory put in zippers. By specializing in a task, workers become very good at what they do.

3 MANAGERS
Managers are needed when many people work together within an organization. One of a manager's most important functions is to assign jobs to workers so that the company produces its goods efficiently.

JOB SCOPE Job scope refers to the number of operations involved in a job. In a job with narrow scope, a worker performs a small number of operations and repeats them frequently. Assembly-line workers who only adjust tires, for example, have very limited job scope. People with limited job scope often become bored with their jobs, and the quality of their work declines.

People with a broad job scope perform many job functions. Account managers for advertising firms, for example, meet with clients, develop strategies, brainstorm creative ideas, track market changes and advances with the competition, and produce commercials. Most people find a job with broad scope more satisfying than one with narrow scope.

JOB DEPTH Job depth is the freedom employees have to plan and organize their work, interact with co-workers, and work at their own pace. Corporate sales representatives, for example, often are given considerable freedom to perform their jobs. Many decide for themselves which customers or potential customers they want to call on and how much of their budget they want to spend trying to win a new account. Their days are much less regulated than those of many office workers.

RESPOND

What role does a manager play in improving the effectiveness of an organization?

▲ **TEAM BUILDING** This team of Honda workers is responsible for a large number of functions. *Why do you think Honda uses teams of workers rather than the traditional assembly-line approach, in which workers perform a few highly specialized tasks?*

Improving Communication

Members of an organization need to communicate with each other to help their organization achieve goals. Managers must communicate goals, strategies, policies, and procedures to their staff. Employees must communicate ideas, results, and problems to their managers.

Organizational structure allows companies that employ hundreds or thousands to communicate with their employees in an organized manner. This is done through meetings, memos, e-mail, telephone conversations, and informal encounters between employees. Communication ensures that all employees understand company expectations.

What Makes an Organization Effective?

No single formula guarantees success for an organization. Many successful organizations do share certain characteristics that are shown in **Figure 12–2**.

Knowing Your Customers and Responding to Their Needs

The success of a business ultimately depends on identifying what customers want and providing it. To do so, companies need to understand customers and respond quickly to their needs.

Kodak owes much of its success to commitment to the customer. George Eastman, company founder, created the first simple camera for general use in 1888. This camera was introduced with the slogan, "You push the button, we do the rest." Cameras became accessible to everyone, not just professionals.

▲ MEETING CUSTOMER NEEDS To succeed in the business world, companies must change to keep up with customer needs. *What are some ways that Kodak has done this?*

Figure 12–2	CHARACTERISTICS OF HIGHLY EFFECTIVE ORGANIZATIONS

- Responsive to the market

- Customer centered

- Committed to maintaining networks and alliances

- Developed around a vision

- Focused on creating top-quality products and services

- Dedicated to positive learning and change

- Attentive to meeting responsibilities to customers, employees, suppliers, and society

- Committed to measuring their progress against world-class standards of excellence

- Able to respond to changing market conditions quickly

Successful organizations are committed to meeting the needs of their customers. *Why do you think such a commitment is important?*

Kodak chairman and CEO Daniel Carp has continued this tradition of meeting customer needs. Kodak has held to the belief that photography should allow all people to capture their most important memories. Computer technology, and its popularity in both business and personal lives, has had a major impact on the way photographs are taken and processed. Kodak has met the changing customer needs with the introduction of the digital camera, the Advantix system, photo CDs, and Photo-Net online picture service. Kodak continues to take cutting-edge technology and make it accessible, so that people can "Take pictures. Further."

Decentralization

During the nineteenth and early twentieth centuries, many U.S. companies were highly centralized. Power was held by a few senior managers who were responsible for making the most important decisions. Today, most U.S. companies find that a decentralized organization is more effective. Managers at all levels make decisions in these organizations.

ADVANTAGES OF DECENTRALIZATION Organizations decentralize for several reasons. First, decentralization increases an organization's ability to respond to market changes by allowing decisions to be made by managers who are close to their customers. Second, decentralization frees senior managers from many day-to-day tasks. It permits them to devote more time to higher-level issues, such as planning. Finally, giving decision-making authority to lower-level managers increases their job scope. This increases the level of responsibility and makes their jobs more interesting.

Nordstrom's, the upscale department store chain, does an outstanding job of meeting its customers' needs. Each department in each store is responsible for its own purchasing. Although it might be more efficient to have a single buyer responsible for shoe departments all over the country, Nordstrom's prefer to allow each store to make its own decisions about which shoes to purchase.

▲ **DECENTRALIZATION** In certain chain stores, department managers decide which products to stock. *What are some of the advantages of decentralizing decision making to the store level?*

DISADVANTAGES OF DECENTRALIZATION Critics of decentralization point to two potential problems. First, decentralization can result in a loss of managerial control. Corporate managers at Nordstrom's, for example, do not determine which products their stores stock because these decisions are left largely to store managers. Corporations that are not comfortable letting lower-level managers make decisions may be reluctant to decentralize.

A second potential problem involves duplication of effort. At Nordstrom's, each of the company's shoe store managers must determine which shoes to purchase. In contrast, at Borders Books, a highly centralized company, a single buyer makes purchasing decisions for all of the company's stores.

Section 12.1 Assessment

 FACT AND IDEA REVIEW

1. List and explain the three benefits of organizing.
2. Why do businesses organize their workforces?
3. Describe four characteristics of well-organized companies.
4. What is job scope? Why is it important?
5. True or false—Businesses are more centralized today than they were 100 years ago.

 ASSESSING WRITING SKILLS

You are a senior manager at a highly centralized record company. Write a one-page essay explaining why you believe the company should be decentralized. What benefits will decentralization bring to the organization.

CRITICAL THINKING

1. **Predicting Consequences:** What are the advantages of having a clearly defined chain of command?
2. **Analyzing Information:** Why do businesses decentralize their operations? What are some of the disadvantages of decentralization?

 CASE ANALYSIS

You just purchased a 35,000-square foot retail store, which you plan to turn into a gourmet shop and catering company. To staff your new business, you will need to hire several dozen people.

Apply: Think about how to structure the chain of command at your new business. Then create an organizational chart showing who will report to whom.

DELEGATING RESPONSIBILITY AND AUTHORITY

WHAT YOU'LL LEARN

➤ Three benefits of delegating.
➤ Five reasons some managers are reluctant to delegate.
➤ How managers delegate effectively.

WHY IT'S IMPORTANT

Managers cannot and should not make all decisions themselves.

KEY TERMS

- delegate
- responsibility
- subordinate
- unity of command
- span of management
- accountability

Maintaining Authority

Student council president Wayne Forte spends every afternoon in the student council office. He also spends most weekends working on student council affairs. Wayne has good ideas and spends plenty of time working to implement his ideas. However, he has not been an effective student leader.

Last year's president, Kristin Hernandez, put in less time on the student council. However, she did a very good job of involving other students. By assigning tasks to others, she achieved much more than hard-working Wayne.

Wayne had a lot of authority in his organization, but he failed to use it effectively. He tried to keep all of the authority to himself, rather than delegate some responsibility to others. To **delegate** is

▲ **DELEGATING TASKS** People who manage other people must learn to delegate responsibility and authority. *What kinds of tasks do you think this movie director delegates to others?*

to assign responsibility and authority for a task to another person. **Responsibility** is the obligation to perform assigned duties. Delegating responsibility to a **subordinate**, or a person holding a lower position within an organization, means that the manager obligates the subordinate to carry out certain duties. The subordinate has been given the ability to act and make decisions.

Kristin Hernandez did a good job of delegating authority. She asked the student council treasurer to take responsibility for raising $2,000 to finance student activities. She asked the head of the security committee to conduct a survey of students' concerns about safety at school. By delegating authority and responsibility, she achieved more than she could have herself.

Enforcing the Unity of Command Principle

The **unity of command** principle states that an employee should have only one immediate supervisor. The principle is based on the notion that confusion is likely to result when a person has to report to two people at the same time.

To see why the unity of command principle is important, consider the situation faced by production supervisor for personal electronics, Max Lyman. His immediate supervisor is production manager Rick Huganir. Each week, Mr. Huganir sets production targets for hair dryers. Last month, Mr. Lyman learned that the new quality control supervisor, to whom he also reports, plans to check the quality of the hair dryers that each production supervisor turns out. To meet the quality control supervisor's standards, Mr. Lyman will need to slow down his workers, so that fewer errors are made. However, slowing down the assembly line will mean that Mr. Lyman will not produce enough hair dryers to meet the weekly production goals.

Mr. Lyman can meet the standards set by the production supervisor, or he can meet the standards set by the quality control supervisor. He cannot meet the standards set by both supervisors. He is in a no-win situation. Whatever he does, one of his superiors will be dissatisfied with his work.

To avoid this kind of problem, organizations adopt the principle of unity of command. In the case of Mr. Lyman, the organization needs to restructure its organization so that he reports to a single manager, whose standards he can then try to meet.

QUESTION

What is the definition of a *principle?*

All About

ATTITUDE

BOSSY BOOTS
Even if your boss seems difficult to get along with, don't take it personally. He or she may be simply pushing you to do a better job. Your boss needs to accomplish his or her own work, oversee a department, and provide performance evaluations as well. Simply show appreciation for any feedback given.

CONNECT

Have you ever been in a situation at home, work, or school where the unity of command principle would have prevented a frustrating conflict of expectations? Explain.

Establishing an Appropriate Span of Management

RESPOND

Why is it important to control the number of subordinates managers supervise?

HEY, COACH!

Most likely you'll receive some coaching to get where you're headed in business. As you become more skilled in your daily routines, take the time to coach others on your areas of expertise. Pass down your experiences along the way to help your organization grow.

Another way that organizations maintain authority is by controlling the number of people who report to each manager. The **span of management**, or *span of control*, defines the number of subordinates a manager can effectively control.

Several factors determine how many subordinates a manager can handle. These include:

- the complexity of the jobs subordinates perform
- the quality of the people who fill the positions
- the ability of the manager

Managers with too many subordinates may feel overwhelmed. Their span of control may not allow them to manage their staff effectively.

Managers with too few subordinates may have too little to do. A manager with just two subordinates, for example, may be unnecessary. The organization could eliminate the manager's position and have the subordinates report to the next level of management within the organization.

Many businesses are moving away from this traditional span of management and toward a team structure of organization (see Chapter 13). This change is part of a new emphasis in management that emphasizes flexibility in order to meet customer needs. **Figure 12–3** contrasts the traditional view of the manager with the contemporary view.

▲ **SUPERVISION** A manager in a telemarketing firm may supervise dozens of telemarketers. *What factor makes it possible for these managers to supervise such a large number of subordinates?*

Figure 12–3	THE TRADITIONAL MANAGER VERSUS THE TEAM MANAGER	
Traditional Manager	**Team Manager**	
Thinks of self as a manager or boss	Thinks of self as a sponsor, team leader, or internal consultant	
Follows the chain of command	Deals with anyone necessary to get the job done	
Works within a set organizational structure	Changes organizational structure in response to market changes	
Makes most decisions alone	Invites others to join in decision-making	
Hoards information	Shares information	
Tries to master one discipline	Tries to master a broad array of managerial disciplines	
Demands long hours	Demands results	

WORKING WITH CHARTS	The team manager represents one who is more of a team player than a boss. *What are the benefits of this new type of management?*

"The New Non-Managers," *Fortune*, February 12, 1993.

Giving Subordinates the Authority to Make Decisions

Managers cannot delegate responsibility without delegating the authority to perform the task. Consider Paula Brookes, a departmental manager who delegates the responsibility for purchasing office supplies to her administrative assistant, Leslie Wong. Paula delegates responsibility to Leslie, but she does not give her the authority to actually purchase the supplies. As a result, every time Leslie needs to order new supplies, she must go to Paula for approval. Paula has delegated responsibility without having delegated the necessary authority to meet that responsibility. As a result, she finds herself having to make decisions that could have been made by her assistant.

Ensuring Accountability

Managers cannot simply delegate responsibility to their subordinates. They must also ensure that their subordinates will actually perform the tasks that have been delegated to them. To do so, managers must be able to hold their subordinates accountable for their actions. **Accountability** is the obligation to accept responsibility for one's actions.

BusinessWeek

Management Model

DOUGLAS K. SMITH

"Taking Charge of Change"

Douglas K. Smith, an expert on organizational change and also on teamwork, discussed his book, "Taking Charge of Change," with *BusinessWeek*.

Q: A huge proportion of companies that try to change fail to do it successfully. Why?

A: The most prevalent reason for such failures has to do with not understanding the "how" part of change.

Q: How does teamwork fit into the concepts of successful change?

A: Team performance is one of the 10 basic principles for managing profound change.

Q: What is the best way to teach the team concept to staff?

A: First, focus on what performance goals or challenges might require teams. Then, decide whether the goals in question truly need real-time integration of many people or can be accomplished through the sum of individual best performances. Then, if teams are needed, have the teams learn about the discipline of a team in pursuit of their real goals, not just in training classes.

Q: Do you believe in incremental or revolutionary change?

A: Both. First, distinguish between organizational change that requires hundreds of people to change and organizational change that depends on a big decision like a downsizing. If it is behavior-driven change, then it must happen at the individual level. What is profound behavioral change for individuals may not seem revolutionary to companies. But unless hundreds of individuals learn new things, the revolutionary change the company seeks won't happen!

Q: List some effective methods for motivating staff to need to be part of the team.

A: First, strong perfor-

mance goal-setting and management. Second, the team must be in control, not the boss. Third, if the organization depends on teams performing, then career paths must reflect team skills and opportunities.

Q: How do you measure the readiness of an organization for change?

A: First, look who signs up for specific performance challenges. Second, talk with people involved and figure out what their reluctance stems from.

Excerpted with permission from BusinessWeek, *January 3, 1996.*

CRITICAL THINKING

Explain what Smith means when he states that the most prevalent reason why companies fail to change has to do with not understanding the "how" part of change.

DECISION MAKING

The corporation you work for is downsizing. As a manager, which of Smith's theories of change will help you instigate change in your company?

Accountability allows managers to monitor the work of subordinates. The administrative assistant who purchases the department's office supplies is accountable for the money he or she spends. The manager has the right to ask the subordinate to account for all funds spent in order to ensure that money is not being spent inappropriately.

Why Delegate?

Managers delegate for several reasons. First, sometimes a task is simply too time-consuming for a manager to handle alone. In this case, managers have no choice but to delegate responsibility to subordinates.

Second, some tasks are too routine to warrant a manager's attention. Allowing a lower-level employee to handle such tasks frees up the manager's time for more important tasks. Managers who use their time wisely, for example, allow subordinates to take care of such routine tasks as tracking sick leave and ordering supplies.

In the 1970s, President Jimmy Carter was widely criticized for his failure to delegate responsibility for minor tasks. According to press reports, the President personally handled the scheduling of court time on the White House tennis courts. Carter's reported failure to delegate such duties raised doubts about his managerial skills.

Third, sometimes a task requires special skills that a manager may not possess. In this case, the manager needs to delegate responsibility to subordinates with the appropriate job skills. Lyn Stein is a mid-level manager in charge of developing a new light aircraft for a major aerospace company. Lyn's background is in engineering, but she is not an expert in metal strength. She delegates all responsibility for issues relating to metal strength to the metal expert on her staff, who is better qualified than she is to make the appropriate decisions.

Companies benefit enormously when managers delegate effectively because it means that decisions are made by people with the most direct knowledge of issues. It improves a business's ability to respond to customer needs.

Delegating also has a positive effect on staff. Employees who are given responsibility and authority know that their

▲ **DELEGATING RESPONSIBILITY** Reportedly President Carter had difficulty delegating responsibility for some minor tasks, such as scheduling tennis court time at the White House. *Why is it important for managers to delegate routine responsibilities to their subordinates?*

CONNECT

Imagine that you are the general manager of a movie theater. What tasks would you delegate to your employees? What skills would you look for in the employees to whom you assigned the tasks?

managers have confidence in them. As a result, they are more likely to feel a sense of commitment to the organization. Delegating also increases employees' job skills and knowledge of an organization.

Learning to Delegate

To delegate successfully, managers must identify which tasks can be delegated. To do so, they need to analyze how they spend their time. They should look for tasks that could be handled by subordinates. Once they identify these tasks, they then need to determine which subordinates could best handle them. Finally, they need to make sure that the subordinate to whom they delegate understands and accepts responsibility for the task he or she is being given.

Managers who delegate responsibility must clearly define the objectives of all tasks and set standards that subordinates need to meet. They also need to provide

◀ **COMMUNICATION** To delegate successfully, managers must make sure that their subordinates clearly understand the objectives of the tasks they are assigned. *What else must managers do to make sure their subordinates perform their duties appropriately?*

Figure 12–4	**REASONS MANAGERS RESIST DELEGATING**

- Fear that subordinates will not perform the task well

- Fear that subordinates will do the job too well, showing up the manager

- The belief that it is easier to perform the task oneself than to delegate it to someone else

- The natural tendency to want to hold on to power

- Comfort in performing the tasks one is used to performing

Many managers are unwilling to delegate authority and responsibility. *What are some reasons for their resistance?*

appropriate training so that subordinates are able to take on additional responsibility.

Resistance to Delegating

Failure to delegate can cause catastrophic results for businesses. As you learned in Chapter 2, Henry Ford's lack of confidence in his subordinates and his unwillingness to share power almost destroyed the company he founded. Managers resist delegating authority for a variety of reasons, as **Figure 12–4** shows. Managers need to let go of some of their control and have confidence in their subordinates. They should evaluate whether doing particular tasks would take away from their management functions, and delegate those tasks that do interfere.

Tips from Robert Half

In business, success is usually a team effort. Help out whenever your help is necessary, even if it is "not your job." Show initiative, and take credit for the group when someone compliments a job well done.

Section 12.2 Assessment

FACT AND IDEA REVIEW

1. What is the unity of command principle?
2. Name three factors that control the number of subordinates that a manager can handle.
3. Give three reasons why it is important for managers to delegate.
4. Explain the process by which managers determine which tasks to delegate.

CRITICAL THINKING

1. **Analyzing Information:** How does delegation help a company respond to customer needs?
2. **Understanding Cause and Effect:** Why do you think entrepreneurs who start their own companies sometimes have trouble delegating responsibility and authority?

ASSESSING LANGUAGE ARTS SKILLS

Write a one-page essay describing why it is important to delegate authority and responsibility. Use the text for ideas, but use your own words to write the essay.

CASE ANALYSIS

Jim Waters is a detail man. Despite heading up a 30-person marketing department for a major corporation, he types all of his own correspondence, keeps track of all employees' sick and vacation days, and makes all of his own travel arrangements. As his supervisor, you are concerned that he is spending too much time on tasks that could be handled by his assistant.

Apply: Write a one-page memo explaining how and why you would like Mr. Waters to delegate some of his responsibilities.

CHAPTER 12 ASSESSMENT

REVIEWING VOCABULARY

Define each of the following terms and use each in a sentence.

organization	job depth
authority	delegate
chain of command	subordinate
division of labor	unity of command
job rotation	span of management
job scope	accountability

Section 12.1

▶ Organizations help individuals work together efficiently and effectively.

▶ A well-defined chain of command defines who is in charge for all members of an organization.

▶ The division of labor assigns specific tasks to individuals or groups.

▶ Companies prevent boredom in specialized workforces by rotating jobs, widening job scope, and increasing job depth.

Section 12.2

▶ Managers should delegate authority and responsibility for decision-making to subordinates.

▶ The unity of command principle states that an employee should have one immediate supervisor.

▶ The span of management defines the number of subordinates a manager can effectively control.

▶ In successful delegation managers identify tasks to be delegated, choose a subordinate to handle tasks, and establish expectations.

RECALLING KEY CONCEPTS

1. Why are organizations necessary?
2. What is a chain of command?
3. What can happen to productivity if workers become bored with their jobs?
4. Why do managers need to learn to delegate responsibility and authority?
5. Give two reasons why some managers are reluctant to delegate.

THINKING CRITICALLY

1. Why is authority important in an organization?
2. Do you think centralized organizations or decentralized organizations are more effective in meeting customer needs? Explain your answer.
3. Is it possible to manage successfully with delegating? Why or why not?
4. Why is it important for businesses to get close to their customers?

CHAPTER 12 ASSESSMENT

MATH SKILLS Cindy Giovanetti earns $6.25 an hour as a cashier at a video store. The manager of the store, Jon Laughlin, earns $12.00 an hour. Last week Jon put in 10 hours of overtime stocking the shelves with new products. He was paid $18.00 an hour. How much would the company save if Cindy had stocked the shelves during her regular working hours?

● APPLYING MANAGEMENT PRINCIPLES

SOLVE THE PROBLEM You have just been promoted to production manager of a company that manufactures picture frames. Your department employs 25 workers on an assembly line. One set of workers cuts wood for the frames. Another sands the edges, while a third nails the four pieces of wood together. A fourth group of workers dusts the frames and packs them into cartons. Turnover and absenteeism are high, and the quality often is unsatisfactory.

Language Arts What changes would you make that might reduce the high level of turnover and absenteeism? How would you improve the quality of work that the company produces? Write a step-by-step plan of your ideas for implementing change in a two-page report.

● PREPARING FOR COMPETITIVE EVENTS

Answer true or false to the following statements. Explain your answers.

a. Rotating employees from job to job reduces productivity.

b. Unity of command states that employees often need many managers.

BusinessWeek ONLINE

In this chapter you read the *BusinessWeek* Management Model about an expert on organizational change and teamwork. For more information, go to *BusinessWeek* online at: **www.businessweek.com**

Find several articles on teamwork. Then make a list of the advantages and disadvantages of teamwork in a business. Share your list with the class.

CHAPTER 13

ORGANIZATIONAL STRUCTURE

LEARNING OBJECTIVES

When you have completed this chapter, you will be able to:

- Read an organizational chart.
- List the four types of organizational structures and explain the advantages and disadvantages of each type.
- Name the factors that affect the type of structure an organization adopts.
- Describe the roles of the chief executive officer and the board of directors.

READING STRATEGIES

As you read

- **PREDICT** what the section will be about.
- **CONNECT** what you read with your own life.
- **QUESTION** as you read to make sure you understand the content.
- **RESPOND** to what you read.

"MANAGEMENT TALK"

"Our company today is leaner, faster, more flexible and more efficient—in short much more competitive. But our journey is far from finished. Building upon our recent success and momentum, we are determined to drive GM to the next level—to sustained success."

—Rick Wagoner, General Motors, Chairman and CEO

WORKPLACE CONNECTIONS

Understanding Management

General Motors has a long, proud history of being one of the biggest car manufacturers in the world. By the 1980s and 1990s, however, the company was losing profits to newer, more efficient manufacturers. Since then, the company has updated its factories and streamlined its operations in order to reduce costs.

Analyzing Management Skills

How would consolidating six divisions help General Motors improve service and cut costs? What are the possible drawbacks of merging the separate divisions?

Applying Management Skills

Have you ever been in a situation at home or work where there were too many people in charge of completing a task? What suggestions would you make to simplify the process?

BusinessWeek ONLINE

For further reading on managers and management go to:
www.businessweek.com

UNDERSTANDING HOW ORGANIZATIONAL STRUCTURES WORK

WHAT YOU'LL LEARN

➤ How to read an organizational chart.
➤ The four main types of organizational structures.
➤ The difference between staff and line functions.
➤ The benefits of adopting a matrix or team structure.

WHY IT'S IMPORTANT

Without an appropriate organizational structure, a business will not succeed.

KEY TERMS

• organizational chart
• line function
• staff function
• matrix structure
• team structure
• flat structure
• tall structure

What Is Organizational Structure?

Some organizations, such as a high school volunteer club, exist to help people in need. Other organizations, such as a student council, exist to give students a voice at school. Business organizations exist to earn profits. To meet their goals, they organize their employees into some kind of structure.

Companies adopt organizational structures in order to minimize confusion over job expectations. Having an organizational structure helps them coordinate activities by clearly identifying which individuals are responsible for which tasks.

▲ **ORGANIZATIONAL STRUCTURE** Chief executive officers cannot make all decisions themselves. They need to organize their companies so that other managers can share in decision making. *How does an organizational structure help a company earn profits?*

Types of Organizational Structures

Companies generally adopt one of four organizational structures. These include:

- line structure
- line and staff structure
- matrix structure
- team structure

CONNECT

Do you belong to any organizations? If so, how are they structured?

Each of these different types of organizational structures can be shown in an organizational chart. An **organizational chart** is a visual representation of a business's organizational structure. It shows who reports to whom within the company. It also shows what kind of work each department does.

Line Structure

In a *line organization*, authority originates at the top and moves downward in a line (see **Figure 13–1**). All managers perform **line functions**, functions that contribute directly to company profits. Examples of line functions include production managers, sales representatives, and marketing managers.

| Figure 13–1 | LINE STRUCTURE |

Chief Executive Officer

Senior Managers

Mid-level Managers

Lower-level Managers

Nonmanagement Employees

WORKING WITH CHARTS In a line structure organization, managers make all decisions affecting their departments. *What kinds of companies usually have line structures?*

Senior Engineer

■ Nature of the Work

Senior engineers manage people and projects for a variety of industries. For example, they oversee the design and production of electrical and electronic equipment, industrial machinery, aircraft, and motor vehicles. They work in scientific, medical, and construction fields as well. State, local, and federal agencies employ many engineers at all levels.

Senior engineers supervise engineering and support staff, meet with upper management, and establish budgets and completion schedules for projects. They write reports for management and government inspectors. They see that projects conform to government guidelines and industry standards. Senior engineers often troubleshoot a project when problems develop.

■ Working Conditions

Senior engineers work in offices, laboratories, or industrial plants. They work 40 hours a week or longer, and may travel to outside sites to inspect projects.

■ Training, Other Qualifications, and Advancement

To become a senior engineer, you need a bachelor's or master's degree in engineering, plus several years experience. Engineers whose work affects life, health, or property, or who offer services to the public must register in the state in which they work. Registration requires a degree from a college or university accredited by the Accreditation Board for Engineering and Technology (ABET), four years of experience, and successful completion of a state exam.

■ Salary Range

Senior engineers earn $99,200 to $120,000+, depending on experience, responsibilities, and industry.

CRITICAL THINKING

What skills and abilities might be useful to a senior engineer?

STANDARD &POOR'S

INDUSTRY OUTLOOK

The aerospace industry is the largest exporter in the United States. In 2002, the industry had a net trade balance of $30 billion. Civil aerospace exports totaled $47 billion, military exports were $9.4 billion, and engine and other parts comprised $17 billion. Imports of aerospace products were $27 billion for the year.

BUSINESS MANAGEMENT Online

For more information on management careers, go to:

busmanagement.glencoe.com

Line managers collect and analyze all of the information they need to carry out their responsibilities. Production managers, for example, hire and fire all of the assembly-line workers in their departments. They also order all of the supplies their department needs.

Line organizations are common among small businesses. Larger companies usually require a different kind of organizational structure.

Line and Staff Structure

In mid-sized and large companies, line managers cannot perform all of the activities they need to perform to run their departments. In these companies, other employees are hired to help line managers do their jobs. These employees perform staff functions (see **Figure 13–2**).

Staff functions advise and support line functions. Staff departments include the legal department, the human resources department, and the public relations department. These departments help the line departments do their jobs. They contribute only indirectly to corporate profits. Staff people are generally specialists in one field, and their authority is normally limited to making recommendations to line managers.

LEADING THE WAY

LEAVE THE COMPETITION BEHIND
Different departments within an organization may not always be following the same operating rules of success. Always focus on the goal of satisfying customers. Internal rivalry wastes time and lessens morale. Compete with your competitors, not your co-workers.

QUESTION

Would a line structure be more compatible with a continuous flow or intermittent flow operating system?

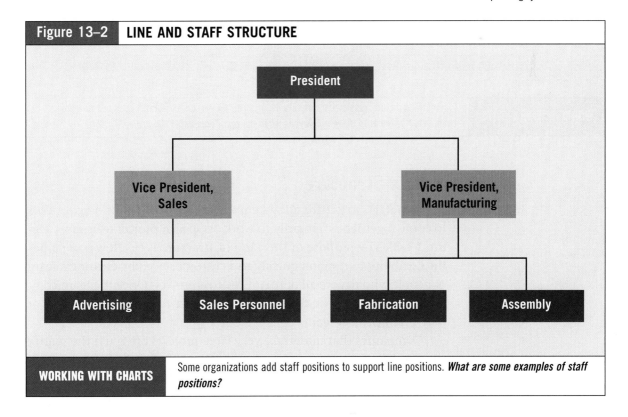

| Figure 13–2 | LINE AND STAFF STRUCTURE |

President

Vice President, Sales

Vice President, Manufacturing

Advertising

Sales Personnel

Fabrication

Assembly

WORKING WITH CHARTS Some organizations add staff positions to support line positions. *What are some examples of staff positions?*

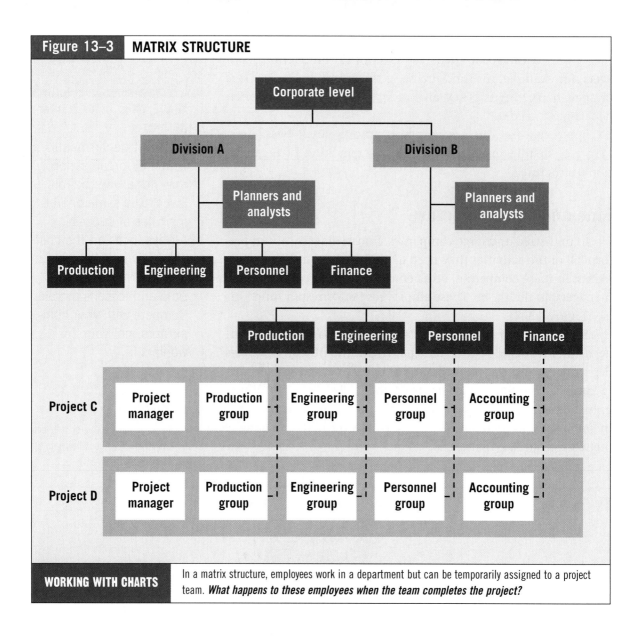

Figure 13–3 MATRIX STRUCTURE

In a matrix structure, employees work in a department but can be temporarily assigned to a project team. *What happens to these employees when the team completes the project?*

Matrix Structure

A **matrix structure** allows employees from different departments to come together temporarily to work on special project teams (see **Figure 13–3**). The purpose of this kind of structure is to allow companies the flexibility to respond quickly to a customer need by creating a team of people who devote all of their time to a project. Once the team completes the project, the team members return to their departments or join a new project team.

Companies that undertake very large projects often use the matrix structure. Boeing, for example, regularly assigns employees to project teams it creates to design new aircraft. Large high-tech firms also frequently use the matrix structure.

Team Structure

Many companies have abandoned the line and staff approach to organizational structure in favor of the team approach. A **team structure** brings together people with different skills in order to meet a particular objective (see **Figure 13–4**). More and more companies are using the team structure. They believe this structure will allow them to meet customer needs more effectively than the traditional structure.

The team structure is very different from the traditional organizational structure. In the traditional structure, each level of management

▲ **TEAM BUILDING** Many companies have moved away from the traditional organizational structure. *How does organizing a company into teams help it compete?*

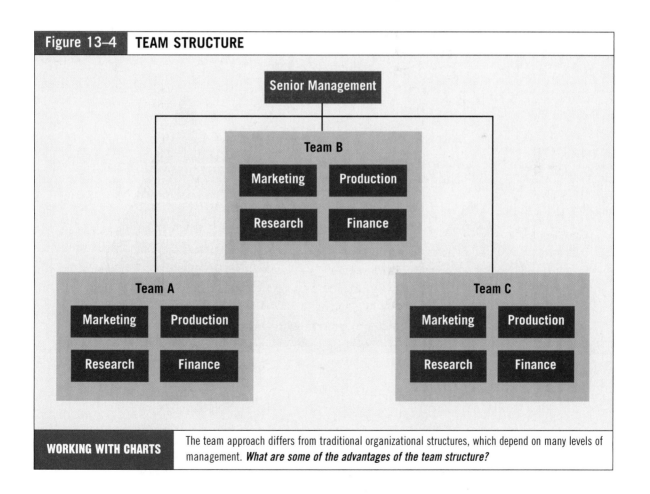

Figure 13–4 | **TEAM STRUCTURE**

Senior Management

Team B
- Marketing
- Production
- Research
- Finance

Team A
- Marketing
- Production
- Research
- Finance

Team C
- Marketing
- Production
- Research
- Finance

WORKING WITH CHARTS The team approach differs from traditional organizational structures, which depend on many levels of management. *What are some of the advantages of the team structure?*

reports to a higher management level. In this kind of organization, senior managers need not approve decisions by lower-level managers. Instead, teams have the authority to make their own decisions. Employees often prefer the team structure because of its focus on completing a project rather than performing a particular task.

One company that has successfully used teams is IBM. Beginning in 1990 the company introduced self-directed management teams that it organized around customer needs. Each team tries to determine what the customer is looking for and develop strategies with which to meet those needs. The approach helps the company respond quickly in competitive markets.

RESPOND

Would you prefer to be an employee in an organization with a tall structure or a flat structure?

Flat vs. Tall Structures

In the previous chapter we looked at the importance of a manager's span of management—the number of employees who report to a

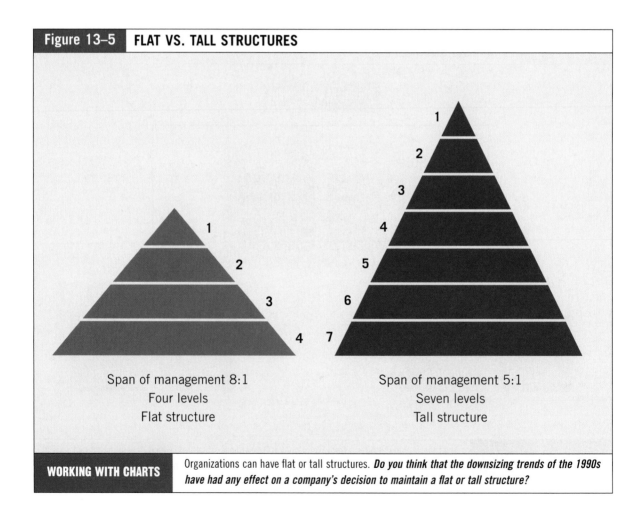

Figure 13–5 **FLAT VS. TALL STRUCTURES**

Span of management 8:1
Four levels
Flat structure

Span of management 5:1
Seven levels
Tall structure

WORKING WITH CHARTS Organizations can have flat or tall structures. *Do you think that the downsizing trends of the 1990s have had any effect on a company's decision to maintain a flat or tall structure?*

manager. In a similar fashion, organizations can be classified as being either tall or flat.

A **flat structure** is an organization that has a small number of levels and a broad span of management at each level. This calls for a good deal of delegation on the part of the manager. Employees have more power within the company. A **tall structure** is an organization that has many levels with small spans of management. In this case, power is centralized on the top levels and there is more employee control. **Figure 13–5** illustrates the breakdown of management levels that occur in a flat or a tall structure. Some advantages of a flat structure include greater job satisfaction, more delegation, and increased communication between levels of management. Some advantages of a tall structure are greater control and better performance.

Section 13.1 Assessment

FACT AND IDEA REVIEW

1. What is the purpose of an organizational chart?
2. What is a line function?
3. What is a staff function?
4. What is a matrix structure?
5. How does the team structure differ from the line and staff structure?
6. True or False: A tall structure allows for greater employee power through delegation.

CRITICAL THINKING

1. **Analyzing Information:** Why do businesses need organizational structures?
2. **Drawing Conclusions:** Why do some companies prefer to organize by teams?
3. **Predicting Consequences:** In a business with a line and staff structure, why might conflict arise between line managers and staff managers?

ASSESSING MATH SKILLS

Labyrinth Technologies, a high-tech company that specializes in computer graphics, has decided to reorganize its corporate structure into a team structure. By organizing into teams, Labyrinth expects to be able to eliminate three mid-level managers, each earning $82,000 a year. It also expects to hire two additional entry-level employees, to be paid about $25,000 a year each. If the cost of the reorganization itself is $75,000, how much can the company expect to save after two years?

CASE ANALYSIS

You are the manager of a manufacturing company that employs 500 people. The owner of the company has given you free rein to reorganize the company however you want.

Apply: Write a one-page paper that describes whether you would recommend adopting a line, line and staff, matrix, or team structure.

CREATING AN ORGANIZATIONAL STRUCTURE

WHAT YOU'LL LEARN

▶ The different ways in which companies organize their departments.
▶ Why a company's structure needs to change as the company grows.
▶ The role of the chief executive officer.
▶ The role of the board of directors.

WHY IT'S IMPORTANT

Managers both help create and work within organizational structures.

KEY TERMS

• committee
• chief executive officer
• board of directors

Factors Affecting Organizational Structure

The organizational structure a company chooses depends on the nature of its business. A structure that is appropriate for a high-tech company that employs 50,000 people in eight countries will not be appropriate for a small retail business with just a dozen employees.

Many factors affect the choice of organizational structure. The most important factors are the size of the business and the kinds of products or services it produces.

Size

The size of a business has a very important effect on the organizational structure that a management adopts. Very small, single-person businesses need no organizational structure at all. Companies with only a few employees can also function well without a formal structure.

Once a business employs more than just a few employees, however, a formal structure is necessary. Moreover, for a business to be successful, its structure must change as the business continues to grow.

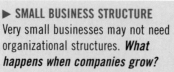

▶ SMALL BUSINESS STRUCTURE
Very small businesses may not need organizational structures. *What happens when companies grow?*

Figure 13–6

ORGANIZATIONAL LIFE CYCLE STAGES

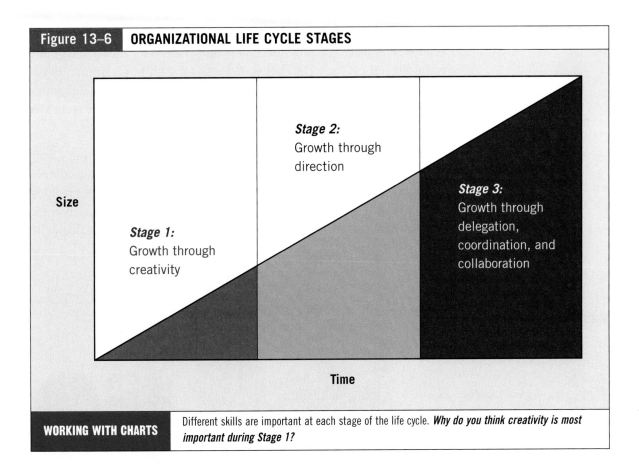

Stage 2:
Growth through direction

Stage 3:
Growth through delegation, coordination, and collaboration

Size

Stage 1:
Growth through creativity

Time

WORKING WITH CHARTS Different skills are important at each stage of the life cycle. *Why do you think creativity is most important during Stage 1?*

Typically, businesses go through three organizational life cycle stages. As **Figure 13–6** shows, these stages include growth through creativity; growth through direction; and growth through delegation, coordination, and collaboration.

STAGE 1: GROWTH THROUGH CREATIVITY During the first stage of growth, entrepreneurs with new ideas create products or services for which there is a market (see **Figure 13–7**). Their businesses tend to be small. They usually lack formal structures, policies, and objectives. The company founder is involved in every aspect of the business and makes all decisions.

During this stage of development, management skills are much less important than they are later on, because there are very few employees to manage. Having an idea that appeals to consumers is very important.

STAGE 2: GROWTH THROUGH DIRECTION Once a company grows, it enters the second stage of its growth cycle. During this stage, the company grows in size, and the company founder is no longer solely responsible for all decision making. Instead, the company relies on professional managers. The managers are responsible for various functions, including planning, organizing, and staffing.

PREDICT

At what point do you think a company will make the shift from Stage 1 to Stage 2 growth?

As a company grows, its managers usually create written policies, procedures, and plans. They establish rules and systems for hiring, firing, and rewarding employees. They set up systems for communicating information among employees. They set up financial controls, which determine how much each department can spend. Employees who once were able to make decisions spontaneously must now follow formal rules.

STAGE 3: GROWTH THROUGH DELEGATION As we discussed in Chapter 12, sometimes a company's structure becomes too rigid, and decision making becomes too centralized. Lower-level employees feel left out of the decision-making process. Top executives find themselves too far removed from the customer to make good decisions. To deal with

FIGURE 13–7

The Changing Nature of a Company's Organizational Structure

A company's organizational structure must adapt as the company grows and different skills are needed at each stage of the cycle. Look at how the needs of Apple Computer have changed over time.

1 STAGE 1
When a company is young, it depends heavily on creativity. Steven Jobs and Steve Wozniak were technical geniuses who had a brilliant idea for a user-friendly desktop computer. They turned this idea into a multimillion dollar company by introducing the Apple II computer in the 1970s.

these problems, companies often move to the next stage of the organization life cycle, stage 3.

In stage 3, businesses delegate more responsibility to lower-level employees in an attempt to decentralize decision making. Delegating authority helps businesses in two ways. First, it motivates people at lower levels, whose jobs become more interesting. Second, it allows senior executives to devote more of their time to long-term management issues, such as what kinds of products their companies should offer five and ten years down the road.

As you can see, businesses grow for many reasons and in many different ways. **Figure 13–7** illustrates the growth of one company through the three stages.

2 STAGE 2
As a company grows, it needs managers with excellent managerial skills. To continue to grow, in the 1980s Apple Computer replaced its co-founder, Steven Jobs, with a professional manager. The new chief executive officer, John Sculley, helped introduce the company's Macintosh computer.

3 STAGE 3
In the third stage of the organizational life cycle, managers learn to delegate authority. In 1996 company founder Steven Jobs returned to Apple as interim chief executive officer in an effort to breathe new life into a company that had fallen on hard times. Apple's organizational structure allowed it to introduce several important products in the 1990s, including the iMac.

Type of Product or Service

The type of product or service a company produces is another important factor affecting its organizational structure. In general, the number of levels within an organization increases as the level of technical complexity increases. This means that a company that produces sophisticated electronic equipment is likely to have more levels of management than a company that produces garden tools. Companies that produce technically complicated products also are likely to have a larger percentage of managers and supervisors than companies that produce simpler products.

The president of a large water company that has 7,500 employees aptly summed up this relationship between product and organizational complexity. He noted, "We don't need more management than a toy store does." A company with just a few layers of management has a flat organizational structure.

▲ FUNCTIONAL DEPARTMENTATION
This graphic artist works in the marketing department, together with all of the company's other marketing professionals. *What are some of the advantages of organizing a company in this way?*

Organizing a Company into Departments

All but the smallest companies are organized into departments. These departments may be based on work functions, products, geography, or customers.

General Electric has several major divisions, including aircraft engines, consumer products, insurance, commercial finance, NBC, and Power Systems. A senior manager heads each of these divisions.

Organizing Departments by Work Functions

Some businesses organize their departments by function (see **Figure 13–8**). These functions include production, marketing, finance, and human resources.

- *Production* refers to the actual creation of a company's goods or services.
- *Marketing* involves product development, pricing, distribution, sales, and advertising.
- *Finance* refers to maintaining a company's financial statements and obtaining credit so that a company can grow.
- *Human resources* deals with hiring employees and placing them in appropriate jobs.

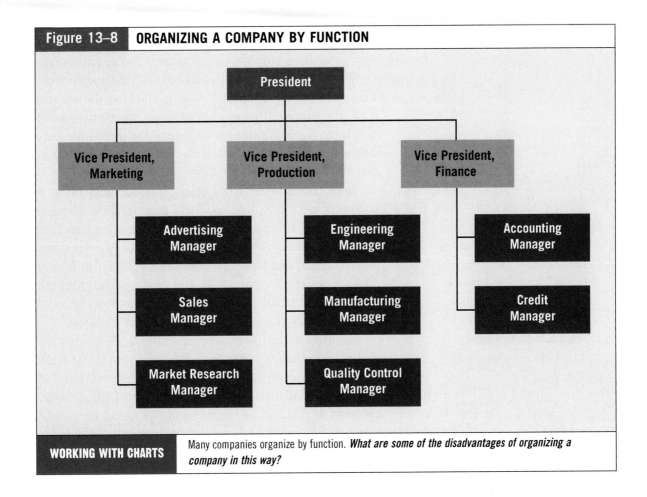

Figure 13–8 ORGANIZING A COMPANY BY FUNCTION

President

Vice President, Marketing

Vice President, Production

Vice President, Finance

Advertising Manager

Engineering Manager

Accounting Manager

Sales Manager

Manufacturing Manager

Credit Manager

Market Research Manager

Quality Control Manager

WORKING WITH CHARTS Many companies organize by function. *What are some of the disadvantages of organizing a company in this way?*

Each of these basic functions includes various positions. Marketing, for example, includes advertising, sales, and market research. Production includes engineering, manufacturing, and quality control. Finance includes accounting and credit.

The primary advantage of organizing a company by functions is that it allows for functional specialization. One group of professionals can devote all of its time to accounting. Another can become experts in advertising or engineering. Organizing a company by functions also may save a company money by allowing it to use its equipment and resources most efficiently.

Organizing a company by function can have some negative effects, however. Conflicts may develop between departments with different goals. The production department, for example, may be more concerned about product quality than the marketing department.

Organizing a company by functions also may hurt a company by creating managers whose scope is relatively narrow. For example, a marketing manager may know a great deal about marketing, but he or she may be completely unfamiliar with the other aspects of the company's business. Where managers need to have a much broader scope, a different organizational structure may be more appropriate.

QUESTION

Which of these four functions are line functions and which are staff functions?

Organizing Departments by Product

A second way in which a company can organize its departments is by product (see **Figure 13–9**). Under this kind of organizational structure, a single manager oversees all the activities needed to produce and market a particular product. This type of organizational structure allows employees to identify with the product rather than with their particular job function. It often helps to develop a sense of common purpose.

Structuring a department by product also helps a company identify which products are profitable. General Motors (GM), for example, can easily determine which of its divisions is earning the most money because the company is organized in independent units. Each unit produces a different product. If GM had instead adopted functional departments, it would be difficult to know if Chevrolets were earning more profits than Cadillacs.

Another advantage of organizing departments by products is that it provides opportunities for training executive personnel by letting them experience a broad range of functional activities. The head of the Pontiac Division at GM, for example, understands all aspects of the division, not just those related to one particular function. He or she is in a better position to become the chief executive officer of GM than a manager who had spent his or her entire career working in a single functional department.

Organizing a company by products also can cause problems, however. Departments can become overly competitive, to the detriment of

Tips from Robert Half

With the growing number of small businesses, chances are good that you'll work for one. Take advantage of the opportunity at a small firm to learn about marketing, sales, public relations, and computers.

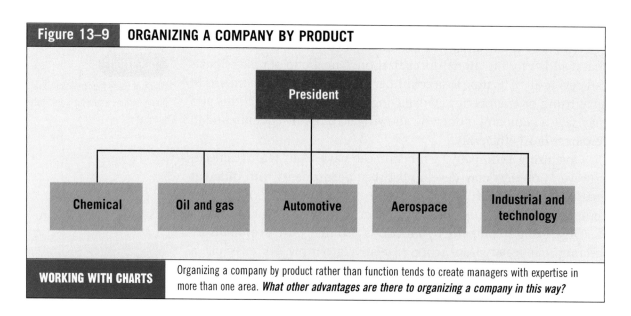

| Figure 13–9 | ORGANIZING A COMPANY BY PRODUCT |

WORKING WITH CHARTS — Organizing a company by product rather than function tends to create managers with expertise in more than one area. *What other advantages are there to organizing a company in this way?*

▲ **PRODUCT ORGANIZATION** At many packaged-goods manufacturers, managers are responsible for every aspect of a particular brand. *What are the advantages to organizing a company in this way?*

the company as a whole. Organizing the company by product also means that activities are duplicated across departments. GM, for example, has a marketing department for each division, rather than a single marketing department for the company as a whole.

Organizing Departments in Other Ways

Companies can organize in other ways as well. Some companies, for example, organize their operations by geographical region. One senior manager might be responsible for all of a company's activities within North America. Another might be in charge of all activities in Asia.

Companies also can organize by type of customer. A large computer company, for example, might have one division responsible for sales to governments, another to for-profit businesses, and another to nonprofit organizations.

Q&A WITH THE VISIONARY-IN-CHIEF

A Talk with Chairman Bill Gates on the World Beyond Windows

BusinessWeek speaks to Bill Gates about the company's sweeping reorganization.

Q: Microsoft's financials have never looked better. So why reorganize?

A: Companies fail when they become complacent and imagine that they will always be successful. So we are always challenging ourselves: Are we making what customers want and working on the products and technologies they'll want in the future? Are we staying ahead of all our competitors? Are we organized most effectively to achieve our goals? Even the most successful companies must constantly reinvent themselves.

Q: What are the three key principles of the reorganization?

A: First, our vision had always been a computer on every desk and in every home. But it was also clear that we needed to build on that vision. Although the PC is still at the heart of computing, it is being joined by a large number of new devices—from palmsize PCs to smart telephones. At the same time, the Internet has

changed everything by giving the world a level of connectivity that was undreamed of just five years ago. So we needed a new vision centered around the Internet.

Second, the new structure puts the customer at the center of everything we do by reorganizing our business divisions by customer segment rather than along product lines.

Third, we're now holding the leaders of our new business divisions accountable to think and act as if they are independent businesses. That will give us even more flexibility to respond to changes in technology and the marketplace.

Q: Which three companies do you consider to be your biggest competitors today?

A: In 25 years in this industry, I have never seen so much competition in every single area. I can probably narrow today's list down to IBM, Sun, AOL/Netscape, Novell, Linux, and Oracle.

There's an unchanging competitor too—ourselves. Customers can choose whether to stay with the software they have or upgrade to our new products. We have to ensure that all new releases are much, much better than our previous products. If they aren't, customers won't upgrade.

Excerpted with permission from BusinessWeek, *May 17, 1999*

CRITICAL THINKING

Explain what Gates means when he states, "Even the most successful companies must constantly reinvent themselves."

DECISION MAKING

As a manager at Microsoft, decide whether it would be best to use customer departmentation or product departmentation.

Understanding the Role of Company Leadership

Organizational structures often appoint individuals or groups in leadership positions for the company. Three examples of such leadership roles are committees, chief executive officers, and boards of directors.

Committees

A **committee** is an organized group of people appointed to consider or decide upon certain matters. Committees can be permanent or temporary. You might have been part of a committee at school, planning for the homecoming dance or a Thanksgiving drive to collect food for the poor. A committee might be formed in a company to work on a new budget, or to plan for the relocation of an organization.

Managers can do many things to increase the efficiency of a committee. In order to produce the optimal results, there are guidelines that should be followed when choosing and managing a committee. These guidelines are

- clearly define the committee's function
- establish authority figures within a committee
- set clear goals for members to attain
- decide on the limits of a committee's power

Chief Executive Officer

Senior managers initiate or approve all of a company's major decisions. These include decisions about producing new products, expanding internationally, or building new factories. These managers are led by a **chief executive officer**, the most important executive in a company.

The chief executive officer, or CEO, is the top executive in a company. Together with other senior managers, the CEO

- sets the company's objectives
- makes decisions about meeting the company's objectives
- determines who fills senior management positions
- develops the company's long-term strategies
- attends the company's annual stockholders' meeting and answers questions about the company's activities
- takes charge of the company in a crisis
- works with the board of directors

CONNECT

Imagine that you are in charge of organizing a committee to oversee your school's homecoming activities. What would you do to increase the committee's efficiency?

WORKPLACE DIVERSITY

TURKEY

Age is highly honored in Turkey. The Turkish defer to elders to offer advice and make decisions, especially since so many Turkish businesses are family owned. Elders are shown respect by being introduced first, served first, and allowed to go through doors first.

Board of Directors

In companies owned by stockholders, a board of directors approves all major management decisions. A **board of directors** is the legal representative of a company's stockholders. In this role, a board of directors serves several important functions. Headed by a chairperson, the board approves the most important decisions made by the company's chief executive officer. It examines all major decisions to ensure that they are in the best interest of the company's stockholders.

The presence of a board of directors makes it more difficult for corporate managers to act in ways that benefit them personally at the expense of the company's owners.

If, for example, management proposed to increase executive salaries by 300 percent, the board of directors would likely veto the move. It would approve the increase if it believed that such a move was somehow in the interest of stockholders.

In a small business, the board of directors may consist entirely of family members. In a larger company, the board usually includes both people from the company and people from outside the company.

RESPOND

Do you think it's important for members of a company's board of directors to have expertise in the company's type of business? Why or why not?

▲ **CORPORATE DECISIONS** During his tenure as CEO of Home Depot, Arthur Blank (right) initiated or approved all major corporate decisions. *What are some of the decisions Blank was likely to face?*

Senior company managers who serve on the company's board of directors are known as *inside board members*. Directors who do not work for the company are known as *outside board members*.

Outside board members often include senior executives of other businesses, heads of cultural or educational institutions, and former public servants. At PepsiCo, for example, the board of directors includes the former CEOs of IBM and AT&T, as well as the CEO of a public television station and the former president of a major university. Such outside directors often bring a fresh perspective to analyzing a business's decision-making process.

Boards of directors usually meet four to six times a year. They focus on a company's major decisions, leaving day-to-day company operations to the company's managers.

Section 13.2 Assessment

FACT AND IDEA REVIEW

1. What are the three organizational stages a company will go through?
2. Name two different ways a company can organize its departments.
3. Explain some of the duties of a chief executive officer.
4. What is the difference between an inside board member and an outside board member?
5. How can a manager increase committee efficiency?

CRITICAL THINKING

1. **Making Comparisons:** What are the advantages and disadvantages of organizing a company by function? By product?
2. **Analyzing Information:** What is the purpose of a board of directors? Why is it important for a company to have outside directors on its board?

ASSESSING COMPUTER SKILLS

Choose a major U.S. company, such as Compaq Computer, Texas Instruments, IBM, Coca-Cola, or General Mills. Using the Internet or library resources, find out how the company you selected is organized and identify the top six managers. If you can, obtain a copy of the company's organizational chart.

CASE ANALYSIS

Johnson Office Supply is a large wholesale supplier of office supplies. The company sells to office supply stores, government agencies, and other institutions. Currently, the company is organized geographically, with senior managers responsible for each of the company's four major regions. The president of Johnson Office Supply suspects that this structure may not be appropriate. She has asked you to come up with a proposal for reorganizing the company.

Apply: Prepare a one-page report explaining how and why you would reorganize Johnson Office Supply.

CHAPTER 13 ASSESSMENT

CHAPTER SUMMARY

Section 13.1

▶ Companies use organizational charts to visually represent their organizational structures.

▶ Businesses generally adopt one of the following four organizational structures: line structure, line and staff structure, matrix structure, or team structure.

Section 13.2

▶ The type of structure a company adopts depends on many factors, including the company's size and its products or services.

▶ Many companies are organized by work functions. Others are organized by product, region, or customer.

▶ An organization may form a committee to decide upon certain matters.

▶ Senior management, led by the company's chief executive officer, initiates or approves all of a company's major decisions.

▶ A board of directors approves all major decisions made by corporate management.

REVIEWING VOCABULARY

Write a paragraph that demonstrates your understanding of the following vocabulary words:

organizational chart	flat structure
line function	tall structure
staff function	committee
matrix structure	chief executive officer
team structure	board of directors

RECALLING KEY CONCEPTS

1. Describe a line and staff organizational structure.
2. How does a business's structure change as it grows in size?
3. What are some factors that determine the kind of organizational structure a company adopts?
4. How does a board of directors affect the decision-making process of a business?

THINKING CRITICALLY

1. Why do businesses need organizational structures?
2. Why is it important for a company's structure to evolve as the company grows?
3. What skills are most important at each stage in a company's development?
4. Why is it important for a company's management to work well with its board of directors?
5. Explain the difference between a tall structure and a flat structure.

CHAPTER 13 ASSESSMENT

ASSESSING ACADEMIC SKILLS

ART Choose two of the organizational structures described in this chapter. Make a poster showing how a company would be organized under each type of structure.

APPLYING MANAGEMENT PRINCIPLES

SOLVE THE PROBLEM You are a member of the board of directors of a major importer of tropical nuts. Recently, some of the company's stockholders have expressed their concern that the company may be contributing to the depletion of the Amazon rain forest. As a board member, how would you respond to their concerns?

Public Speaking Present your ideas on responding to environmental concerns to the other members of the board. End your presentation with a proposal to company management.

PREPARING FOR COMPETITIVE EVENTS

To display the authority structure within an organization, use a/an

  a. bar chart.
  b. line graph.
  c. organizational chart.
  d. pictogram.

BusinessWeek ONLINE

In this chapter you read the *BusinessWeek* Management Model about Bill Gates. Using the Internet or library resources, find current articles on Microsoft's corporate organization, Bill Gates' role in the company, and the government's impact on Microsoft's organization. Write a two-page summary of the articles and present your findings to the class. For more information, go to *BusinessWeek* online at: **www.businessweek.com**

CHAPTER 14

UNDERSTANDING WORK GROUPS

LEARNING OBJECTIVES

When you have completed this chapter, you will be able to:

- Explain the difference between formal and informal work groups.
- Discuss group norms, group cohesiveness, and group conformity.
- Understand why individuals conform to group norms.
- Recognize the importance of work groups to an organization.
- Suggest ways to build effective work groups.

READING STRATEGIES

As you read

- **PREDICT** what the section will be about.
- **CONNECT** what you read with your own life.
- **QUESTION** as you read to make sure you understand the content.
- **RESPOND** to what you read.

Lucent Technologies
Bell Labs Innovations

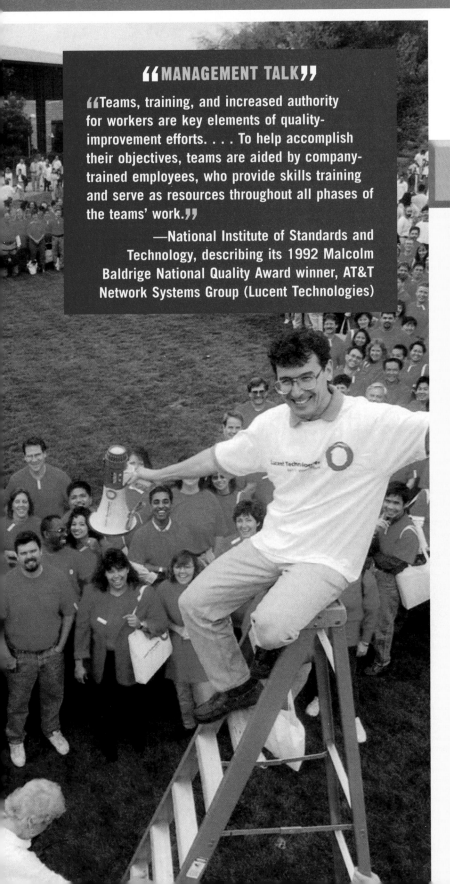

WORKPLACE CONNECTIONS

Understanding Management

When Lucent technologies spun off from its parent company, AT&T, it gained the freedom to organize its workforce differently. Most Lucent employees work in teams designed to foster efficiency, creativity, and innovation. This approach gives employees the flexibility to solve problems and invent new products. In fact, Lucent can boast of earning about two patents per working day, as well as the Malcolm Baldrige National Quality Award.

Analyzing Management Skills

Why would it be important for team members to receive continual training?

Applying Management Skills

If you were on a team responsible for inventing a communications system, what qualities would you appreciate in your team members?

BusinessWeek ONLINE

For further reading on managers and management go to: www.businessweek.com

HOW GROUPS BEHAVE

Groups Within Organizations

All organizations depend on groups to achieve success. In organizations, a group is two or more people who interact to meet a shared goal. In your high school, groups of students may form the student council or organize fundraising or social events. A shared sense of purpose sets a group apart from just a gathering of people. In general, organizations contain two kinds of groups: formal work groups and informal work groups.

Formal Work Groups

Management establishes **formal work groups** to carry out specific tasks. Formal groups may exist for a short or long period of time. A task force is an example of a formal group. These groups have a single goal, such as resolving a problem or designing a new product.

▲ **INFORMAL GROUPS** People who work together often join informal groups for social reasons. *What are some of the positive and negative aspects of belonging to such a group?*

A different type of formal work group is the *command* or *functional* group. This group consists of a manager and all the employees he or she supervises. Unlike a task group, the command group's work is ongoing and not confined to one issue or product.

Informal Work Groups

Informal work groups are formed voluntarily by members of an organization. They develop from personal contacts and interactions among people. Groups of employees that lunch together regularly and office cliques are examples of informal work groups.

PREDICT

Why would employees form informal work groups?

A special type of informal group is the *interest group*. Its members share a purpose or concern. For example, women executives might form a group to share ideas about issues that women in management face.

Work is a social experience. Employees interact while performing job duties in offices, factories, stores, and other workplaces. Friendships emerge naturally from these contacts. Informal groups formed around mutual interests fill important social needs. In earlier centuries, groups like extended families, churches, and small towns met these needs. Today people socialize mostly with people they meet at work.

Informal work groups affect productivity, the morale of other employees, and the success of managers. They can be the result of—and

▲ **RESEARCHING WORK** In the first half of the twentieth century, researchers studied the way factory workers behaved on the job. *Why do you think factory owners and managers wanted to know how workers behaved?*

can help create—a shared sense of loyalty. This is especially prevalent in high-risk occupations, such as fire fighting and police work.

Informal work groups often develop in areas where employees work close together (such as offices with cubicles) and among employees in the same field (such as accounting or graphic design). Employees may band together to share fears or complaints. In such cases, informal groups work against organization goals.

Studies have identified the power of informal work groups in organizations. The 1924 Hawthorne studies (see Chapter 2) discovered that groups may set their own productivity levels and pressure workers to meet them. In one group, workers who produced more or less than the acceptable levels met with name-calling, sarcasm, ridicule, and in some cases, a blow on the arm. The Hawthorne studies concluded that informal organizations with their own social systems exist within formal organizations.

In general, management does not recognize informal groups that revolve around friendships, interests, or shared working space and tasks. Yet an understanding of these groups can improve managers' work with formal groups. Employees join informal groups to meet a social need. They often gain great satisfaction from these groups. Managers seek to duplicate this satisfaction in formal work groups.

Group Norms

Group norms are the informal rules a group adopts to regulate the behavior of group members. They may be extremely simple—a group that lunches together may maintain a rigid seating order. They may include expectations that group members will remain loyal to each other under any circumstances. Whatever the norms, group members are expected to hold to them. Members who break the rules often are shut out.

Norms don't govern every action in a group, only those important for group survival. For instance, a working group's norms would affect its productivity levels, operating procedures, and other work-related activities. Norms may not be written down or even spoken. Rather, group members use their actions to show new members how to behave.

CONNECT

Describe an informal group at your school. What are the group's norms?

▲ **CULTURAL VALUES** Group norms may be based on shared cultural values. *What cultural values make work groups successful?*

Labor Relations Manager

Nature of the Work

Labor relations managers are vital in companies that employ union workers. However, in most industries, union membership is declining, and, more often, labor relations managers are working with non-unionized employees.

Labor relations managers prepare the information used during collective bargaining. They must know economics, labor law, and collective bargaining trends. Their staff sees that grievances, wages, salaries, healthcare plans, and pensions are administered according to the contract. Directors of industrial relations develop labor policy, oversee labor relations, and negotiate collective bargaining agreements.

Working Conditions

Labor relations managers work in many different industries, usually in clean, pleasant surroundings. They tend to work more than 40 hours a week and face extreme pressure during contract negotiations.

Training, Other Qualifications, and Advancement

Labor relations managers need a bachelor's degree in liberal arts with emphasis in human resources, personnel administration, business or labor law, or industrial relations. A master's degree is required for top management positions. Internships or work-study programs are useful.

Labor relations managers must have integrity, strong speaking and writing skills, and experience working with people of all backgrounds. They must be fair and able to function well under pressure.

Salary Range

Labor relations managers earn $25,300 to start with a bachelor's degree; $39,900 with a masters; directors of industrial relations, $100,000+ depending on the size and type of industry, and experience.

CRITICAL THINKING

Why must labor relations managers have integrity?

STANDARD &POOR'S

INDUSTRY OUTLOOK

When labor negotiations break down in the transportation industry, it can have a devastating effect on the U.S. economy. Nearly 7 million businesses rely on the U.S. transportation network to conduct commerce, and more than 100 million U.S. households rely on freight transportation to access goods and services.

BUSINESS MANAGEMENT *Online*

For more information on management careers, go to:
busmanagement.glencoe.com

Group Behavior

Think about the informal groups of friends and classmates you have belonged to at school or in your neighborhood. However they develop, informal work groups share similar types of behaviors. They include cohesiveness, conformity, and groupthink.

Group Cohesiveness

Group cohesiveness is the degree of attraction among group members, or how tightly knit a group is. The more cohesive a group, the more likely members are to follow group norms. A number of factors affect the cohesiveness of informal work groups—size, success, status, outside pressures, stability of membership, communication, and physical isolation.

Size is a particularly important factor in group cohesiveness. The smaller the group, the more cohesive it is likely to be. A small group allows individual members to interact frequently. Members of large groups have fewer chances to interact, therefore these groups tend to be less cohesive.

Think about how two close friends operate when they study together. Because they know each other well and talk easily, they have no trouble working together. Now imagine three new people in the study session. Everyone might not agree on the best way to cover material. It may be hard to work with different people. This might cause the study group to fall apart.

Success and status affect group cohesiveness. The more success a group experiences, the more cohesive it becomes. Several factors contribute to a group's status. For instance, highly skilled work groups tend to have more status than less-skilled groups. Like groups that meet their goals, high-status groups tend to be more cohesive than other informal work groups. These relationships are circular—success and status bring about cohesiveness, and cohesiveness brings about status and success.

Outside pressures, such as conflicts with management, can increase group cohesiveness. If a group sees management's requests as a demand or threat, it becomes more cohesive. In these situations, members may develop an "us against them" mentality.

A stable membership and easy lines of communication improve group cohesiveness. Long-standing members know each other well and are familiar with group norms. Employees who work in the same area socialize easily. In a production line, however, conversation is difficult and groups are less cohesive.

Finally, physical isolation from other employees may increase group cohesiveness. The isolation forces workers into close contact with each other and strengthens bonds.

▲ **GROUP COHESIVENESS**
Many businesses are abandoning offices in favor of cubicles. *Do you think cubicles increase group cohesiveness?*

Group Conformity

Group conformity is the degree to which group members accept and follow group norms. A group generally seeks to control members' behavior for two reasons. First, independent behavior can cause disagreements that threaten a group's survival. Second, consistent behavior creates an atmosphere of trust that allows members to work together and socialize comfortably. Members are able to predict how others in the group will behave.

Individual members tend to conform to group norms under certain conditions:

- when group norms are similar to personal attitudes, beliefs, and behavior
- when they do not agree with the group's norms but feel pressure to accept them

GROUP PRESSURE AND CONFORMITY Researchers have studied the influence of group pressure on individual members. One study of group conformity took place at a textile firm in Virginia. A textile employee began to produce more than the group norm of 50 units per day. After two weeks, the group started to pressure this worker to produce less, and she quickly dropped to the group's level. After three weeks, all the members of the group were moved to other jobs except for this worker. Once again, her production quickly climbed to double the group norm (see **Figure 14–1**).

QUESTION

Overall, is conformity to group norms a positive or negative habit? Explain your answer.

All About

ATTITUDE

SHYNESS DOESN'T SHINE

Part of your job is informing others of your actions and knowledge base. Keeping an open channel of communication allows information to flow freely throughout your organization. Speak up and don't be silent. Your input on situations is important.

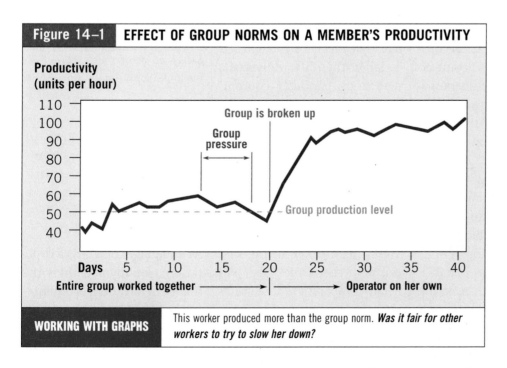

Figure 14–1 | **EFFECT OF GROUP NORMS ON A MEMBER'S PRODUCTIVITY**

Productivity (units per hour)

Group is broken up

Group pressure

Group production level

Days 5 10 15 20 25 30 35 40

Entire group worked together ————→ | ——→ Operator on her own

WORKING WITH GRAPHS This worker produced more than the group norm. *Was it fair for other workers to try to slow her down?*

The Global Corporation Becomes the Leaderless Corporation

The trailblazing corporate superstar will become a thing of the past. And follow-the-leader is a game companies will no longer play. The path to success will be paved by teams.

We are all angels
*   with only one wing.*
We can only fly
*   while embracing each other.*
*   —Luciano de Crescenzo*

The 20th century Italian poet's metaphor wasn't about the 21st century corporation, but it might as well have been. The coming century will be unfriendly to superhero CEOs who try to wing their companies heavenward by sheer force of will. Success will belong to companies that are leaderless— companies whose leadership is so widely shared that they resemble beehives, ant colonies, or schools of fish.

Today, democratic decision-making in corporations is still confined largely to factory floors and new-product laboratories, far from the top of organizational pyramids. That is hardly surprising. In a nation that loves superheroes, people

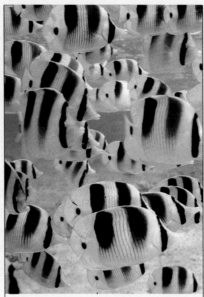

cling to the myth of what management guru Warren Bennis calls "the triumphant individual." The media celebrate CEOs as larger-than-life individuals who single-handedly communicate a vision and lead the way, earning millions for themselves in the process.

Cool the hero worship. In the 20th century, the Soviet Union collapsed because its command-and-control economy couldn't keep up with the West's free market. In the 21st century, the same fate will befall companies whose CEOs attempt to control everything.

Teams at the top will make more sense than a single outrageously paid CEO.

The Internet allows companies to be more leaderless because information can be shared horizontally rather than funneled up to the CEO's office and back down again.

Team leadership is ideally suited for this new reality. When the landscape is changing daily, it's crucial to react fast—something bureaucratic, top-down organizations don't do well. Most urgent projects require the coordinated contributions of many talented people working together.

Excerpted with permisssion from BusinessWeek, *August 30, 1999*

CRITICAL THINKING

According to the writer, what is the key component for a company's success in the 21st century?

DECISION MAKING

As a manager of a large corporation, would you employ the theory of a leaderless organization? Explain.

GROUPTHINK When group members lose their ability to think as individuals and conform at the expense of their good judgment, **groupthink** occurs. Members become unwilling to say anything against the group or any member, even if an action is wrong. William Golding explored the concept of groupthink in his novel *The Lord of the Flies*. This book illustrates what can happen when individuals are removed from society and are left to create their own rules.

Keeping a group together under any circumstance is a goal in itself. Groups with this goal believe that the group is indestructible and always right. Group members justify any action, stereotype outsiders as enemies of the group, and pressure unwilling members to conform. In business, groupthink is disruptive because it affects employees' ability to make logical decisions.

CONNECT

Imagine that you are the new manager of a department that has succumbed to groupthink. What steps would you take to encourage individual thinking?

Section 14.1 Assessment

FACT AND IDEA REVIEW

1. What is the major difference between formal and informal groups?
2. Name two things that often cause employees to join or initiate informal work groups.
3. Give three factors that influence a group's cohesiveness.
4. Describe two situations in which group members are likely to conform to group norms.

CRITICAL THINKING

1. **Predicting Consequences:** Do you think it is possible to eliminate the need for informal work groups? Explain.
2. **Drawing Conclusions:** Some employees are described as "marching to the beat of a different drummer." After reading this section, what do you think that statement means?

ASSESSING SPEECH SKILLS

You have been a member of many formal and informal groups in your life. Examples of such groups may include a youth group, a sports team, co-workers at a summer or part-time job, or neighborhood friends. Some of the groups have been effective and some have not. Think about the most effective and ineffective groups you have been in. Prepare a brief presentation describing the characteristics of each group.

CASE ANALYSIS

You have been hired for the summer to help raise money for a local environmental group. The group has two teams that telephone people in the evenings to solicit donations. The group has raised a respectable sum of money. The problem is that one team member, Marcia, is pulling in most of the donations on a nightly basis. The rest of the team feels they are not doing the job well. You decide to talk to the team leader about the situation.

Apply: With several other students, decide what you are going to say to the team leader. Consider the options carefully. For instance, is there some way Marcia can contribute to raising group productivity?

MANAGING FORMAL GROUPS

WHAT YOU'LL LEARN

▶ The importance of formal work groups.
▶ How managers can influence group cohesiveness and conformity.
▶ Methods of encouraging teamwork in formal groups.
▶ The characteristics of successful group leaders.

WHY IT'S IMPORTANT

Formal work groups are an important way of organizing work, and managers must help them succeed.

KEY TERMS

• linking-pin concept
• team building
• idiosyncrasy credit
• quality circle

The Importance of Formal Work Groups

Formal work groups play an important part in helping an organization meet its goals. Groups have more knowledge and information than individuals. They make communicating and solving problems easier. This creates a more efficient and effective company.

The importance of managing groups effectively is becoming recognized in the business world. Employees must work closely to improve production and maintain a competitive edge. Changes in the work force are bringing men and women from different backgrounds together. Managers must work with groups to overcome cultural and gender differences. These, and other factors, make managing work groups one of management's most important tasks.

▲ TEAM WORK Honda's team sometimes spends 18 months working together on the design of a new car. *Why is a team a better choice for this task than an individual?*

Influencing Work Groups

Studies at the Hawthorne plant, where researchers documented the existence of informal work groups, looked at the effects of various changes on workers' productivity. Researchers varied job factors, including the way workers were paid and supervised, lighting, the length of rest periods, and the number of hours worked. Productivity rose with each change.

This result led to the coining of the term *Hawthorne effect*. As you may remember from Chapter 2, the Hawthorne effect states that giving special attention to a group of employees changes the employees' behavior. The results of the studies show that when groups of employees are singled out for attention, they tend to work more efficiently.

Building Effective Work Groups

Members of informal work groups often develop a shared sense of values and group loyalty. Formal groups rarely share these qualities because they are assigned to them rather than voluntary. Managers are responsible for developing shared values and group loyalty in formal work groups.

The linking-pin concept is one way of describing management's role in work groups. The **linking-pin concept** holds that because managers are members of overlapping groups, they link formal work groups to the total organization. Managers improve communication and ensure that organizational and group goals are met. In other words, managers themselves are the linking pins (see **Figure 14–2**).

Figure 14–2 | LINKING-PIN CONCEPT

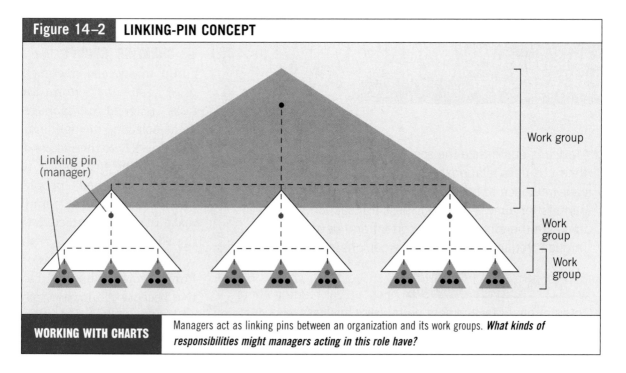

Linking pin (manager)

Work group

Work group

Work group

WORKING WITH CHARTS — Managers act as linking pins between an organization and its work groups. *What kinds of responsibilities might managers acting in this role have?*

► **ENVIRONMENT** Work groups need a place to meet and work that is comfortable and has the equipment they need. *Why do you think environment is so important to a work group?*

Building effective formal work groups often is called team building. **Team building** is the process of establishing a cohesive group that works together to achieve its goals. A team will be successful only if its members feel that working conditions are fair to all. A team can fail, even in a supportive organization, if a manager does not encourage fair play.

The success of a group or team can be measured in the same way as the success of organizations. Successful organizations and groups both meet their goals by using their resources well. Managers encourage teamwork by selecting group members carefully, creating a positive work environment, building trust, and increasing group cohesiveness.

CREATING GROUPS For a group to succeed, members must be able to perform the tasks assigned by management. Selecting the right individuals is key to the success of a group. The first step is to identify qualified people. Then management must make the group attractive to these individuals.

For most employees, a formal work group is attractive because it increases pay and offers some satisfaction. If employees see that joining

International Management

MEXICO

Mexicans emphasize the social and personal aspects of their business relationships. The government has significant influence in private business matters and requires permits for almost every business transaction. Connections are therefore vitally important and developed through frequent and warm interpersonal transactions.

BusinessWeek *ONLINE* For further reading about International Management go to: **www.businessweek.com**

a formal group can provide them with the same satisfaction that an informal group can, they are more likely to participate willingly.

Environment also can be important to the success of a group. An important requirement for meeting group goals is a suitable place to work. How the office is laid out and other physical factors will affect the group's ability to work together successfully.

BUILDING TRUST Trust is essential among group members and between groups and management. A successful group effort means sharing responsibilities and making decisions together. Group members must feel that the entire group is willing and able to work together successfully to achieve goals. Without trust, groups can't set or stick to production norms.

Bill Gates of Microsoft relies on small teams that work on their own. He says, "You've got to pick a few people and really trust them." Managers must have faith in their employees. They also must recognize the interests of the organization, the group, and the employees. Effective managers should become personally involved, take a real interest in group members, share information, and exhibit honesty.

INFLUENCING GROUP COHESIVENESS AND CONFORMITY

Think about teams you have belonged to at school or summer camp. These successful teams often are highly competitive and eager to succeed. Effective work groups share these characteristics. Both types of groups also draw their primary satisfaction from a sense of accomplishment, which comes from a job well done.

▲ **SMALL TEAMS** Huge corporations often use small teams to develop products such as computer software. *How might small teams of workers benefit the company?*

Managers can affect formal group performance levels by studying the degree of group conformity. Formal groups must be cohesive and dedicated to high performance norms in order to succeed. Managers can influence group cohesiveness by

- keeping groups small
- selecting group members carefully
- finding a good personality fit between new and old employees
- developing an office layout that improves communication
- creating clear goals
- inspiring group competition
- rewarding groups rather than individuals
- isolating groups from each other

RESPOND

How would you feel if a manager asked you to sacrifice your individual goals for the sake of team goals? What would a manager have to do in order to persuade you to do this?

Basketball coach Phil Jackson has an approach to management that is based partly on his Zen Buddhist outlook and partly on team building. Jackson claims his approach gave the Chicago Bulls and the L.A. Lakers several NBA championships over the past ten years. When

◄ **TEAM BUILDING** The team concept stresses the good of the group over the good of the individual. *What is required of workers to make a team succeed?*

asked what Zen Buddhism has to do with management, Jackson replies, "Whether on the court or off, what I call for in my people is full awareness and attention."

Jackson's approach teaches individuals to value the needs of the team. High individual performance with poor team performance is not what winning is about, either in sports or in business. Individuals must surrender their egos so that the end result is bigger than the sum of its parts. When this happens, the team works together like fingers on a hand.

Some members of groups will always be permitted to depart from group norms. This phenomenon is known as the idiosyncrasy credit. The **idiosyncrasy credit** occurs when individuals who have played a significant role in a group are allowed some freedom within the group. People in this position have often helped develop a group's norms. Because the group's norms often are the same as their own, those who could use the idiosyncrasy credit often do not.

Quality Circles

One type of formal work group is the quality circle. A **quality circle** is a group of employees from a single work unit (such as a department) who share ideas on how to improve quality. The goal of a quality circle is to involve employees in decision making. Membership is almost always voluntary and members share a common bond—they perform similar tasks.

Japan has used quality circles since the early 1960s. The idea arrived in the United States after executives from Lockheed Corporation visited Japan in the 1970s and saw the circles in action. Lockheed used quality circles to improve quality and save several million dollars.

Quality circles have benefits other than increasing employee participation. They encourage communication and trust among members and managers. They are an inexpensive way to provide employees with training while giving them a sense of control over their work lives. Most importantly, however, they may solve problems that have been

THERE'S NO "I" IN TEAM
Working in a team environment means that everyone contributes toward a common goal. Although you may be working independently, let others know they can count on you for assistance or clarification at any time.

QUESTION
Are quality circles more consistent with Theory X or Theory Y management philosophies?

FIGURE 14–3

Team Building

Managers can build effective teams in three ways: by selecting the right individuals and providing a positive environment for them, by building trust, and by encouraging group cohesiveness and conformity.

1 SELECTING INDIVIDUALS
The first step in building an effective team is finding the right people. Group members need to have the right skills and the right personality fit.

2 TRUST-BUILDING
The second step is to build trust among group members and between the group and management.

3 ENCOURAGING GROUP COHESIVENESS
The third step is to develop a cohesive group that conforms to group norms. Managers can improve group cohesiveness by keeping groups small, giving them clear goals, and rewarding them as a team.

around for years. Quality circles create strong lines of communication. "Me" becomes "us" in a good quality circle.

Groups and Leaders

When an informal group selects a leader, members choose the person most capable of satisfying the group's needs. The group gives this leader authority, and can take this authority away at any time. This leader needs strong communication skills, especially in setting objectives for the group, giving directions, and summarizing information.

To see how informal groups choose leaders, imagine a group of people shipwrecked on an island. The group's first goal is to find food, water, and shelter. The individual best equipped to help the group survive would naturally become the leader. Later, the group's goal might change to getting off the island. The original leader may no longer be the best person to help meet this new goal, and a new leader could emerge. The process may continue through several leaders.

▲ **QUALITY CIRCLES** Automakers use the quality circle to focus on issues of quality. *Why do you think these groups are able to solve problems individuals have not been able to solve?*

Gaining Acceptance

Managers assigned to formal work groups must work to gain acceptance as leaders. They generally do not have the same authority as leaders of informal groups. The formal authority granted by top management is no guarantee that a manager will effectively guide a group.

Think about how you respond to your teachers. You respect teachers who know their subject well, communicate information effectively, treat students with respect, and make fair judgments. Managers working with formal groups can use these same behaviors to gain the trust and respect of employees.

Managers must keep track of those changes within the organization that might affect the group. At times, they may have to modify group goals to meet new organizational goals. For example, an organization faced with strong competition may need to make decisions rapidly rather than rely on groups to come up with a solution. In these cases, managers must be ready to make immediate decisions for the group.

RESPOND

In general, what qualities would make an effective group leader?

Encouraging Participation

Building an effective team requires a nontraditional managerial approach. In a traditional organizational structure, managers direct the employees who work for them. As part of a team, however, managers encourage participation and shared responsibility, acting more like a coach than a manager.

One way of encouraging team spirit is to provide the group with a vision. People who organize groups to support social causes often use this approach. For example, one person may rally a community around a project such as reclaiming a vacant lot for a park. In the business world, managers can offer team members the possibility of designing a state-of-the-art product or service.

Managers lead by example. Their attitude and performance become the standard for group norms. A manager who believes that a group must listen to and support all members might create a group of top managers who share this feeling. Employees who see managers functioning within a cohesive group are more likely to work effectively in groups themselves.

Section 14.2 Assessment

 FACT AND IDEA REVIEW

1. Why are work groups important?
2. What two things attract employees to formal work groups?
3. Why is trust essential in a group?
4. Describe two methods managers can use to encourage group participation.

 CRITICAL THINKING

1. **Analyzing Information:** Draw on your own experience to explain why you think the Hawthorne effect does or does not exist.
2. **Evaluating Information:** Do you think leading by example is a good way to motivate people? Why or why not?

 ASSESSING PHYSICAL EDUCATION SKILLS

Within the class, organize teams to compete in a game of volleyball or other sport. Have each group select a captain, then work together to create cohesiveness. Methods may include practicing together, engaging in a group activity, or sharing personal information. Keep a record of the methods your group uses. Once the games have been completed, compare your methods with those of the other teams. What methods did the winning team use that might have made it successful?

 CASE ANALYSIS

Darren Washington, an employee at AT&T, wants to start a volunteer tutoring program at a local school. His supervisor, Jackie, is pleased by this idea. AT&T encourages volunteerism and allows employees time to participate. Jackie wants to ensure that Darren will be an effective group leader.

Apply: Make a list of questions Jackie can ask that will help her determine whether Darren is a good candidate for team leader.

CHAPTER 14 ASSESSMENT

REVIEWING VOCABULARY

With a group of students, role-play a meeting of managers who are trying to find ways to make their work groups more productive. Use each of the vocabulary words in your role play.

formal work group	groupthink
informal work group	linking-pin concept
group norms	team building
group cohesiveness	idiosyncrasy credit
group conformity	quality circle

CHAPTER SUMMARY

Section 14.1

▶ Organizations have two kinds of work groups, formal and informal.

▶ Informal work groups develop around friendship, shared interests, or similar work responsibilities.

▶ Informal groups have their own norms, are cohesive, and develop ways to maintain conformity.

Section 14.2

▶ Formal work groups often lack the loyalty and shared values that characterize informal groups, so managers work hard to encourage participation.

▶ Managers can build effective teams by selecting the right candidates, building trust, and encouraging group cohesiveness.

▶ In order to be good team leaders, managers must be accepted by the group, understand how to provide a vision, and lead by example.

RECALLING KEY CONCEPTS

1. Name two types of formal work groups.
2. Give two reasons groups try to control member behavior.
3. Name three ways managers can influence group cohesiveness.
4. What two things do managers accomplish when they act as linking pins between work groups and management?
5. Some people who could use the idiosyncrasy credit in a group often don't. Why not?

THINKING CRITICALLY

1. Explain why members of formal work groups often don't share informal groups' loyalty and common sense of values.
2. Why is it important for managers to have faith in their employees and work groups?
3. What are the reasons for wanting a good personality fit when selecting people for a work group?
4. Why don't managers of formal work groups have the same authority as informal group leaders?
5. Do you think work groups always respond best to a participatory management approach? Why or why not?

CHAPTER 14 ASSESSMENT

ASSESSING ACADEMIC SKILLS

WRITING You are a manager at a family-oriented restaurant chain. In the past year, two new restaurants have opened in the area. Both of them have done poorly, despite good locations. You must put together a task force to find ways to boost the new restaurants' revenues. Decide where you would find people for the task force. Then compose a memo for senior management presenting your proposal and explaining your reasons for choosing these employees.

APPLYING MANAGEMENT PRINCIPLES

SOLVE THE PROBLEM The insurance company where you work is purchasing new software for the billing department. As head of the Information Technology Department, you are to lead the six-member team that will choose the new software. During the first two meetings, members of the group bickered constantly, and no one made any realistic suggestions. What can you do to make the team more effective?

Public Speaking In groups of five, discuss possible reasons for the group's behavior. Then discuss ways of building a more effective team that addresses those reasons. Prepare a presentation that describes your plan to create a more effective group.

PREPARING FOR COMPETITIVE EVENTS

Answer true or false and explain your answer.

Group members affected by groupthink won't say anything against the group or any member of it, even if an individual or the group does something wrong.

BusinessWeek *ONLINE*

In this chapter you read the *BusinessWeek* Management Model about global corporations becoming leaderless corporations. For more information, go to *BusinessWeek* online at: **www.businessweek.com**

Using the Internet or library resources, find current articles on companies that use this theory. Write a two-page summary highlighting the changes that led to a leaderless organization. Share your summaries with the class.

CHAPTER 15

WORKING WITH EMPLOYEES

LEARNING OBJECTIVES

When you have completed this chapter, you will be able to:

- Understand the methods that organizations use to select employees.
- Explain the difference between a transfer, promotion, and separation.
- Identify different methods of training employees.
- Understand the methods that organizations use to measure performance.
- Explain the process of Management By Objectives.
- Understand the importance of rewarding employees.

READING STRATEGIES

As you read

- **PREDICT** what the section will be about.
- **CONNECT** what you read with your own life.
- **QUESTION** as you read to make sure you understand the content.
- **RESPOND** to what you read.

Trusted Gear. Expert Advice. Since 1938.

www.rei.com

WORKPLACE CONNECTIONS

Understanding Management

REI (Recreational Equipment Inc.) has repeatedly been named to *Fortune* magazine's list of "100 best companies to work for in America." The outdoors and sporting goods retailer has earned this distinction by offering employees a unique set of benefits, including flexible health, life, and disability insurance plans, an employee profit-sharing plan, and a "challenge grant" program that encourages employees to test REI products on wilderness adventures.

Analyzing Management Skills

Why would employee enthusiasm be important to a company like REI?

Applying Management Skills

If you were publishing a list of the 10 best companies to work for in your town, what things would you take into consideration?

BusinessWeek ONLINE

For further reading on managers and management go to: **www.businessweek.com**

MEETING PERSONNEL NEEDS

WHAT YOU'LL LEARN

▶ How companies use methods such as interviewing and testing to select employees.
▶ How the human resources department handles employees leaving positions.
▶ What training techniques companies develop to teach new concepts.

WHY IT'S IMPORTANT

A successful manager must develop effective processes to select, train, and maintain employees.

KEY TERMS

- human resources
- job description
- halo effect
- exit interview
- layoff
- termination
- job rotation
- vestibule training
- apprenticeship

How Companies Select Employees

Paul Ling is graduating from college in the spring. He is searching for a job in which he can develop his graphic design skills. Paul has scheduled three interviews during his upcoming spring break. To prepare for a successful interview, Paul has thoroughly researched each company. He had no idea searching for a job would be such hard work!

The process of finding a job requires time and effort from the applicant. However, the process of recruiting, selecting, and training employees is no easy task for an organization.

In most organizations, the **human resources** department recruits employees, manages training and compensation, and plans for future personnel needs. When a company has an open position, human resources will advertise, select from the applicants, and then fill the position. However, this is just one function of human resources.

▲ **RECRUITING STRATEGIES** Some organizations seek out new employees through signs, as in this photograph. *What are other ways that human resources can recruit potential employees?*

Human resources managers must consider the company's business goals and the business environment. With these in mind, human resources will then develop an employment plan. The first step is to create a **job description**, or a written statement identifying the type of work and necessary qualifications for a job. The job description sets the standards against which applicants can be rated.

Once the job description is prepared, the next step is to determine the target applicant pool and advertise the position. Traditional methods of job recruiting include placing an advertisement in the newspaper or attending a job fair. Technological changes have increased the value of the Internet in the job search. Web sites like monster.com and careerpath.com allow job seekers to search databases of classified ads and post résumés on the Internet. Companies search résumés to find qualified candidates.

QUESTION

Why is it important for a manager to put careful thought into the creation of a job description?

The Selection Process

A standard selection procedure helps a company choose the most qualified applicants. There are four steps that make up this process. These steps are

1. preliminary screening
2. testing
3. employment interview
4. personal judgment

Preliminary Screening

The first step in any selection procedure is *preliminary screening*. Hundreds of letters and résumés may arrive in response to one advertisement. The human resources department may sort these applications for the hiring manager, determining which applicants have the necessary education or experience. Southwest Airlines receives 129,000 résumés and hires approximately 3,411 people every two years.

When the preliminary screening has narrowed the applicant pool, a manager might seek input from team members. At this stage, the organization may check the applicant's references and credentials. If an applicant makes it this far, he or she will be contacted to schedule an interview or test.

▲ **PRINT RECRUITING** Newspaper advertisements may include very brief job descriptions. *What effect does this have on the applicant pool?*

Testing

The next step may include a test. For any job, there are often applicants with similar credentials. Tests provide a uniform evaluation of the qualifications of a prospective employee. Some different kinds of employment tests are highlighted in **Figure 15–1.**

A recent trend in employee testing is the Predictive Index (PI), created by Arnold Davies in the 1950s. This ten-minute personality test is used for effectively hiring and working with employees. It identifies an individual's strengths and weaknesses. More than 3,000 companies currently use this test, including IKEA, Budget Rent-A-Car, and even some college and professional sports teams.

Employment tests must meet requirements of *validity* and *reliability*. A test is valid if it measures factors relevant to the job. A test is reliable if the same person or group of people taking it again under similar circumstances get similar results. This helps to remove the element of chance from the testing program.

RESPOND

Do you think tests provide an accurate prediction of an employee's potential performance? Why or why not?

Figure 15–1	COMMON EMPLOYMENT TESTS
Aptitude Test	Measures capacity to learn a particular subject or skill.
Psychomotor Test	Measures strength, dexterity, and coordination.
Job Knowledge Test	Measures knowledge related to a particular job.
Proficiency Test	Measures performance on a sample of the work required in the job.
Interest Test	Categorizes applicant's interests relative to the job.
Psychological Test	Attempts to define personality traits.
Polygraph Test ("lie detector test")	Records changes in physical response as a person responds to questions to determine whether responses are truthful.

Students spend a good deal of time preparing for and taking tests. *What are some examples of tests? What are the purposes of those tests?*

Personnel Manager

■ Nature of the Work

Personnel managers oversee all the needs of employees. In small companies, they may recruit, interview and hire potential employees, as well as develop and coordinate personnel programs and policies. In larger firms, personnel managers oversee lower-level managers who specialize in different aspects of personnel management, such as hiring, wages, benefits, training, or employee relations. Personnel managers at all levels may help their firms develop training programs to enhance employee skills, and improve the company's employees' satisfaction with their jobs.

■ Working Conditions

Personnel managers work in clean, pleasant, comfortable offices. They work a 35 to 40 hour week. Companies in all industries and of all sizes hire personnel managers.

■ Training, Other Qualifications, and Advancement

To become a personnel manager, you need a bachelor's degree in liberal arts, with an emphasis on human resources or business administration. Some companies prefer that personnel managers have a background in the industry. A master's degree is required for top management positions.

Personnel managers must like and work well with people of all backgrounds. They must have strong speaking and writing skills, be fair-minded, and have integrity.

■ Salary Range

Entry-level positions for employees with a bachelor's degree starts at $25,000; with a master's degree, $40,000. Personnel managers earn about $91,000. Salary varies with location, company, and experience.

CRITICAL THINKING

In what situations would a personnel manager be required to be fair-minded? What kinds of ethical dilemmas might a personnel manager face?

STANDARD &POOR'S

INDUSTRY OUTLOOK

One growing industry that will demand a number of human resource managers is the exploding field of online security. Companies who share information or make sales online must secure the safety of their networks and transactions. To do so, they will hire and train vital personnel to develop and/or monitor anti-virus, firewall, encryption, and authentication products.

For more information on management careers, go to:
busmanagement.glencoe.com

Employment Interviews

Interviews are another step in the selection process. Companies use several types of interviews, including the structured and unstructured interview. In many cases, a potential applicant who looks promising will be called back for a *second interview*. A second interview may be more in-depth than an initial screening interview, because managers can spend more time with a smaller number of candidates. See **Figure 15–2** on the importance of preparing for an interview.

THE STRUCTURED INTERVIEW In the *structured interview*, the interviewer prepares a list of questions. Structured interviews are useful

FIGURE 15–2

Preparing for an Interview

Interviews are an important step in the employee selection process. They allow the employer to learn more about the applicant than can be conveyed in a résumé or cover letter.

1 SETTING ASIDE SPACE
Before the applicant arrives there should be a place set aside for the interview. If a private room is not available, the interview must take place out of earshot of any other job applicants.

when interviewing many applicants for one position because they provide uniform information for each applicant. They also remind the interviewer to cover each question, for example why the applicant wants to change jobs, or where he or she wants to be in five years.

THE UNSTRUCTURED INTERVIEW The *unstructured interview* is a conversation between employer and applicant in a relaxed atmosphere. The employer asks open-ended questions, such as "Why did you leave your previous job?" Then the applicant has the opportunity to ask questions about the organization.

Unstructured interviews are not always reliable because all pertinent questions may not be covered and the possibility of bias. It is

2 **PUTTING THE APPLICANT AT EASE** Conducting an effective interview begins with the interviewer, who should be an outgoing person trained in interviewing skills. It is helpful to put the applicant at ease first with a cup of coffee or some small talk.

3 **TAKING CONTROL OVER THE INTERVIEW** The interviewer should take notes during the interview to record important points. While the applicant should be encouraged to talk, the interviewer must control the direction of the discussion.

BE FAIR
Reward team members equally. If a team does well, everyone deserves credit. If a team is not performing, call a team meeting to discuss expectations. Singling out individuals will only weaken the rest of the team's spirit.

natural for people to form first impressions based on personal attributes. A qualified computer programmer who arrives for an interview wearing a nose ring might be rejected based on appearance alone. For this reason, most people dress conservatively for interviews. They recognize the importance of first impressions.

In the **halo effect**, a single characteristic dominates the interviewer's impression of the applicant. For example, if the applicant has a pleasant personality, the employer may overlook other concerns. A pleasant personality, however, is no guarantee that the applicant is qualified. In addition, people are generally on their best behavior during interviews. The employee may turn out to be grumpy and difficult in the workplace.

Personal Judgment

The final step in the selection process is personal judgment—choosing which individual gets the job. If more than one applicant is qualified, the employer must make a value judgment as to who would be most successful. If the previous steps have been performed correctly, this should not be a difficult decision.

Occasionally, none of the applicants is qualified. In this case, a higher salary might be offered to attract more applicants. The company may re-advertise in a different newspaper or Web site. It is best to wait for a qualified candidate rather than settle on a mediocre applicant.

Legal Considerations in Selection

Supreme Court decisions have had an impact on employment testing procedures. Legal action may result when tests are used without ensuring fairness, validity, and reliability. Results must be evaluated objectively based on job-related attributes, not on attributes such as race, religion, or sex.

Griggs v. Duke Power Company

The *Griggs v. Duke Power Company* case was brought by a group of African American employees at a power-generating plant. The employees objected to the requirement of a high-school diploma or the passing of intelligence tests as conditions of employment in or transfer to jobs at the plant.

The court decided that if a test negatively impacts female or minority group applicants, then the company must prove validity and prevalence to job requirements. Even if a company does not mean to discriminate, it may unintentionally select an unfair test.

Albemarle Paper Company v. Moody

In *Albemarle Paper Company v. Moody*, the North Carolina paper mill was seeking the reversal of a Court of Appeals decision that eliminated its testing program and awarded back pay to a group of African American employees. The managers argued that in addition to creating diversity programs, they had statistical proof that their testing was job-related. A lower court noted that they had made efforts to deal with segregation.

The Supreme Court agreed with the Court of Appeals that the intentions of the company were not the main issue. It held that it was not enough to show that the best workers did well on the tests, or that a testing program improved the overall quality of the work force. Any tests had to be specifically related to performing the job in question.

Transfers, Promotions, and Separations

Human resources planning must account for employees leaving positions, as well as new employees being hired. Employees may leave their positions through transfers, promotions, or separations.

Transfers

A *transfer* moves an employee into another position within the company. The employee generally maintains the same level of responsibility and pay. Transfers are a good way for an employee to learn different functions in an organization. For example, when one engineering project is finished, employees may be transferred to a new project.

Promotions

A *promotion* involves moving to a position of greater responsibility, with higher status and pay. Promotions are merit-based and encourage performance. When considering an employee for a promotion, organizations weigh merit and *seniority*, or

▲ **JOB TRANSFER** In a large company with offices in many locations, a promotion may involve a move to a different geographical location. **What are some benefits of a promotion?**

length of service. Most union contracts require that seniority be a factor when determining promotions.

In promotions, it is important to consider not only how an employee performs in the current job, but also how he or she will adapt to a new one. An organization that does not consider this becomes subject to the Peter Principle. The Peter Principle states that it is possible for employees to be promoted until they reach a level at which they can no longer perform.

Suppose a management position opens up in the Quarkville Advanced Physics Laboratory. Michelle Grayson is selected for the job based on her performance as a senior scientist. When she becomes lab chief, it is clear that she has poor management skills.

The laboratory has gained a mediocre supervisor and lost an excellent working scientist. It is unlikely that Michelle will be considered for further promotions, based on her performance. She has "risen to her level of incompetence." This can be avoided by considering the aptitudes and interest of candidates for promotion, in addition to performance in their current job.

WORKPLACE DIVERSITY

SWITZERLAND

The Swiss expect fashionable but conservative dress. Slouching in a chair would convey a poor image and humor is not acceptable in business negotiations. Managers are expected to be multilingual, well-educated and highly qualified. The business structure requires respect for tradition and seniority.

Separations

The final way in which an employee leaves a position is through separation. Separation may be voluntary or involuntary. A *voluntary separation* occurs when an employee resigns. The voluntary separation process usually includes an exit interview. An **exit interview** pinpoints reasons why an employee is leaving, such as a noncompetitive pay structure.

Involuntary separations include layoffs and terminations. **Layoffs** occur when there is not enough work for all employees. For example, factory layoffs may follow a cut in production. If the workload increases again, the laid-off employees can be called back. Sometimes layoffs are the result of *downsizing*, or transitioning to a smaller number of employees to increase efficiency.

In a **termination**, the employee is asked to leave because of poor performance or failure to follow company rules. Training, counseling, and disciplinary action are all solutions to personnel problems. However, if these fail, termination is necessary.

Termination should be a last resort. In addition to upsetting employees, it wastes company resources and the time invested in hiring and training that individual. Instead of terminating an unproductive employee, the company L.L. Bean will reassign the worker to a less stressful work site with a lower volume of sales.

CONNECT

Have you, or has a friend or family member, ever left a job through voluntary separation? If so, for what reasons?

How to Keep Rising Stars From Straying

The news stunned investors. On April 21, 1999, Black & Decker Corp. announced that Joseph Galli, 41, head of the company's $2.9 billion power-tool business had quit, sending the stock price down nearly 8%. The once struggling company had rebounded in part because of Galli's new-product launches at the division, which brings in 65% of sales.

It wasn't the first time the Towson (Md.) company has lost key talent: Three other top executives have quit B&D for CEO posts elsewhere this decade. But if B&D appears to have problems holding on to rising stars, it is hardly alone. With high-end job-hopping rampant amid a perceived leadership shortage, retaining the best is tougher than ever. That means companies must focus more on the care and feeding of their top brass.

TOO BRIGHT. So how to avoid the disruptions and costly searches that occur when the pipeline is suddenly vacant? While there are many things companies can do to motivate high performers, first they must find them. Dennis C.

Carey, vice-chairman of Spencer Stuart U.S., says that boards should do regular audits to identify talent.

Once identified, keeping the best and the brightest loyal usually starts with compensation. After the 1997 merger of Bell Atlantic Corp. and Nynex, the new board gave special retention bonuses to five top executives. If they stay at least three years, they earn payouts above $1 million. Not one of them has left.

PASTURES GREEN. Yet even the best-laid plans may not be enough to prevent a company from having to make a tough choice when an ambitious underling is itching to move into the corner office. Rather than lose a top-notch heir, for some the answer lies in accelerating the transition.

Whether that is the best option, of course, depends on many things, not least of which are the ages of the CEO and the heir, as well as their relative managerial strengths. In the case of B&D, the company is unable—or unwilling—to make enough room for both parties. While letting Galli leave may have been the right call, it's hardly an ideal solution. The lesson for any company looking to avoid B&D's troubles: Never forget that keeping your stars motivated is a far tougher job than recruiting them in the first place.

Excerpted with permission from BusinessWeek, June 7, 1999.

CRITICAL THINKING

What are two ways to maintain talented employees?

DECISION MAKING

Which of the methods cited in this article would you employ as a manager? Why?

Training Employees

Training is a way for employees to learn new concepts, gain new skills, or update existing ones. It may be individualized, such as when a supervisor introduces an employee to a new job function. Training also may take place in a class or group setting. **Figure 15–3** (on page 354) shows some of the training methods businesses use.

Occasionally, a particular type of training must be provided to the entire organization. For example, if a company switches from a paper-based timesheet system to a computerized system, everyone must learn the new way to report their hours.

Outback Steakhouse, the Australian-themed franchise, holds monthly video conference meetings with all kitchen staff. These meetings are a forum to discuss cooking and menus. Videotapes train workers on everything from serving techniques to food handling.

On-the-Job Training and Job Rotation

An employee's supervisor administers *on-the-job training*. The employee works and trains under close supervision until he or she understands the task and performs it correctly. On-the-job training is less disruptive than removing the employee for off-site training. However, the pressures of the workplace may result in incomplete and unorganized training.

▶ **EMPLOYEE TRAINING** Training is necessary for employees to stay aware of company procedures. *Can you think of an example when training would be necessary?*

▲ **ON-THE-JOB TRAINING** Many companies prefer on-the-job training to traditional classroom training. *What are some benefits of on-the-job training for a company?*

Job rotation (also called *cross-training*) is a form of on-the-job training that exposes employees to several jobs within an organization. Employees perform each job for a fixed period. They often enjoy cross-training because it allows them to master many skills.

Vestibule Training

In **vestibule training**, a training area, or *vestibule*, is set up with equipment similar to that used in the actual job. The employee learns and practices in a simulated work environment. Vestibule training is used to train cashiers, bank tellers, clerks, and technicians.

While vestibule training is a good way to get hands-on training, creating the training area can be expensive. The costs can be the same as installing the original facility because it simulates the actual working environment. The employee will need to adapt to working in the "real" environment, with all its pressures, when training ends.

Apprenticeship Training

Apprenticeship is a time-tested form of on-the-job training. In an apprenticeship, an experienced worker passes on skills to an assistant. Modern organizations adapt the system by assigning an experienced worker as a *mentor* to a new employee.

Apprenticeship programs are common in skilled occupations. Professional internships, such as those in which newly graduated physicians begin their medical practice under supervision, are an apprenticeship.

Classroom Training

Classroom training presents general information about the organization, rules, safety, and job concepts in a classroom setting. An expert in the subject lectures, answers questions, and encourages discussion. This form of training is often used to train technical, professional, and managerial employees. IBM employees spend at least 40 hours a year in the classroom, discussing new products and job concepts.

Classroom training allows information to be shared with large groups for a low cost. However, it is not effective for learning hands-on tasks because employees do not get to practice skills.

RESPOND

What training method would you prefer? Explain your reasoning.

Computer-Based Training

Computer-based training (or *Internet training*), in the classroom or on an individual basis, contributes to employee development at a low

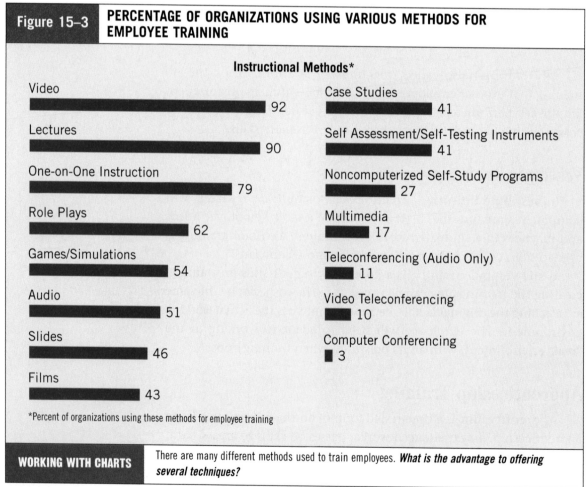

Figure 15–3 | **PERCENTAGE OF ORGANIZATIONS USING VARIOUS METHODS FOR EMPLOYEE TRAINING**

Instructional Methods*

Method	Percent
Video	92
Lectures	90
One-on-One Instruction	79
Role Plays	62
Games/Simulations	54
Audio	51
Slides	46
Films	43
Case Studies	41
Self Assessment/Self-Testing Instruments	41
Noncomputerized Self-Study Programs	27
Multimedia	17
Teleconferencing (Audio Only)	11
Video Teleconferencing	10
Computer Conferencing	3

*Percent of organizations using these methods for employee training

WORKING WITH CHARTS | There are many different methods used to train employees. *What is the advantage to offering several techniques?*

Source: Adapted from B. Filipczak, "What Employers Teach," *Training* 29, no. 10 (1992) p. 46.

Reprinted with permission. © 1992 Lakewood Publications, Minneapolis, MN. All rights reserved.

cost. Employees view material at individual computer workstations and answer questions at their own pace. According to the International Data Corporation, the market for electronic learning will grow to approximately $23.7 billion by 2006.

Daniella Varsak is working on the employee newsletter at the financial consulting firm where she works. She needs to learn the computer program Adobe Photoshop, but does not have time to take a class. The Internet offers online courses through companies such as Digital Think and Learning University. With services like these, Daniella can learn the program, finish tutorials, and take quizzes during her free time.

To make all types of training meaningful, managers need to provide positive reinforcement. Feedback regarding progress is critical to effective learning. Managers should encourage learning by setting standards and measuring performance.

Section 15.1 Assessment

 FACT AND IDEA REVIEW

1. What are the first two steps in an employee selection procedure?
2. Name three kinds of employment tests.
3. What is the difference between a structured and an unstructured interview?
4. Give two examples of involuntary separations.
5. Identify a benefit and challenge of vestibule training.

 CRITICAL THINKING

1. **Analyzing Information:** How can an employer ensure test reliability? Why is reliability necessary?
2. **Drawing Conclusions:** In a structured interview, is it possible for an interviewer to be misled by the "halo effect"?

 ASSESSING SOCIAL STUDIES SKILLS

Apprenticeship has been utilized as a job training method for thousands of years. Drawing on library and Internet research, discuss the historical role of apprenticeship as well as the place that apprenticeship programs have in the modern workplace. Then discuss the role of contemporary mentor programs.

CASE ANALYSIS

Curtis Long manages a local sports-equipment store that supplies the local high-school athletes and coaches. Curtis needs to hire a part-time assistant to help with the day-to-day operations of the store, such as taking inventory, predicting what new products the store should carry, and handling customer requests in the store and on the telephone.

Apply: Prepare a job description for the assistant position. Then, write a classified ad to place in the local newspaper. Finally, develop five interview questions to determine qualification.

REWARDING PERFORMANCE

WHAT YOU'LL LEARN

➤ Four different methods of evaluating employee performance.
➤ Why it is important to provide feedback to employees.
➤ How to connect a reward system to performance evaluation.

WHY IT'S IMPORTANT

Reward systems are developed to maintain employee motivation. It is necessary to evaluate performance and provide feedback to produce positive results.

KEY TERMS

• Management By Objectives (MBO)
• intrinsic rewards
• extrinsic rewards

How Is Performance Measured?

Rewarding employees for good performance encourages them to do their best. A company must show appreciation to retain qualified employees. America West Airlines offers employees a $50 bonus for every month in which the company ranks in the top three major airlines in either on-time performance or lack of customer complaints. Many trucking companies, such as Evans Trucking, offer bonuses based on safe and timely delivery and other gauges of driver performance.

Performance assessments identify problem areas. An employer must assess how well employees are meeting goals and employees must understand company's expectations. Performance assessments should guide an employee's future efforts.

Performance measures an employee's degree of accomplishment and results in job-related tasks. It is related to, but not the same as, the effort that an employee exerts on the job. However, an employee may work very hard without getting positive results.

▲ TRAINING OPPORTUNITY Sometimes an employee might give a job his or her best effort, but still not get good results. *What are some ways to remedy the situation?*

The employee's understanding of his or her part in an organization's work is called *role perception*. Role perception problems can often be solved through discussions between the employee and his or her supervisor. Motivated employees have excellent potential. However, feedback is necessary to perform effectively.

Organizations use several different methods to evaluate employee performance. These include Management By Objectives, production standards, essay appraisal, and critical-incident appraisal.

Management By Objectives

Management By Objectives (MBO) is a process often used in quality improvement and goal setting for the whole organization. It is equally valuable in goal setting and performance appraisal for individuals. See **Figure 15–4** for sample objectives.

Management By Objectives empowers employees by involving them in personal goal setting. This motivates employees to achieve those goals. The typical MBO process

- establishes well-defined job objectives
- develops an action plan for achieving objectives
- allows employees to implement the action plan
- evaluates achieved performance-based objectives
- takes necessary corrective action
- establishes new objectives for the future

MBO objectives should be clear and straightforward. Effective objectives challenge employees and provide incentives for improvement. The manager and employee should agree on objectives that are fair and realistic.

CONNECT

How would you use the Management By Objectives process to form an achievement plan for the rest of your school year?

All About

ATTITUDE

BURNING BRIDGES

"Why should I be nice to them? They're just interns." You never know who may rise above you within your own organization. A co-worker may be part of an accelerated career path at your company. People who cross your path today may some day be a superior or even a customer. Always be considerate.

Figure 15–4	SAMPLE OBJECTIVES

- To answer all customer complaints in writing within three days of receipt of complaint.

- To reduce order-processing time by two days within the next six months.

- To implement the new computerized accounts receivable system by August 1.

It is important for objectives to be challenging but obtainable goals. *How do these sample objectives meet that standard?*

Production Standards

Companies use the *production standards* approach when producing something that can be counted or measured. Goal setting for employees involves setting an expected level of output. Finally, employees compare their production with this standard.

To be effective, reasonable standards must be developed, based on the normal output of an average worker. Once standards have been established, this method has the advantage of objectivity. However, for many jobs it is difficult to set production standards because the job results cannot be quantified.

Essay Appraisal

In the *essay appraisal* method, the manager describes the employee's performance in a written narrative. Often the manager is provided with a form, which may include questions such as "Describe, in your own words, this employee's performance. What are his or her strengths and weaknesses?"

Essay appraisals may give a more complete picture of the employee's strengths and weaknesses than other methods. However, the essay appraisal's effectiveness depends on the writing skills of the supervisor. It may be subjective and difficult to defend against accusations of unfairness.

Critical-Incident Appraisal

The *critical-incident appraisal* method requires the manager to record specific situations that reflect the employee's performance, behavior, and attitudes on the job. These incidents are then used as the basis for performance appraisal and feedback.

This method produces a large volume of material and recording it all can be time-consuming. Subjectivity is another problem. A supervisor who likes an employee may record positive incidents and overlook negative ones. Conversely, a supervisor who does not get along well with a certain employee may draw attention to negative incidents.

QUESTION

List the four types of performance appraisal and describe the advantages of each one.

Providing Feedback

In an appraisal interview, the supervisor must communicate the performance appraisal results to the employee. Managers must carefully explain results to employees, particularly when there is negative feedback. The interview should provide motivation for the employee to improve. **Figure 15–5** lists the factors necessary for a successful appraisal interview.

Figure 15–5 | THE SUCCESSFUL APPRAISAL INTERVIEW

The following factors contribute to the success of the appraisal interview:

- employee involvement in the appraisal and goal-setting process

- recognition and praise of good performance

- improvement goals that are set by the manager and employee together

- discussion of problems that hinder performance

- avoidance of heavy criticism

- encouragement for the employee to voice his or her opinions

- opportunity for the employee to prepare for the interview

- employee perception that good performance will be rewarded

The goal of the appraisal interview is to motivate an employee to improve. *How could these factors help to achieve that goal?*

Legal Considerations

Title VII of the Civil Rights Act requires that an organization's performance appraisal system be "bona fide." A bona fide appraisal does not have a disproportionately negative effect upon minorities, women, or older employees.

In order to make its performance appraisal system fair and legally defensible, an organization should

- base its appraisal system on job descriptions
- emphasize performance rather than personal traits
- communicate appraisal results to employees
- allow employee response during appraisal interview
- train managers in conducting proper evaluations
- ensure that appraisals are written and documentation is retained
- make personnel decisions consistent with performance appraisals

PREDICT

What steps should a company take in order to make sure its performance evaluations are fair to all employees?

Organizational Reward System

The *organizational reward system* includes everything that an employee receives from an organization. **Intrinsic rewards** are intangible and internal to the individual, such as personal growth and job

Figure 15–6	INTRINSIC VERSUS EXTRINSIC REWARDS
Intrinsic Rewards	**Extrinsic Rewards**
Sense of achievement	Formal recognition
Feelings of accomplishment	Fringe benefits
Informal recognition	Incentive payments
Job satisfaction	Base wages
Personal growth	Promotion
Status	Social relationships
WORKING WITH CHARTS	Job can have intrinsic and extrinsic rewards for a worker. *Why is it important for there to be a balance of both on the job?*

satisfaction. **Extrinsic rewards** are controlled and distributed by the organization. The outerwear company Patagonia provides extrinsic rewards such as child care, a sand volleyball court, twice-weekly yoga classes, and surfing in the nearby Pacific Ocean. See **Figure 15–6** for a longer list of examples of intrinsic and extrinsic rewards.

Relating Rewards to Performance

A *free enterprise system*, such as the economy of the United States, is based on the idea that rewards should be related to performance. The theory is that people will be motivated to improve their performance in order to achieve greater rewards.

◄ **MERIT PAY** While a merit pay system is the most effective way to tie rewards to performance, many companies do not use this system. *What challenges does a company face in developing a merit pay system?*

However, many extrinsic rewards that companies provide are not tied directly to performance. In particular, benefits such as insurance plans are usually awarded to all employees on an equal basis. Other benefits, such as vacation days, are based on seniority.

A *merit pay* system, in which salary increases are based on performance appraisals, effectively ties rewards to performance. However, most U.S. companies do not employ this tactic. Many organizations award an *across-the-board pay increase* of a fixed percentage. In other cases, a union contract may require distribution of increases by seniority.

Employees should have a clear picture of how performance affects their pay. Merit increases should be distinguishable from seniority pay and cost-of-living adjustments. Finally, managers should be trusted to foster an environment in which employees can succeed.

Section 15.2 Assessment

 FACT AND IDEA REVIEW

1. What is role perception?
2. What are the criteria for objectives when using MBO?
3. What guarantees a successful appraisal interview?
4. What is the difference between a merit pay system and an across-the-board pay increase?

 CRITICAL THINKING

1. **Predicting Consequences:** What might happen if a manager and an employee have different role perceptions of the employee's job?
2. **Drawing Conclusions:** Why is it necessary for managers to provide feedback to an employee after an appraisal interview?

ASSESSING MATH SKILLS

You are a manager at an electrical sales company that produces light switches. It is time for a six-month performance appraisal, which establishes raises. Cherie Espinoza works in inside sales. Based on her performance, the estimated raise is 9% to her $29,000 salary. The quality of the work of Marcus Wells, three-year project manager, has decreased in the past six months. You believe he deserves a 3% raise to his $38,000 salary. The company has considered adopting an across-the-board pay increase of 5%. How much would the company save on these two employees' raises if they implemented a 5% raise for everyone? How much more money would Cherie make with the merit-based pay raise?

 CASE ANALYSIS

You recently opened a store, "Sweet Tooth," that sells homemade chocolates. You predict increased business during the holidays, and you meet with your five store employees to discuss the most effective way to handle the increased sales.

Apply: Use the Management By Objectives principles to your company, focusing on holiday goals. This includes establishing objectives, developing an action plan for these objectives, and deciding on methods to evaluate performance.

CHAPTER 15 ASSESSMENT

 REVIEWING VOCABULARY

A manager at a local publishing house needs to fill two recently vacated positions. Write a conversation between this manager and the head of human resources regarding the process of employees leaving, and the steps that need to be taken to hire two new individuals. Use all of the vocabulary terms listed below.

human resources	vestibule training
job description	apprenticeship
halo effect	Management By
exit interview	Objectives
layoff	intrinsic rewards
termination	extrinsic rewards
job rotation	

CHAPTER SUMMARY

Section 15.1

▶ The employee selection procedure includes screening, testing, and interviewing.

▶ Employees may leave a position through transfers, promotions, or separations.

▶ Methods of employee training include on-the-job training, vestibule training, apprenticeship, classroom training, and computer-based training.

Section 15.2

▶ Performance is the degree of accomplishment in completing job-related tasks measured by results.

▶ Performance can be evaluated by Management By Objectives, production standards, essay appraisal, and critical-incident appraisal.

▶ Supervisors should provide feedback to employees.

▶ The organizational rewards system includes intrinsic and extrinsic rewards.

▶ Rewards should be based on performance.

 RECALLING KEY CONCEPTS

1. What is a job description?
2. How can an organization ensure test reliability?
3. What are two employee benefits of a transfer?
4. What is the production standards approach to evaluating performance? When is it most effective?

 THINKING CRITICALLY

1. Explain the importance of *Griggs v. Duke Power Company*.
2. Why is subjectivity a problem in the critical-incident appraisal approach to evaluating performance?
3. How can employees "rise to their level of incompetence"?
4. Explain which method of training might be most effective for an electrician and why.

CHAPTER 15 ASSESSMENT

⬤ ASSESSING ACADEMIC SKILLS

SOCIAL STUDIES Using the Internet or resources at a local library, research the impact on corporate organizations by one of the following: *Griggs v. Duke Power Company, Albemarle Paper Company v. Moody,* or Title VII of the Civil Rights Act. What brought about the legal movement? How did it affect businesses? Present your research in a 300-word essay.

⬤ APPLYING MANAGEMENT PRINCIPLES

SOLVE THE PROBLEM You are the head of human resources at a monthly travel magazine. The overseas department needs a new assistant editor. You posted an ad in local newspapers and have received résumés and writing samples from many qualified applicants. Still, the interviewing editor has turned down every potential employee that she has interviewed. Her interviewing style is informal, and you believe that this is the problem.

Writing Write a one-page memo to the interviewing editor explaining the potential dangers of the informal interview, including some sample interview questions. Then, propose the alternative of a more formal interview. Finally, explain why you think this method may provide positive results in the search.

⬤ PREPARING FOR COMPETITIVE EVENTS

Answer true or false to the following statements and explain your answers.

a. Performance is the effort that an employee puts into a job.

b. The Peter Principle states that sometimes employees can be promoted until they reach a level at which they are not able to perform.

In this chapter you read the *BusinessWeek* Management Model about the importance of companies retaining talented employees. For more information, go to *BusinessWeek* online at: **www.businessweek.com**

Using your local newspaper, read 10 to 15 job listings in an industry that interests you. Then make a list of the top 10 traits you find from the advertisements and share it with the class.

CASE STUDY 5

Effective Organization

OVERVIEW

Many companies are growing and changing in today's business world. While some are merging with other companies, others are downsizing. Many more are outsourcing and trying different working arrangements such as telecommuting and work sharing. Managers must deal with such changes in company arrangements and continue to lead their businesses to operate efficiently. Managers who can maintain an effective organizational structure and good communication practices will succeed in changing times. This case study explores difficulties managers face as they try to successfully organize their workforce.

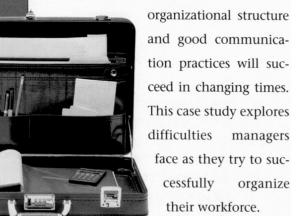

RESOURCES

■ envelopes
■ business periodicals
■ word processor
■ Internet (optional)

PROCEDURES

◆ STEP A ◆

Structuring an Organization

When a business becomes larger, its organizational structure is altered, and it encounters new challenges. Both the chain of command and the line of communication might become unclear. Leaders of a business should be concerned with the type of structure required to accommodate changes.

Identifying Information:

1. In small groups of two to four students, list four types of organizational structures discussed in this unit.

2. Explain the characteristics of each type of organizational structure.

3. Identify 10 challenges that businesses encounter as they strategically plan for growth.

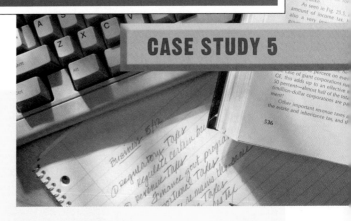

CASE STUDY 5

◆ STEP B ◆

Leadership and Communication

It is important to have effective leadership and communication within a large organization. As a business expands and new organizational structures are created, it's important for managers to communicate the changes that affect their employees.

Organizing Information:

1. Get into small groups assigned by your teacher. As a group, designate a leader.

2. Your teacher will give the teams a set of six cards, each bearing a different symbol. Each leader will also be given a sealed envelope containing the proper arrangement of these cards, along with a set of written commands. The envelope is not to be opened until your teacher directs you to do so.

3. The object is for the team members to put the cards in the proper order under the commands of the team leader. There is to be no talking during the game.

4. You are ready to start the game. Follow your teacher's instructions on how to play the game. There will be two parts to this game.

5. After you finish discuss as a class what happened during the game.

6. Discuss the role of leadership and communication and how they affect your work performance. What are the pros and cons of using an organizational structure? What did you learn? Is there anything you wish you had done differently?

◆ STEP C ◆

Management Report

To demonstrate how effective leadership is the main element in successfully restructuring a company, write a 3- to 5-page research paper that includes the following:

1. List the challenges that managers face as they try to match a new company strategy with an appropriate organizational structure. Use your experiences in the game to support your answer.

2. Include the key elements of your group discussion about the importance of leadership and effective communication.

3. Also include current examples of how a chief executive officer has played a key role in guiding his or her company through a restructuring effort into the future.

Leadership Skills

Chapter 16

Motivation and Leadership

Chapter 17

Managing Conflict and Stress

Chapter 18

Managing Change, Culture, and Diversity

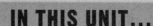

IN THIS UNIT...

You will be introduced to the concept of leadership and how strong leadership skills are essential to any effective manager. You will see how leaders can motivate employees, handle conflict in the workplace, and encourage diversity.

Journal Writing

In your journal, assess your knowledge of
management by writing about the following:

1. How can a good leader motivate others to
   work to their potential? List the five most
   important qualities of a good leader.
2. How do you manage stress during exams?
3. Do you think that your school culture is
   diverse? Explain why or why not.

CHAPTER 16

MOTIVATION AND LEADERSHIP

LEARNING OBJECTIVES

When you have completed this chapter, you will be able to:

- Explain five theories of motivation.
- Understand how managers use motivation theories to motivate employees.
- Identify the difference between power and authority.
- Describe three styles of leadership.
- Identify the leadership skills necessary for effective management.

READING STRATEGIES

As you read

- **PREDICT** what the section will be about.
- **CONNECT** what you read with your own life.
- **QUESTION** as you read to make sure you understand the content.
- **RESPOND** to what you read.

Understanding Management

Over the course of his life, the late Sam Walton saw his tiny Arkansas five-and-dime grow into the successful nationwide chain of Wal-Mart stores. Walton's success was aided by his charismatic leadership style. He was known for pulling outrageous stunts in order to motivate his employees. In one of his stunts, he promised his associates that he would do a hula dance on Wall Street if they exceeded performance goals. They did, and he danced.

Analyzing Management Skills

Why do you think Wal-Mart employees responded to Walton's leadership style?

Applying Management Skills

Imagine that you own two coffee shops. Shop one is losing money. Shop two is doing very well. What would you do to motivate workers at shop one? Shop two?

BusinessWeek *ONLINE*

For further reading on managers and management go to: **www.businessweek.com**

"MANAGEMENT TALK"

"A paycheck and a stock option will buy one kind of loyalty. But all of us like to be told how much somebody appreciates what we do for them. We like to hear it often, and especially when we have done something we're really proud of. Nothing else can quite substitute for a few well-chosen, well-timed, sincere words of praise. They're absolutely free—and worth a fortune."

—Sam Walton, Wal-Mart, Founder

MOTIVATION

WHY IT'S IMPORTANT

To be able to motivate the people who work for them, managers need to recognize what drives individuals' behavior.

KEY TERMS

• motivation
• positive reinforcement
• negative reinforcement

What Is Motivation?

Lori Ayeung, the manager of a four-person product team, gets to work at 7:30 every morning. When her team is up against a deadline, she stays late. She also has been known to spend weekends at the office.

Carlos Lomaz, a manager at the same company, often shows up late for work. He takes little pride in his work and does not seem to understand the importance of completing tasks on time. Carlos' teammates find it frustrating to work with him because of his obvious disinterest.

What explains the difference between the behavior of these two managers? It lies in **motivation**, or the factors that give people a reason to act. Motivation is concerned with three sets of issues:

• what makes people act
• why people try to achieve particular goals
• what makes individuals stick with their goals

▲ **MOTIVATION** Successful athletes understand the importance of motivation. *What do you think motivates this baseball team?*

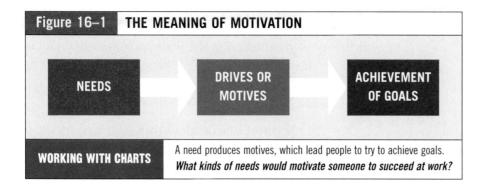

Figure 16-1 | **THE MEANING OF MOTIVATION**

NEEDS ➤ DRIVES OR MOTIVES ➤ ACHIEVEMENT OF GOALS

WORKING WITH CHARTS | A need produces motives, which lead people to try to achieve goals. *What kinds of needs would motivate someone to succeed at work?*

As **Figure 16–1** shows, motivation begins with a need. One person might be motivated by the need to earn a lot of money. Another might be motivated by the need to work with interesting people. Yet another might be motivated by the need to live abroad.

Psychologists believe that needs produce drives or motives, which then lead people to try to achieve goals. The desire to live abroad, for example, might motivate an individual to study a foreign language. To fulfill this need, individuals might set goals, such as mastering a foreign language, researching the culture and traditions of the country of their choice, and saving money for travelling.

CONNECT

Recall a time you felt especially motivated about completing a task. Explain the circumstances that made you feel that way.

What Motivates People?

Researchers have studied how people perceive their needs, set their goals or accept those set for them, and take action. They have come up with various theories about what motivates people.

Maslow's Hierarchy of Needs

One theory of motivation is Maslow's *hierarchy of needs*. As you learned in Chapter 2, according to Maslow, most people seek to meet lower-level needs before they address higher-level needs. A person will fulfill the need for shelter before that of personal satisfaction, for example.

Managers apply Maslow's principles by recognizing that employees seek to meet some needs before others. They should ensure that the physical working conditions are adequate before concerning themselves with creating interesting and satisfying jobs.

▲ **MASLOW'S HIERARCHY OF NEEDS** According to Maslow, people need to fulfill lower-level needs before they can address higher-level needs. *What basic needs does this construction worker need to fulfill before he will want to meet higher-level needs?*

Herzberg's Motivation-Maintenance Model

A second theory of motivation is the *motivation-hygiene theory* of Frederick Herzberg. According to Herzberg, people are motivated by two sets of factors, as **Figure 16–2** shows. *Motivators,* or *job content factors,* are factors that lead to job satisfaction. These include

- the opportunity to achieve through work
- the opportunity for promotion
- the chance to grow, learn, and take on new responsibilities

Hygiene, or *context, factors* are primarily negative factors. They are taken for granted until something goes wrong. When these factors are unsatisfactory, people become dissatisfied with their jobs.

Hygiene factors include

- pay
- benefits
- physical working conditions

Herzberg concluded that job satisfaction and dissatisfaction are caused by two different sets of factors. People are satisfied at work if they encounter positive content factors, or motivators. They are unhappy if they encounter negative context factors, or hygiene factors.

All About

ATTITUDE

DON'T JUST DO YOUR JOB. DO IT BETTER!

In today's workplace, simply showing up isn't good enough. Floating by and doing the minimum amount of work expected is a thing of the past. Challenge yourself to improve constantly upon your abilities. Your boss, co-workers, and customers will all appreciate your effort!

QUESTION

What is the difference between motivators and hygiene factors in Herzberg's Model?

Figure 16–2	HERZBERG'S MODEL OF MOTIVATORS AND HYGIENE FACTORS	
Motivators		**Hygiene Factors**
• Achievement		• Company rules and policies
• Recognition		• Quality of supervision
• Work itself		• Interpersonal relations
• Responsibility		• Working conditions
• Advancement possibilities		• Salary and benefits
• Growth on the job		• Status
		• Job security
WORKING WITH CHARTS	People who work in unpleasant physical surroundings are likely to be dissatisfied with their jobs. *According to Herzberg, what factors account for job satisfaction?*	

Training and Development Manager

■ Nature of the Work

Training and development managers plan, organize, and direct the training of new and seasoned employees. They arrange for on-the-job training for those who are new to the workforce. They develop programs to keep the skills of veteran employees honed. In large companies, training and development managers may spend more time developing training policies and overseeing training staff than they do actually training.

Training and development managers play an important part in business. Employees who are properly trained develop and improve the skills necessary to help a company compete in a technology-driven market. Well-trained employees are more productive, and they produce work that is of higher quality. They have better morale and are more loyal to the company.

■ Working Conditions

Training and development managers work in clean, pleasant, comfortable surroundings, usually for 35 to 40 hours a week. They are employed in many kinds of industries.

■ Training, Other Qualifications, and Advancement

Training and development managers need a bachelor's degree in human resources, personnel administration, or business. Special knowledge of a technical field may be necessary, but for most training managers, a broad background is more useful. A master's or doctoral degree may be necessary for top management.

■ Salary Range

Entry-level training managers with a bachelor's degree earn $25,000. Those with a master's degree can earn $40,000. Training and development managers earn $86,600. Salaries vary with location, company, and experience.

CRITICAL THINKING

Why would good training improve employee loyalty and morale?

STANDARD &POOR'S

INDUSTRY OUTLOOK

Intense competition at home has forced automotive manufacturers to move into new markets around the world. This has led to higher quality products and lower costs for cars, vans, and light trucks. Employee training will be vital to companies that want to keep their production edge.

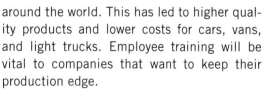

BUSINESS MANAGEMENT *Online*

For more information on management careers, go to:
busmanagement.glencoe.com

Herzberg's research has important implications for managers. It suggests that all work environments must establish positive hygiene factors. Employees will be dissatisfied with their jobs in a work environment in which they are poorly paid, inadequately supervised, and unable to interact with others.

Meeting these minimum standards does not mean that employees will be motivated to work hard, however. Even if people are well paid and work in pleasant surroundings, they will lack motivation if their jobs do not have positive content factors.

McClelland's Achievement-Power-Affiliation Approach

David C. McClelland developed a third approach to motivation, as illustrated in **Figure 16–3**. According to McClelland, people are motivated by three needs:

- the *need for achievement,* or the desire to accomplish something or to do something new
- the *need for power,* or the desire to influence people and events
- the *need for affiliation,* or the desire to have close relations with other people

Everyone aspires to fulfill all of these needs to some degree. However, some people have stronger needs in one area than in others. To be effective, according to McClelland, managers must identify a person's strongest need and seek to meet that need.

Carmen Sanchez is the manager of the marketing department at a large pharmaceutical company. Carmen works hard to identify what motivates each of her employees. She has noticed that one employee, Winston Brown, has a very strong need for affiliation. Last week, Carmen was asked to assign a member of her staff to a company-wide committee. Carmen chose Winston for the job because she recognized his appreciation for working with others. She believes that Winston's need to work with people will motivate him to work hard on the committee.

FIGURE 16–3

McClelland's Motivation Needs

In order to motivate effectively, managers need to recognize the needs of their employees.

1 THE NEED FOR POWER
Some people are strongly motivated by the need for power. They are likely to be happiest in jobs that give them control over budgets, people, and decision making.

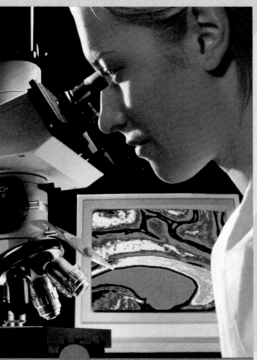

2 THE NEED FOR ACHIEVEMENT
Other people are strongly motivated by the need for achievement. They are likely to be happiest working in an environment in which they can create something new.

3 THE NEED FOR AFFILIATION
Some people are strongly motivated by the need for affiliation. These people usually enjoy working with other people. They are motivated by the prospect of having people like them.

Sheila Fagan, who also works on Carmen's staff, is not as people-oriented as Winston is. She has a much stronger need to achieve, however. Recognizing Sheila's need, Carmen assigns her tasks that will give her a strong sense of accomplishment. Last week, for example, Carmen asked Sheila to take charge of the annual report the marketing department prepares for senior management. She knows that Shelia's need to achieve will motivate her to prepare a well-written report.

Expectancy Theory

A fourth theory of motivation is the *expectancy approach*. According to this theory, motivation depends on employees' beliefs about how effort and performance affect outcomes. If employees believe that extra effort will result in better performance, they are likely to be motivated to work. If they believe that regardless of hard work they are unlikely to succeed, they are not likely to be highly motivated.

Remy was accidentally placed into French IV, even though the language he has studied for two years is Spanish. He is not motivated to study very hard for this class because he assumes his studying would

▲ **EXPECTANCY THEORY** These bond traders are motivated to work hard because they receive hefty year-end bonuses if they do well. *According to expectancy theory, what other factor affects motivation?*

make no difference. If instead he were placed in French I, he would probably study very hard. He would recognize that this class is not beyond his level and that his hard work would help him achieve a high grade.

Managers try to ensure that employees see a relationship between effort and performance by placing people in jobs they are able to perform. They avoid hiring people who are not up to the job, and they assign tasks that people will be able to complete.

Another important aspect of expectancy theory is the belief that improving performance will lead to rewards, such as a raise or extra vacation days. Employees who believe their work will be rewarded are more likely to work harder than employees who do not see this connection. Many Wall Street companies, for example, pay large end-of-the-year bonuses to employees who perform well. The knowledge that working hard will result in a large bonus motivates many people on Wall Street to work very hard.

Reinforcement Theory

Reinforcement theory, or *operant conditioning,* is the idea that punishing or rewarding people will affect their future behavior. Parents apply this theory when they reward children for being good or discipline them for misbehavior.

L EADING THE W AY

STORYTELLERS
Leaders often use different tactics to motivate others. The use of stories to communicate ideas is one of them. A parable or symbolism can help bring a difficult situation into a clearer picture of what needs to be accomplished. Shed new light on a subject by telling a story that your audience can relate to.

RESPOND
Of the five approaches to motivation described in this chapter, which do you think is most important?

◄ **REINFORCEMENT THEORY**
Dog trainers use both positive and negative reinforcement of behavior to train dogs. *Which type of reinforcement do many managers consider more effective?*

Reinforcement theory uses two kinds of reinforcement—positive and negative. **Positive reinforcement** involves rewarding people who engage in behavior that the manager wishes to encourage. **Negative reinforcement** involves punishing or reprimanding people who engage in behavior that the manager hopes to discourage.

Managers use positive reinforcement when they praise their employees for work well done, give them a raise, or offer extra vacation days. Employees who receive this kind of reinforcement are likely to be motivated to behave in the same way again.

Managers use negative reinforcement by reprimanding their employees or not giving them raises. Employees who receive this kind of reinforcement may be motivated not to engage in the behavior again.

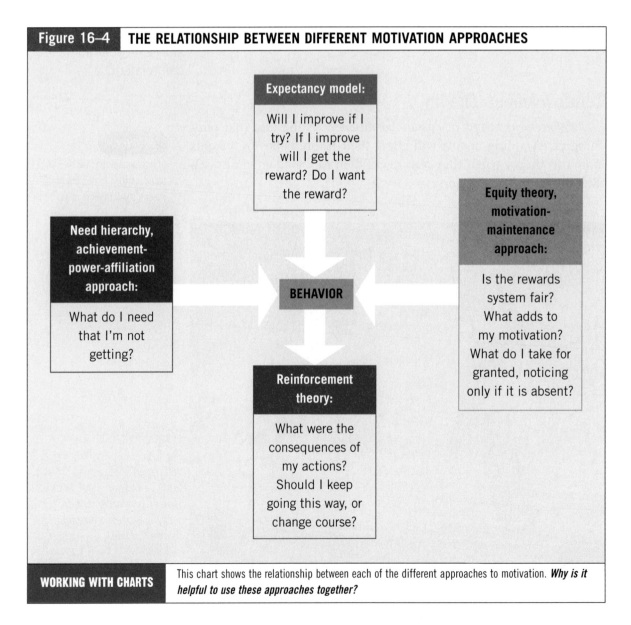

| Figure 16–4 | THE RELATIONSHIP BETWEEN DIFFERENT MOTIVATION APPROACHES |

Expectancy model:

Will I improve if I try? If I improve will I get the reward? Do I want the reward?

Need hierarchy, achievement-power-affiliation approach:

What do I need that I'm not getting?

BEHAVIOR

Equity theory, motivation-maintenance approach:

Is the rewards system fair? What adds to my motivation? What do I take for granted, noticing only if it is absent?

Reinforcement theory:

What were the consequences of my actions? Should I keep going this way, or change course?

WORKING WITH CHARTS This chart shows the relationship between each of the different approaches to motivation. *Why is it helpful to use these approaches together?*

Many managers believe that positive reinforcement is more effective than negative reinforcement. They believe that rewarding employees for good work, as opposed to punishing them for mistakes, is more likely to motivate them.

Integrating the Approaches to Motivation

There are many ways to look at motivation. Each approach emphasizes different contributors to motivation, or sees the same contributors from a different perspective (see **Figure 16–4**). No single approach provides all the answers, so it is sometimes necessary to utilize more than one approach.

Tips from Robert Half

Money is not all a company can offer. Some companies offer benefits such as advancement opportunities, stock options, tuition reimbursement, training, telecommuting, flex-time and child care. Employees who feel valued work harder.

Section 16.1 Assessment

FACT AND IDEA REVIEW

1. Name three theories of motivation and briefly describe each.
2. According to Herzberg, what kinds of factors account for job satisfaction?
3. According to McClelland, what are the three main forces that motivate people?
4. Give one example of positive reinforcement and one example of negative reinforcement.

CRITICAL THINKING

1. **Analyzing Information:** How would a manager use expectancy theory to motivate employees?
2. **Predicting Consequences:** Why do you think positive reinforcement is more effective than negative reinforcement or punishment?

ASSESSING SOCIAL STUDIES SKILLS

Using the Internet or resources at your public library, write a short biography of Ivan Pavlov (1849–1936), the Russian physiologist who studied the affect of conditioning on behavior.

CASE ANALYSIS

You are the manager of a 14-person telemarketing team. Some of your workers show up on time and work hard all day. Others are often late and slack off while at work.

Apply: Use the ideas of expectancy and reinforcement theory to come up with a plan for motivating all of your employees.

POWER, AUTHORITY, AND LEADERSHIP

Distinguishing Between Power and Authority

The production supervisor John Quiggin rushes onto the factory floor, barking out orders to his employees. Malcolm Jefferson, the warehouse supervisor, quietly gives instructions to the people he manages. Both men are using their **power**, or the ability they have to make other people act in certain ways. However, each has a different style of using power.

Managers derive power from various sources, as shown in **Figure 16–5**. An important source of power is that managers determine their subordinates' incomes. This kind of power is known as *reward power*.

There are other important sources of power. Bill Gates, chairman and co-founder of Microsoft, is powerful not only because he has the power to fire his employees, but also because he is a well-respected computer software expert. This kind of power is known as *expert power*. If Bill Gates was not respected as an expert in his field, his power would be much more limited.

Figure 16–5	SOURCES OF POWER
Source of Power	**Basis of Power**
Reward power	Ability to provide rewards
Coercive power	Ability to punish
Legitimate power	Position in the organizational hierarchy
Expert power	Skill, expertise, or knowledge
Personality power	Characteristics that attract others
WORKING WITH CHARTS	Personalities often affect the way people handle power. *Which kind of power do you think is most important in a product design department?*

◄ **AUTHORITY** Clark Clifford, a lawyer who advised many U.S. Presidents, had no authority to make decisions. Yet, he had considerable power. *What was the source of his power?*

Authority is the right to issue directives and expend resources. Power and authority often are related. Sometimes, however, people with power have no actual authority. An advisor to the President of the United States, for example, may have no authority to make decisions. If the person has influence over the President, however, he or she may have significant power.

PREDICT

In your own words, explain the difference between power, authority, and leadership.

What Is Leadership?

Leadership is the ability to influence people. Some people seem to be born natural leaders. Others are happy following their lead. However, leadership skills can be learned. Understanding what makes a good leader can make any manager stronger.

Leaders use their power to guide other people's behavior. To be effective, leaders must have a vision for the future, develop strategies for achieving that vision, and motivate employees to implement them. They also must develop a leadership style.

Framework for Classifying Leadership Studies

Leadership studies can be classified by whether they take a universal or contingent approach. The **universal approach** assumes there is one way to lead, regardless of the circumstances. The **contingent approach** assumes that the best approach to leadership depends on the situation. These studies also can be classified by a focus on traits or behaviors. *Traits* are characteristics the leader possesses. *Behaviors* refer to what the leader does. The most important studies we will examine are classified in **Figure 16–6.**

Trait Theory

Early research focused on what a leader was like, rather than what a leader did. This stress on personal traits is called *trait theory.* Personality traits (originality, persistence, and enthusiasm), social traits (tact, patience, and sympathy), and even physical characteristics (height and weight) are examined to determine good leadership.

Based on trait theory, those qualities most often associated with excellent leaders include

- loyalty
- courage
- stamina
- empathy
- decisiveness
- timing
- competitiveness
- self-confidence
- accountability
- charisma

Trait theory is not useful in identifying effective leadership. Some traits may seem important to leadership in a particular situation. However, they might not ensure an effective leader under different circumstances. For example, the captain of last year's field hockey team was enthusiastic and empathetic. While those qualities were helpful, it is not reliable to base the decision for this year's captain on those two traits alone.

Figure 16–6	**FRAMEWORK FOR CLASSIFYING LEADERSHIP STUDIES**	
Focus	**Approach**	
	Universal	*Contingent*
Traits	Trait theory	Fiedler's contingency theory
Behavior	Leadership styles	Path-goal theory
WORKING WITH CHARTS	Over time, many different kinds of leadership studies have attempted to classify leader types and attitudes. *What is the importance of these studies?*	

BusinessWeek

In My Company You Can't Make Leaders

"Train Anyone to Become a Leader," shouted the brochure's big, bold headline. I sighed as I tossed it into the wastebasket. But the headline kept popping into my mind at unexpected moments. Now I know why it bothered me: It's simply not true. Not everyone is meant for leadership.

In our family business making plastic bags, we have tried to make leaders out of some of our best employees—with disastrous results. They may be tops when it comes to fixing machinery, but when it's people and organizational skills, forget it. And no amount of training seminars or mentoring has worked.

DISILLUSIONED. When I came into my family business 2½ years ago, I had a more democratic vision of leadership that counted on everyone leading and everyone taking responsibility for his or her work.

We recently promoted a longtime employee who had proven himself adept with machinery and at teaching others his skill. We knew he was less effective in disciplining employees or providing

direction. Still, when a management slot came open, we decided to give him a chance. Lord knows, he tried. We sent him to classes on how to supervise and gave him books about getting organized. But when the going got tough, he fell into old patterns.

By contrast, take Evelyn Martin. For most of her 25 years here, Martin, 53, had simply packed bags into boxes. But she had always been a de facto leader.

So when sagging production and poor morale called for a leadership change, Martin got the job as production foreperson. With no formal training,

she has turned her unit around. Production has risen 25%, and absenteeism on her shift has plummeted. She has succeeded, in part, because she has a vision of how she wants her department to run. If crew members don't follow through, she holds them accountable, telling them clearly where they failed. She also rewards her crew for success.

Since I can't clone Evelyn, I try to stay close to employees, as she does. I talk to them, soliciting their ideas. I look over daily reports and attend meetings to see who's vocal. It's an imperfect method for identifying leaders, but it has helped me find some promising candidates.

Excerpted with permission from BusinessWeek, *December 7, 1998*

CRITICAL THINKING

Why does the writer believe not everyone is meant to be a leader?

DECISION MAKING

As a manager in a company, what traits would you look for in a leader?

Styles of Leadership

Researchers have identified three basic styles of leadership. They include autocratic leadership, laissez-faire leadership, and democratic leadership.

AUTOCRATIC LEADERSHIP *Autocratic leaders* are leaders who do not listen to other people but make all decisions themselves. These leaders make most decisions alone because they have little trust in the people they work with.

RESPOND

Imagine three different classrooms. one lead by an autocratic teacher, one a laissez-faire teacher, and the other a democratic teacher. Which classroom would you prefer? Why?

Few people enjoy working for an autocratic leader. There is little room for initiative. Autocratic leaders are unlikely to acknowledge their subordinates' work or give them credit for their achievements. While autocratic leaders can be effective when they are present, performance and productivity are likely to decline when the leader is away from the work site.

A generation ago, most managers were autocratic leaders who simply told their subordinates what to do. Although some autocratic managers still exist today, the trend has been toward different leadership styles.

LAISSEZ-FAIRE LEADERSHIP *Laissez-faire* means hands off. Laissez-faire leaders are leaders who choose not to lead. This situation can occur when someone is thrust unexpectedly, or unwillingly, into a leadership position. These leaders often lack confidence in their leadership abilities and allow other people in the group to make decisions. They fail to set goals for the group and provide no real leadership.

The effects of laissez-faire leadership usually are negative. Productivity is low, and the completed work is sloppy. Individuals have little motivation to succeed, lack enthusiasm, and avoid teamwork.

▲ **AUTOCRATIC LEADERSHIP** In life and death situations, it may be necessary to follow orders without question. This leadership style usually does not work in the business environment, however.
Can you think of situations in which some form of autocratic leadership might be necessary?

DEMOCRATIC LEADERSHIP *Democratic leaders* are often the best kind of leaders. This kind of leader listens to other people's opinions and encourages the exchange of ideas. Democratic leadership helps develop a feeling of responsibility among group members.

When democratic leaders make a decision, they will explain the reasoning behind their actions. This creates a group that feels empowered. Democratic leadership usually results in high productivity, strong morale, and good teamwork.

Fiedler's Contingency Studies of Leadership

Early leadership studies attempted to identify universal principles that could be applied to any situation. However, in performing these studies, researchers began realizing the difficulty of generalizing, for example between a military unit and a PTA committee. Even within the business environment alone, leadership practices appropriate to the production floor might not work in the executive suite.

Later studies looked at leadership styles specific to particular situations. This is called the *contingency approach*. Fred Fiedler conducted one of the first contingency studies. He studied the match between a leader's personality and the situation. Fiedler defined two basic leadership traits:

- *Task-motivated leaders* gain satisfaction from the performance of a task.
- *Relationship-motivated leaders* gain satisfaction from interpersonal relationships.

This study helped to evaluate leadership styles against particular situations. An autocratic, task-oriented leader, for example, would probably not be a good match for an unstructured environment in which good leader-group relations are important.

Path-Goal Theory of Leadership

Path-goal theory addresses the relationship between a leader's behavior and subordinates' performance and job satisfaction. Leader behavior affects employees' perception of their work environment.

This model categorizes leaders into four basic types. One of these types is the autocratic style discussed earlier in this chapter. The types are as follows:

- *Role classification* leaders let group members know what is expected of them, establish the methods to use, coordinate work within the group, and maintain standards of performance. Such clarification is helpful to employees engaged in unstructured tasks.

▲ **DEMOCRATIC MANAGEMENT** In the democratic leadership style, new ideas from the group are welcomed. *What are some benefits of this style of management?*

QUESTION

Why is it important to take specific management situations into account when evaluating the effectiveness of a leadership style?

RESPOND

If you were a manager, what type of a leader would you be according to the path-goal theory?

- *Supportive* leaders create a pleasant work environment and are approachable. This is satisfying to those working on highly structured tasks, as friendliness can lighten an oppressive routine.
- *Participative* leaders consult with subordinates in the decision-making process. These discussions improve the performance of employees working on ambiguous tasks.
- *Autocratic* leaders issue orders that subordinates are not expected to question. This leadership style hurts job performance and satisfaction in most situations.

Developing Good Leadership Skills

With so many different theories on leadership, it may be difficult to find the one that works for you. Regardless of which theory you choose, there are many good leadership skills that are effective in most situations. To become effective leaders, managers need to master the following set of skills:

▲ **LEADERSHIP SKILLS** Good leaders serve as examples to the people on their teams. *What are some other leadership skills leaders try to master?*

1. *Plan.* Managers must have a good sense of what their departments are trying to achieve. They need to come up with detailed plans on how their team will meet the established goals. Effective managers involve their subordinates in developing plans of action.
2. *Become a teacher.* Effective managers help their employees succeed. They work with employees individually when possible to help them learn good problem-solving techniques.
3. *Delegate.* As you learned in Chapter 12, managers need to delegate responsibility. Good leaders surround themselves with people they can trust so that they are comfortable delegating responsibility.
4. *Encourage independent thinking.* Good leaders encourage their subordinates to come to them with problems and solutions. They help their subordinates think through solutions.
5. *Build a team.* Good leaders see themselves as captains of teams. The team captain inspires confidence in team members by striving for excellence and encouraging others to contribute.

6. *Set an example.* People tend to imitate the behavior of others. To benefit from this tendency, good leaders strive to set an example. They treat other people with respect. They listen to other people's views. They meet deadlines. They remain cool under pressure.
7. *Share credit with subordinates.* Good leaders accept full responsibility when things go wrong. They share credit with others when things go right.

With dynamic forces at work in the marketplace, managers and employees must continually adapt to new situations. The need to improve performance under conditions of constant change challenges managers continually to improve their motivation and leadership skills.

Section 16.2 Assessment

 FACT AND IDEA REVIEW

1. Name three types of power and explain what each means.
2. What is the difference between the universal approach and the contingent approach to leadership?
3. What is a laissez-faire leader?
4. Name four skills a manager needs to master to become an effective leader.

CRITICAL THINKING

1. **Analyzing Information:** How can a person with no authority have power?
2. **Predicting Consequences:** Why do you think most people fail to perform well under autocratic leaders?

 ASSESSING MATH SKILLS

Last year Ray Watson took over as manager of the production department. Under Ray's leadership, production increased from 42,000 to 57,000 units a month. By what percentage did output increase? If output were to increase by the same percentage next month, how many units would the department produce?

 CASE ANALYSIS

Michelle Young has just joined a large company as a marketing manager. Michelle takes a relaxed attitude toward her job, often taking long lunches and leaving early on Fridays. She offers subordinates little guidance and seems unclear on departmental goals. Within a month of joining the company, Michelle is fired.

Apply: Explain why Michelle showed poor judgment as a manager and describe some of the things she should have done to provide leadership to her department.

CHAPTER 16 ASSESSMENT

CHAPTER SUMMARY

Section 16.1

▶ Motivation is concerned with what makes people act, what makes them try to achieve goals, and what makes them stick with their goals.

▶ There are numerous theories about what motivates individuals. These include: hierarchy of needs, motivation-management model, achievement-power-affiliation approach, expectancy theory, and reinforcement theory.

Section 16.2

▶ Power is the ability to make others act in a certain way, while authority is the right to issue directives.

▶ Leadership is the ability to influence people.

▶ Leadership studies can be classified by whether they take a universal or contingent approach, as well as if they focus on traits or behavior.

▶ Regardless of which leadership theory one uses as an example, there are many leadership qualities that are helpful in all situations.

REVIEWING VOCABULARY

Write a sentence definition for each term. Then write a second sentence giving an example of each term.

motivation
positive reinforcement
negative reinforcement
power
leadership
universal approach
contingent approach

RECALLING KEY CONCEPTS

1. What are the three areas with which motivation is concerned?
2. How do people's expectations about the relationship between effort and performance affect their motivation?
3. True or false: The different approaches to motivation cannot be used together. Explain your answer.
4. What is trait theory?
5. How did Fiedler's study differ from the earlier universal leadership studies?

THINKING CRITICALLY

1. Discuss the following statement: "Leaders are born; they cannot be developed."
2. Which style of leadership generally is the most effective? Explain your answer.
3. Why are employees who do not understand job expectations less motivated than those who understand what their managers expect of them?
4. Why is it important for good leaders to share credit for success with their subordinates?

CHAPTER 16 ASSESSMENT

ASSESSING ACADEMIC SKILLS

SOCIAL STUDIES In a hereditary monarchy, a leader gains position by right of birth. Most modern hereditary monarchs have mainly ceremonial roles. However, in earlier times they had a great deal of power. Research a noted historical monarch, and write an essay addressing the following questions.

- Were these "leaders from birth" always "born leaders"? Were they always good leaders? Defend your answer.
- Skilled leaders can still be bad rulers if they lead their people to destructive ends. Give examples.
- Why do you think people sometimes follow a leader beyond all reason?

APPLYING MANAGEMENT PRINCIPLES

SOLVE THE PROBLEM You have just been given a $90,000 increase in your salary budget. You could use the money to give everyone a raise, or you could use the money to raise some employee's salaries but not others. Alternatively, you could use the extra money to put a new bonus program into place.

Public Speaking Use what you know about motivation to come up with a plan for spending the increased salary budget. Back up your recommendations with what you learned in this chapter. Then present your plan to the class. After everyone is finished, vote on the most convincing speech and the best plan of action.

PREPARING FOR COMPETITIVE EVENTS

Answer true or false to the following statement. Explain your answer.

Good leaders involve their subordinates in developing plans of action to achieve collective goals.

BusinessWeek ONLINE

In this chapter you read the *BusinessWeek* Management Model about a manager who believes that not everyone can become a leader. What do you think? What traits make up a great leader? Using the Internet or library resources, locate an article about a leader you admire. Write a two-page paper addressing why you admire this person and discuss the steps the person took to become a great leader. For more information, go to *BusinessWeek* online at: **www.businessweek.com**

CHAPTER 17

MANAGING CONFLICT AND STRESS

LEARNING OBJECTIVES

When you have completed this chapter, you will be able to:

- Understand the sources of conflict that exist in the workplace.
- Recognize how managers can resolve conflicts among their employees.
- Understand the sources and effects of stress and burnout in the workplace.
- Identify the kinds of programs businesses set up to deal with employee problems.
- Know how to use stress-management techniques to reduce the level of stress.

READING STRATEGIES

As you read

- **PREDICT** what the section will be about.
- **CONNECT** what you read with your own life.
- **QUESTION** as you read to make sure you understand the content.
- **RESPOND** to what you read.

"MANAGEMENT TALK"

"UPSers remain among the most loyal service providers in American business. That is an immensely valuable asset, and one that we feverishly protect through a host of career development programs. . . . That's also why our management was so careful during the strike to protect the equity and loyalty that exists between our drivers and our customers. It's why we chose to take the 'high road' in our public communications, and even with the benefit of hindsight, there is little we would change."

—John W. Alden,
Vice Chairman of United Parcel Service

WORKPLACE CONNECTIONS

Understanding Management

In 1997, operations at United Parcel Service were severely hampered when unionized drivers and truck loaders went on strike. Unable to provide timely services, UPS was in danger of losing its customers. Recognizing the importance of individual contact between customers and drivers, UPS was careful not to create negative images of its striking drivers. The company survived the strike and is once again profitable.

Analyzing Management Skills

What might have happened if UPS had used press coverage of the strike to portray its drivers negatively?

Applying Management Skills

Have you ever witnessed a dispute between friends or co-workers that turned out badly? Create a set of rules for successfully resolving a similar dispute.

BusinessWeek *ONLINE*

For further reading on labor issues go to:
www.businessweek.com

CONFLICT IN THE WORKPLACE

WHY IT'S IMPORTANT

Managing conflict reaps benefits for all members of an organization. Unresolved tensions between employees reduce productivity and create a poor work environment.

KEY TERMS

- conflict
- interpersonal conflict
- intergroup conflict
- organizational conflict

Effects of Conflict

Chris Morris storms out of his boss's office, furious over a decision in which he was not involved. Later the same day, raised voices are heard coming from the boss's office. Little work gets done in the office, as everyone in the department tries to figure out what is going on.

People who work together do not always get along or agree with one another. In fact, **conflict**, or the struggle between people with opposing needs, wishes, or demands, is a common feature of business life.

Managers once thought conflict within organizations should be avoided at all costs. Today, however, many managers recognize that some conflict can have a positive effect. Today's managers understand that not all conflicts create winners and losers. Conflict can actually help bring about desirable changes. Some myths and truths about conflict in the workplace are shown in **Figure 17–1**.

Figure 17–1	MYTHS AND TRUTHS ABOUT CONFLICT
Myth	**Truth**
Conflict in the workplace is always dysfunctional.	Conflict is a normal part of life within an organization.
All conflicts can be resolved.	Most conflicts can be managed.
Conflict tends to go away if it is ignored.	Conflict can motivate change.
Conflicts always result in winners and losers.	Conflict can help build relationships between people.
WORKING WITH CHARTS	Conflict in the workplace is not always negative. *What are some of the positive effects of conflict?*

Adapted from *Resolving Conflicts on the Job*, Jerry Wisinski, 1993 American Management Association.

Positive Effects of Conflict

Conflict can play a useful role within a business organization. It can, for example, force people to confront situations they might otherwise have ignored. As entrepreneur William Wrigley, Jr., the founder of the giant chewing gum company, once said, "When two men in business always agree, one of them is unnecessary."

Conflict has additional positive effects:

- *Conflict energizes people.* Even if all of the activity generated by conflict is not constructive, conflict motivates people.
- *Conflict is a form of communication.* Resolving conflict may open up new channels of communication. Departments that once had little contact with each other may develop formal and informal ways of communicating once a conflict is resolved.
- *Parties to a conflict can learn from the experience.* Conflict can make people more aware and raise understanding of other people's functions and challenges in an organization.

Max Caswell, the head of the marketing department at a large retail chain, faced bitter conflict between the graphic artists and copywriters. The graphic artists complained that the copywriters regularly made minor changes to the advertising copy at very late stages of production. The changes required the artists to redo their work. The copywriters insisted that they had the right to make changes to all copy at any stage of production and resented the artists' complaints.

QUESTION

What are some common myths about conflict in the workplace?

LAUGH A LITTLE

Don't take yourself too seriously. When you feel stressed, try to view the situation in a healthy manner. Placing humor into the mix can help to ease tensions in a room. It can also be used to connect with others in the same situation.

◄ **HANDLING CONFLICT**
Not all conflict hurts an organization. *What are some of the benefits that might emerge from this group's conflict?*

PREDICT

At what point does workplace conflict become too intense to be positive?

RESPOND

Have you ever been in a situation where conflict made you feel less productive? If so, explain why conflict hindered your work.

▼ **STRIKES** Different groups of employees often have misconceptions about each other. *Why is it important for all groups to have realistic ideas about each other?*

Resolution of the conflict helped the copywriters understand how much extra work their minor changes entailed. It also helped the artists understand why the copywriters felt they needed to make the changes they made. As a result of the conflict, both groups tried to accommodate the other's needs more than they had before the conflict erupted.

Negative Effects of Conflict

Although some kinds of conflict can be positive, unresolved conflict can create an unproductive work environment. Anger can make it difficult for people to continue to work together. Resentment can make it difficult for employees to accept other people as managers.

Unresolved conflicts also can distort reality. For example, union members whose demands are ignored by management may come to believe that management does not value their work. Managers who oppose the union's demands may start to question workers' commitment to the company. Misconceptions on both sides may strain relations between the two groups.

Finally, ongoing conflict makes it difficult for people to concentrate on their jobs. Conflict distracts employees from their work and causes them to use their time unproductively. It also makes it difficult for employees to commit themselves to working for the good of the company.

Hotel Manager

■ Nature of the Work

Hotel managers are responsible for the efficient and profitable operation of their establishments. In a small hotel, motel, or inn with a limited staff, the manager may direct all aspects of operations. However, in large hotels with hundreds of workers, there may be a number of assistant managers to oversee various departments.

General managers may set room rates, approve expenditures, and establish standards for service, decor, housekeeping, food quality, and banquet operations. They use computers to track guests' bills, reservations, room assignments, meetings, and special events. They make reports to the hotel's owners.

■ Working Conditions

Hotel managers usually work in comfortable surroundings, but hours are long, and work is often stressful.

■ Training, Other Qualifications, and Advancement

To become a hotel manager, you need a bachelor's degree in liberal arts plus hotel experience, or a bachelor's degree in hotel or food management. Internships, work study, or part-time work in hotels or food service is useful.

A hotel manager must be able to work with people under stressful conditions, solve problems, concentrate on details, organize, and direct the work of others. Communication skills are essential.

■ Salary Range

Assistant hotel managers average $40,000; general managers, $39,000 to $81,000. Hotel managers may receive housing, meals, laundry, and other services. Salary varies according to responsibilities, experience, and the size and location of the hotel.

CRITICAL THINKING

What kinds of stressful situations might a hotel manager be called on to resolve? Why would a hotel manager need excellent communication skills?

STANDARD & POOR'S

INDUSTRY OUTLOOK

According to the Travel Industry Association of America (TIA), U.S. residents are forecasted to take more than 122 million business trips in 2004 and nearly 127 million business trips in 2005. Overall domestic traveler and international visitor spending is forecasted to be $568 billion in 2004 and reach $594 billion in 2005.

BUSINESS MANAGEMENT Online

For more information on management careers, go to:
busmanagement.glencoe.com

Types of Conflict

Conflict within a business organization can take several different forms:

- **Interpersonal conflict** is conflict between individuals that arises when individuals perceive or value situations differently.

FIGURE 17–2

The Nature of Workplace Conflict

Conflict in the workplace usually stems from disputes between individuals, between groups, or between groups of individuals and the organization itself. Managers need to know how to address each of these types of conflicts.

1 INTERPERSONAL CONFLICT
Interpersonal conflict is a major source of conflict in the work environment. Different values and personality traits can make it difficult for some people to work together. Interpersonal conflict also can arise over policy issues, such as how to allocate business tasks.

- **Intergroup conflict** is conflict between groups or departments that causes friction in an organization.
- **Organizational conflict** is conflict between employees and the organization itself.

The different types of workplace conflict are shown in **Figure 17–2**.

2 INTERGROUP CONFLICT
In intergroup conflict, different groups within organizations disagree because they have different goals. This designer might resent the marketing department's concern with marketability and cost. The marketing department might resent the design department's inability to create better looking cars.

3 ORGANIZATIONAL CONFLICT
Organizational conflict pits employees against the organization itself. Changes in policies are one source of such conflict. Reorganizations and corporate downsizing, or laying off workers, are also major causes of organizational conflict. Lack of resources also can be a source of organizational conflict.

Managing Conflict

All managers have to deal with conflict. How they do so affects department effectiveness.

Some minor conflicts can be avoided by smoothing over tensions without addressing the underlying problem. Other conflicts can be resolved by asking one side to give in to the other.

In other cases, however, managers need to force the conflicting parties to meet to resolve the conflict. When they do, they need to take a positive approach to conflict resolution.

Create the Appropriate Atmosphere

Effective managers start by establishing an atmosphere that promotes partnership and problem solving among their employees. They meet

CONNECT

Identify two conflicting groups at your school. What would you do in order to resolve the conflict between those groups?

▲ **RESOLVING CONFLICT** Conflict resolution is a process that involves cooperation from all parties involved. *What is one thing that this manager could do differently?*

with all parties to the conflict in a quiet, neutral place, such as a meeting room. Good managers express confidence that the two sides can come up with a solution in order to encourage the parties to the conflict to work together.

Keep an Open Mind

Good managers listen to alternative options with an open mind. They prepare for discussions by coming up with several specific new options that meet the needs of both sides. Rather than present these options as final solutions, however, good managers use them to help the parties to the conflict brainstorm other solutions.

Good managers also look for common ground between the two sides to a conflict. They listen actively and acknowledge the points made by each side. Managers should be empathetic with both sides and make sure to be fair and nonjudgemental.

Section 17.1 Assessment

 FACT AND IDEA REVIEW

1. Identify two positive effects of workplace conflict.
2. Identify two negative effects of workplace conflict.
3. Describe the three types of conflicts that occur in the workplace.
4. What are some things managers can do to help resolve conflict?

 CRITICAL THINKING

1. **Making Comparisons:** What is the difference between good and bad workplace conflict?
2. **Predicting Consequences:** What kinds of conflict do you think might arise if a company announced a plan to replace all offices with cubicles?

 ASSESSING WRITING SKILLS

Interview adults or students who work, and find examples of each of the three types of workplace conflict. Then write a one-page paper describing the three types of conflict, giving at least one example of each.

 CASE ANALYSIS

You are the chief executive officer of a health maintenance organization (HMO) that employs 1,400 people. Recently you have noticed growing tension between the health-care professionals and the company's accountants and financial analysts.

Apply: Describe what you would do to reduce tension between the two departments, and explain why doing so is important.

STRESS IN THE WORKPLACE

WHAT YOU'LL LEARN

▶ The positive effects of workplace stress.
▶ The negative effects of workplace stress.
▶ The sources and causes of workplace stress.
▶ How and why some employees experience professional burnout.
▶ How businesses help their employees manage and prevent stress and related problems.

WHY IT'S IMPORTANT

In order to get the most out of their employees, managers must recognize the signs of stress among employees and take steps to change the environment if necessary.

KEY TERMS

• stress
• burnout
• employee assistance program (EAP)
• wellness program

What Is Stress?

Just about everyone experiences stress in life. It might be caused by midterms, a tough work schedule, chores, or balancing extra-curricular school activities with academic work. **Stress** is any physical, chemical, or emotional factor that causes bodily or mental tension. Stress comes from many sources including health and money worries, problems with family members, and concerns over the future.

Many people suffer from work-related stress. According to Dr. Paul J. Rosch, former president of the American Institute of Stress, "Stress in the workplace may well be the number one health problem for the working adult population in the United States."

▶ STRESS Job-related stress costs businesses millions of dollars every year. *How does stress in the workplace affect businesses?*

Companies Hit the Road Less Traveled

It's Spiritual Unfoldment time at the World Bank. Every Wednesday at 1 P.M., a group of bank employees sits in a semicircle in a conference room at the Washington-based agency and connects. Today, it's standing-room only. There's no stereotyping this crowd of about 60, which includes senior managers and young assistants. Group founder Richard Barrett, an engineer at the bank, leads the meeting, which begins with a moment of silence. Today's topic: "Ten Strategies for Attaining Soul Consciousness." After an hour of talk about such things as realigning ego and soul, even staffers who arrived looking wilted leave smiling.

SOUL SEARCH. Get used to it. Spirituality is creeping into the office. Having survived downsizing and reengineering, overworked employees are stealing a moment and asking: "What does all this mean? Why do I feel so unfulfilled?" And companies are turning inward in search of a "soul" as a way to foster creativity and motivate leaders.

It may sound flaky, but a growing number of companies are setting off on spiritual journeys. It's not about bringing religion into the office or requiring that employees chant mantras at their workstations. Rather, the spirituality movement in the corporation is an attempt to create a sense of meaning and purpose at work and a connection between the company and its people.

CASH FROM KARMA? While still very new, the trend is starting to go beyond fringe companies or vaguely foreign institutions like the World Bank. Lotus Development Corp. has a "soul committee" that makes sure the company lives up to its stated values. Boeing Co. recruited poet David Whyte to read poems and regale top managers with fables as part of a program to revitalize their spirits on the job. And some divisions of AT&T are referring managers to a training program intended to reenergize them at the job. Says Lawrence Perlman, CEO of Minneapolis-based Ceridian Corp. and an advocate of the spirituality trend: "Ultimately, the combination of head and heart will be a competitive advantage."

Excerpted with permission from BusinessWeek, June 5, 1995

CRITICAL THINKING

Explain what Perlman means by "Ultimately, the combination of head and heart will be a competitive advantage."

DECISION MAKING

As a manager of a company with stressful deadlines, come up with one method for helping employees to manage stress.

◀ SOURCES OF STRESS Millions of American workers suffer from job-related stress. *What factors might make this airline ticket agent experience stress?*

Positive Effects of Stress

Like conflict, stress can be a positive force. In fact, too little job stress can cause boredom and depression at work. Many people enjoy the excitement that comes with working in high-stress jobs. They like the constant pressure and the need to perform well at all times.

Stress also can motivate people to work harder than usual. Deadlines, for example, force people to get work done within a set period of time. Without such sources of stress, many people would have difficulty getting motivated.

Negative Effects of Stress

While some stress can be beneficial, too much stress can be harmful. Job-related stress can cause a variety of emotional and physical problems (see **Figure 17–3**). These problems

Figure 17–3	EMOTIONAL AND PHYSICAL PROBLEMS CAUSED BY STRESS	
Emotional Problems		**Physical Problems**
• Impaired concentration		• Headaches
• Depression		• Backache
• Insomnia		• High blood pressure
• Loss of appetite		• Muscle tightness
• Substance abuse		• Diarrhea
• Mood swings		
• Loss of motivation		
WORKING WITH CHARTS		Stress can cause serious emotional and physical problems. *As a manager, how might you recognize that one of your employees was under too much stress?*

Figure 17–4	SOURCES AND CAUSES OF STRESS IN THE WORKPLACE
Source of Stress	**Possible Cause**
Job mismatch	• Job demands skills or abilities employee does not possess. • Job does not provide opportunity for employee to use his or her skills fully.
Conflicting expectations	• Company's concept of expected behavior differs from employee's concept.
Role ambiguity	• Employee is uncertain or unclear about what is expected. • Employee is unclear or uncertain about relationship between job performance and expected rewards and penalties.
Role overload	• Employee is not able to perform job effectively.
Poor working conditions	• Job environment is unpleasant. • Job involves long or erratic work hours.
Unsatisfying working relationships	• Employee has trouble working with superiors, peers, and/or subordinates.
Alienation	• Employee lacks opportunities for social interaction and decision making.
WORKING WITH CHARTS	Employees who are either overqualified or underqualified for their jobs often suffer from stress. *What are some other causes of job-related stress?*

can lead to absenteeism, job turnover, and reduced productivity.

As **Figure 17–4** shows, workplace stress is caused by many factors. Some employees suffer from stress because their jobs are too demanding. These people feel overwhelmed by their jobs.

Others suffer from stress because their jobs are not demanding enough. The boredom they feel at work makes them unhappy and concerned about the future.

Work-related stress can also lead to burnout. **Burnout** occurs when excessive stress causes a person to lose interest in his or her job. Managers need to reduce burnout by first identifying jobs with the highest potential for burnout. Once those jobs are identified, managers should work to redesign the jobs, clarify

RHI Robert Half International Inc.

Tips from Robert Half
Communication is very important in a team-oriented work environment. Learn to communicate your ideas to others through written memos or verbal updates. Always keep your supervisor updated on the status of your projects.

Figure 17–5 **THE PATH TO PROFESSIONAL BURNOUT**

Difficult Working Conditions	Cause	Leading to	Ending in
Constant pressure	Unfulfilled expectations	Stress	Burnout
Lack of job security	Lack of challenge	Fatigue	
Competition	Lack of meaning	Frustration	
Overspecialization	Lack of control	Helplessness	
Conflict	Limited mobility	Guilt	
Economic worries	Overwork		
Health problems	Poor decisions		
Alienation			
Uncertainty			
Isolation			

WORKING WITH CHARTS Professional burnout occurs when difficult working conditions cause an employee to lose interest in his or her job. *What are some of the signs that an employee may be burning out?*

expectations, improve working conditions, and train the employees who hold these jobs. The process through which burnout takes place is shown in **Figure 17–5**.

Managing Stress

RESPOND

Why do you think workplace stress would contribute to problems such as alcohol and drug abuse?

Many organizations, both large and small, are attempting to help employees with stress, burnout, and other personal problems. These problems include alcohol and drug abuse, depression, anxiety, domestic trauma, and financial problems.

Employee Assistance Programs

Years ago, most business organizations avoided getting involved with employee problems that were not job related. Instead of helping employees deal with these problems, most companies simply tried to get rid of problem workers.

Today, many companies consider employees' personal problems to be private, until they affect their job performance. Once personal problems reduce job effectiveness, those problems become a matter of concern for the organization.

Many businesses set up employee assistance programs. **Employee assistance programs**, or EAPs, are company-sponsored programs that help employees deal with personal problems. Such programs put employees in touch with professionals who diagnose the problem and refer them to an appropriate agency or clinic for treatment.

Businesses support EAPs because these programs help increase productivity by reducing absenteeism, tardiness, friction among employees, and employee grievances. EAPs also reduce a company's insurance costs by reducing illness and accidents.

Wellness Programs

Many companies have also set up wellness programs. **Wellness programs** are company-sponsored programs designed to prevent illness and enhance employee well-being. These programs can include such things as

- periodic medical examinations
- clinics to quit smoking
- education on nutrition, hypertension detection and control, weight control, exercise, stress management, and accident-risk reduction
- exercise facilities
- immunizations
- cardiopulmonary resuscitation (CPR) training

Companies support wellness programs because they reduce sick days, lower medical costs, and may make

All About

ATTITUDE

HELP!
Every now and then, you'll run into a difficult situation that seems to have no end in sight. If you're up against a brick wall, there's no point in banging your head against it. Start mapping out options to overcome the barrier. Solicit help from others inside and outside of your organization.

► **WELLNESS PROGRAMS** Many businesses provide exercise facilities for their employees. Why do you think they provide such facilities?

employees more productive. An organization that has adopted a wellness program is Adolph Coors Company. Coors claims that its wellness center has helped the company save over $2 million annually.

Stress Management Techniques

QUESTION

List seven job-related sources of stress.

To prevent burnout among their employees, business managers need to recognize when employees may be facing too much stress.

Figure 17–6	**REDUCING STRESS BY APPROACHING NEW SITUATIONS POSITIVELY**
Negative Reaction	**Positive Reaction**
I'll never get this project in on time.	If I stay focused and take it one step at a time, I'll make steady progress.
My supervisor didn't say good morning. She's probably displeased with my work, and I'll get a bad evaluation.	My supervisor may be in a bad mood. So far all my evaluations have been positive, so unless I get some negative feedback, I'll assume my supervisor is pleased with my work.
I can't get my mistake on page 53 out of my mind. The report is ruined. I have disappointed everyone.	No one is perfect. I did my best. I'm overreacting to one mistake when the overall report is fine.

WORKING WITH CHARTS Negative thinking can be a cause of stress. *What is one way that employees can learn to deal with their stress?*

Source: www.stressrelease.com, copyright © 1999 Center for Anxiety and Stress Treatment/Stress Release Health Enterprises, from *Overcoming Panic, Anxiety & Phobia*, by Shirley Babior and Carol Goldman (Whole Person Press, 1996). Reprinted by permission.

Then they must take actions to improve the work environment for them. These actions could include redesigning jobs, clarifying expectations, improving physical working conditions, and providing additional training.

In addition to looking out for their employees, managers need to manage their own stress. To cope with stress, managers need to take a positive attitude toward change. They need to view setbacks as challenges, not catastrophes (see **Figure 17–6**).

Managers who are unable to cope with stress need to recognize that they are anxious and try to pinpoint the source of their anxiety. Once this source is identified, they must then try to figure out what they can do to eliminate or minimize the situation so that it becomes less stressful.

RESPOND

What techniques do you use to relieve stress in your daily life?

Section 17.2 Assessment

FACT AND IDEA REVIEW

1. What are some of the positive effects of stress in the workplace?
2. What are some of the negative effects of stress in the workplace?
3. What are some of the causes of workplace stress?
4. What is burnout and what causes it to occur?
5. What is an employee assistance program (EAP)? What are some other ways businesses help their employees manage stress?

CRITICAL THINKING

1. **Evaluating Information:** What steps can managers take to cope with stress?
2. **Drawing Conclusions:** Why do you think businesses support employee assistance and wellness programs?

ASSESSING MATH SKILLS

As head of the human resources department at your company, you have been asked to conduct a study on the annual cost of absenteeism. Your research reveals that your company loses 88,000 hours of work a year to absenteeism. If the average worker earns $16.75 an hour, what is the annual cost of absenteeism? How much would your company save if it could reduce absenteeism by 15 percent?

CASE ANALYSIS

You have just taken over as chief executive officer of a mid-size electronics company. One of the first things you notice is the high level of stress at the company. You are concerned that the stress level at your new company may be reducing your employees' ability to perform their jobs well and may even motivate them to leave the company.

Apply: What steps would you take to reduce the level of stress?

CHAPTER 17 ASSESSMENT

REVIEWING VOCABULARY

Working in groups of three, create a word-find puzzle that uses each of the following vocabulary words:

conflict

interpersonal conflict

intergroup conflict

organizational conflict

stress

burnout

employee assistance program (EAP)

wellness program

Chapter Summary

Section 17.1

▶ Some conflict is beneficial, while some creates an unproductive work environment.

▶ Three types of conflict that businesses may face are interpersonal, intergroup, and organizational.

▶ Good managers help promote partnership and problem-solving among their employees.

Section 17.2

▶ Job-related stress is a problem for millions of Americans.

▶ Some stress can be positive, but too much stress may cause emotional and physical problems.

▶ Burnout occurs when excessive stress causes a person to lose interest in his or her job.

▶ Companies set up employee assistance and wellness programs to help employees.

▶ Managers must be able to handle personal stress.

RECALLING KEY CONCEPTS

1. What are some of the positive and negative effects of workplace conflict?
2. What are some of the positive and negative effects of workplace stress?
3. What causes some employees to burn out? What can managers do to prevent burnout?
4. Describe employee assistance and wellness programs. Why do companies set up these programs?

THINKING CRITICALLY

1. What should a manager do if he or she notices that an employee is regularly showing up late for work and seems unable to complete his work?
2. How might an employee feel if her manager failed to explain her job duties to her? Why might she feel this way?
3. Describe one situation in which stress has a positive effect on employees and one situation in which stress has a negative effect.
4. What are some ways that people can cope with stress?

CHAPTER 17 ASSESSMENT

ASSESSING ACADEMIC SKILLS

ART Identify five causes of stress. Then prepare a chart in which you illustrate and label each cause.

APPLYING MANAGEMENT PRINCIPLES

SOLVE THE PROBLEM Since March, the product development team at your company has been working 70 to 80 hours a week to get a new software product out on the market before the end of the year. In November, you notice that the morale of many of the team's most enthusiastic members seems low. You also notice that although the entire department continues to put in long hours, it is no longer making progress at the same rate it had in the spring.

Writing Analyze what you think may be happening. Then write a one-page memo describing the steps you plan to take to deal with the problem.

PREPARING FOR COMPETITIVE EVENTS

When both sides in an argument change their position to reach an agreement, this is called

a. a conflict.
b. a compromise.
c. an uncertainty.
d. a code of conduct.
e. distancing.

In this chapter you read the *BusinessWeek* Management Model about a growing number of companies using spiritual journeys to create a sense of meaning for its employees. For more information, go to *BusinessWeek* online at: **www.businessweek.com**

Using the Internet or library resources, locate an article about stress management at work. Write a two-page summary of the article, highlighting the strategies used at the company.

CHAPTER 18

MANAGING CHANGE, CULTURE, AND DIVERSITY

LEARNING OBJECTIVES

When you have completed this chapter, you will be able to:

- Recognize the sources of change managers face.
- Explain why it is important for managers to adapt to change.
- Discuss the reasons people resist change.
- Describe the steps managers can take to reduce resistance to change.
- Understand corporate culture and how it is created.
- Explain the importance of diversity in the workplace.

READING STRATEGIES

As you read

- **PREDICT** what the section will be about.
- **CONNECT** what you read with your own life.
- **QUESTION** as you read to make sure you understand the content.
- **RESPOND** to what you read.

Understanding Management

The high-tech equipment and software manufacturer Hewlett-Packard is known for its strong, supportive corporate culture. After experiencing the pressures of raising his two daughters on his own, former CEO and Chairman, Lewis Platt, changed some of HP's personnel policies to help attract and retain a diverse group of talented employees.

Analyzing Management Skills

Explain why a diverse group of employees might give a company like Hewlett-Packard a competitive advantage over less diverse companies.

Applying Management Skills

Visually survey the scene at your school lunch hour. Do groups of people tend to sit together? How diverse are the groups? What actions would you propose to get different groups to mix with each other?

BusinessWeek ONLINE

For further reading on managing diversity go to:
www.businessweek.com

"MANAGEMENT TALK"

"We must become a model of inclusion around the world. We need the creative talents, the enthusiastic commitment, the ideas and contribution of every HP employee. Invention requires creativity; creativity requires true diversity."

—Carly Fiorina, Hewlett-Packard Company, Chairwoman and CEO

MANAGING CHANGE

Sources of Change

Change affects all companies, even the most successful. Just ask Andrew Grove, the chairman of Intel Corporation, the maker of the Pentium® processor. During the 1970s, Intel was a leading manufacturer of computer memory chips. By the mid-1980s, however, Japanese producers had taken over the market. To adapt to the change, Intel took a radical approach. It cut its workforce by about a third and closed several plants to focus on a new product line—microprocessors. Today the company leads the market, remaining alert to profit-threatening changes.

Business managers are constantly confronted with change. Consumers lose interest in some products and flock to new ones. Technological advances leave once-popular products obsolete. Prices of raw materials change, forcing manufac-

▶ **CHANGE** Changes in styles and tastes can affect a clothing business. *What happens to fashion businesses that fail to keep up with the times?*

turers to adjust production processes or change prices. Companies that fail to respond to change may find themselves out of business.

Businesses face two kinds of changes. **Internal changes** are changes that occur within a business organization. **External changes** are changes caused by forces outside the company. See **Figure 18–1** for the types of changes affecting organizations.

PREDICT

Describe some general types of internal and external changes.

Internal Changes

Internal changes occur constantly in management, policies, procedures, and organizational structure. A company may change its policy on extending credit to customers. It may eliminate a layer of management to reorganize structure. These are internal changes.

Managers must learn to adapt to internal changes. It is necessary that they help employees adapt to these changes as well.

External Changes

External changes are changes that take place outside a company. Two important sources of external change are changes in technology and changes in the environment within which a business operates.

Figure 18–1	TYPES OF CHANGES AFFECTING ORGANIZATIONS	
Internal	**Technological**	**Environmental**
• Policies	• Products	• Consumer tastes
• Procedures	• Machines	• Social trends
• Methods	• Equipment	• Fashion trends
• Rules	• Processes	• Political trends
• Reorganization	• Automation	• Interest rates
• Budgets	• Computers	• Competition
• Organizational structure	• Raw materials	• Suppliers
• Personnel	• Robots	• Population trends
• Management		• Laws
• Ownership		• Taxes
• Products/services sold		

WORKING WITH CHARTS	All businesses are affected by circumstances over which they have no control. *What happens to businesses that fail to adapt to change?*

▶ **TECHNOLOGY** Teenagers today spend hours communicating with friends through e-mail, a technology that was barely used a decade ago. *How do changes in technology affect businesses?*

CHANGES IN TECHNOLOGY A hundred years ago, businesses that produced buggies and horse whips thrived. The invention of the automobile made these products obsolete. No matter how well-managed these companies were, they could not succeed. External change forced these companies out of business.

Changes in technology also affect a company's production processes. The rise in data-processing systems and robotics in the second half of the twentieth century forced large companies to automate many functions they once performed manually. Companies that failed to adopt the new technologies could not compete effectively.

CHANGES IN THE ENVIRONMENT Environmental changes refer to all non-technological changes that occur outside an organization. They include changes in consumer tastes, social trends, economic conditions, and government regulations.

These changes have tremendous impact on a business. For almost 150 years, the Singer Company sold sewing machines to American women. As women began to work outside the home, however, they had less time to sew. Fewer American women purchased sewing machines. This change produced disastrous results for Singer, which declared bankruptcy in 1999.

Changes in government regulations also affect businesses. Manufacturers of lead paint developed new products after the government determined that lead caused developmental disabilities in children. Babywear manufacturers had to find new fabrics when the government banned certain materials found to be flammable.

Adapting to Change in the Twenty-First Century

Businesses have always needed to adapt to change. However, the pace of change is more rapid today. In the four hundred years after Gutenberg invented movable type in the 1400s, technology remained virtually unchanged. Today, software programs may become obsolete within months, and computers are considered unusable a decade after representing the cutting edge.

Technology has changed more than a business's products and production methods. It also has changed the way businesses compete. By making it easier to communicate with customers around the world, technology has created a global economy. In the **global economy** businesses from around the world compete with each other. Managers must respond quickly to change because of the competitive global economy.

CONNECT

What are some significant advances in technology that have taken place in your lifetime?

Resistance to Change

Most people resist change, especially when it affects their jobs. Some people do so in an open manner. Others do so subtly. The employee who quits a job because of a change in a policy demonstrates resistance explicitly. The employee who stays at the job but no longer works hard is resisting passively.

Reasons for Resistance

Employees resist change for several reasons:

- *Fear of the unknown.* Many changes involve outcomes that are not known. People fear that these changes will produce negative results.
- *Fear of losing one's job or income.* Sometimes employees resist change because they fear that it will threaten their jobs or incomes. Production workers, for example, may oppose new standards that reduce their number of overtime hours.
- *Fear that skills and expertise will lose value.* Everyone likes to feel valued by others. For this reason, people resist changes that have the potential to reduce their value. Assembly-line workers are likely to resist the introduction of robots, which may make their skills unnecessary.
- *Fear of loss of power.* Many employees, especially managers, fear that change may diminish their power. They prefer to maintain the status quo.

QUESTION

List six fears that can lead to an employee's resistance to change.

• *Fear of inconvenience.* Many changes result in personal inconveniences. Employees may resist acquiring new skills needed to perform their jobs.

• *Fear of threats to relationships.* Most people feel comfortable working with people they know. Changes that threaten ongoing working relationships are likely to meet resistance.

Reducing Resistance to Change

The way in which managers implement change often has a significant impact on the way in which the change is accepted. To encourage employees to accept changes, managers need to take the following steps:

1. *Build trust.* If employees have trust and confidence in management, they are much more likely to accept change. If an atmosphere of distrust exists, employees are likely to resist change strongly.

2. *Discuss upcoming changes.* Fear of the unknown is a major barrier to change. Managers should explain what changes are planned and why they have been proposed. They should also outline the likely impact the change will have on each employee.

3. *Involve employees.* Involving employees means more than discussing upcoming changes with them. It should involve them in the process by considering employee feedback.

The specific approach to breaking down resistance that a manager will use depends on the nature of the situation. **Figure 18–2** identifies six possible strategies.

To understand how managers overcome resistance to change, consider the case of Vista Systems, a large computer systems company. Until recently, Vista's salesforce was organized by geographical region.

Last month, senior management reorganized the sales department by industry. Under the reorganization, one group of sales people will specialize in hospitals. Another will handle manufacturing companies, while a third will call exclusively on government agencies.

▲ **OVERCOMING RESISTANCE** Involving people in the change process can reduce resistance to change. *What other strategies can managers use to encourage employees to accept change?*

Figure 18–2	STRATEGIES FOR OVERCOMING RESISTANCE TO CHANGE		
Approach	**Appropriate Situation**	**Advantages**	**Drawbacks**
Education + communication	Where there is a lack of information or inaccurate information and analysis	Once persuaded, people will often help implement change.	Can be very time-consuming if many people are involved
Participation + involvement	Where the initiators do not have all the information they need to design the change, and where others have considerable power to resist	People who participate will be committed to implementing change, and any relevant information they have will be integrated into the change plan.	Can be time-consuming if participators design an inappropriate change
Facilitation + support	When people are resisting because of adjustment problems	No other approach works as well with adjustment problems.	Can be time-consuming and expensive and still fail
Negotiation + agreement	Where someone or some group will clearly lose out in a change and where that group has considerable power to resist	Sometimes it is a relatively easy way to avoid major resistance.	Can be too expensive; in many cases it alerts others to negotiate for compliance.
Manipulation + co-optation	Where other tactics will not work or are too expensive	Relatively quick and inexpensive	Can lead to future problems if people feel manipulated
Explicit + implicit coercion	Where speed is essential and the change initiators possess considerable power	Speedy and can overcome any kind of resistance	Can be risky if it leaves people mad at the initiators

WORKING WITH CHARTS	Before choosing a strategy for reducing resistance to change, managers must identify the source of resistance. *What strategy would you use to overcome resistance by employees who are confused about the implications of a proposed change?*

Source: "Choosing Strategies for Change," John P. Kotter and Leonard A. Schlesinger, *Harvard Business Review*, March–April 1979.

Last week Lisa Wong, the manager of Vista's sales department, presented the new reorganization to her staff. Opposition was fierce. Salespeople already had established good relationships with customers, which they would lose. The new plan meant more traveling, as customers would now be all over the country. It also involved training, which many resisted.

Lisa expected that her salespeople would resist the plan. To overcome resistance, she used the strategy of negotiation plus agreement (see **Figure 18–2**). Recognizing that the reorganization would probably reduce salespeople's earnings in the short run, she convinced management to guarantee staff's salaries for 18 months. Her approach addressed the most important source of resistance—fear of reduced earnings.

To help overcome resistance, Lisa took two additional steps. Rather than simply assign industries to the people on her staff, Lisa met with all 20 salespeople to find out which industries they preferred to cover. Involving them in the change, rather than imposing the change upon them, helped reduce their resistance.

Lisa also explained to her staff why management had adopted the new plan. In the end, she convinced them that in the long run commissions would increase as they became experts in their industries. Because she was not afraid of change, Lisa was able to find a strategy to help her staff adapt to the reorganization successfully.

Section 18.1 Assessment

FACT AND IDEA REVIEW

1. What are two basic types of change that a business faces?
2. Identify four sources of change over which businesses have no control.
3. Name three reasons many people resist change.
4. List three steps managers can take to reduce resistance to change.

CRITICAL THINKING

1. **Predicting Consequences:** How might a major increase or decrease in people's income affect a business?
2. **Distinguishing Fact from Opinion:** Does change always represent a threat to business?

ASSESSING HISTORY SKILLS

Using the resources at your public library, research the history of the Internet. Identify when and where it was invented and how it was first used. Write a one-page report summarizing your findings.

CASE ANALYSIS

Your company has introduced a job-sharing program. Under this new program, two employees who prefer to work part time can share a job by each working three days a week. You recognize that although the new policy will please some of your employees, it is likely to concern others.

Apply: Explain how you would introduce this change to your staff. Identify the techniques you would use to reduce resistance to the change.

Food and Beverage Manager

■ Nature of the Work

Food and beverage managers oversee food service in hotels and restaurants. They are responsible for hiring, firing, training, scheduling, and supervising workers. They plan menus, decide the numbers of meals to be prepared, estimate costs, and order and schedule food deliveries. They see that sufficient supplies, such as paper goods, are on hand at all times. They arrange for maintenance of equipment and furniture. Managers may help with cooking, clearing tables, and other tasks. They also resolve customer complaints.

■ Working Conditions

Food and beverage managers work in busy, often hectic conditions, up to 50 or 60 hours a week, especially in hotels holding conventions. They may work weekends and evenings.

■ Training, Other Qualifications, and Advancement

Food and beverage managers need a bachelor's degree in hotel, restaurant, or food management. Internships, work study, or part-time work in hotels or restaurants is useful.

Food and beverage managers must be able to work with people under stress, problem solve, concentrate on details, organize and direct the work of others. Bookkeeping, accounting, payroll preparation, communica-

tion, and computer skills are essential. Managers must be clean and neat in appearance.

■ Salary Range

Food and beverage managers earn $30,000 to $50,000 and may receive benefits and an annual bonus of between $2,000 and $10,000. Salaries vary with location, company, responsibilities, and experience. Meals may be included.

CRITICAL THINKING

Why would a clean, neat appearance be important for a food and beverage manager?

STANDARD &POOR'S

INDUSTRY OUTLOOK

The market for natural and organic foods has been growing 4 to 5 times as fast as the market for conventional foods. In 2002, natural and organic food and beverage sales totaled $14.4 billion, up 9 percent from 2001. Future annual growth is expected to be a very healthy 8 to 10 percent.

BUSINESS MANAGEMENT Online

For more information on management careers, go to:

busmanagement.glencoe.com

MANAGING CORPORATE CULTURE AND DIVERSITY

Understanding Corporate Culture

Jamie Wyatt didn't know quite what to think when she arrived for a job interview at a San Francisco-based Internet company. Having worked in banking, she found it odd to see professionals dressed in blue jeans and secretaries calling bosses by their first names. Jamie was familiar with a conservative culture, in which narrowly defined norms of behavior were strictly observed. The culture she had entered was a much more open culture, in which a wider range of behavior was welcomed.

▲ **CORPORATE CULTURES** Nontraditional offices like this one are common in high-tech companies, particularly on the West Coast. *What does this office suggest about the company's corporate culture?*

A **culture** consists of a set of customs, traditions, and values that members of a community share. Nations and ethnic groups have cultures. Corporations develop cultures as well.

A corporation's culture can be compared with a person's personality. Just as people's personalities differ, company cultures vary as well. Some, such as the company at which Jamie interviewed, are informal places that value creativity. Others might be rigid institutions, where policies dictate most activities.

RESPOND

In what type of corporate culture would you feel most comfortable?

Senior management transmits an organization's culture to employees. At the Walt Disney Company, executives reportedly pick up litter on the grounds of the company's theme parks without thinking. This is because of the Disney commitment to cleanliness.

At TBWA/Chiat/Day, an advertising agency based in Los Angeles, management values creativity and independence above all else. Employees know that they will be given little guidance. They are expected to make their own decisions. People who are not comfortable with ambiguity will not fit in at TBWA/Chiat/Day because the culture there thrives on freedom.

Factors that Determine Corporate Culture

What causes an organization to develop a particular type of culture? Many organizations trace their culture to the company's founder. Harley Procter of Procter & Gamble, Thomas J. Watson, Sr., of IBM, and Walt Disney of Walt Disney Corporation all left their imprints on the organizations they headed.

▲ **FACTORS DETERMINING CORPORATE CULTURE** Walt Disney established the corporate culture that still dominates the company he founded. *What other factors determine a company's culture?*

BREAKING THE ICE

When you're placed into a situation of meeting new employees for the first time, try to find something in common to discuss with your peers. Whether it's sports or fashion, some common interest can break the ice. Birds of a feather flock together!

In most cases, corporate culture is not affected by the founder's values, however. Instead, four factors contribute to an organization's culture: the company's history, environment, selection process, and socialization process.

HISTORY Awareness of a company's past often helps create its corporate culture. Employees at J.P. Morgan Chase & Company have a strong sense of the important role their bank has played since the nineteenth century. This sense of tradition increases their sense of commitment. It also motivates them to act in ways that will carry on the great traditions of their company.

ENVIRONMENT Most corporations develop their cultures in response to the environment in which the business operates. Banks on Wall Street, for example, have fairly formal corporate cultures. Men are expected to wear suits, and women are expected to wear formal office attire. This part of bank culture reflects expectations of how bankers should carry themselves.

▲ **COMPETITION** Long-distance companies today compete vigorously for customers. *What change made the industry competitive?*

In contrast, West Coast-based high-tech companies often encourage their employees to dress casually. This culture reflects the creative nature of high-tech industries, as well as the more laid-back attitude of the West Coast.

One of the environmental factors that affects a company's culture is government regulation. Before the 1980s, the telecommunications industry was highly regulated. The telephone company faced few incentives to innovate, because it had no competition and all costs were passed on to customers. Deregulation of the industry in the 1980s changed the culture overnight. Today, the telecommunications industry is competitive and dynamic. As a result, prices are lower and consumers have a wider range of service options.

International Management

HONG KONG

Hong Kong Chinese expect to be trained on the job and will not work on their business skills outside the office. But, managers and workers respond favorably to training courses offered during office hours at company expense.

BusinessWeek ONLINE For further reading about International Management go to: **www.businessweek.com**

STAFFING Organizations tend to hire, retain, and promote people who are similar to their current employees. They do this to find people whom they believe will fit in. This "fit" criterion ensures that new employees will accept the company's values. People who might challenge the status quo will be screened out.

For many years, Danette Garcia worked as an accountant for a private accounting firm. Last year, Danette left her job to become a manager for a different company. The fit was not a good one. Danette expected her staff to work past 7 P.M. every evening and was surprised to find that no one worked weekends. Unable to adapt to the new culture, she quit her job and searched for one where she was more comfortable.

ENTRY SOCIALIZATION Companies with strong cultures attach great importance to the process of introducing and indoctrinating new employees. This process is called **entry socialization**. Entry socialization reduces threats to the organization from newcomers. It also educates new employees about company expectations.

Entry socialization may be handled formally or informally. At many large corporations, new employees attend a full-day orientation session. This orientation involves speeches by managers and multimedia presentations about the company. This kind of orientation gives new employees a sense of the company's values and attitudes.

QUESTION

What are the potential benefits and drawbacks to hiring, retaining, and promoting people who are similar to a company's current employees?

Strong and Weak Corporate Cultures

A strong corporate culture is clearly defined, reinforces a common understanding about what is important, and has the support of management and employees. Such a culture contributes greatly to an organization's success by creating an understanding about how employees should behave. **Figure 18–3** identifies the characteristics of a strong corporate culture.

Weak cultures have the opposite characteristics. In a weak corporate culture, individuals often act in ways that are inconsistent with the company's way of doing things.

Characterizing Corporate Cultures

A company's culture is reflected in seven key attributes:

1. *Individual autonomy.* The degree of responsibility, independence, and opportunities for exercising initiative given to individuals in the organization.
2. *Structure.* The number of rules and the amount of direct supervision used to control behavior.
3. *Support.* The degree of assistance and warmth provided by managers to their subordinates.
4. *Identification:* The degree to which members identify with the organization as a whole rather than with their particular work group.
5. *Performance-reward.* The degree to which reward allocations (such as salary increases and promotions) are based on performance.

Figure 18–3	STRONG CORPORATE CULTURE

The characteristics of a strong corporate culture are

- Organizational members share clear values and beliefs about how to succeed in their business.

- Organizational members agree on which beliefs about how to succeed are most important.

- Different parts of the organization have similar beliefs about how to succeed.

- The rituals of day-to-day organizational life are well organized and consistent with company goals.

Companies with strong corporate cultures share certain characteristics. *Why is a strong corporate culture important?*

Adapted from Terrence E. Deal and Allan A. Kennedy, *Corporate Cultures: The Rites and Rituals of Corporate Life.*

6. *Conflict tolerance.* The degree of conflict present in relationships between peers and work groups as well as the willingness to be open about differences.

7. *Risk tolerance.* The degree to which employees are encouraged to be aggressive, innovative, and risk seeking.

Corporate cultures can be characterized by the degree of risk associated with the organization's activities and the speed with which the organization receives feedback on the success of decisions. **Figure 18–4** shows a matrix based on these two factors.

Few companies fit neatly into one category. In fact, various cultures may co-exist within different departments of the same company. A company's payroll department, for example, may represent a process culture, while the new product development department may represent a bet-your-company culture.

MACHO CULTURE The macho culture is characterized by individualists who take high risks. In a macho culture, employees receive quick feedback, which identifies decisions as right or wrong. Teamwork is not important in a macho culture because every colleague is a potential rival. The value of cooperation is ignored.

The macho culture does not allow the chance to learn from mistakes. People who function best in this type of culture are those who need to gamble and are willing to tolerate all-or-nothing risks for instant feedback. Traders at the New York Stock Exchange function within a macho culture.

Figure 18–4	**GENERIC TYPES OF ORGANIZATIONAL CULTURE**	
Speed of Feedback	**Degree of Risk**	
	High	*Low*
Rapid	Tough-guy, macho culture	Work-hard/ play-hard culture
Slow	Bet-your-company culture	Process culture
WORKING WITH CHARTS	Four basic types of organizational cultures can be distinguished. *How is the process culture characterized?*	

▲ **WORKPLACE** Different work environments reflect different types of culture. *Which of the four types of cultures best describes this workplace?*

CONNECT

Describe a few local examples of macho, work-hard/play-hard, bet-your-company, or process culture companies.

WORK-HARD/PLAY-HARD CULTURE The work-hard/play-hard culture encourages employees to take few risks and to expect feedback. In this culture, activity is the key to success. People who are persistent and fulfill needs succeed in this kind of culture. Because of the need for volume, outgoing team players thrive. People who work for management-consulting firms function within a work-hard/play-hard culture.

BET-YOUR-COMPANY CULTURE The bet-your-company culture requires large-stakes decisions. In this culture, considerable time passes before results are known. Pressures to make the right decisions are always present in this environment. Managers of aerospace companies, whose decisions today affect production a decade from now, work in a bet-your-company culture.

RHI Robert Half International Inc.

Tips from Robert Half

Many companies look for leadership potential in new employees. Look beyond your immediate area of responsibility. Help your colleagues, learn what motivates and inspires people, and take on new challenges.

PROCESS CULTURE The process culture involves low risk coupled with little feedback. Employees must focus on how things are done rather than on outcomes. Employees in this atmosphere become cautious and protective. Those who thrive are orderly, punctual, and detail oriented. People who work in insurance companies might function within a process culture.

Managing Diversity

An important change in today's work environment is the increasing diversity of the workforce. **Diversity** in the workforce means including people of different genders, races, religions, nationalities, ethnic groups, age groups, and physical abilities.

The increasing diversity of the workplace represents a major social change in the United States. According to the U.S. Department of Labor, minorities are expected to rise from one in every four Americans to one in every two by 2050, and by 2010, Hispanics will likely become the largest minority group in the country. Growth rates for Hispanic and Asian populations are expected to top 2 percent each year until 2030.

The trend toward greater diversity is expected to continue over the next 50 years, as the proportion of nonwhites and immigrants in the U.S. population grows. In fact, diversity is increasing so quickly in the United States that the percentage of nonhispanic whites is projected to fall from 71.8 percent in 2000 to just 52.8 percent by 2050 (see **Figure 18–5**).

This change in the work environment has important implications for managers. According to *The Wall Street Journal,* in the twenty-first century, "managers will have to handle greater cultural diversity" to be effective.

Figure 18–5	PROJECTED U.S. POPULATION, BY DEMOGRAPHIC GROUP, 2000–2050 (PERCENT OF POPULATION)					
Demographic group	**2000**	**2010**	**2020**	**2030**	**2040**	**2050**
Nonhispanic white	71.8	68.0	64.3	60.6	56.6	52.8
Nonhispanic black	12.2	12.6	12.9	13.1	13.3	13.6
Hispanic	11.4	13.8	16.3	18.9	21.7	24.5
Nonhispanic American Indian, Eskimo and Aleut	0.9	0.7	0.8	0.8	0.8	0.9
Nonhispanic Asian and Pacific Islander	3.9	4.8	5.7	6.6	7.5	8.2
Total	100.0	100.0	100.0	100.0	100.0	100.0
WORKING WITH CHARTS	The demographic makeup of the U.S. population is projected to change dramatically over the next 50 years. *Which demographic groups are growing?*					

U.S. Census Bureau, http://www.census.gov/populations/nations/nsrh/nprh9600.txt.

Reasons for Creating Diverse Workforces

Companies are seeking diverse workforces because

RESPOND

Imagine that you are in charge of a marketing firm located in a culturally diverse city, such as Los Angeles or New York. What would you do to tap into the diverse marketplace successfully?

- employee population is increasingly diverse
- customer population is increasingly diverse
- retaining top talent means recruiting individuals from all backgrounds
- increasing diversity minimizes the risk of litigation

By creating a culture that is open to different behavioral styles and that incorporates a wide range of views, diversity can improve corporate decision making. Greater diversity allows a company to respond to diverse groups of customers (see **Figure 18–6**).

Diversity Training

Sometimes employees have difficulty working with people who are different from them. To address this problem, many companies, including Allied Signal, Black & Decker, Corning, and IBM, offer seminars on diversity. These seminars help employees understand the value of diversity in the workplace and marketplace. They help managers create workplaces in which all employees feel that they can participate, add value, and make a difference.

▶ **AMERICANS WITH DISABILITIES ACT** Since the passage of the Americans with Disabilities Act in 1990, more people with disabilities have begun working for companies outside of their homes. *Why is including people with diverse backgrounds necessary for business organizations?*

FIGURE 18–6

The Changing American Workplace

Advances in civil rights and demographic changes in the United States have made the workplace much more diverse than it was 30 years ago. Today, managers must understand how to work with people from diverse backgrounds.

1 **THE WORKPLACE IN THE 1960S**
Until the 1970s, white males dominated most businesses in the United States. For the most part, managers managed people who came from backgrounds that were similar to their own.

2 **THE WORKPLACE IN THE YEAR 2000**
By the year 2000, most workplaces included women and minorities. Increasing diversity has helped companies understand the needs of their increasingly diverse customer bases.

3 **THE WORKPLACE IN THE MID-TWENTY-FIRST CENTURY**
By the middle of the twenty-first century, minorities will make up almost half of the population. In response to these changes, the workplace is expected to become even more diverse than it is today.

DIVERSITY RULES

It's No Easy Task for a Business Owner to Keep the Melting Pot from Boiling Over

Want a glimpse into the world of diversity? Try the men's bathroom in any American factory. What a shock the day in March that I checked out our plant men's room at the urging of a concerned employee. Every imaginable racial and ethnic slur was scrawled across the surface of the largest stall. I asked myself, Is this what people really think? How are they ever going to work together if they feel this way?

Wandering the factory floor, though, you'd never guess the writing on the wall. Anglos bend over machines helping Spanish-speaking workers repair timing belts. Koreans mix inks for African American printing-press operators. Women and men spell one another on the packing lines. Everyone seems to be working together to get the job done at our vegetable-bag printing plant.

GRIPES AND GRUDGES. But look more closely and the picture gets more complex. At lunchtime, the ethnic and gender groups largely go their own way, then privately air

their biases about the others, I hear.

How's a small business to cope? Mostly, we manage diversity by insisting on rules that keep people's uglier impulses at bay. Last year, at the urging of our labor attorney, we assembled an employee handbook, the first few pages of which spell out tough harassment and equal opportunity policies. We passed out literature on sexual harassment. Anybody found guilty of breaking the rules is dealt with harshly.

This seems to have improved things considerably. Still, rules only get you so far. We had to do more to communicate our commitment. Last year, I urged a longtime female bag packer to apply for an assistant foreperson's job. And earlier

this year we promoted our first Hispanic to head mechanic and elevated an African American to press-department foreperson.

We're also experimenting. Later this year we'll offer Spanish classes to our managers, which we hope will improve communication with the half of our employees who are Spanish-speaking. Next year, English lessons will be available for all non-native speakers. We're also rolling out a course on teamwork. It will emphasize respect for people from different cultures and teach how cultural differences can shape perceptions.

Excerpted with permission from BusinessWeek, *September 1, 1997*

CRITICAL THINKING

Evaluate the author's methods for handling cultural differences.

DECISION MAKING

As a manager for a small company, develop an employee handbook that defines your harassment and equal opportunity policies.

Diversity training increases acceptance of diversity by breaking down stereotypes, which reflect ignorance. People who have never worked with people with physical disabilities, for example, may assume that these workers are less capable. People who have never worked with people from other countries often make incorrect assumptions about the way foreigners think and act.

To bring together all of the people who work for them, managers must avoid stereotyping. They must create a work environment in which prejudice is not tolerated and diversity is welcomed and respected. Employees need to feel that they are valued and respected for who they are. Managers should always be sensitive to the backgrounds of their workers, and should foster a diverse and understanding corporate culture.

Section 18.2 Assessment

 FACT AND IDEA REVIEW

1. Explain how the environment affects a business's culture.
2. List three characteristics of strong corporate cultures.
3. How do companies use the hiring process to reinforce their corporate culture?
4. What advantages does a diverse workforce give a company?

 CRITICAL THINKING

1. **Predicting Consequences:** What do you think happens when an employee rejects the values embodied in a company's corporate culture?
2. **Drawing Conclusions:** Why is it more important today than it was 50 years ago for managers to be able to work with a diverse group of people?

 ASSESSING COMPUTER SKILLS

Using the Internet, locate the home pages of two of the following companies: Dell, General Mills, Microsoft, State Farm Insurance, Texas Instruments. Then find statements that give you a clue as to what kind of corporate culture characterizes each company.

 CASE ANALYSIS

You are the manager of a department that processes mortgage applications. Last week you interviewed a woman who previously worked for a daily newspaper. However, you are not sure if she would fit in with the culture at your company—a process culture. You invite her back for a second interview before you make a decision.

Apply: Make a list of questions to determine if she would fit in at your company.

CHAPTER 18 ASSESSMENT

C HAPTER SUMMARY

Section 18.1

▶ Internal changes occur within an organization, while external changes are caused by outside forces.

▶ Managers reduce resistance to change by building trust, discussing changes with staff, and involving employees in the process.

Section 18.2

▶ Corporate culture is the corporate personality.

▶ Strong corporate cultures are clearly defined, reinforce what is important, and have support.

▶ The four types of cultures are macho culture, work-hard/play-hard culture, bet-your-company culture, and process culture.

▶ As the U.S. population becomes more diverse managers must learn to work with people of different genders, races, religions, nationalities, ethnic groups, age groups, and physical abilities.

● REVIEWING VOCABULARY

Give examples of each of the following:

internal change
external change
environmental change
global economy
culture
entry socialization
diversity

● RECALLING KEY CONCEPTS

1. What are three examples of internal change?
2. Why is it important for employees to have confidence in their manager?
3. What four factors affect corporate culture?
4. What is the macho culture? Give an example.
5. How can training increase acceptance of diversity?

● THINKING CRITICALLY

1. Technological changes in the past century revolutionized business organizations. What kinds of changes do you think that businesses can expect in the next ten years?
2. Why do individuals resist those changes that might threaten existing relationships?
3. What is the difference between a macho corporate culture and a bet-your-company culture?
4. What is likely to happen to a workforce made up entirely of one kind of person?

CHAPTER 18 ASSESSMENT

ASSESSING ACADEMIC SKILLS

MATH The population of the United States is much more diverse today than it was 50 years ago. Using the Internet or the resources at your public library, collect statistics on the ethnic makeup of the population in 1950, 1960, 1970, 1980, and 1990. Then create a bar chart showing how the population has changed.

APPLYING MANAGEMENT PRINCIPLES

SOLVE THE PROBLEM You are the manager of a department that includes two Asian Americans, four Mexican Americans, five African Americans, and 26 nonhispanic whites. Last week, there was a nasty exchange between two employees that showed you that some employees hold stereotypical views of people from different ethnic groups.

Writing Write a one-page memo explaining how you plan to deal with the problem this incident revealed.

PREPARING FOR COMPETITIVE EVENTS

Which of the following is *not* an example of an external change?

a. computers

b. competition

c. management

d. taxes

e. consumer tastes

BusinessWeek ONLINE

In this chapter you read the *BusinessWeek* Management Model about diversity in the workplace. Using various business magazines, locate an article about an organization handling cultural differences in the workplace. What methods do businesses use to handle diversity issues? Write a brief summary of your findings and then share them with the class. For more information, go to *BusinessWeek* online at: **www.businessweek.com**

CASE STUDY 6

Managing Conflict

OVERVIEW

An effective manager is also an effective leader. One way to define leadership is *the ability to help others focus, work together, and make quality decisions*. Successful leaders can work well with others. They have good human relations skills. They also must be skilled in dealing with conflict.

In this case study, you will have a chance to use and expand your human relations skills. You will also learn more about working with and being responsible for others.

RESOURCES

- paper
- pen or pencil
- calculator
- word processor (optional)

PROCEDURES

◆ STEP A ◆

Leadership and Conflict

In order for a manager to be successful, he or she must possess leadership skills. Leadership is the ability to influence people. An effective leader can use his or her influence to guide other people's behavior. When a group of peers has more than one leader, conflict might occur. Resolving such conflicts requires human relations skills that are essential to all managers and leaders.

Identifying Information:

1. In small groups of three to five students, list the three basic styles of leadership discussed in this unit.

2. Define each type of leadership style.

3. Review the material on managing conflict. List the three basic types of conflict that might occur in a group.

4. Discuss ways to manage conflict.

CASE STUDY 6

◆ STEP B ◆

The Committee Funding Task

You and your group members are the Medical Research Funding Committee at Got-A-Heart, Inc., a nonprofit organization. Your company gives money to professionals in the health field. The money funds projects that will improve the health of people in your county. Your committee must decide how to distribute $2 million among four grant proposals that total $13 million.

No one in your group is a medical expert. Each of you serves on this committee because you have made wise choices when faced with difficult decisions in the past. Today members of the committee must make difficult decisions that will challenge leadership and human relations skills.

Analyzing Information:

1. In class your teacher will give you copies of four proposals from medical professionals who are asking for money from your committee. This information is in the teacher's material only. Read the proposals and rank them in order of funding priority (e.g., 1 is for the proposal that most deserves funding, 2 is for the next most deserving proposal, etc.). Write down the reasons for your rankings. You will need these reasons for the next step in the activity.

2. Get into groups of four or five. In your group, discuss how to distribute Got-A-Heart, Inc.'s $2 million. Be sure all members explain their rankings and reasoning.

3. As a group come up with a unanimous recommendation for the distribution of funds. Then discuss your choices as a class.

◆ STEP C ◆

Management Report

To illustrate the importance of leadership and human relations skills in avoiding and resolving conflicts, prepare a 3- to 5-page report that includes the following:

1. Analyze the group's unanimous recommendation about how the money should be distributed and your reasons for your choice.

2. Explain how the decision was reached. Describe any challenges your group experienced.

3. Address the role of leadership and human relations skills in managing conflict.

4. Compose a letter to the individuals who will receive the funding. Explain why your committee will fund their proposal and how much money you plan to give them.

5. Compose a letter to the individuals who will not receive funding from Got-A-Heart, Inc.

Quality Control Skills

Chapter 19
Management Control

Chapter 20
Operations Control

Chapter 21
Management Information Systems

IN THIS UNIT...

You will be introduced to methods used for management and operations control and information management. Included in this unit are chapters on management control, operations control, and management information systems.

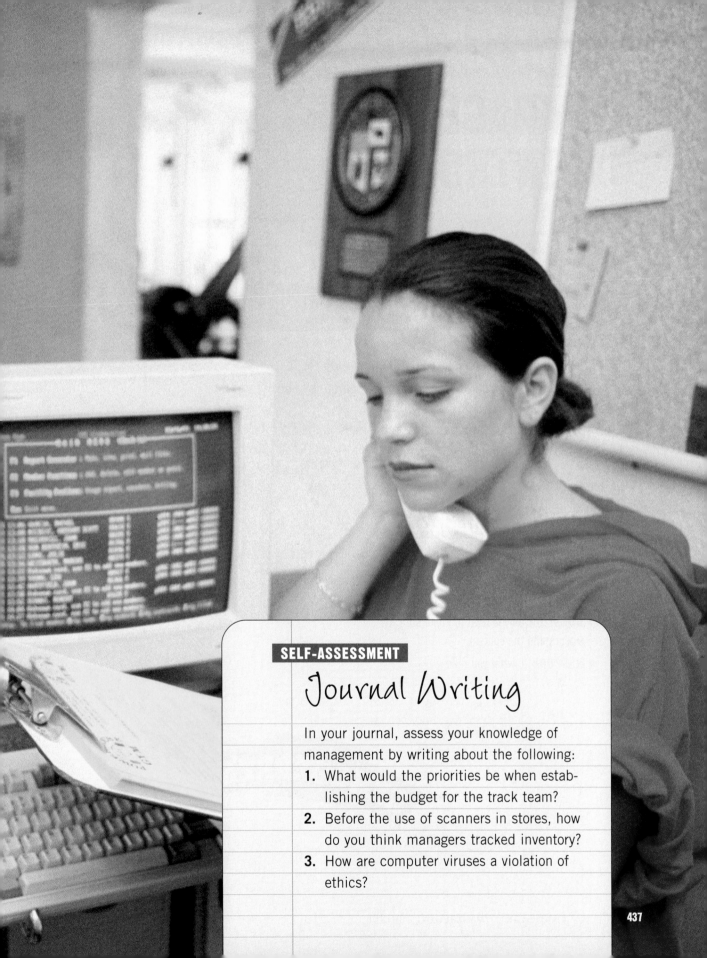

Journal Writing

In your journal, assess your knowledge of
management by writing about the following:
1. What would the priorities be when establishing the budget for the track team?
2. Before the use of scanners in stores, how
   do you think managers tracked inventory?
3. How are computer viruses a violation of
   ethics?

MANAGEMENT CONTROL

LEARNING OBJECTIVES

After studying this chapter, you should be able to:

- Explain the importance of the management control process.
- Discuss the three types of management control.
- List five methods of management control.

READING STRATEGIES

As you read

- **PREDICT** what the section will be about.
- **CONNECT** what you read with your own life.
- **QUESTION** as you read to make sure you understand the content.
- **RESPOND** to what you read.

Understanding Management

Ben & Jerry's is known for its innovative ice cream flavors, as well as its commitment to social causes. But even a company as creative as Ben & Jerry's must pay attention to the bottom line. In 2000, Ben & Jerry's was sold to Unilever. The company founders, Ben Cohen and Jerry Greenfield, said in a statement that "we hope that, as part of Unilever, Ben & Jerry's will continue to expand its role in society."

Analyzing Management Skills

How might the Unilever acquisition advance Ben & Jerry's social mission?

Applying Management Skills

If you had a set budget for clothing, entertainment, and savings for college, how much would you allocate for each category? What factors would influence your decision?

BusinessWeek ONLINE

For further reading on expense management go to:
www.businessweek.com

"MANAGEMENT TALK"

"Ben & Jerry's is definitely not the same Company in 2002 that it was in 2000. While the Company may have lost some of its earlier irreverence, it remains committed to its social mission. And as a result of its Unilever connection, Ben & Jerry's is much better positioned today to execute its mission, and, with Unilever's help, to leverage the impact."

—James E. Heard, social performance auditor for Ben & Jerry's

THE MANAGEMENT CONTROL PROCESS

WHAT YOU'LL LEARN

▶ Why management controls are needed.
▶ The basic principles of a feedback system.
▶ The three basic requirements for management control.

WHY IT'S IMPORTANT

Controls give a manager ways to uncover and correct problems before they damage the business. Controls can also provide the information necessary to improve business functions.

KEY TERMS

• control
• feedback loop
• standard

The Importance of Management Control

Managers organize activities on the assumption that everything will run smoothly. At the same time, good managers should anticipate and prepare for problems.

Joanne Williams has a small jewelry store. She uses *controls* to keep track of her valuable inventory and analyze her sales figures. Controls help Joanne plan future orders from her suppliers and ensure that she can meet her customers' demands.

In business, **control** means looking at a business activity, comparing it to what is supposed to be happening, and addressing any problems that are found. When controlling, managers assess the current

▲ **ADDRESSING PROBLEMS** Early warning of a problem helps to solve it before it gets too big. *Can you think of examples of problems in the workplace that grow if they are ignored?*

▲ **TECHNOLOGY** Changes in the environment may require a company to adjust the way it does business. *What are some examples of these changes?*

situation, compare it to the objectives for the activity, and decide how to proceed.

PREDICT

How can controls help a company prevent waste and theft?

Why Controls Are Needed

Managers need controls to alert them to problems in their area. Senior managers must know if the company is meeting its goals. Managers at all levels are accountable for performance in their area of responsibility. Good managers use controls to give them the information to monitor the progress of their activities. With this information, they can:

- *Prevent crises.* Small problems are more easily solved before they grow into big problems.
- *Standardize outputs.* When products and services can be reproduced dependably, processes and procedures can be used to improve their quality.
- *Appraise employee performance.* Good controls are objective so that employees can be evaluated fairly.
- *Update plans.* Changes in conditions both inside and outside the company can require changes in plans. Controls allow managers to react quickly to a changed environment.
- *Protect the organization's assets.* Controls protect assets from waste and theft.

L EADING THE W AY

SURPRISE!
Bad news is no fun to relay but it must be done. Let everyone know at the earliest possible moment when bad news arises. Don't keep bad news from your group hoping that a solution will mysteriously appear. Bring your group together and turn the activity into a positive discussion.

Feedback Systems

In the control process, managers evaluate their organizations' performance to determine necessary changes. The performance, or *output*, helps managers decide how to proceed. A **feedback loop** occurs when the output of a system is used to drive its subsequent operation.

For example, Alex is listening to his stereo with his sister, June. June complains that the music is too soft, so Alex increases the volume. Then Alex's mother yells that the music is too loud, so he turns it down again. Alex uses the reactions of others as *input* to determine how to adjust the stereo to the right volume.

A key point about feedback systems is that there will be a certain amount of back and forth movement about the desired point. No one starts complaining until the music is too loud or not loud enough. Similarly, a management control system helps managers identify a need for change when the control system detects problems. A well-designed system catches the problems while small corrective changes are all that are necessary.

CONNECT

Imagine that you are the manager of a company that rents laptop computers to college students. Describe a feedback system that would help you monitor the company's operations.`

Three Requirements for Control

There are three steps that are necessary in a control process:

- setting standards
- monitoring performance
- correcting deviations

The first step, setting standards, is done as part of planning goals for the company. The addition of the other two steps provides a control process. All three steps are essential to effective control.

Robert Half International Inc.

Tips from Robert Half

When focusing on a management career, don't forget to learn a second language. Among executives surveyed, 63 percent said Spanish is the most important language to know as business becomes more global.

Setting Standards

A **standard** outlines what is expected of the employee or organizational unit. Standards may come directly from organizational objectives. For example, a lighting wholesaler wants to boost sales by 10,000 lamps, or increase market share by 10 percent over the next year. In order to increase sales, the marketing department strives to develop three new brochures within six months.

The more specifically a standard can be defined and the more precisely it can be measured, the more useful it will be in driving a control system. Some examples of standards that are often used in management controls include output per hour, revenues, and inventory levels.

◄ STANDARDS Fast-food restaurants operate in a competitive environment and serve hundreds of meals every day. *What are some standards that might be useful in this business?*

Monitoring Performance

A control system is only as good as the information it runs on. Managers monitor performance to gather data and detect problem areas. They must strive to do the right amount of monitoring. If managers gather too little information, there will not be enough data to detect problems. On the other hand, too much monitoring is expensive and irritating to employees.

Managers often strike a balance by concentrating on monitoring activities or outputs that are relevant to the standards. Monitoring should occur often enough that problems can be caught quickly, but not so often that the monitoring interferes with getting the job done.

If an engineering team leader spends one day a week meeting with upper management to present detailed progress reports, the managers certainly will gather much data about the engineering project. However, this amount of monitoring means that the engineering team is only supervised four days a week. A weekly summary delivered by e-mail might provide senior managers with the information they need with less disruption to the project.

All About

ATTITUDE

LOOSE LIPS SINK SHIPS
Spreading rumors distracts everyone from concentrating on his or her work. If necessary, do your part to clarify what is true, what's false, and get to the bottom of it. Even if you're listening to gossip, you're not being a part of the solution.

Correcting for Deviations

A common mistake in management control is to collect a lot of reports but fail to make appropriate changes. This results in paying for monitoring costs with no benefits in return. If a standard is not being met, the problem is usually in performance. However, sometimes the standard may be unrealistic or improperly defined. **Figure 19–1** lists some potential causes of performance deviation.

FIGURE 19–1

Causes of Performance Deviation

There are many reasons why performance may fail to meet standards. Management controls help managers detect these deviations.

2 INSUFFICIENT COMMUNICATION
Insufficient communication within an organization leaves employees wondering what is expected of them. Managers may not be aware of issues affecting performance.

1 FAULTY PLANNING
Faulty planning can show up in many ways, including incorrect estimates of demand for a product or service.

Managers should address the cause of a problem rather than simply try to fix the symptoms. For example, software development projects often proceed more slowly than planned. Demanding that programmers produce more lines of code per week does not result in a better product or a closer completion date. The problem is often that the plans were unrealistic, the overall design is defective, or the requirements keep changing.

4 LACK OF MOTIVATION Lack of motivation reduces efficiency and prevents employees from meeting their objectives.

3 TRAINING The need for training employees in new tasks means that performance may decline slightly during the learning period.

5 UNFORESEEN FORCES Unforeseen forces outside the organization can include anything from new government regulations to natural disasters.

The Control Pyramid

When implementing controls in an organization, managers usually begin with simple ones and then move on to more complex control processes. The increasing complexity of control systems can be illustrated using a control pyramid, shown in **Figure 19–2**.

Foolproofing

The first controls managers should implement are those involving *foolproofing*. Rather than trying to monitor if employees remember to keep both hands on the operating levers of a dangerous machine, a plant manager might install special switches that prevent the machine from being operated at all unless both levers are being gripped. The manager only needs to monitor that the switches are operational.

Automatic Controls

The second level of controls to implement would be *automatic*, requiring little intervention once set up. Mechanical feedback loops such as a thermostat are examples of automatic controls. Modern factory equipment often monitors its own condition with automated diagnostic systems. The equipment then issues warnings when maintenance is necessary.

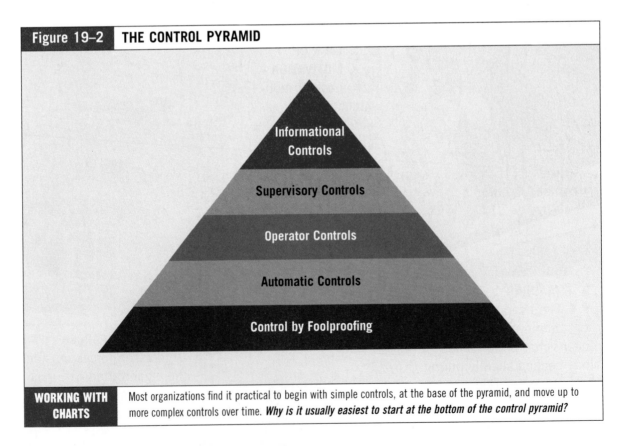

Figure 19–2	THE CONTROL PYRAMID

Informational Controls

Supervisory Controls

Operator Controls

Automatic Controls

Control by Foolproofing

WORKING WITH CHARTS Most organizations find it practical to begin with simple controls, at the base of the pyramid, and move up to more complex controls over time. *Why is it usually easiest to start at the bottom of the control pyramid?*

Medical Office Manager

■ Nature of the Work

Doctors in private practice or in an office with other physicians need office managers. Although the physicians establish office policy, the manager handles day-to-day business affairs. In larger offices, the manager may advise on business strategies and policies as well as coordinate day-to-day activities in the office. Medical office managers generally supervise several other office staff. They use accounting and bookkeeping skills to oversee billing, collection, budgeting, planning, and equipment purchases. They must develop a system to ensure efficient patient flow.

■ Working Conditions

Medical office managers usually work in clean, pleasant surroundings. Their jobs may be stressful since they need to coordinate all office activities and to accommodate emergencies that arise.

■ Training, Other Qualifications, and Advancement

Many medical office managers get training through office experience, on-the-job training, or a one to two-year certificate or diploma program in medical office management at a community college. However, many offices prefer managers to have a bachelor's degree. Office managers need good communication skills, organizational skills, bookkeeping, accounting, and computer skills.

■ Salary Range

Medical office managers earn $56,000 to $77,000, depending on the size and type of office, location, responsibilities, and experience.

CRITICAL THINKING

What personality traits would contribute to making a person a good medical office manager? What kinds of computer skills might a medical office manager need?

STANDARD &POOR'S

INDUSTRY OUTLOOK

With further education, medical office managers with bachelor's degrees may go to work in nursing homes, an expanding segment of the healthcare industry. These facilities provide services to patients with long-term care needs, such as meals, medical supplies, and recreation.

BUSINESS MANAGEMENT *Online*

For more information on management careers, go to:

busmanagement.glencoe.com

Operator Controls

The third level represents *operator controls*, in which the person doing the work also does the monitoring. For example, a salesperson at Sears might be expected to count inventory on the racks in his or her department. The salesperson's counts are then compared against sales figures to check for theft or loss. In order for this to be effective, the control should be practical to monitor and meaningful for the operator.

Supervisory Controls

The next level, *supervisory controls*, involves those monitored by the operator's manager. In many companies, supervisors are responsible for checking the time reports submitted by their employees.

Informational Controls

The final area involves *informational controls*, such as management summary reports. These are complex controls to implement because they involve gathering information from a number of sources to get a complete picture of the organization's position. For example, a manager at Wal-Mart needs to look at reports that compare sales figures for different product lines.

How Much Control?

In considering the number and types of controls to implement, a manager must consider both economic and behavioral factors. While economic concerns may be easier to anticipate and quantify, behavioral considerations are equally important.

Economic Considerations

Control systems cost money to install and operate. Most require human supervision and intervention. Others may require expensive equipment or software. Control systems are useful only if they save more money than they cost.

THE COST-BENEFITS ANALYSIS A cost-benefits analysis for management controls determines the point at which increasing controls will no longer increase performance or reduce costs proportionally. A minimum level of controls must be in place before any benefits are seen at all. Then there will be a range in which increased controls leads to increased performance. Finally, the organization will have reached a point where spending more money on controls will lead to no more improvement, or too small an improvement to justify added costs.

▲ **COST CONTROL** Sophisticated electronic control systems can be very costly. *What can a manager do if improvements are still needed, but the costs of additional equipment cannot be justified?*

For example, the Acme Chemical Company must control the temperature of its production line to ensure product quality. Traditionally, employees checked thermometers and adjusted burner settings. Then the plant manager installed an automatic control system that could hold the temperature within one degree of its desired value. The new system was expensive but justified because fewer products were wasted. A few years after installing the system, the plant manager saw an advertisement in a trade magazine for a new, improved automatic control system that can hold the temperature to within one tenth of a degree. She did not purchase it, because temperature differences of that size do not make a difference in product quality.

CONTROL AND RISK Risk must be factored into this analysis as well. When Boeing builds jet engines, it must evaluate the cost of controls differently than if it were manufacturing motors for household appliances. The potential human and economic cost of a jet engine failure is much higher than that of a household appliance.

Behavioral Considerations

Managers must be aware of the impact a proposed control system might have on their staff. Employees do not like to feel that they are being watched and questioned. Employees traveling on business do not like to justify the amount of money they spend on each meal. As

QUESTION

What are the five basic types of controls in order from the simplest to the most complex?

a result, many organizations employ a per diem system in which they provide a fixed amount of money for meals each day, which employees can spend as they choose. This substitutes a foolproof control for a supervisory control, making it easier to implement.

Employees may view attempts to increase productivity by restricting breaks for coffee, snacks, or personal phone calls as petty and intrusive. At the same time, most people do not enjoy working in a control-free environment. In this situation they are left to guess what is expected of them. The goal for a manager is to find a proper balance.

RESPOND

How is your own motivation affected when you work in an environment where there are many rigid rules for behavior?

Many managers tend to implement rigid rules when things are not going according to plan. This often results in an increase of tension within the organization. Employees may then find ways to work around or sabotage the controls.

A better approach is to motivate employees to work toward organizational goals. To do this, managers should

- Make sure their controls are realistic.
- Involve employees in the control-setting process.
- Use controls only where needed.

An effective manager may use different types of controls with different groups of employees. For example, in an automobile dealership, the performance of salespeople is reflected in their sales volume. Their compensation is tied directly to their results by means of a *commission*, or percentage of sales. Since the salespeople's income is directly

▲ **ORGANIZATIONAL GOALS** Rigid rules enforcing productivity are not necessary when employees are committed to organizational goals. *How can such an environment be encouraged in more routine jobs?*

dependent on their performance, they might not require the same controls on time usage as the salaried workers in the service area.

Who Has Control?

The traditional view of hierarchical organizations keeps control in the hands of senior management. In such organizations, decisions and controls tend to be centralized, as you learned in Chapter 13.

Today, decentralized operations have become more common. A trend toward empowerment has encouraged managers to allow employees to decide how to do their jobs. This has been most successful when employees are also given the opportunity to implement controls at their own levels. This helps employees understand why controls are necessary and keeps managers from being overwhelmed with details. Finally, people who have the authority to control their own work are unlikely to resent the controls.

Section 19.1 Assessment

FACT AND IDEA REVIEW

1. List three reasons why management controls are needed.
2. Describe a feedback loop.
3. What are the three functions that make up a control?

CRITICAL THINKING

1. **Analyzing information:** Describe the leadership style of a manager who might do a good job in an environment with decentralized controls.
2. **Predicting consequences:** Is it possible to run an organization using only the bottom three levels in the control pyramid (foolproofing, automatic controls, and operator controls)? Defend your answer.

ASSESSING SCIENCE SKILLS

Feedback loops are very common in biological systems. Consider the feedback loop by which your body regulates its own temperature. What is the standard? How is the condition monitored? How is deviation corrected?

CASE ANALYSIS

You are the supervisor of a large warehouse store. Your costs for salaries keep increasing, yet as you walk through the store, many of the departments do not seem to be well staffed. You suspect that some of your employees may be punching the time clock and then wandering off, or punching the time clock for absent friends.

Apply: What types of controls might you implement to deal with this problem?

METHODS OF MANAGEMENT CONTROL

WHAT YOU'LL LEARN

➤ The difference between behavior control and output control.

➤ Three points in a business process to implement controls.

➤ Five ways of implementing controls.

WHY IT'S IMPORTANT

In order to implement or evaluate control systems well, managers need to be familiar with different ways of controlling.

KEY TERMS

- behavior control
- output control
- preliminary control
- concurrent control
- post-action control
- budget
- zero-based budgeting
- audit

Types of Control

Businesses are complex organizations, and no one type of control fills all their needs. Controls may monitor different things, or they may be used at different times during the work process. They all have the same basic purpose: to improve the way the company works, and to find problems early so they can be fixed.

Behavior Controls and Output Controls

Control methods can be grouped by what is being monitored. In one type of management control, the control system monitors an

▲ CONTROLLING BEHAVIOR Behavior controls can be used to limit costs and reduce waste. *What kinds of behavior controls are employed in your household for this purpose?*

employee's personal activities. Such a control involves direct surveillance of the employee, and is called a **behavior control**. Behavior control might monitor office Internet use to ensure that only work-related sites are accessed.

Output control is based on the measurement of something that is produced by the employee or work unit. Output control takes count of the actual physical or intellectual products, such as number of cars built or brochures written. It can also monitor a financial measure or milestones relating to a project.

Output and behavior controls serve different organizational needs. Output controls provide an accurate measure of performance. Behavior controls are used to promote efficiency, limit costs, and keep employees focused on their work. In most situations, organizations need to use a mix of output and behavior controls because each type of control serves different organizational needs.

QUESTION

Why are preliminary controls useful to managers and employees?

Preliminary, Concurrent, and Post-Action Controls

Another way of classifying control methods is by the timing of their use. Organizations integrate three types of controls to successfully monitor all aspects of their processes. These management controls may be preliminary, concurrent, or post-action.

- **Preliminary control** methods are designed to prevent problems from occurring. Requiring prior approval for purchases of all items over a certain value is an example of a preliminary control.
- **Concurrent controls** focus on things that happen during the work process. They are designed to pick up problems as they occur. A supervisor watching as employees serve customers at an elegant restaurant is an example of a concurrent control.
- **Post-action controls** detect problems after they occur, but before they become a crisis. Post-action controls provide management with useful information to solve problems and to reward employees for good performance. A weekly status report is a post-action control.

WORKPLACE DIVERSITY

PERU

Peruvians maintain a high level of formality. The cultural decorum of politeness requires indirect speech. Many Peruvians will tell you what they think you want to hear. Since blunt, frank

speech is not valued, it is important to listen to subtleties and avoid the hard-sell approach.

Tools for Control

There are many methods of implementing controls. These include budgets and other financial controls, direct observation, written reports, and audits.

Budgets

Budgets are probably the most widely used control devices. A **budget** is a statement of expected results or requirements expressed in financial terms. Preparing the budget is a function of the planning process. When a budget is actually used as a management tool, it is part of the control process.

TYPES OF BUDGETS. When one does household budgeting, one thinks about how much income is available to spend on food, rent or mortgage, utilities, and other items. This type of budgeting is also crucial to businesses and is called the *revenue and expense budget*. However, there are many other types of budgets, the most common of which are listed in **Figure 19–3**.

Figure 19–3	TYPES AND PURPOSES OF BUDGETS
Type of Budget	**Purpose**
Revenue and expense budget	Provides details for revenue and expense plans.
Cash budget	Forecasts cash receipts and disbursements.
Capital expenditure budget	Outlines specific expenditures for plant, equipment, machinery, inventories, and other capital items.
Production, material, or time budget	Expresses physical requirements of production capabilities, material, or time for the budget period.
Balance sheet budgets	Forecasts assets, liabilities, and net worth at the end of the period.
WORKING WITH CHARTS	Different budgets are used for different purposes. *When would you use a cash budget?*

BusinessWeek

COMMENTARY:

Smoke, Mirrors, and the Boss's Paycheck

It's not every day that a corporate chieftain offers to give up a full year's salary if his company fails to meet an earnings target. By making that pledge, Union Carbide Chairman and Chief Executive William H. Joyce made headlines last week. News reports indicated that Joyce, who earned $2.1 million last year, would forfeit his base salary—currently $850,000—if his company does not earn at least $4 a share in 2000.

CLEVER PUBLIC RELATIONS.
Before anyone anoints Joyce a pay-for-performance hero, however, a closer look at his pay plan is in order. Chalk this one up to clever public relations. "People are so cynical about executives having their snouts in the trough that anyone who raises his head for a few moments is considered a hero," says Graef "Bud" Crystal, the executive pay consultant and critic.

If Carbide misses its target, Joyce will lose that money. But in return, he stands to gain far more. Joyce will get "additional incentive compensation" up to eight times the

salary he is forsaking if earnings hit $4.75 a share in 1999 and 2000. And the payoff could be even higher because that pay will be converted into "phantom shares" of stock at current prices. If he delivers the goods, he'll benefit from any uplift in the market.

WHAT STICK? It's also far from clear that Joyce's pay will really take a hit. Joyce could more than make up any salary loss with cash bonuses and stock plans. Last year, these alone paid him $1.4 million, not including options on 130,000 shares. If Carbide stock rises by 10% a year over the 10-year

option term, they would be worth $9.5 million.

Under a meaningful plan, a CEO would no longer be paid millions simply for riding the cyclical wave of an industry upturn or a bull market. Such a plan would base compensation on goals set against an industry peer group over multiple years. Every cent beyond his base salary would then be paid only if he outperformed Carbide's main rivals on key targets such as return on equity or assets.

Few boards of directors and still fewer CEOs want to put that much on the line. Until then, we'll have to do with gestures that have more public-relations value than real impact.

Excerpted with permission from BusinessWeek, *October 13, 1997*

CRITICAL THINKING

Why is Joyce forfeiting his base salary?

DECISION MAKING

Do you think Joyce's strategy is effective? Why or why not?

Some budgets may be expressed in figures other than dollars. For example, a time budget attempts to estimate the workload a task will require in hours, weeks, months, or years. A material budget uses units of quantity such as pieces, gallons, or tons. As part of the overall budgeting process, these quantities are generally converted to dollars, such as cost per ton or average employee salary plus overhead.

BUDGET MISUSE Budgets are an essential business tool, but they can be misused. One problem is inflexibility. Particularly in a fast-changing marketplace, progress sometimes requires spending money in order to keep up. Budget rigidity can result in passing up the opportunity to make $500 in order to save the $5 over budget it would cost.

Hector Garcia is a freelance computer programmer who works in Visual Basic. His current work involves maintaining programs for clients whose systems use older versions of the software. Hector did not budget for upgrading his own software until next year. At a conference, he meets a prospective client with a big job that would provide him with steady work for about three months. The work involves developing a new system, and the client wants the latest version of the language to be used. If Hector decides not to overspend his budget, he would lose this lucrative job.

In another misuse of the budget process, meeting the budget becomes the primary goal of the organization. This results in misplaced priorities and makes the budget an end in itself, rather than the tool it should be. Each department should be primarily focused on its part in the organization's mission—service to some group of customers or clients. Organizations should not exist for the purpose of getting their own paperwork to balance out at the end of the year.

CONNECT

Do you have a budget for your expenses? How would you go about making a budget to save for college costs?

ZERO-BASED BUDGETING Budgeting can be a difficult and time-consuming process. To make the process easier, managers often take the budget from the year before and modify it as necessary. It would be foolish to ignore past budgeting experience. However, there are problems with developing a budget this way.

Sometimes, a specific item from the previous budget is automatically included in the new one, despite changed situations. Last year's level of expenses may be accepted without considering cost reduction. The result is that inefficiencies may be passed along from one year to the next. To prevent this, some organizations have implemented a process called zero-based budgeting.

Zero-based budgeting requires each manager to justify each budget request in detail. Managers need to show why each expense is necessary. Each year, the importance of every activity, such as equipment upgrades or sending employees for training, is evaluated and ranked. Each activity must compete for a share of the organization's available resources.

▲ **ZERO-BASED BUDGETING** In an effort to reduce federal spending, Congress employed zero-based budgeting techniques. As a result, the elimination of entire government agencies or departments has been called for. *What are the advantages and disadvantages of this approach?*

Financial Controls

Managers use other financial information for control purposes. This information includes balance sheets, income statements, and financial ratios. Financial information generally is not meaningful out of context. For example, how does a manager know whether revenues of $500,000 are acceptable or not? Financial information must either be compared to historical performance figures for the organization itself (such as last year's income), or weighed against those of similar organizations. Because an organization's performance may vary for internal as well as external reasons, an industry average generally is used for comparison.

FINANCIAL RATIOS There are four basic types of financial ratios: profitability, liquidity, debt, and activity ratios. Profitability ratios indicate how efficiently the organization is being managed. Liquidity ratios measure the ability to meet short-term obligations, such as payroll and accounts payable. Debt ratios indicate the ability to meet long-term obligations. Activity ratios measure how effectively the organization manages its basic operations.

Direct Observation

Managers may control using direct observation, ranging from supervision of a junior employee to a company president's plant tour. A certain amount of observation is necessary to get an accurate picture of an organization. However, direct observation can be time-consuming and subject to misinterpretation because people are on their best behavior when being observed. The manager may also bring biases to the process.

Written Reports

Written reports are management controls that may be prepared on a periodic or "as necessary" basis. There are two basic types of written reports: informational and analytical. Informational reports present a series of facts. Analytical reports also provide an interpretation of the facts they present.

Preparing a report is a multistep process, including

1. planning what is to be done
2. collecting the facts
3. organizing the facts
4. interpreting the facts (this step is omitted for informational reports)
5. writing the report

Most reports should be prepared for the benefit of the reader and not the writer. In most cases, the reader wants useful information not previously available.

Audits

An **audit** is a detailed look at an organization's financial or other practices. External audits often are performed by outside accountants who examine a company's financial records. Accountants evaluate whether the company's accounting methods are fair, consistent, and in accordance with regulations and customary practice. Internal audits are performed by members of an organization itself.

Management audits look at areas other than finance and accounting. A company may audit its personnel procedures to ensure compliance with equal opportunity laws. Management audits may be conducted either by internal staff or outside consultants. Internal audits may be less expensive; however, there is a greater risk of bias.

QUESTION

When would an audit be more useful than a written report?

Section 19.2 Assessment

 FACT AND IDEA REVIEW

1. Describe the difference between behavior and output controls.
2. Give one example for each of the following: a preliminary control, a concurrent control, and a post-action control.
3. List five methods or tools for implementing controls.

 CRITICAL THINKING

1. **Analyzing Information:** A manager is concerned that payments have not been coming in as quickly as expected from customers. Holiday bonuses to employees will soon be due. What control might the manager use to address his concerns?
2. **Predicting Consequences:** A new manager abolishes all personal controls. Employees' performance will be appraised strictly on output. Do you think the overall performance of the department will get better or worse? Defend your answer.

 ASSESSING LANGUAGE ARTS SKILLS

You are the president of a large clothing manufacturer. Your company has factories in many locations. One of the factories has just automated several of its production-line activities, and many employees had to be transferred. Write a memo to the plant manager to arrange a date for a visit, and provide instructions for planning a productive visit.

 CASE ANALYSIS

You are a school principal and your overall responsibility includes the education of all students at your school, the running of an organization of more than 100 employees, and the maintenance of the physical plant. Because the district installed computer systems several years ago, you have been able to request a number of management reports without burdening your staff.

Apply: Develop a list of at least six reports that would be useful to you in your job.

CHAPTER 19 ASSESSMENT

CHAPTER SUMMARY

Section 19.1

▶ Management controls are needed to detect and correct problems before they become crises.

▶ The necessary steps in a control process are setting standards, monitoring performance, and correcting deviations.

▶ The ideal number and type of controls to be used depends on economic and behavioral considerations.

▶ Organizations generally get the best results when employees are given the means and opportunity to implement many of their own controls.

Section 19.2

▶ Controls can be classified by whether personal behavior or work outputs are being monitored.

▶ Controls can be implemented before, during, or after the work or other action is performed.

▶ Control types include budgets and financial controls, direct observation, written reports, and audits.

REVIEWING VOCABULARY

Write a sentence definition for each term in the context of this chapter.

control	concurrent control
feedback loop	post-action control
standard	budget
behavior control	zero-based budgeting
output control	audit
preliminary control	

RECALLING KEY CONCEPTS

1. Describe how management controls help to prevent business crises.
2. What is a feedback system?
3. Describe the control pyramid.
4. Differentiate between the purposes of preliminary, concurrent, and post-action controls.
5. What is a management audit?

THINKING CRITICALLY

1. Is a manager's job easier when his or her employees are empowered to implement their own controls? Why or why not?
2. Consider the process of learning to operate a new video game. Describe this process in terms of a feedback loop.
3. Why do you think written reports are among the most commonly used management controls?
4. What happens to an organization that makes the budget its top priority?

CHAPTER 19 ASSESSMENT

ASSESSING ACADEMIC SKILLS

LANGUAGE ARTS You are starting a software company with four hand-picked employees with whom you went to college. Write a paragraph or two, using and underlining all the words in the chapter vocabulary list, describing the control methods you would and would not put in place.

APPLYING MANAGEMENT PRINCIPLES

SOLVE THE PROBLEM You are the manager of a research and development department in a company that manufactures electronic hardware. The travel budget is centrally controlled, and primarily used by the sales representatives for another department. Occasionally you can get one or two of your engineers to a conference early in the year, but the one most applicable to their work is held in the fall, when travel money is very tight.

You want to convince upper management to delegate the control of the travel budget to the individual departments. You expect to get less than the sales department. You simply want to know what your share is, and budget it for the year.

Public Speaking
Present your argument for moving this control down a level in the hierarchy. Explain to senior management why it would be good for the company as a whole, as well as your concerns for your engineers.

PREPARING FOR COMPETITIVE EVENTS

Answer true or false to the following statements. Explain your answers.

a. With zero-based budgeting, managers use last year's budget to create this year's budget.

b. A control system consists of a standard and a monitoring process.

BusinessWeek ONLINE

In this chapter you read the *BusinessWeek* Management Model about a CEO who was willing to forfeit his salary if his company failed to meet a target. For more information, go to *BusinessWeek* online at: **www.businessweek.com**

Locate an article about a successful company. Find out what strategies the company used to have good public relations. Write a brief summary of the article and share it with the class.

CHAPTER 20

OPERATIONS CONTROL

LEARNING OBJECTIVES

When you have completed this chapter, you will be able to:

- Identify four types of operating costs.
- Learn how businesses keep track of their inventory.
- Understand what operations managers mean by the term "quality."
- Explain how total quality management can increase the quality of a company's products.

READING STRATEGIES

As you read

- **PREDICT** what the section will be about.
- **CONNECT** what you read with your own life.
- **QUESTION** as you read to make sure you understand the content.
- **RESPOND** to what you read.

amazon.com.

on.co

"MANAGEMENT TALK"

"I constantly remind our employees to be afraid, to wake up every morning terrified. Not of our competition, but of our customers. Our customers have made our business what it is, they're the ones with whom we have a relationship, and they're the ones to whom we owe a great obligation. And we consider them to be loyal to us— right up until the second that someone else offers them a better service."

—Jeffrey P. Bezos,
Amazon.com CEO

Understanding Management

In a few short years, Amazon.com grew from a small start-up business to an international corporation selling books and music to millions of customers. With e-commerce sites multiplying rapidly, customers can easily choose between several Internet booksellers. As Amazon.com CEO Jeffrey Bezos notes, customer service makes the difference between a quick sale or a lost opportunity.

Analyzing Management Skills

What things can an Internet retailer like Amazon.com do to make customers' buying experiences satisfying?

Applying Management Skills

As a customer, have you ever been frustrated by poor service? What things would have made your buying experience more positive?

BusinessWeek ONLINE

For further reading on e-commerce and customer service issues go to:
www.businessweek.com

Section 20.1

MANAGING COSTS AND INVENTORY

WHAT YOU'LL LEARN

- The four types of direct operating costs.
- The six types of holding costs.
- What the ABC classification system is.
- How businesses keep track of their inventory.

WHY IT'S IMPORTANT

Controlling operational costs increases a business's profits and allows it to remain competitive.

KEY TERMS

- **direct costs**
- **inventory**
- **finished goods**
- **holding costs**
- **safety stocks**
- **economic order quantity**
- **physical inventory**

Controlling Operational Costs

Dan Rosenberg, the operations manager of a large cosmetics company, recently learned that one of the company's main suppliers was raising its prices 6 percent. Mr. Rosenberg responded immediately, contacting other suppliers to check their prices.

Making sure that his company controls its costs is one of Mr. Rosenberg's main responsibilities. Like most operations managers, he is concerned primarily with **direct costs**, the labor, materials, and overhead costs associated with production (see **Figure 20–1**).

Figure 20–1 TYPES OF DIRECT COSTS

Type of Cost	Components
Labor	Wages and salaries of employees engaged in production
Materials	Items that become a tangible part of the finished product
Variable production overhead	Training new employees, safety training, salaries of departmental supervisors and clerical workers, overtime premiums, shift premiums, payroll taxes, vacation and holiday benefits, retirement benefits, insurance, supplies, travel, repairs, maintenance
Fixed production overhead	Travel, research and development, utilities, rent, depreciation, property taxes, insurance
WORKING WITH CHARTS	Direct costs include labor, materials, and overhead. ***Under which category of expense would the maintenance of a first-aid station in a factory fall?***

Direct labor costs include the wages and salaries of employees directly involved in producing the company's products—from assembly-line workers to production supervisors. It does not include the salaries of support staff, such as secretaries or bookkeepers.

Direct materials costs include the cost of materials that become part of the final product. The direct materials used to produce a refrigerator, for example, include steel, glass, plastic, and insulation. The oil used to lubricate the assembly line is not a direct materials cost because it is not part of the final product.

Instead, the oil used to keep the assembly line moving would be an example of a direct overhead cost. *Direct overhead costs* include all other expenses associated with production. The cost of training new production workers is a direct overhead cost. So are the costs of electricity, rent, and taxes.

To control costs, companies budget a certain amount of money for each of the four categories shown in **Figure 20–1**. They keep careful records showing how much they spend on each category. Managers then compare actual and budgeted spending to identify areas where costs appear to be excessive.

Controlling Inventory

Businesses that produce goods must carry enough inventory to meet customer needs. **Inventory** includes the raw materials, partially finished goods, and finished goods that a company keeps in stock. **Finished goods** are products that are ready to be shipped to customers.

◀ **MANUFACTURING INVENTORY** Manufacturing businesses can keep millions of dollars of inventory on hand. *What kind of inventories do they hold?*

QUESTION

What types of companies generally use continuous-flow operating systems? What types of companies use intermittent-flow systems?

Inventories are maintained to ensure that customer demand is met. All companies keep inventories of materials on hand in order to produce goods. As you learned in Chapter 11, companies that use continuous-flow operating systems keep inventories of finished-goods on hand. Companies that use intermittent-flow operating systems often keep no finished-goods inventories in stock. They immediately ship out all of the custom-made goods they produce.

The Problem of Holding Inventory

Holding inventory is expensive. In fact, inventory costs run as high as 20 to 30 percent a year of the value of the inventory. This means that holding $1 million worth of inventory could cost a business $200,000 to $300,000 a year.

PREDICT

Why must managers make careful decisions about how much inventory to keep on hand?

To see how holding inventory costs companies money, consider Gillette's situation. Before it earns a single dollar selling razors and razor blades, the company spends millions of dollars on steel and plastic. It pays suppliers for these materials before receiving payment for sold goods. Gillette also spends money storing the raw materials and finished products. Gillette has to cover all of these expenses before it begins to earn revenues from the manufactured products.

The costs of keeping inventory in stock are known as the **holding costs**. Holding costs include storage and handling charges, interest, taxes, insurance, and the risks of obsolescence and deterioration associated with keeping inventory in stock.

▲ **INVENTORY COSTS** Holding inventories can cost businesses millions of dollars. *Why is holding inventory so expensive?*

◄ **INVENTORY RISKS** Many products must be sold before a certain date. Companies that purchase large quantities of inventory risk having to destroy products they do not sell before the expiration date. *What other risk does a business face when purchasing inventory?*

STORAGE AND HANDLING CHARGES One of the most significant holding costs is storage and handling. These costs include the cost of renting warehouse space to store the inventory and the staff time involved in keeping track of the inventory.

INTEREST CHARGES Businesses must pay for the inventory they purchase. To do so, they borrow money from banks or investors or use money they would otherwise have invested. If they borrow, they pay interest on loans. If they use money they could have invested, they lose the interest they could have earned.

Ken Jackson, the owner of a large gourmet food shop, is considering purchasing $50,000 in inventory. To purchase the inventory, Ken would have to use all of the cash he had planned on investing. If he decides not to purchase the inventory, he could put $50,000 in a savings account and earn 3 percent interest, or $1,500 a year. By purchasing these inventories and holding them for a year, he is losing the interest. The interest component of his holding costs is $1,500 a year. As a result, the investment in his shop is $51,500.

TAXES Taxes on inventory also add to the cost of holding inventory. Many states, cities, and counties impose taxes on business inventories. A company that holds significant levels of inventory will have to pay more in taxes than a company with low inventory levels.

INSURANCE Businesses purchase insurance to protect their inventories against burglary, theft, and natural disasters. This cost varies directly with the value of the inventory. A company that holds millions of dollars of inventory will pay more for insurance than a company with minimal inventory levels.

OBSOLESCENCE Businesses that keep large stocks of inventory on hand take the risk that their inventory might become obsolete. Inventory can become obsolete when new products come on the market or tastes change. Ken Jackson, for example, might purchase $2,000 worth of imported herbal teas just as consumers lose interest in these products. When purchasing this large quantity, Ken risks spending thousands of dollars on products that will not be sold.

DETERIORATION Many products have limited *shelf lives*. This means that after a certain date, a product can no longer be used. If Ken fails to sell his tea products before they expire, he will have to destroy them. This risk of deterioration adds to his holding costs.

Managing Inventory Levels

Operations managers control costs by not maintaining unnecessary inventories. Knowing how much inventory to keep is tricky. Keeping too much inventory is expensive while keeping too little may prevent a business from filling orders (see **Figure 20–2**).

The cost of materials determines the level of raw materials inventories. If the cost of holding raw materials is low, businesses tend to keep high levels of inventory. Making glass, for example, requires large quantities of sand. Because sand is inexpensive and glass production cannot proceed without it, most glass-making factories keep large quantities of sand on hand.

If the cost of raw materials is high, businesses hold lower levels of inventory. Jewelers, for example, do not keep large stocks of diamonds on hand because they are too expensive. Instead, they purchase a small number of diamonds and reorder regularly.

MAINTAINING SAFETY STOCKS Running out of inventory can be costly. A business that runs out of raw materials could have to stop production temporarily. A business that runs out of finished goods inventory could lose an important order. To protect against running out of stock, businesses keep extra inventories on hand called **safety stocks**.

Safety stocks prepare businesses for unanticipated situations. These stocks allow a company to respond immediately if a large order arrives unexpectedly. Holding safety stocks protects businesses against shortages or delays from suppliers or the receipt of unusable materials.

Robert Half International Inc.

Tips from Robert Half

Temporary positions give you a chance to sample companies, industries, and positions. It's a good way to get experience that will be useful when you look for a permanent position or start consulting.

FIGURE 20–2

Maintaining the Level of Inventory

Maintaining the proper level of inventory is one of the operations manager's most important tasks. Keeping too much inventory in stock means a business is spending too much on holding costs. Holding too little inventory may prevent a company from filling orders.

1 **TOO MUCH INVENTORY**
This company appears to be holding too much inventory given its limited warehouse space. It needs to reduce inventory levels or obtain more storage space.

2 **TOO LITTLE INVENTORY**
This company is losing money because it has run out of merchandise to sell. It needed to keep larger stocks of inventory on hand.

3 **THE RIGHT AMOUNT OF INVENTORY**
This production line appears to be running smoothly. The operations manager has made sure that inventories of raw materials are sufficient.

MAINTAINING SEASONAL STOCKS Many businesses experience seasonal variations in sales. Sales of outdoor furniture, for example, are higher in spring and summer than in fall and winter. To prepare for increased sales, outdoor furniture manufacturers increase their raw materials and finished goods inventories.

USING THE ABC CLASSIFICATION SYSTEM A simple and widely used system for managing inventories is the ABC approach. The *ABC classification system* manages inventories based on their value. Classification of an item depends on the item's cost and the amount kept in inventory. This system is described in **Figure 20–3**.

The ABC system allows managers to control closely inventory levels of those items that are most important to their operations. Operations managers using this system would monitor inventory levels of Group A items very closely, Group B items less carefully, and items in Group C only occasionally.

To see how the ABC system works, consider a full-service gas station. The manager of the station divides all items she sells into three groups—Group A, Group B, and Group C.

- Group A includes the station's most important product, gasoline, which she monitors daily.
- Group B includes tires, batteries, and transmission fluid, which she monitors weekly.
- Group C includes windshield wiper blades, fan belts, and car wax. The manager might check these inventory levels every two or three months.

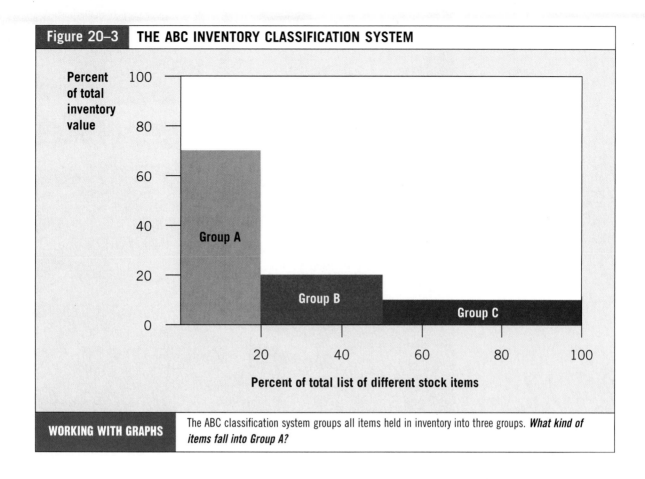

Figure 20–3 | **THE ABC INVENTORY CLASSIFICATION SYSTEM**

Percent of total inventory value

100
80
60
40
20
0

Group A

Group B

Group C

20   40   60   80   100

Percent of total list of different stock items

WORKING WITH GRAPHS | The ABC classification system groups all items held in inventory into three groups. *What kind of items fall into Group A?*

A shortcoming of the ABC method is that some Group C items may be important to a business's operations. An inexpensive jack may be critical to some auto repairs, for example. Running out of this item could prevent the station from servicing some vehicles. Companies handle this problem by grouping very important items as Group A items, regardless of their cost or usage.

Many companies use computers to keep track of each group of inventory items. Using computers helps operations managers monitor the level of inventory and make decisions about reordering supplies.

QUESTION

Why must managers classify and prioritize different kinds of inventory?

Determining When to Reorder

Operations managers use two basic methods to determine when to order:

- *Fixed-order quantity method*—Orders are placed whenever inventory reaches a predetermined level.
- *Fixed-order period method*—Orders are placed at predetermined intervals, regardless of how much inventory is on hand.

▲ **KEEPING INVENTORY** This store receives fresh bread every morning, regardless of how much bread it has in inventory. *Which method of reordering is it using?*

Using the fixed-order period method, an operations manager might reorder supplies on the last day of every month. This system is convenient, because it is not necessary to keep track of inventory in stock. If, however, the company uses up its inventories more rapidly than usual, it could find itself out of inventory before new supplies arrive.

Using the fixed-order quantity system, the operations manager keeps track of inventory in stock and reorders when the level falls. This method ensures that the company will not run out of inventory. Because it requires tracking inventory levels, however, it is best suited to companies that can continually monitor their inventories with computers.

To see the difference between the two methods of ordering, think about retailers in your community. The manager of the local hair salon may check the supply of hair products at the end of every week to determine what to reorder. This manager is using the fixed-order quantity method. In contrast, the local grocer receives fresh bread every morning, regardless of how much bread remains from the previous day. This manager is using the fixed-order period method.

Determining the Economic Order Quantity

Operations managers need to know when to reorder supplies and materials. They also need to know how much to order. When determining the optimal number of units to order, managers must consider

- how much it costs to place an order, including the cost of preparing and shipping the order
- how much it costs to keep the item in inventory, including all holding costs

By placing small orders, a manager can keep holding costs low. However, frequent reordering can become costly. Ordering in small quantities may prevent businesses from taking advantage of *scale discounts*, or discounts given for ordering in bulk.

To keep costs as low as possible, operations managers calculate the economic order quantity. The **economic order quantity** is the number of units at which ordering costs equal holding costs. **Figure 20–4** shows how managers calculate this quantity.

CONNECT

If you were in charge of inventory at a small coffee shop, what would be the best way to handle the inventory of coffee, baked goods, and paper products?

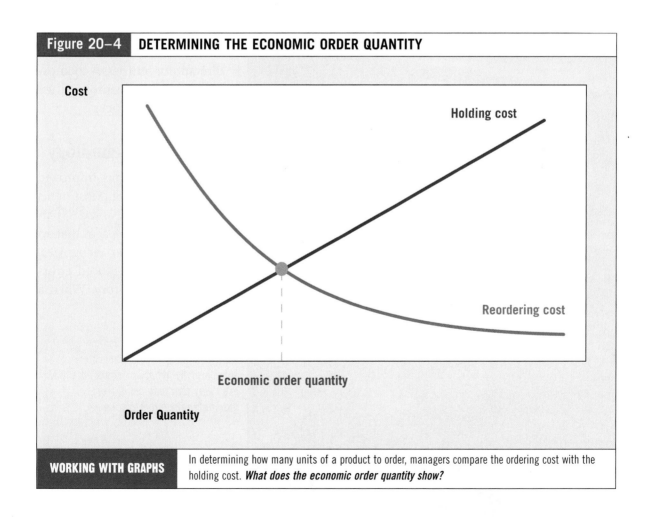

| Figure 20–4 | DETERMINING THE ECONOMIC ORDER QUANTITY |

WORKING WITH GRAPHS In determining how many units of a product to order, managers compare the ordering cost with the holding cost. *What does the economic order quantity show?*

Carlton Long is the operations manager of a company that produces 25,000 glass jars a month. To determine how many lids to purchase each month, Carlton calculates the cost of reordering and compares it with the cost of holding extra lids in inventory. Carlton estimates that keeping 35,000 lids in stock costs him about $40 a month in holding costs and the same in ordering costs. The economic order quantity is 35,000.

Tracking Inventory

Before computers, tracking inventory was a tedious and time-consuming task. It was difficult to keep accurate inventory records. Employees recorded every sale and purchase, and a bookkeeper would subtract all sales and add all purchases at the end of the week. This determined how much inventory remained in stock.

However, employees often forgot to record transactions. Bookkeepers frequently made mistakes computing figures. Both kinds of errors made it difficult for businesses to know how much inventory they actually had in stock.

Bar Code Technology

Technology has improved inventory tracking. Most items are marked with *bar codes*, patterns of bars and spaces that an electronic scanner recognizes. Bar coding has reduced errors in tracking inventory. When a

◀ **TRACKING INVENTORY** Scanners allow businesses to track inventory automatically. *What are some potential problems that may come from automated inventory tracking?*

company purchases or sells an item, an employee scans the item's bar code. A computer program recognizes the information contained in the bar code and automatically adds or subtracts the item from inventory.

Physical Inventory

Even if computers track inventory, managers need to take physical inventory. A **physical inventory** involves actually counting the number of units of inventory a company holds in stock. Most businesses perform a physical inventory once or twice a year.

Managers need to conduct physical inventories because actual inventory is often different from the level of inventory tracked. The discrepancy may reflect errors or unauthorized withdrawals, including theft. Managers who do not adjust their inventory occasionally may experience shortages.

Section 20.1 Assessment

 FACT AND IDEA REVIEW

1. What are the four types of direct costs?
2. List six types of holding costs.
3. What are safety stocks and why do businesses keep them on hand?
4. Explain how the ABC inventory classification system works.
5. How do managers calculate the economic order quantity?

 CRITICAL THINKING

1. **Drawing Conclusions:** What do you think would happen to the volume of a company's raw materials inventory if the price of the raw material doubled? Explain your answer.
2. **Predicting Outcomes:** What happens if companies hold too much or too little inventory?

 ASSESSING ART SKILLS

Make a poster illustrating the six types of costs associated with holding inventory.

 CASE ANALYSIS

You have just taken over as the operations manager of a mid-sized company that produces kitchen appliances. To keep the assembly line running, you need to make sure that you keep enough steel, plastic, rubber, oil, and glass shelving in stock. Your company's warehouse has limited space, and your company is concerned about tying up too much cash in inventory.

Apply: Explain how you would decide how much of each item to keep in inventory. Your analysis should include discussion of holding costs, safety and seasonal stocks, the ABC inventory classification system, the fixed-order quantity and fixed-order period reordering methods, and the economic order quantity.

QUALITY MANAGEMENT

WHAT YOU'LL LEARN

▶ What operations managers mean by the term "quality."

▶ The three steps involved in managing for quality.

▶ How total quality management can increase the quality of a company's products.

WHY IT'S IMPORTANT

To meet their customers' needs, businesses must maintain certain standards of quality.

KEY TERMS

• quality
• quality planning
• quality control
• quality assurance

What Is Quality?

To consumers, the word "quality" refers to how well a product is made. A high-quality product is reliable and attractive. However, to operations managers the term **quality** refers to how well a product meets certain predetermined standards.

All businesses set quality standards. Some businesses set high quality standards and charge high prices for their goods. Other companies set lower quality standards so that they can afford to sell their products at lower prices.

A business needs to ensure that established quality standards are met. A manufacturer of inexpensive watches, for example, may establish a quality standard that demands that no more than 2 percent of the watches fail to function. The operations manager's job is not to produce high-quality watches, but to ensure that only 2 percent of the products are defective.

◀ QUALITY STANDARDS
Manufacturers of luxury goods set very high quality standards but charge high prices for their products. Manufacturers of lower-priced goods set lower standards in order to sell products at lower prices. *Which type of company needs to maintain quality standards?*

Retail Manager

Nature of the Work

Retail managers may oversee one department, several departments, one store, or several branches. They supervise sales associates and often work on the sales floor. They prepare work schedules for store employees and assign tasks. They may interview, hire, train, and fire employees.

Retail managers may establish policies and procedures for their store or department, or implement those established by the company. Store managers review inventory and sales records and develop merchandising strategies. They are called on to resolve customer complaints.

Working Conditions

Retail managers usually work in pleasant surroundings. Their hours may be long, irregular, and include weekends and evenings. Some work in offices, but the job often involves long hours of standing. Their job can be stressful at holidays, sales, during inventory, and when working with customer complaints.

Training, Other Qualifications, and Advancement

To become a retail manager, it would be helpful to take courses in business accounting, marketing, administration, management, and sales. Many retail managers learn through experience, starting as sales associates, customer service representatives, or cashiers. Many stores provide management training.

Salary Range

Retail managers earn $12,900 to $50,400, depending on the size and type of store, location, experience, and responsibilities. They may receive commission in addition to salary, or a percentage of the sales of the department, as well as bonuses and benefits.

CRITICAL THINKING

Considering the long, irregular hours, and stressful work, what are the advantages of retail management?

STANDARD &POOR'S

INDUSTRY OUTLOOK

In the next millennium, retailing will change significantly as an increasing number of people make their purchases via the Internet. In 2001, total online retail sales were $36 billion, or 1 percent of total retail sales. Analysts estimate that by 2006, this figure will reach approximately $110 billion, or 2.5 percent of total retail sales.

BUSINESS MANAGEMENT *Online*

For more information on management careers, go to:

busmanagement.glencoe.com

PREDICT

What does the term "quality" mean to customers? To managers?

RESPOND

What level of service would you expect from the following motels or hotels: Hilton, Motel 6, Ritz-Carlton, Travelodge?

Managing for Quality

Most consumers have certain expectations about the products that they buy. Customers who buy clothing at discount stores do not expect garments to be hand-stitched. They do expect the clothing to last more than a few months, however. If the quality of the outlet's products deteriorates below a certain level, customers will shop elsewhere. For this reason, companies need to maintain the quality of their products at, or above, the level that customers expect.

Ensuring that a company's products meet standards involves three processes: quality planning, quality control, and quality improvement. Each process involves several steps, as shown in **Figure 20–5**.

Quality Planning

Quality planning involves establishing goals that will help a company produce goods customers want to buy. Sometimes goals are market driven. Customers who purchase high-end running shoes, for example, demand certain performance, comfort, and durability features. Producers who compete in that market must meet these standards to find customers.

Sometimes quality goals are driven by government regulations. Airlines, for example, must meet safety regulations set by the Federal

Figure 20–5	COMPONENTS OF MANAGING FOR QUALITY	
Quality Planning	**Quality Control**	**Quality Improvement**
• Identify customers	• Evaluate actual quality performance	• Establish a program for improving quality
• Determine customer needs	• Compare actual performance to quality goals	• Identify specific areas that require improvement
• Develop product features that respond to customer needs	• Take steps to narrow the gap between actual performance and goals	• Establish project teams to diagnose the causes of the problem, develop solutions, and establish controls for implementing the solutions
• Develop processes that are able to produce those product features		
• Establish quality goals		
• Establish process controls		

WORKING WITH CHARTS Managing for quality involves three processes: quality planning, quality control, and quality improvement. *Why do businesses need to manage for quality?*

▲ **QUALITY CONTROL** In some companies, quality-control inspectors check every unit the company produces. In others they check just a sample of the company's output. *Which procedure do you think this company uses?*

Aviation Administration. Meat packers must meet health regulations set by the U.S. Department of Agriculture.

Senior managers play an important role in setting a company's quality goals. Once the goals have been established, operations managers bear much of the responsibility for seeing that they are met.

Quality Control

Quality control is the process by which a company measures actual performance against set quality standards. Companies control for quality in many ways, including quality inspection and quality assurance.

QUALITY INSPECTION Many companies control for quality by inspecting products to ensure that they meet quality standards. At some companies, quality control inspectors check every unit the company produces. This kind of quality-control system is used when the consequences of a single defective unit could be enormous. Manufacturers of heart and lung machines, for example, must inspect every machine they produce because a single defect could have deadly consequences.

All About

ATTITUDE

THE 80/20 RULE

Eighty percent of getting your job done is in having the right attitude. Activities can be repetitive or unique, great or small. The way in which you hold yourself while accomplishing your tasks can make you a well-respected and more productive employee.

BusinessWeek

A NICE BUSINESS BUILT ON BEING NICE

Generosity Is the Hallmark of Thriving Boston Duck Tours

A lot of experts tell Andrew Wilson he doesn't understand business: His prices are too low, his pay scale too high. But the 41-year-old founder of Boston Duck Tours, which offers land/water sightseeing trips in World War II-era amphibious vehicles known as DUKWs, or "Ducks," has built a flourishing company in just four years by swimming against the current.

Buoyed by Boston's recent tourism boom, Wilson has made his entertaining tours stand out. His colorful flock of 16 Ducks take visitors on a fun yet fact-packed trip that cruises along the Charles River as well as around the city's fabled sights.

The 80-minute excursion costs adults $20. Boston Duck Tours carried 300,000 passengers from April to October, 1997, when the Small Business Administration named Wilson Massachusetts Entrepreneur of the Year. That traffic produced revenues of $4.4 million—and profits of $900,000.

But what makes this former investment bank vice-president a rare bird is the way he operates. Wilson won't raise prices, even though he turned away 250,000 customers last year because of limited capacity. "It'd be greedy," says Wilson, who relies on word-of-mouth and customer satisfaction to generate business. "People remember when you've gouged them." The situation has made Boston Duck Tours a B-school case study. At Harvard University, the professors thought he should expand outside Boston. But Wilson thinks the city's calm river and compact historical district are uniquely suited to the business.

PRACTICAL. Then there's his attitude toward profits. Last year, he donated 10% of pre-tax profits, or about $90,000, to community projects such as cleaning up the Charles. He also paid out about $1.1 million in bonuses—to everyone but himself. His own salary is "significantly under six figures," he says. All 50 or so employees enjoy benefits almost unknown in seasonal work: year-round medical, dental, and life insurance, plus a 401(k). Such largesse is practical, Wilson argues, citing the success of employee-oriented Southwest Airlines Co.: "Ultimately, this business is about people. If they're enthusiastic, it works."

Excerpted with permission from BusinessWeek, *September 14, 1998*

CRITICAL THINKING

Why doesn't Wilson raise his prices?

DECISION MAKING

As a manager for Wilson's company, develop a written customer service policy that outlines your strategies for satisfying customers while still making a profit.

When the consequences of selling a defective product are less serious, quality control inspects only a sample of products. A manufacturer of inexpensive jewelry, for example, does not check every earring it produces. The consequences of selling a defective earring are minor and the cost of inspecting each earring is high.

QUALITY ASSURANCE Many companies have employees who specialize in inspecting for quality control. Others build quality control into the production process, a concept known as *quality assurance*. **Quality assurance** makes quality the responsibility of all employees, not just of the quality-control inspectors. It emphasizes preventing defects and mistakes rather than correcting them. Adopting quality assurance increases productivity.

Quality Improvement

If a company fails to meet its quality standards, it must determine the source of the problem in order to improve quality. In some cases, quality standards may be unrealistic. If so, the standards, rather than the production process, need to be changed.

A production department may fail to meet the company's quality standards because of circumstances beyond its control. An outbreak of the flu, for example, which causes employees to miss work could affect production. In this case, a temporary factor, rather than the production process, is to blame. The production process does not need to be modified.

When quality standards are realistic and performance is not affected by uncontrollable factors, the production process itself may need to be changed if it does not allow quality standards to be met. A change in the production process can have an enormous effect on productivity and can help a company meet standards.

Because of the many different ways quality can affect an organization, it can be difficult to determine precisely the costs associated with different quality levels. In addition, customers are willing to pay for quality only up to a point. Some managers have instituted a quality program driven by customer responses.

International Management

GREECE

In Greece, the contract is considered a part of overall negotiations that will cease only when the work is completed. Rather than a final written agreement, the contract signals intention for serious negotiations. Managers expect to make adjustments as the contract is fulfilled.

BusinessWeek *ONLINE* For further reading about International Management go to: **www.businessweek.com**

▲ **TOTAL QUALITY MANAGEMENT** All employees need to get involved if a total quality management program is to be successful. *What is the purpose of TQM?*

CONNECT

How might Total Quality Management be adopted to improve the quality of instruction at your school?

LEADING THE WAY

IT'S YOUR COMPANY
Perhaps you don't own the business you work for. As a manager, you should learn to treat the company as if you were the owner. Your loyalty and pride will translate into a desire to manage situations effectively.

TOTAL QUALITY MANAGEMENT One of the most popular approaches to improving quality is total quality management. As you learned in Chapter 2, *total quality management* (TQM) is a system of management that involves all employees in improving quality and productivity by improving work methods.

TQM represents a company-wide effort to ensure that a commitment to quality becomes part of the company's corporate culture. It has helped many companies reduce defects, empower and train workers, implement suggestion programs, listen to customers, and measure processes and progress.

TQM involves the following steps:

1. Find out what customers want by using surveys, focus groups, interviews, or other technique.
2. Design a product that will meet or exceed what customers want.
3. Design a production process that gets the job done correctly the first time.
4. Keep track of results, and use those results to figure out how to improve the system.
5. Extend these concepts to suppliers and distribution.

Many large companies, including Motorola, Texas Instruments, and L.L. Bean, have adopted TQM programs. Smaller companies also have benefited from TQM. Moss Tent, Inc., a 55-person company that produces expensive nylon tents, enjoyed a 38 percent increase in productivity after it adopted TQM.

Before adopting TQM, Moss used an inefficient production process that resulted in waste. The company used an assembly-line approach in which some workers cut, others stitched, and others assembled tents. Once the tents were completed, inspectors checked for defects. The production process was inefficient—one out of every four tents failed inspection. This cost the company thousands of dollars in wasted materials and labor.

Under the TQM system, Moss organized into teams of workers that start and finish the production of a tent. Work is inspected at each stage of production. Self-inspection has led to such high quality that the company almost never discards a completed tent.

Section 20.2 Assessment

 FACT AND IDEA REVIEW

1. What is quality planning?
2. Why do some companies inspect only a sample of the products they produce?
3. What is quality assurance?
4. What is total quality management (TQM)?

 CRITICAL THINKING

1. **Predicting Outcomes:** What do you think happens to businesses that consistently fail to meet their quality standards?
2. **Analyzing Information:** What kind of quality-control inspection do you think is used by a company that produces basic screwdrivers? Why?

 ASSESSING LANGUAGE ARTS SKILLS

Using the Internet or resources at your public library, research W. Edwards Deming, the father of total quality management. Then write a one-page report that provides some biographical information and a description of Deming's ideas.

 CASE ANALYSIS

You are the CEO of a company that produces car radios. You are concerned that product quality has been slipping. To improve quality, you would like to adopt a total quality management program. Some employees like the idea, but others are unconvinced that the program will improve quality.

Apply: Write a one-page memo to a supervisor explaining why you think your company should adopt a TQM program. Be sure to explain the benefits you believe such a program would bring.

CHAPTER 20 ASSESSMENT

CHAPTER SUMMARY

Section 20.1

▶ Operations managers control operating costs.

▶ Businesses maintain inventories to meet product demand.

▶ The ABC classification system classifies inventories in three groups based on relative value.

▶ Managers use the fixed-order quantity method or the fixed-order period method to determine when to reorder.

▶ Many businesses use computers to track inventory and take physical inventory once or twice a year.

Section 20.2

▶ To operations managers, quality refers to how well a product meets certain predetermined standards.

▶ Businesses manage for quality through quality planning, quality control, and quality improvement.

▶ Total quality management (TQM) involves all employees in improving quality and productivity.

REVIEWING VOCABULARY

Together with a partner, discuss the meaning of each of the following terms:

direct costs	physical inventory
inventory	quality
finished goods	quality planning
holding costs	quality control
safety stocks	quality assurance
economic order quantity	

RECALLING KEY CONCEPTS

1. What are holding costs?
2. What is a physical inventory? How often does it take place?
3. What do operations managers mean by "quality"?
4. What is involved in quality control?

THINKING CRITICALLY

1. What risk does a company take by not maintaining safety stocks of inventory?
2. What is the importance of keeping seasonal stocks? Name some examples of items that would be maintained in seasonal stock.
3. How have computers simplified inventory for managers?
4. What is the difference between having quality inspectors control for quality and adopting a quality assurance program?

CHAPTER 20 ASSESSMENT

ASSESSING ACADEMIC SKILLS

MATH The average wage in your furniture factory is $13.54 an hour. If it takes 8.5 hours and $62 worth of materials to manufacture one armchair, what are the direct costs associated with producing 100 chairs?

APPLYING MANAGEMENT PRINCIPLES

SOLVE THE PROBLEM Your factory employs 24 production workers, one quality control inspector, three supervisors, three clerical workers, one full-time bookkeeper, and one operations manager. Production costs (direct labor, direct materials, variable production overhead, and fixed production overhead) are so high that the company is not earning profits. All production workers belong to a union, which means that you cannot cut their wages to reduce costs. Unless you are able to cut costs, however, your company will be unable to stay in business.

Writing Propose several ways to reduce your company's costs. Write a one-page memo that summarizes your ideas.

PREPARING FOR COMPETITIVE EVENTS

Answer true or false to the following statements. Explain your answers.

a. All companies need to keep three months worth of raw material inventory in stock.

b. Only companies that produce high-quality products need to establish quality programs.

BusinessWeek ONLINE

In this chapter you read the *BusinessWeek* Management Model about the importance of sastisfying customers. For more information, go to *BusinessWeek* online at:
www.businessweek.com

If you were in charge of creating a written customer service policy for a retail store, what 10 strategies would you develop? Share your list with the class.

CHAPTER 21

MANAGEMENT INFORMATION SYSTEMS

LEARNING OBJECTIVES

When you have completed this chapter, you will be able to:

- Describe the general evolution of computers since the early 1960s.
- Distinguish between data and information.
- List the basic components of a management information system (MIS).
- Explain what a decision support system (DSS) and an executive information system (EIS) can do.
- Understand what expert systems can do.
- Explain criticisms of MISs.

READING STRATEGIES

As you read

- **PREDICT** what the section will be about.
- **CONNECT** what you read with your own life.
- **QUESTION** as you read to make sure you understand the content.
- **RESPOND** to what you read.

Understanding Management

Companies of all sizes rely on computer systems to communicate information, manage inventory, and make business transactions. Some businesses, like Yahoo!, depend almost entirely on computers and communications technology. A manager working in such a field must be aware of the latest developments in technology in order to stay ahead of competitors.

Analyzing Management Skills

Why is it important for a company like Yahoo! to offer the most innovative and highest quality products to Internet users?

Applying Management Skills

Imagine that you work at a job that uses computers to make sales and track inventory. What can go wrong when the computer system is not working properly?

BusinessWeek *ONLINE*

For further reading on Internet service providers and management information systems go to: **www.businessweek.com**

"MANAGEMENT TALK"

"Our strategy to continue taking the business forward is to leverage the power of the Yahoo! global network to create the most innovative, highest quality products for users and to provide the most efficient and effective marketing platform for businesses."

—Terry Semel, Yahoo! Inc., Chairman and CEO

TOOLS OF THE INFORMATION AGE

The Information Explosion

A business manager needs to get and use information wisely. For example, the owners of a toy store need to know how many families with children live nearby. A supermarket manager should track the sales of meat. Businesses of every kind must be able to understand their financial position and control their operations accordingly.

Computers have revolutionized the way most businesses work by making information more organized and available. They also have changed the way managers decide what information they need, how to gather it, and the best ways to work with it.

Fifty years ago, most business information was exchanged at face-to-face meetings or in print. This information could be accessed later, but searching through files of memos and meeting notes was time-consuming and expensive. For data about customers and competitors,

➤ **POINT-OF-SALE SYSTEMS** In addition to the amount of the sale, today's computerized point-of-sale systems also store information about items that are bought. *How can a store manager use this information for future planning?*

managers often had to rely on out-of-date reference materials. Much of the information they wanted was unavailable.

Information Overload

Today, managers have a different problem. Automation has made it easy to record and exchange data about anything. The Internet has grown quickly into the world's largest information source. Cable television has created hundreds of channels, and more books and magazines are being printed than ever.

Many managers are experiencing **information overload**. They are flooded with more data, text, and images than they can process. Instead of figuring out how to get enough information, they now must decide what is useful and what is not.

The Development of Computers

Computers can filter information to avoid the problem of information overload. Managers have not always had immediate access to computers, however. The first electronic computer, ENIAC, was developed in 1946 at the University of Pennsylvania, in cooperation with the U.S. Army. The room-sized ENIAC weighed about 30 tons. Setting it up to run a program took two days. Its vacuum tubes and complex wiring needed constant maintenance. No one at that time could have predicted that someday there would be a computer on almost every desktop!

In the 1960s, government agencies and some of the largest corporations had large central computers called *mainframes* to handle their accounting data. Mainframes were expensive, and only trained specialists could operate them. Programs were typed out one line at a time on stacks of *punch cards* and used to process information stored on magnetic tape.

The Spread of Smaller Computers

Smaller and less expensive systems called *minicomputers* were developed in the 1970s. For the first time, smaller businesses could afford to computerize. In larger companies, individual departments began buying their own computers.

Electronic parts continued to get smaller. By the late 1970s the "brain" of a computer could be etched onto a tiny silicon chip. Today, desktop *microcomputers*—far more powerful than the old mainframes—cost less than a thousand dollars. Software has improved over the years, becoming more **user-friendly**, or easier to learn and use. It also allows first-time users to perform functions, such as word processing and graphic design.

Management Information Systems in Use

A **management information system (MIS)** is a computerized system that transforms data into information managers can use. *Data* includes facts that have not yet been analyzed about people, places, things, or events. *Information* is data that has been interpreted in some way to make it useful. An MIS filters, organizes, and interprets data so that managers can access and use it in a timely manner.

The United Parcel Service (UPS) is the world's largest package delivery company, used in more than two hundred countries. UPS has integrated an MIS system through the software provider Peoplesoft. This enables UPS to save all order and shipping information from the time the information is entered until the package reaches the shipping docks. The system uses the information to create labels and specialized tracking numbers to simplify delivery. All of this information is transmitted to the Peoplesoft operating system where it can be accessed in the event of customer service problems.

The automobile maker BMW utilizes a program developed by SAP AG, a software provider that helps companies to benefit from computer technology. At the BMW facility in South Carolina, three hundred cars are produced daily in a 16-hour production cycle. This happens with the help of the SAP R/3 information system. This system allows coordination between services including production planning and control and plant maintenance.

MIS and Data Processing

It is important to distinguish between an MIS and a data processing system. **Data processing** is the capturing and storing of data, while an MIS uses the data to produce information for management. A data processing system provides the raw material on which the MIS works. For example, in a megaplex cinema, a data processing system records ticket sales. An MIS uses the data to determine which types of movies are most popular for daytime and evening showings on weekdays and weekends.

Transaction processing, a type of data processing, substitutes computer processing for record keeping procedures people previously did by hand. These include payroll, billing, and inventory record-keeping. In most organizations, a transaction processing system provides the data for the MIS to work on. Other organizations have a transaction processing system but have not yet implemented an MIS. **Figure 21–1** shows the relationship between a data processing system, transaction processing system, and an MIS.

QUESTION

What sorts of information can an MIS tell the manager of a fast-food restaurant?

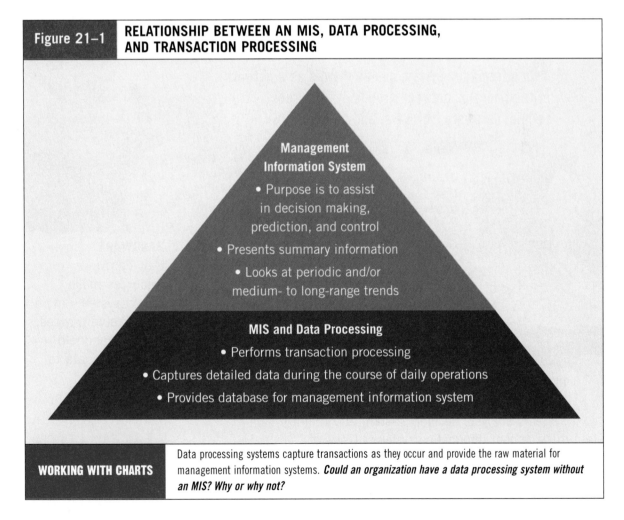

| Figure 21–1 | RELATIONSHIP BETWEEN AN MIS, DATA PROCESSING, AND TRANSACTION PROCESSING |

Management Information System

• Purpose is to assist in decision making, prediction, and control

• Presents summary information

• Looks at periodic and/or medium- to long-range trends

MIS and Data Processing

• Performs transaction processing

• Captures detailed data during the course of daily operations

• Provides database for management information system

WORKING WITH CHARTS   Data processing systems capture transactions as they occur and provide the raw material for management information systems. *Could an organization have a data processing system without an MIS? Why or why not?*

MIS Components

An MIS needs several components to function: hardware, software, data, and people. **Figure 21–2** shows the interaction between these components.

Hardware

Hardware refers to all the equipment that makes up the computer. Hardware includes the *central processing unit*, which is the "brain" of the computer. It also includes the keyboard, monitor, data storage devices, printer, modem, and any other physical components. Hardware has become smaller, more powerful, and less expensive as technology has developed.

FIGURE 21–2

Components of an MIS

An information system can be viewed as a network of relationships between groups of resources: people, hardware, software, and data.

2 HARDWARE
New hardware resources make information systems more flexible. Portable devices, such as this handheld computer, allow data to be recorded easily.

1 PEOPLE
Specialists such as programmers and systems analysts develop, install, and maintain management information systems. Users of the system can provide feedback that specialists can use to improve it.

Software

Software is the name for the instructions, or *programs*, that tell the computer what to do. Examples of software programs are Microsoft Word, QuarkXpress, and Powerpoint. Today, managers can purchase most of the software that they need. Some special-purpose applications require custom-written software.

Data

Suppose a computer runs accounting software that adds up a list of sales figures. The program knows how to add, but it doesn't know what the sales figures are. It needs the data from the company's database.

A **database** contains data about an organization's operations, such as sales, prices, employee salaries, and expenses. To be useful, it

3 SOFTWARE
Occasionally a new software resource revolutionizes management information systems. In the 1970s, spreadsheet programs allowed managers to look at different possibilities and see how they would affect their company's financial picture.

4 DATA
Data resources include product descriptions, customer records, employee files, transaction records, and inventory databases. The rapidly growing quantity of data maintained by organizations has encouraged the development of hardware that can provide fast, cost-effective access to it.

Management Analyst and Consultant

■ Nature of the Work

Management analysts and consultants work with businesses, government agencies, and other organizations. They analyze and suggest solutions to management problems, such as designing new inventory systems, purchasing a computer system, and reorganizing after an acquisition or merger. In the process, they collect, review, and analyze information, interview managers, observe the current operation, and prepare written and oral reports for management. They may help the organization implement their recommendations.

The work varies from project to project, although they usually specialize in a particular industry or a particular function, such as accounting or human resources. They may work independently, with the organization's managers, or with a team of management consultants.

■ Working Conditions

Management analysts and consultants work 40 hours a week; however, there may be much uncompensated overtime. About 45 percent of management analysts and consultants are self-employed.

■ Training, Other Qualifications, and Advancement

To become a management consultant, you need a master's degree in business administration or related discipline, and at least five years experience in the field. Government analysts are hired at the entry level with a bachelor's degree and no experience.

■ Salary Range

Management analysts and consultants earn $30,000 to $100,000+, depending on the industry, experience, and skills.

CRITICAL THINKING

Why do you think the demand for management analysts and consultants will grow?

STANDARD &POOR'S

INDUSTRY OUTLOOK

Many companies use cost-effective intranets. These "little Internets" connect most or all of a firm's computers. Access is usually limited to the company's employees. Intranets enable firms to distribute and share information quickly, easily, cheaply, and reliably among offices around the world.

BUSINESS MANAGEMENT *Online*

For more information on management careers, go to:
busmanagement.glencoe.com

must be stored and accessed easily. In an MIS, the software acts on the data to produce information in the form of reports and graphs.

People

Specialists such as computer programmers and systems analysts contribute to a management information system. *Programmers* are specialists in computer languages who write software. *Systems analysts* study an organization's computing needs and decide what type of software should be written. Computer specialists also help integrate purchased software packages so that they work together, configure them for the specific environment of the organization, and maintain them.

Managers are another important component of an MIS. Managers must be familiar with the information needed in the MIS. They also need to use and improve upon this information. Senior managers who provide adequate resources and utilize the MIS in their decision-making process contribute to the overall effectiveness of the system.

Section 21.1 Assessment

 FACT AND IDEA REVIEW

1. List two major differences between the computers of the early 1960s and those of today.
2. Describe the difference between data processing systems and management information systems.
3. Name four components of a management information system.

 CRITICAL THINKING

1. **Predicting consequences:** Using scanners and other methods has allowed store managers to record purchases made by each customer. How can this information gathering benefit the customer? What potential negative effects can it have?
2. **Making comparisons:** Which will be more successful, a company in which upper management supports the MIS or one in which management is less supportive? Why?

 ASSESSING SOCIAL STUDIES SKILLS

In the library or on the World Wide Web, look up the early history of computers and focus on a company or government agency that was among the first to use them. Write a few paragraphs about the organization, how it used its computer, and the effect the computer had on it.

 CASE ANALYSIS

You are a mid-level manager in a company that has a well-developed data processing system but no MIS. You believe that there is a lot of useful information hidden in your company's database that could help you and other managers plan for the future and get an edge over your competition.

Apply: Prepare a presentation for upper management describing why an MIS would be worth the money they would have to spend on it.

IMPLEMENTING AN MIS

WHAT YOU'LL LEARN

▶ Strategies for implementing an MIS.
▶ How special-purpose systems are used to support decision making and executive information needs.
▶ Four criticisms of MISs.

WHY IT'S IMPORTANT

Understanding the methods and challenges of implementing management information systems will prepare managers to work with them effectively.

KEY TERMS

- outsourcing
- decision-support system (DSS)
- groupware
- executive information system (EIS)
- expert system

Implementation Strategies

Implementing an efficient MIS creates many challenges. Managers must decide what types of systems are needed. They also need to convince others in the organization that adopting the system is worth the expense and the difficulty of changing the way things are done.

Many organizations have problems implementing management information systems. Sometimes the difficulty is technical, for example, getting new software to work properly with older equipment. More often, however, difficulties are related to training users to operate the system and convincing them to use it.

▲ **IMPLEMENTATION** Training is one important way to gain user acceptance of a new management information system. *What are some other ways?*

Building and implementing a successful MIS takes the cooperation of many groups of people. Several strategies can help increase support for the MIS.

- *Get top management involved.* Not only does top management provide the resources, but the rest of the organization will sense their enthusiasm and respond accordingly.
- *Sell the need.* Make sure both the people who operate the MIS and the users understand the benefits of using the system.
- *Get users involved.* Many people resist change. Involving employees in the design process will reassure them that the system will be simple to use.
- *Provide training.* Users often feel insecure about trying new ways of doing things. This insecurity alone may cause opposition to the MIS. If you help them understand the system's purpose and show them how to use it, they will approach it with more confidence.
- *Consider user attitudes.* If users are forced to accept the system by management pressure, they will use it, but not willingly or effectively. Establishing an incentive, financial or otherwise, for successful implementation of the system is a better way to gain cooperation.
- *Provide a simple system.* The system may be complex, but it should not be difficult to use.
- *Remember its purpose.* Managers need to be involved in building the system so that it will meet the organization's needs. Computer specialists within an organization must be open to feedback from users, who are in a better position to judge which functions are most important.

Tips from Robert Half

Temporary employees help companies to be more flexible. A company may have a permanent employee take on the complex tasks and hire temps for routine tasks, or a company may hire a high-level contract manager only for specialized aspects of the job.

QUESTION

What are the seven strategies for successfully implementing an MIS?

Outsourcing

Developing and maintaining an MIS involve highly specialized tasks. Constant retraining is needed to keep up with new technologies. The turnover among computer specialists also tends to be high. Many organizations pay another company to manage the MIS for them in an arrangement called **outsourcing**.

An example of outsourcing is the relationship developed in 1988 between Peoplesoft software provider and six corporations, including KPMG Peat Marwick and USinternetworking. The advantage of outsourcing is that the company offering the services specializes in information technologies. It stays on top of the latest developments and hires the specialized staff, leaving its customers free to concentrate on what they do best.

CONNECT

If you were the manager of an auto supply store chain, would you outsource your MIS system? Why or why not?

How the costs of outsourcing compare to in-house development varies widely. The outsourcing firm must make a profit to stay in business. However, it tries to remain competitive by offering greater efficiency than the customers could achieve on their own. Generally, customers pay a monthly fee for complete service, including equipment, to an outsourcing firm.

Information Centers

Many managers do not have the time or interest to become computer experts. They want and need access to information without a hassle.

For these managers, an information center may be a solution. An *information center* is an in-house unit that a company establishes to teach managers how to use information systems. Many large companies, such as Exxon and New York Telephone, have established them.

Information centers are staffed by specialists whose job is to support non-specialists. They provide hands-on training so that managers can learn to generate their own reports. The information center staff must develop a constructive relationship with the managers they serve. Some managers are reluctant to try something new or are uncomfortable asking for help. If they can overcome these issues, the information center works well.

Special-Purpose Systems

As management information systems evolved, some of their specialized functions have become regarded as separate systems. These include decision-support systems, executive information systems, and expert systems.

Decision-Support Systems

A **decision-support system (DSS)** helps an individual manager or a small group solve problems. Like an MIS, it provides information as input to decisions. The difference between a DSS and an MIS is that the DSS also provides suggestions to the decision maker.

A DSS generally has a much smaller scope than an MIS. Instead of dealing with information for the entire company or an entire function, it handles a specific issue, such as finding a good location for a new factory. These kinds of issues are *semi-structured;* that is, they have some elements that are well defined and can be calculated, and other elements that cannot. A properly designed DSS

- solves parts of the problem
- provides its results to the decision maker
- helps isolate points where experience and judgment are required

GROUP DECISION SUPPORT SYSTEMS A group decision support system, often called **groupware**, is a type of DSS that combines communication, computing, and decision-support technologies. The goal is to improve group decision making by making the same information available to everyone in the group.

Groupware has the potential to revolutionize business decision making. Its effectiveness will depend on how widely it is accepted.

WORKPLACE DIVERSITY

NIGERIA
Successful business in Nigeria requires patience. Conducting business by phone or mail is considered trivial and unimportant. Significant business transactions require personal meetings to develop friendly and respectful relationships. Managers should offer or accept refreshments at meetings and expect invitations for a meal.

▲ **GROUP DECISION MAKING** Group decision-support systems can aid in group decision making. *How is this accomplished?*

BusinessWeek

Management Model

Knowledge Management: Taming the Info Monster

Now, coping with data overload—both inside and outside the company—is a matter of survival.

"Getting a handle on information was always a challenge for companies," says Michael Sullivan-Trainor, vice-president of Internet research for International Data Corp. "But with the Internet, companies now have a means by which to control this information and make it work for them."

What's involved? For many companies, no less than a sweeping change in corporate culture. So-called knowledge management means tearing down walls between departments and individuals, inside and outside the company. For starters, that might mean something as simple as pinpointing who knows what inside the company and posting it on the company's intranet.

The really hard part is convincing employees to share what they know rather than horde knowledge to protect their standing in the organization. Says Jack Welch, chairman of industrial giant General Electric Co.: "An organization's

ability to learn, and translate that learning into action rapidly, is the ultimate competitive business advantage."

Cadence Design Systems Inc., a San Jose-based supplier of automated design software, was able to get new sales representatives up to speed and out into the field two to four months faster. How? By creating an in-house Web site that included a step-by-step guide through the sales process, product specs, and profiles of potential and existing customers. Market researcher International Data Corp. estimates the company could save up to $7.6 million over three years.

But knowledge management isn't just for high-tech companies.

Temporary employment agency Manpower currently makes free computer-based training courses available on its Web site. The agency will train potential recruits if they note those courses in résumés. The idea: Manpower cultivates talent, which can be called upon to fill client needs.

The lesson: Companies shouldn't wait too long to dive in. In an era where information is a commodity, the companies that prosper will be those that can use the Net to harness their know-how to competitive advantage.

Excerpted with permission from BusinessWeek, *June 22, 1998*

CRITICAL THINKING

Why is knowledge management important to a company?

DECISION MAKING

As a manager, what might you include on your company's intranet?

Executive Information Systems

An **executive information system (EIS)** is an interactive tool that provides high-level managers with access to information about the general condition of the business. An EIS has enough flexibility built in for managers to obtain a range of reports on demand.

An EIS must be user-friendly and require little help from a technical or administrative assistant. The system must be created for executives' needs and provide access to a variety of data presented in different formats, such as graphs and spreadsheets.

Expert Systems

An **expert system** is a computer program that gives advice about a decision that is usually made by a person with special expertise. It can provide valuable assistance in cases where such expertise is not immediately available.

For example, some automated equipment now comes with expert systems that help operators diagnose and fix problems. Sometimes the situation can be resolved without calling a repair technician. If not, at least the operator can give the technician more information over the telephone.

An expert system differs from a DSS because, although it asks for information about the problem, it does not expect any judgment calls from the user. It also explains the logic behind its reasoning.

MIS Security

With the increase in computer use in organizations has come an increase in abuse. Four of the most common misuses are theft, illicit use, hacking, and spreading viruses.

The theft of computer hardware is a problem that has grown as computers themselves have become smaller. Software also may be stolen, as when an employee duplicates copyrighted software for home use. Data also can be stolen, such as when a salesperson takes a list of prospects to a new employer, or provides sensitive business data to a competitor.

▲ **USAGE POLICIES** Playing computer games during office hours is an example of illicit computer use. *What are some other examples?*

Illicit use of computers is also common. It would be hard to find an office today in which no one has ever played a computer game during office hours or sent e-mail to a friend.

These problems are not unique to computers. Companies have always encountered theft and personal use of office technology, including telephones and photocopiers. However, computer misuse can cause serious damage to files and company information in new ways, such as hacking and spreading viruses.

Hackers

Hacking refers to the practice of gaining unauthorized access to a computer system or database. Hackers might seek to do harm by destroying or altering software or data. Hackers are often motivated by curiosity, such as in cases where a payroll file is accessed for purposes of comparing salaries. Finally, some hackers regard their activity as a sort of puzzle and do it for fun.

Viruses

A programming code that can copy itself and spread via diskettes or over the Internet is known as a *virus*. For example, if someone uses a normal diskette on a computer with a virus, the virus will spread to the diskette. Then the diskette transmits the virus to any other

Figure 21–3	CRITICISMS OF MANAGEMENT INFORMATION SYSTEMS	
Criticism	**Underlying Weakness**
"I get information, but I can't get the information that I need."	System developers do not understand or have adequate information about the managers' roles and information needs.
"All those systems are run out of another department. I can't get them to listen to my priorities."	Information development may be too centralized. It is possible for a centralized information systems organization to meet a company's overall needs, but they have to work at it.
"I can't get that thing to work."	The system is not user-friendly, and/or users have not been adequately trained.
"I keep telling the programmers what I need, but nobody's listening."	Inadequate communication between users and developers, and failure to deal with user feedback.

WORKING WITH CHARTS	Management information systems generally have a positive effect on organizational performance. *What are some criticisms of MISs?*

computer that uses it. The spread of viruses has increased as file exchanges over the Internet have gained popularity.

While some viruses are harmless, simply displaying an annoying message, others can destroy data or programs or erase a disk. Many companies install anti-virus software, such as the Norton Anti-Virus program, to help to detect viruses and correct damaged files.

Criticisms of MISs

Management information systems can have a very positive effect on organizational performance. Nonetheless, they are subject to frequent criticism, which often addresses problems in implementation. Another criticism is that computer systems are rigid and impersonal. Good MISs should be well designed and user-friendly, and should assist rather than replace human decision making. Some frequent complaints are listed in **Figure 21–3**.

Section 21.2 Assessment

 FACT AND IDEA REVIEW

1. List seven strategies for implementing a successful MIS.
2. Explain how a decision-support system differs from an MIS.
3. Give four problems in implementing an MIS that often cause it to be criticized.

 CRITICAL THINKING

1. **Analyzing information:** Who is likely to be more reluctant to use an information center, a new employee or a senior manager? Defend your choice.
2. **Predicting consequences:** A company's information operation is outsourced. How can the outsourcing firm make sure it understands the customer's needs?

 ASSESSING COMPUTER SKILLS

Imagine you are the manager of a chain of shoe stores. You would like to implement an MIS for your business. Outline the features you would want to build into your MIS.

 CASE ANALYSIS

You were just hired to develop and manage an MIS system for a large wireless communications company. After designing the system, you notice that few managers are using the MIS. Those who do use it are using it incorrectly.

Apply: Analyze the factors that might have caused the managers' reluctance or inability to use the MIS effectively. Develop a plan to correct the situation.

CHAPTER 21 ASSESSMENT

C HAPTER SUMMARY

Section 21.1

▶ Computers today offer employees powerful computer resources on their desktops.

▶ Transaction processing captures detailed data in the course of a company's daily operations.

▶ MISs use data to produce useful knowledge for planning and decision making.

▶ An MIS is made up of computer hardware, software, data, and people, such as computer specialists.

Section 21.2

▶ It is necessary to gain the cooperation of senior managers and users of the system to implement a successful MIS.

▶ Decision-support systems, executive information systems, and expert systems are all special-purpose systems related to management information systems.

▶ Criticisms of management information systems often stem from failure to consider the users' needs.

REVIEWING VOCABULARY

Imagine you are the manager of a clothing retailer. Write a memo to your company's programming department describing your needs for an MIS. Use the following terms in your memo:

information overload	database
user friendly	outsourcing
management informa-	decision-support
tion system (MIS)	system (DSS)
data processing	groupware
transaction processing	executive informa-
hardware	tion system (EIS)
software	expert system

RECALLING KEY CONCEPTS

1. Describe the problem of information overload.
2. What is the difference between data and information?
3. Define the following: management information system, decision-support system, and expert system.
4. List four potential abuses of a company's computer resources.

THINKING CRITICALLY

1. Why can too much information be a problem?
2. What sort of management information system might a company have had before the invention of computers?
3. Give three examples in which the Internet changes the way companies handle information.
4. Why do we say that people are a component of a management information system?

CHAPTER 21 ASSESSMENT

ASSESSING ACADEMIC SKILLS

MATH You are a senior manager in a company with 100 employees and 100 computers. You need to upgrade your information systems, which can be done in-house or with an outsourcing firm. To upgrade in-house would mean a one-time expense of $100,000, plus two additional employees, at a total of $150,000 per year. If you outsource, you won't incur the expenses of upgrading or hiring new employees. The outsourcing firm will charge you $2,000 per year for every computer.

Compute the costs for upgrading and outsourcing over each of the first three years. What are the total costs for each option over this period?

APPLYING MANAGEMENT PRINCIPLES

SOLVE THE PROBLEM You are the president of a medium-sized company. Your chief information officer has complained that she is facing resistance from mid-level managers to providing input for the new management system she has created. They seem to be ignoring it, hoping that it will go away. The annual company luncheon is next week, and she would like you to say a few words in support of the system.

Public Speaking Prepare a brief section of your luncheon remarks in which you explain the advantages of the new system to your managers. Devise an incentive for achieving some milestone related to the system. Deliver your remarks to the class.

PREPARING FOR COMPETITIVE EVENTS

Which of the following is *not* a component of an MIS?

a. software
b. managers
c. data
d. groupware

BusinessWeek *ONLINE*

In this chapter you read the *BusinessWeek* Management Model about the importance of knowledge management. For more information, go to *BusinessWeek* online at: **www.businessweek.com**

Imagine that your are a manager at a major department store. Why would sharing information on the intranet be helpful? Make a list of your ideas and share it with the class.

CASE STUDY 7

Scheduling and Controlling Made As Easy As GANTT!

OVERVIEW

How do you go about planning and completing a task? Do you map out everything in your head? Or do you write a list of all the things you need to do? No matter what your response, all managers must have a detailed plan-of-attack that allows them to schedule, evaluate, and control the operations of their organizations. What do they do? This case study explores a technique that managers can use to guide a project from the beginning to the end.

RESOURCES

- Internet (optional)
- management books
- Microsoft Excel or any spreadsheet software
- poster board
- colored markers

PROCEDURES

◆ STEP A ◆

Understanding GANTT Charts

Today's business planning and scheduling techniques have been used for generations. For example, in 1912, Henry L. Gantt developed a tool called the *Gantt chart*. It is a scheduling chart that analyzes a project, monitors its progress, and determines the time frames needed for completion.

A Gantt chart lists the tasks to be completed on the vertical axis. The time allotted for each task is shown on the horizontal axis. These estimated time requirements are used to determine the scheduling of each activity and of the project as a whole. The

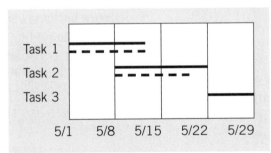

Gantt charts make it easy to compare planned work (solid lines) with actual progress (broken lines).

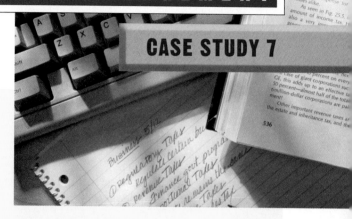

CASE STUDY 7

Gantt chart helps managers schedule employees, purchase materials, and allocate other company resources.

Managers would also need to consider whether an activity on the Gantt chart is dependent or independent. An activity that is dependent on another activity can't be started until the preceding activity is completed. For example, Task 3 in the figure is dependent on Task 2. Activities that are independent, on the other hand, can be scheduled for completion in the same time period.

Analyzing Information:

1. In small groups research the life of Henry L. Gantt and learn about his contributions to the field of management. (Hint: The Gantt chart is not his only contribution.)

2. In your research find one example that illustrates a Gantt chart. Analyze the benefits that are derived from the use of the chart. Then share your research with the class.

◆ STEP B ◆

Microsoft Excel Applications

You can create a Gantt chart with poster board and markers, or with spreadsheet software, such as Microsoft Excel.

Evaluating Information:

1. In your group determine an activity for which a Gantt chart could be used. The activity should have at least six steps.

2. Create a Gantt chart that shows the schedule for your activity.

3. Show how the Gantt chart can be modified based on the progress of the activity.

◆ STEP C ◆

Management Report

In your group create a 15-minute presentation that addresses how a Gantt chart can be used to manage a project. Be sure to speak clearly and professionally. Your presentations should include the following:

1. Discuss Henry L. Gantt's life.

2. Address how Gantt's contributions aided in the development of modern time management principles and techniques.

3. Discuss the business advantages that can be obtained by using a Gantt chart.

4. Integrate your group's Gantt chart in the presentation.

5. Introduce similar tools a business can use for scheduling, controlling, and evaluating projects.

Glossary

A

absolute advantage The ability to produce more of a good than another producer with the same quantity of inputs. (155)

accountability The obligation to accept responsibility for one's actions. (289)

active listening Absorbing what another person is saying and responding to the person's concerns. (205–206)

activity scheduling Creating a detailed production timetable. (267)

aggregate production planning Using an organization's resources to produce enough goods or services to meet demand. (266)

apprenticeship An experienced worker passes on skills to an assistant. (353)

audit A detailed look at an organization's financial or other practices. (459)

authority Power based on the rights that come with a position. (277)

B

balance of trade The difference between the value of the goods a country exports and the value of the goods it imports. (158)

behavior control A control system that monitors an employee's personal activities and involves direct surveillance of the employee. (453)

board of directors The legal representative of a company's stockholders. (316)

brainstorming A group of people come up with as many different ideas as possible, without making judgments about those ideas, to help solve a problem. (193)

brainwriting A group of people write down and then share ideas to help solve a problem. (194)

breakeven analysis Reveals how many units of a good or service a business needs to sell before it begins earning a profit. (143)

breakeven point The point at which revenue is sufficient to cover all costs. (143)

budget A statement of expected results or requirements expressed in financial terms. (454)

burnout Occurs when excessive stress causes a person to lose interest in his or her job. (403)

business cycle Expansion and contraction by many industries at once. (144)

business letters Formal business communication used to communicate with customers and suppliers. (214)

business strategies Plans that pertain to single departments or units within a company. (233)

C

career Series of progressively more responsible jobs in one field or in related fields. (55)

centralization Refers to the concentration of power among a few key decision makers. (44)

chain of command Line of authority within an organization. (278)

chief executive officer Top executive in a company. (315)

chronological résumé Lists work experience and education in reverse order, beginning with most recent job. (70)

code of ethics A document that outlines the principles of conduct to be used in making decisions within the organization. (85)

combination strategy Plan that employs several different strategies at once. (233)

command economy Government decides what goods and services are produced. (135)

committee An organized group of people appointed to consider or decide upon certain matters. (315)

communication The act of exchanging information. (202)

conceptual skills Help managers understand how different parts of a business relate to one another and to the business as a whole. (15)

concurrent control Methods that focus on things that happen during the work process. (453)

conflict The struggle between people with opposing needs, wishes, or demands. (392)

contingent approach Leadership model that assumes the best approach to leadership depends on the situation. (381–382)

continuous-flow system Operating systems that function all the time, regardless of customer orders. (254)

contract An agreement between two parties to carry out a transaction, such as the sale of goods from a seller to buyer. (115)

control Looking at a business activity, comparing it to what is supposed to be happening, and addressing any problems that are found. (440)

copyright The protection provided to a creative work. (112)

corporate strategies *See* grand strategies

corporation A business formed under state or federal statutes that is authorized to act as a legal person. (109)

cover letter Sent with résumé as a brief introduction; emphasizes accomplishments most relative to a job. (70)

culture A set of customs, traditions, and values that members of a community share. (421)

data processing The capturing and storing of data. (491)

database Contains data about an organization's operations. (493)

decentralization Process by which decisions are made by managers at various levels within an organization. (44)

decision-support system (DSS) Management information system that helps an individual manager or a small group to solve problems. (498)

defensive strategy Plan to reverse negative trends in a company, such as sales losses. (232)

delegate To assign responsibility and authority for a task to another person. (286)

depression Business cycle phase in which business activity remains far below normal for years. (146)

differentiation Making a product or service unique. (234)

direct costs The labor, materials, and overhead costs associated with production. (464)

diversity Including people of different genders, races, religions, nationalities, ethnic groups, age groups, and physical abilities in the workforce. (427)

division of labor Assignment of specific tasks to individuals or groups. (280)

economic indicators Data that show how the economy is performing. (149)

economic order quantity The number of units at which ordering costs equal holding costs. (473)

economics Study of how societies decide what to produce, how to produce it, and how to distribute what they produce. (134)

embargo Total ban on the import of a good from a particular country. (161)

employee assistance program (EAP) Company-sponsored program that helps employees deal with personal problems. (405)

employment laws Regulate the relationship between companies and their workers and give workers significant rights and benefits. (120)

entrepreneur Person who launches and runs his or her own business. (22)

entry socialization The process of introducing and indoctrinating new employees. (423)

environmental change All non-technological changes that occur outside an organization. (414)

equilibrium price The price at which supply equals demand. (138)

ethics Set of moral principles or values that govern behavior. (84)

evaluating strategy Process of continuously monitoring the company's progress toward its long-range goals and mission. (244)

executive information system (EIS) Interactive tool that provides high-level managers with access to information about the general condition of the business. (501)

exit interview Pinpoints reasons why an employee is leaving, or voluntarily separating, from a company. (350)

expert system A computer program that gives advice about a decision that is usually made by a person with special expertise. (501)

exports Goods and services sold abroad. (156)

external change Results from forces outside the company. (413)

extrinsic rewards Rewards that are controlled and distributed by the organization. (360)

facilities layout Process of planning the physical arrangement of a facility. (259)

feedback loop Occurs when the output of a system is used to drive its subsequent operation. (442)

finished goods Products that are ready to be shipped to customers. (465)

flat structure Organization that has a small number of levels and a broad span of management at each level. (305)

formal planning Systematically studying an issue and preparing a written document to deal with the problem. (230)

formal work group Established by management to carry out specific tasks. (322)

formulating strategy Developing the grand- and business-level strategies to be used by the company. (237)

for-profit business Firms that operate to earn money for their owners. (67)

free trade area A region within which trade restrictions are reduced or eliminated. (163)

functional strategies Short-range operational plans that support business strategies by emphasizing practical implementation. (234)

glass ceiling Invisible barrier that prevents women and minorities from moving up in the business world. (19)

global economy An economy in which companies compete actively with businesses from all over the world. (162, 415)

goals Concise statements that provide direction for employees and set standards for achieving the company's strategic plan. (241)

grand strategies Provide overall direction for the company and deal with the most important aspects of the company's operations. (230)

group cohesiveness The degree of attraction among group members, or how tightly knit a group is. (326)

group conformity The degree to which group members accept and follow group norms. (327)

group norms Informal rules a group adopts to regulate the behavior of group members. (324)

groupthink Results when group members lose their ability to think as individuals and conform at the expense of their good judgment. (329)

groupware A type of decision-support system that combines communication, computing, and decision support technologies. (499)

growth strategy Plans developed when a company tries to expand sales, products, or number of employees. (232)

halo effect A single characteristic dominates the interviewer's impression of the applicant. (348)

hardware All the equipment that makes up computers. (492)

hierarchy of needs Maslow's grouping and ordering of physical, security, social, and self-fulfillment needs. (38)

holding costs Costs of keeping inventory in stock. (466)

human relations skills The skills managers need to understand and work well with people. (15)

human resources Department that recruits employees, manages training and compensation, and plans for future personnel needs. (342)

idiosyncrasy credit Occurs when individuals who have played a significant role in a group are allowed some freedom within the groups. (334)

implementing strategy Action stage of strategic management in which managers determine and implement the most appropriate company structure, motivate employees, develop short-range goals, and establish functional strategies. (244)

imports Goods and services that are purchased abroad. (156)

income tax A tax levied against a business's profits. (109)

informal work group Formed voluntarily by members of an organization. (323)

information overload The flood of data, text, and images that managers need to process. (489)

intellectual property Ownership of ideas, such as inventions, books, movies, and computer programs. (94)

intergroup conflict Occurs between groups or departments and causes friction in an organization. (397)

intermittent-flow system Operating systems that operate only when an order needs to be filled. (254)

internal change Occurs within a business organization. (413)

international trade Exchange of goods and services by different countries. (154)

interpersonal conflict Occurs between individuals and arises when they perceive or value situations differently. (396)

intrinsic rewards Rewards that are intangible and internal to the individual. (359)

intuitive decision making Making decisions based on intuition or hunches. (180)

inventory Raw materials and finished goods that a company keeps in stock. (465)

job depth The freedom employees have to plan and organize their work, interact with co-workers, and work at their own pace. (282)

job description Written statement identifying the type of work and necessary qualifications for a job. (343)

job design Describes the work an individual or group of individuals is supposed to perform. (262)

job rotation A form of division of labor that involves periodically moving workers from one job to another. A form of on-the-job training that exposes employees to several jobs within an organization; also called cross-training. (280, 353)

job scope The number of operations involved in a job. (282)

law of comparative advantage States that producers should produce the goods they are most efficient at producing and purchase from others the goods they are less efficient at producing. (155)

layoff Occurs when there is not enough work for all employees in the company. (350)

leadership The ability to influence people. (381)

learning styles The different ways people process information. (56)

lifestyle The way you spend your time, energy, and money. (59)

line function Functions that contribute directly to company profits. (299)

linking-pin concept Managers link formal work groups to the total organization because they are members of overlapping groups. (331)

management The process of deciding how best to use a business's resources to produce goods or provide services. (7)

Management By Objectives (MBO) Process that empowers employees by involving them in personal goal setting. (357)

management information system (MIS) A computerized system that transforms data into information managers can use. (490)

market economy Private companies and individuals decide what to produce and what to consume. (136)

materials handling system Network that receives, stores, and moves materials between processing points within a factory. (259)

matrix structure Organization that allows employees from different departments to come together temporarily to work on special project teams. (302)

memos Form of business communication used to communicate with people within the same company. (212)

middle management Responsible for meeting the goals that senior management sets. (8)

mission statement Document that outlines why the company exists, describes the company's basic products, and defines markets and sources of revenue. (238)

monopoly Occurs when one party maintains total control over a type of industry. (34)

motivation Factors that give people a reason to act. (370)

multinational corporation Companies that establish manufacturing and distribution facilities in foreign countries. (166)

negative reinforcement Punishing or reprimanding people who engage in behavior that the manager hopes to discourage. (378)

networking Talking to people who may offer you job leads, contacts, or other information. (63)

nonprofit organization Firms that operate to promote a special interest or cause. (67)

nonverbal cues Pieces of information acquired by observing rather than listening to other people. (209)

operating system The processes and activities needed to produce goods or services. (253)

operational planning Short-range planning that focuses on forming ideas for dealing with specific functions in the company. (230)

operations manager Responsible for the activities involved in producing the goods or services for a company. (252)

opportunity cost The loss associated with the best opportunity that is passed up. (135)

organization A group of people working together in a coordinated effort to reach certain goals. (277)

organizational chart Visual representation of a business's organizational structure. (299)

organizational conflict Occurs between employees and the organization itself. (397)

output control A control system based on the measurement of what is produced by the employee or work unit. (453)

outsourcing Organizations pay another company to perform functions such as managing their information systems. (497)

overall cost leadership strategy Plan designed to produce and deliver a product or service for a lower cost than the competition. (234)

P

partnership An association of two or more persons who jointly own a for-profit business. (108)

patent The document the federal government issues to inventors and companies that gives them the exclusive right to make, use, and sell their inventions for 17 years. (112)

personality The combination of all the unique qualities that make you who you are. (56)

physical inventory Counting the number of units of inventory a company holds in stock. (475)

positive reinforcement Rewarding people who engage in behavior that the manager wishes to encourage. (378)

post-action control Methods that detect problems after they occur, but before they become a crisis. (453)

power The ability managers have to make other people act in certain ways. (380)

preliminary control Methods designed to prevent problems from occurring. (453)

principle A basic truth or law. (16)

professional association Group made up of people in the same field; allows members to exchange information and ideas, promote a positive image for the profession, and provide information to the public. (62)

professional manager Senior, middle, or supervisory manager paid to perform management functions within a company. (22)

property tax A tax levied against the property, buildings, or land owned by a business. (110)

Q

quality How well a product meets certain predetermined standards. (476)

quality assurance Quality control is built into the production process and quality is the responsibility of all employees. (481)

quality circle Group of employees from a single work unit who share ideas on how to improve quality. (334)

quality control The process by which a company measures actual performance against set quality standards. (479)

quality planning Establishing goals that will help a company produce goods customers want to buy. (478)

quota Restrictions on the quantity of a good that can enter a country. (161)

R

rational decision making Making decisions based on factual information and logical reasoning. (182)

recession Phase of the business cycle in which growth falls for two three-month periods in a row. (146)

regulations Rules that government agencies issue to implement laws. (106)

reports Documents that provide a lot of information on a particular topic. (214)

résumé A short document that provides potential employers with information about an individual's specific qualifications for a job. (70)

retrenchment strategy *See* defensive strategy

role A set of behaviors associated with a particular job. (11)

S

safety stocks Extra inventories a business keeps on hand. (468)

scarcity Too few resources available for everyone in the world to consume as much as he or she would like. (134)

scientific management Seeks to increase productivity and make work easier by carefully studying work procedures and determining the best methods for performing particular tasks. (37)

senior management Highest level of management. (8)

site selection Process of selecting a location for a business. (259)

skills résumé Highlights abilities and accomplishments rather than work experience. (70)

small business A company that is independently owned and operated. (26)

social audit A review of a business's social responsiveness. (99)

social responsibility The obligation that individuals or businesses have to help solve social problems. (96)

software The instructions, or *programs,* that tell the computer what to do. (493)

sole proprietorship A business owned by a single individual, or proprietor. (107)

span of management Defines the number of subordinates a manager can effectively control; also called *span of control.* (288)

stability strategy Plan to keep the company operating at the same level that it has for several years. (232)

staff function Functions that advise and support line functions. (301)

stakeholder A company's employees, customers, suppliers, and the community. (97)

standard Outlines what is expected of the employee or organizational unit. (442)

strategic management Application of the basic planning process at the highest levels of the company. (236)

strategic planning Long-range planning done by the highest management levels in the company, including the president, vice president, and chief operating officer. (230)

stress Any physical, chemical, or emotional factor that causes bodily or mental tension. (400)

subordinate A person holding a lower position within an organization than the manager. (287)

supervisory management Lowest level of management; oversees day-to-day operations. (8)

SWOT analysis Technique that evaluates a company's internal strengths and weaknesses and external opportunities and threats; SWOT stands for strengths, weaknesses, opportunities, and threats. (242)

tall structure Organization that has many levels with small spans of management. (305)

tariff Tax on imports. (160)

team building Process of establishing a cohesive group that works together to achieve its goals. (332)

team decision making Process of resolving problems and issues by assigning several people with different backgrounds to a group. (188)

team structure Organization that brings different people with different skills together in order to meet a particular objective. (303)

technical skills The specific abilities that people use to perform their jobs. (15)

termination When an employee is asked to leave because of poor performance or failure to follow company rules. (350)

Theory X Business management theory that assumes people are basically lazy and will avoid working if they can. (42)

Theory Y Business management theory that assumes people find satisfaction in their work. (42)

Theory Z Business management theory that integrates Japanese and American business practices. (48)

total quality management (TQM) A system of management based on involving all employees in a constant process of improving quality and productivity by improving how they work. (45)

trademark Word, name, symbol, or slogan a business uses to identify its own goods and set them apart from others. (112)

transaction processing Type of data processing that substitutes computer processing for record-keeping procedures people previously did by hand. (491)

trend Show changes or movement in a certain area. (61)

trust Giant industrial monopoly. (34)

unions Groups of workers who collectively bargain for rights such as higher wages and better working conditions. (126)

unity of command Principle that states an employee should have only one immediate supervisor. (287)

universal approach Leadership approach that assumes there is one way to lead, regardless of the circumstances. (381)

user-friendly Software that is easy to learn and use. (490)

values Beliefs that guide the way people live. (58)

vestibule training Employee learns and practices job in a training area set up with equipment similar to that used in the actual job. (353)

wellness program Company-sponsored programs designed to prevent illness and enhance employee well-being. (405)

Z

zero-based budgeting Method that requires each manager to justify each budget request in detail. (456)

Index

safety stocks, 468

seasonal stocks, 470

shelf life of, 468

storage and handling costs, 467

tax on, 467

tracking, 474–475

inventory control, 465–474

ABC classification system, 470

economic order quantity, 473–474

holding inventory, 466–468

inventory levels, 468–471

reordering, 471–472

Invisible Hand, 175

involuntary separation, 350

Iron Law of Responsibility, 175

Israel, 171

J

Jackson, Phil, 333–334

Japan

culture, 170

importing from, 157, 158

management practices in, 47–49

quality circles in, 334

silence and discretion in, 398

women's right to work in, 128

job

applying for, 70–75

part-time, 64

job characteristics, 262–263

job content factors, 372

job depth, 282

job description, 343

job design, 262–264

job interview, 209. *See also* interview

job outlook, 61

job rotation (division of labor), 280, 282

job rotation (training), 353

job scope, 282

Jobs, Steven, 308–309

Joyce, William H., 455

K

K.I.S. principle, 217

Koogle, Timothy, 243

L

labor costs, 168, 465

labor, division of, 280–281

labor relations laws, 120, 125–127

laissez-faire leadership, 384

Latin America, 277

law of comparative advantage, 155

laws

benefits, 120, 124–125

commercial, 106, 115–116

competition, 90

consumer, 106, 113–115

consumer protection, 91

corporate, 106–109

employment, 120–129, 348–349

environmental protection, 91–92

Equal Employment Opportunity (EEO), 120–122

ethics-related, 90–91

intellectual property, 94–95, 106, 111–113

labor relations, 120, 125–127

licensing, 106, 117–118

Occupational Safety and Health, 120, 122–123

tax, 106, 109–111

unemployment insurance, 124

wage-hour, 120, 123

workers' compensation, 124

zoning, 106, 117–118

See also government regulation

layoffs, 20, 350

layout, facilities, 259–261

leaders

autocratic, 386

of formal work groups, 336

participative, 386

relationship motivated, 385

supportive, 386

task-motivated, 385

See also leadership

Index

N

National Aeronautic and Space Administration (NASA), 116–117

National Environmental Policy Act (1969), 92

National Labor Relations Act (NLRA), 125–126

needs, hierarchy of, 38–40, 371

negative reinforcement, 378

negotiator, as management role, 14

Netherlands, 85, 171

networking, 63

New York Stock Exchange, 425

Nigeria, 72

nonverbal communication, 208–209

nonverbal cues, 209

norms, 324

North American Free Trade Agreement (NAFTA), 163

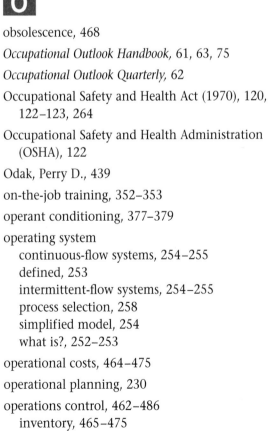

O

obsolescence, 468

Occupational Outlook Handbook, 61, 63, 75

Occupational Outlook Quarterly, 62

Occupational Safety and Health Act (1970), 120, 122–123, 264

Occupational Safety and Health Administration (OSHA), 122

Odak, Perry D., 439

on-the-job training, 352–353

operant conditioning, 377–379

operating system
  continuous-flow systems, 254–255
  defined, 253
  intermittent-flow systems, 254–255
  process selection, 258
  simplified model, 254
  what is?, 252–253

operational costs, 464–475

operational planning, 230

operations control, 462–486
  inventory, 465–475

operational costs, 464–465
  quality management, 476–483

operations management, 250–261
  computer technology for, 255–257
  facilities layout, 259–261
  materials handling, 259–260
  operating systems, 253–255
  process selection, 258
  production planning, 264, 266–267
  role of operations manager, 250, 252–253
  site selection, 258–259

operations manager
  defined, 252
  role of, 250, 252–253

operator controls, 448

opportunity cost, 135

oral communication, 215, 217–218

organizational conflict, 397

organizational reward system, 359–360

organizational structure, 296–319
  changing nature of, 308–309
  creating, 306–317
  departments, 310–313
  factors affecting, 306–310
  flat vs. tall, 304–305
  function, 311
  leadership and, 315–317
  line and staff, 301
  line structure, 299, 301
  matrix, 302
  product or service and, 310
  size of business and, 306–309
  team, 303–304
  types of, 299–304
  what is?, 298

organizations
  changes affecting, 413
  communication in, 282. *See also* communication
  defined, 276–277
  designing, 276–285
  effective, 283–285
  groups in, 322–324
  life cycle stages, 307
  reasons for, 277–278, 280–282
  structure of. *See* organizational structure

organizing, 12. *See also* organizational structure; organizations

Ouchi, William, 48

output controls, 452–453

outsourcing, MIS, 497

overall cost leadership strategy, 233–234

overhead costs, direct, 465

P

participative leaders, 386

partnership, 108–109

part-time job, experience from, 64

patents, 111–112

path-goal theory, 382, 385–386

Pavlov, Ivan, 379

performance
    deviations in, 444–445
    measuring, 356–358. *See also* employee evaluation
    monitoring, 443
    rewarding, 356, 359–361, 424

Perot, Ross, 189

personality, 56, 63

personal strengths, 55–59
    interests and abilities, 55–56
    learning style, 56–58
    lifestyle, 59
    personality, 56
    values, 58

personnel. *See* human resources

personnel plan, 234–235

persuasive skills, 203

Peru, 453

philanthropy, 99

photography industry, 283

physical inventory, 475

planning, 12, 228–235
    aggregate, production, 264, 266
    career, 62–65
    effective, 229–230
    formal, 230
    human resources, 234, 349–350

implementing planning decisions, 231

as leadership skill, 386

operational, 230

production, 234, 264, 266–267

quality, 478–479

reasons for, 228–230

sales and marketing, 234

strategic, 230

Platt, Lewis E., 411

point-of-sale systems, 488

policies, 241

positive reinforcement, 378

post-action controls, 453

power
    authority vs., 380–381
    defined, 380
    expert, 380
    fear of loss of, 415
    need for, 374
    reward, 380
    sources of, 380

Predictive Index (PI), 344

preliminary control, 453

price
    determining, 138–139
    gasoline, 181–182

principle, 16

principles of management, 16–18

problem-solving teams, 188

procedures, 241

process culture, 426

process layout, 260–261

process selection, 258

Procter, Harley, 421

product
    organization structure and, 310
    organizing departments by, 312–313

production department, 310

production plan, 234, 264, 266–267

production standards, 358

productivity
    controls to increase, 450
    group norms and member's, 327
    Hawthorne studies of, 37–38, 331
    improving, 280–282
product layout, 260
professional associations, 62–63
professional managers, 22
profit
    in Corporate America, 145
    defined, 141
    taxes and, 110
profit maximization, 97
programmers, 495
promotions, 349–350
property, intellectual, 94–95
property tax, 110
protectionism, 160–161
    embargoes, 161
    quotas, 161
    tariffs, 160
public domain, 113
publishing industry, 185

Q

quality
    defined, 476
    emphasis on, 44–46
    Malcolm Baldrige National Quality Award, 321
    managing for, 478
    total quality management, 44–46
    of work life, 100–101
quality assurance, 481
quality circle, 334, 336
quality control, 479, 481
quality improvement, 481–483
quality inspection, 479, 481
quality management, 476–483. *See also* quality;
    total quality management
quality planning, 478–479
quotas, 161

R

rational decision making, 182–183
recession, 146–147
regulations
    defined, 106
    See also government regulation; laws
reinforcement theory, 377–379
relationship builder, 14
relationship-motivated leaders, 385
reliability, 344
reports, 214–215, 458
resource allocation, 266–267
resource director, 14
responsibility
    defined, 287
    delegating, 286–293
résumé, 70
    in preliminary screening, 343
    preparing, 72
    types of, 70–72
retail industry, 477
retrenchment strategy, 232–233
revenue, estimating, 141–142
revenue and expense budget, 454
reward power, 380
rewards
    intrinsic and extrinsic, 359–360
    performance, 356, 359–361, 424
risk
    control and, 449
    in decision making, 184
    tolerance for, 425
Rockefeller, John D., 33–34
Roddick, Anita, 100
Roddy, David, 164
role
    decision-making, 14
    defined, 11
    information-related, 14

Index

Index

Index

variable costs, 142–143

vestibule training, 353

vice president, senior, 10

viruses, computer, 502

voluntary separation, 350

volunteerism, 99

W

Waddell, Bill, 164

wage-hour laws, 120, 123

Wagoner, Rick, 297

Walcoff, Carol, 189

Walton, Sam, 369

water treatment industry, 93

Watson, Thomas J., Sr., 421

Wealth of Nations, The (Smith), 280

Web sites
  employment-related, 71, 343
  See also Internet; World Wide Web

Welch, Jack, 500

wellness programs, 405

What Color Is Your Parachute?, 62

Wheeler-Lea Act (1938), 90

Wilson, Andrew, 480

Wilson, Woodrow, 36

wish lists, 194

withholding federal taxes, 110–111

women
  Japanese, 128
  in management, 18–20
  in workplace, 97, 100

work, as social experience, 323–324

workers
  disabilities, 122
  law and, 120–129
  See also employees

workers' compensation laws, 124

workforce, diversity in, 428

Workforce 2000: Work and Workers for the 21st Century, 427

work groups, 320–339
  formal, 322–323. *See also* formal work groups
  informal, 323–324
  See also teams

work-hard/play-hard culture, 426

workplace
  changing American, 429
  conflict in, 392–399
  diversity in, 97
  multicultural, 20
  spirituality in, 401
  stress in, 400–407

work teams, 188. *See also* formal work groups; teams; work groups

World Wide Web, 163. See also Internet; Web sites

Wozniak, Steve, 308

Wrigley, William, Jr., 393

written communication, 210–212, 214–215

Z

Zen Buddhism, 69, 334

zero-based budgeting, 456, 457

Zhao Xiaofan, 164

Zhu Rongji, 164

zoning law, 106, 117–118

Real-World Applications and Connections

Real-World Applications and Connections

Real-World Applications and Connections

Real-World Applications and Connections

Real-World Applications and Connections

Cover Photo

Cover Photograph by: Premium Stock/Corbis/Zenaida Mendoza

Photos

AFP/Corbis 107, 168–9(c), 272(ct), 296–7; Amazon.com 462; Doug Armand/Stone 8, 216; Bill Aron/PhotoEdit 236; Associated Press Boeing Co./AP/Wide World Photos 200; Patrick Aventurier/Liaison Agency 43(br); Paul Avis/Liaison Agency 281(br); Bruce Ayres/Stone 49, 97, 215(b), 346(l), 393, 422; Paul Barton/Corbis 35; Alan Becker/Image Bank 91; Ben and Jerry's 438; Benelux Press/Index Stock Imagery 224(b), 248–9; Bettmann/Corbis 123, 381, 421; Mark Bolster/International Stock 352; Phil Borden/PhotoEdit 92; Daniel Bosler/Stone 10–11(c), 17(bl), 26, 108, 181, 242; Dennis Brack/Black Star/PN 187(cl); Ed Brock/Stock Market 370; Andrew Buurman/FSP/Liaison Agency 100; Bruce Byers/FPG International 332; Cameramann International, Ltd. 264(b); Frank Capri/Archive Photos 22; Steven Castillo/Hewlett-Packard Company 410–1; Steven Castillo/Hewlett-Packard Company 19, 366(b); Chabruken/Getty Images 501; Ron Chapple/FPG International 326; Cindy Charles/Liaison Agency 253(r); John Chiasson/Liaison Agency 316, 336; Jeff Christensen/Liaison Agency 58; Richard Clintsman/Stone 241; Stewart Cohen/Stone 158, 335(cl); John Coletti/Stock Boston 283,292; Corbis 131; Joe Cornish/Stone 170; Court Mast Handout/AP/Wide World Photos 272(cb), 320–1; Rob Crandall/Stock Boston 443; Francisco Cruz/SuperStock 84; Jim Cummins/FPG International 17(tr); Robert E. Daemmrich/Stone 12, 335(tr), 366–7; Mary Kate Denny/PhotoEdit 182; Jody Dole/Getty Images 29; Richard Drew/AP/Wide World Photos 436(c), 462–3; Laima Druskis/Stock Boston 284, 310, 452; DuPont 2(bl), 52, 52–3; Laura Dwight/Corbis 160; Paul Edmondson/Stone 69; Chad Ehlers/Stone 47; Jonathan Elderfield/Liaison Agency 23; Andrew Errington/Stone 383; Ronnen Eshel/Corbis 187(br); Amy C. Etra/PhotoEdit 193, 281(tr); Nicholas Eveleigh/SuperStock 136;

Chris Everard/Stone 6(tr); Barth Falkenberg/Stock Boston 282; Sandy Felsenthal/Corbis 82; Myrleen Ferguson/PhotoEdit 192, 233; Fisher/Thatcher/Stone 433, 496; David Fleetham/FPG International 151; Foodpix 467; Bruce Forester/Stone 206(l); FPG International 32, 96; David Frazier/Stone 195; Tony Freeman/PhotoEdit 115, 147(br), 206–7(c), 234, 276; Robert Frerck/Stone 315; Thomas D.W. Friedman 1997/Mira 499; John Garrett/Corbis 176(b), 200–1; Bassignac Gilles/Liaison Agency 231(cl); Robert Ginn/PhotoEdit 228; Todd Gipstein/Corbis 45; GM Media Services 169, 272(t), 274, 274–5, 296; Brian Gomsak/AP/Wide World Photos 377; The Granger Collection 33, 34, 36, 146; Spencer Grant/PhotoEdit 173, 322; Ernst Grasser/Stone, 385; Jeff Greenberg/PhotoEdit, 184, 191, 342; Jeff Greenberg/Unicorn Stock Photos 398; Timothy Greenfield-Sanders/CORBIS OUTLINE 486-487; Farrell Grehan/FPG International 7; Howard Grey/Stone 445(cl); Charles Gupton/Stock Boston 229, 252–3(c), 474; Charles Gupton/Stone, 398; H. Armstrong Roberts 412; Raoul Hackel/Stock Boston 429(tr); David Hanover/Stone 89(t); David Hanson/Stone 350; William Hart/PhotoEdit 62; Jeff Haynes/AFP Worldwide 252(l); Noel Hendrickson/Masterfile 492; Thomas Herbert/Liaison Agency 141; A. Hernandez/Liaison Agency 135; Hewlett-Packard Company 410; Hirz/Archive Photos 44; Walter Hodges/Stone 103, 204, 250, 303, 335(br), 356, 397(r), 450, 458, 482, 493; B.W. Hoffmann/Unicorn Stock Photos 147(cl); Willie Holdman/Index Stock Imagery 124; Kevin Horan/Stone 397(l); Dave G. Houser/Corbis 112; Paul S. Howell/Liaison Agency 127(r); Hulton Getty Picture Library-Big Picture/Stone 323; Robert Humes/Corbis 231(tr); Richard Hutchings/PhotoEdit 125; IT International ltd./Leo de Wys 218, 445(tr); Jim Sugar Photography/Corbis 207(r); Jimmy Carter Library 291; David Joel/

Stone 24, 396; Chris Johnson/AP/Wide World Photos 444(l); R.W. Jones/Corbis 126(l); Zigy Kaluzny/Stone 405, 429(cr); Kaluzny/Thatcher/Stone 290,499; Arni Katz/Index Stock Imagery 476; Kelly-Mooney Photography/Corbis 231(br); Robert Laberge/AllSport USA 80(tc); Chun Y Lai Photography 43(cl); Rich LaSalle /Stone 154; Yann Layma/Stone 401; Alan Levenson/Stone 256; Alan Levenson 2(t), 4–5; Liaison Agency 55, 309(r); Paul Loven/ Image Bank 453; Lucent Technologies 320; Dick Luria/FPG International 224–5; Dennis MacDonald/PhotoEdit 264(t); David Madison/Stone 406; Tom McCarthy/ PhotoEdit 430; McDonald's Corporation 152; Ryan McVay/Photodisc/Getty Images 111, 469; H.P. Merten/Stock Market 376; Microsoft Corporation/ Rapid Response Team 4; Lawrence Migdale/Stock Boston 89(b), 472; NBAE/Getty Images 132-133; Michael Newman/PhotoEdit 15, 43(tr), 99, 114, 121, 186, 208, 272–3, 324, 346–7(c), 347(r); Johnathan Nourok/Stone 394; Johnathan Nourok/PhotoEdit 360; Richard T. Nowitz/Corbis 436(t), 438–7; Oliver Benn/Stone 159; Jon Ortner/Stone 110; Greg Pease/Stone 492; Chuck Pefley/Stock Boston 263; Jose Pelaez/Stock Market 441; Steven Peters/Stone 188, 298, 402, 429(cl); Richard Pharaoh/International Stock 384; PhotoLibrary of Australia/Index Stock Imagery 98; Robert Pisano/R.E.I. 272(b), 340–1; Joseph Pobereskin/Stone 440; Denis Poroy/AP/Wide World Photos 489; Colin Prior/Stone 94; A. Ramey/Unicorn Stock Photos 286, 371; R.E.I. 340; Ken Reid/FPG International 375(tr); Reuters Newmedia Inc/Corbis 178, 288, 330, 436(b), 486–7; Reuters/Ken Cedeno/Archive Photos 67; Mark Richards/PhotoEdit 6(b), 11(r), 126–7(c), 168(l), 265, 314, 420; Jon Riley/Stone 2–3, 122, 147(tr), 187(tr), 498; Roberts/TSI Imaging/Stone 500; Joel Rogers/Stone 255; Kenneth Rogers/Corbis 465; Micheal Rosenfeld/Stone 163, 257; Mark Rosenfeld/Stone 479; Michael Rosenfeld/Getty Images 353; Andy Sacks/Stone 54, 258, 414; Paul Sakuma/

AP/Wide World Photos 243; Loren Santow/ Stone 10(l), 74; Koji Sasahara/AP/Wide World Photos 176(t), 178–9; Chuck Savage/Stock Market 80–1; Bob Schatz/ Stone 400; Mark Scott/FPG International 416; Jim Scruggs/Liaison Agency 155; Seven Worldwide, Inc. 366(c), 390–1; Jed & Kaoru Share/Stone 90; Allan H. Shoemake/FPG International 269; Stephen Simpson/FPG International 333; Henry Sims/Image Bank 466; Ariel Skelley/Stock Market 101, 343; Don Smetzer/Stone 428; Phillip & Karen Smith/Stone 72; Tom Stewart/Corbis 164; Sun Microsystems 104, 104–5; SuperStock International 21, 41, 60, 93, 119, 140, 167, 185, 213, 239, 251, 279, 300, 325, 345, 373, 395, 419, 447, 477, 494; Starbucks 224(t), 226, 226–7; Sun Microsystems 80(bc); Liba Taylor/Corbis 56; Telegraph Colour Library/FPG International 375(cl), 444(r); Charles Thatcher/Stone 493; Bob Thomas/Stone 260; Arthur Tilley/FPG International 134, 375(br); Travelpix/FPG International 215(t); Robert Trubia/Corbis 113; Peter Turnley/Corbis 166; Tom Uhlman/Liaison Agency 313; United Airlines 30; United Parcel Service, Inc. 390; C. Ursillo/H. Armstrong Roberts 426; Bill Varie/Corbis 266; VCG/FPG International 199, 171; Visuals Unlimited 278, 281(cl); Susan Vogel/Liaison Agency 66; Rudi Von Briel/PhotoEdit 334; D. Walker/Liaison Agency 309(l), 480; Wal-Mart Stores 366(t), 368–7, 368; David Weintraub/Stock Boston 449; Randy Wells/Stone 82–3(c), 457; Randy Wells/Stone 80(b); Ed Wheeler/ Corbis 117; Nik Wheeler/Corbis 2(cl), 30–1; Dana White/PhotoEdit 203; Lee White/Corbis 244; Jim Wilson/Woodfin Camp & Associates 308; Art Wolfe/Stone 328; Robert Yager/Stone 445(br); Michael S. Yamashita/Corbis 80(t), 128, 152–3; David Young-Wolff/PhotoEdit 63(l), 63(r), 162, 165, 176–7, 306, 349, 351, 436–7, 455; Jeff Zaruba/Stone 488; Zephyr Picture/Index Stock Imagery 470; Rex Ziak/Stone 89(c); Zephyr Images 25; Kwame Zikomo/ SuperStock 145.